Development, architecture, and the formation of heritage in late twentieth-century Iran

Manchester University Press

Development, architecture, and the formation of heritage in late twentieth-century Iran
A vital past

Ali Mozaffari and Nigel Westbrook

Manchester University Press

Copyright © Ali Mozaffari and Nigel Westbrook 2020

The right of Ali Mozaffari and Nigel Westbrook to be identified as the authors of this work has been asserted by them in accordance with the Copyright, Designs and Patents Act 1988.

Published by Manchester University Press
Oxford Road, Manchester M13 9PL

www.manchesteruniversitypress.co.uk

British Library Cataloguing-in-Publication Data
A catalogue record for this book is available from the British Library

ISBN 978 1 5261 5015 8 hardback
ISBN 978 1 5261 9561 6 paperback

First published 2020
Paperback published 2026

The publisher has no responsibility for the persistence or accuracy of URLs for any external or third-party internet websites referred to in this book, and does not guarantee that any content on such websites is, or will remain, accurate or appropriate.

EU authorised representative for GPSR:
Easy Access System Europe – Mustamäe tee 50, 10621 Tallinn, Estonia
gpsr.requests@easproject.com

Typeset by
Servis Filmsetting Ltd, Stockport, Cheshire

For

Minoo, whose handwriting adorned my early writings in Iran all those decades ago, and for those whose friendship, care, and intellect have inspired me through the years: Farideh Taslimi (Mozaffari), Victor (You`af) Daresh, Jila Norouzi, Farhad Diba, Seyyed Hamid Nourkeyhani,

and to the memory of

Morteza Mozaffari, Manoutchehr Mozayyeni, Yousef and Shamsi Shariatzadeh, Aligholi Ziaee

Ali Mozaffari

For Sarah, Hannah, and Charlotte

Nigel Westbrook

Contents

List of figures and plates	*page* viii
Acknowledgements	xiv
Note on transliteration	xvi
Introduction – Development, architecture, and heritage: The formation of a collective imagination	1
1 A vital past: Engaging nostalgia	27
2 Canvassing a future: The international congresses of architecture in Iran and the transnational search for identity	55
3 Heritage in the everyday: Housing and collective identity before 1979	82
4 Forming a future from the past: Realizing an everyday Islamic identity	114
5 Forming a national image through public projects: The Shahyad Arya-Mehr Tower	145
6 Tehran's reluctant urban centre: Representing the national capital	180
Conclusion: Design as the mediator of development and heritage	223
Bibliography	239
Index	268

Figures and plates

Figures

1.1 Hossein Amanat, Pasargadae site museum (1973–ongoing) (courtesy of PPRF). 33
1.2 Shiraz Arts Festival, Karlheinz Stockhausen performing at Persepolis, Iran (3 September 1972) (Stockhausen-Verlag, Stockhausen Foundation for Music, www.stockhausen.org, available through Wikimedia CC). 34
1.3 Nader Ardalan, Iran Centre for Management Studies (ICMS)/ Imam Sādegh University (1978). Later phases shown in grey tone (drawn by Nigel Westbrook after Nader Ardalan, based upon Google Earth satellite image). 42
2.1 Delegates exploring site of Persepolis (1970) (source: *Art and Architecture* 1970–71, 2 (8), p. 63). 61
2.2 The Queen opening the 1970 congress (source: Farhad and Bakhtiar 1970, p. 155). 62
2.3 Habitat Bill of Rights, image of traditional and modern habitat (Habitat Bill of Rights, Figures 30 A & B, p. 160). 70
3.1 Shushtar Now, view across rooftops (2015). 83
3.2 Kamran Diba, overall plan of Shushtar Now (drawing by Nigel Westbrook, based upon Google Earth satellite image and original plan drawn by Kamran Diba and published in *Lotus International* 36, 1982). 88
3.3 Kamran Diba, detail of Shushtar Now central area (drawing by Nigel Westbrook, based upon Google Earth satellite image and original plan drawn by Kamran Diba and published in *Lotus International* 36, 1982). 89
3.4 Axonometric view of group of courtyard apartments, Shushtar Now (drawing by Nigel Westbrook, based upon an original drawing by Kamran Diba published in *Mimar Journal* 17, 1985). 90
3.5 View of parkway, Shushtar Now (2015). 91
3.6 Kamran Diba, Jondishapur University, Ahvāz, part of the sports facility (above); general internal space of a faculty (middle); and faculty courtyard (below) (2017). 93

Figures and plates   ix

3.7	Kamran Diba, primary school at Shushtar Now (2015).	94
3.8	Kamran Diba, view of Bazaar courtyard (2015).	95
3.9	Kamran Diba, general view of public garden (2015).	95
3.10	Shushtar Now, view of pedestrian street (2015).	100
3.11	Residents' transformation of the original design in Shushtar Now: (above) a courtyard being covered, and entrance changed; (below) additions to forecourts and entries (2015).	101
4.1	Distribution of housing competitions sites in nine locations (1989) (source: *Competitions* book, p. 36).	117
4.2	Cover of *Competitions* book (1989).	118
4.3	Saremi and Tajeer Architects, project for Isfahan (repeated for Mashhad) (redrawn by Nigel Westbrook from *Competitions* book, 1989, p. 87).	126
4.4	Bāgh-e Melli gate, Tehran (2008).	127
4.5	Arabshabi House, Tehran. Architects: Nasrin Faghih, Taghi Radmard (Bahram Hooshyar Yousefi), Ali Akbar Saremi (redrawn by authors after architects' drawing published in *l'Architecture d'Aujourd'hui* 195, 1978; redrawn after authors by Nigel Westbrook).	128
4.6	Amir Houshang Ardalan and Mandan Consulting Engineers, project for Khuzestan, *Competitions* book (1989) (reproduced from the *Competitions* book).	130
4.7	Nader Kazemi-Nejad of Socnā Engineers, first-prize winning project for Hamedan (redrawn by Nigel Westbrook after the *Competitions* book, 1989, p. 47).	131
4.8	Giti Etemad, Tarh-va-Memari Architects and Planners, second-prize winning project for Hamedan (redrawn by Nigel Westbrook after the *Competitions* book, 1989, p. 55).	132
4.9	Behrouz Ahmadi, Sharestān Consulting Engineers, project for Hamedan (redrawn by Nigel Westbrook after the *Competitions* book, 1989, p. 64).	133
5.1	Official opening ceremony of the Shahyad (courtesy of the National Library of Iran).	146
5.2	The opening of the Shahyad 6 Bahman Museum with the presence of Queen Farah (26 January 1971) (courtesy of the National Library of Iran).	147
5.3	The Shahyad during the uprisings of the Islamic Revolution (courtesy of the National Library of Iran).	148
5.4	Shahyad heritage registration document (available online from http://iranshahrpedia.com/view/16257).	151
5.5	Aerial view of the urban ensemble with Shahyad at its focal point (Google Earth 2017).	152
5.6	The minor north–south arches in the Shahyad (left) and the major east–west arch (right) (2007).	153

5.7	Shayhad, the underside of the east–west arch (left) (2007); mausoleum of Omar Khayyám (right) (adapted by Ali Mozaffari from original photo by Ninara (2011) available in the public domain through WikiCommons; link to original photo: https://flickr.com/photos/37583176@N00/26761782697).	153
5.8	View approximately from north to south (2017). This is the usual casual view of the edifice when one approaches it from the north.	157
5.9	Decorative relief (ribs) that feature underneath the monument are integral to its spatial expression inside and outside (2017).	158
5.10	The 72 Tan Mosque as seen from the upper levels of the Shahyad Tower (left) (2017) and the mosque facing the main avenue with the Shahyad in the background (right) (2017).	159
5.11	A makeshift photo shoot and print shop on the Shahyad platform (left) and the selfie-take statue (right) (2017).	160
5.12	People on the platform; note the 72 Tan Mosque in the background dominating the skyline (2017).	160
5.13	Images selected for random analysis (2017). These were shown to participants in the numbered order here.	162
5.14	One of two main entries of the 72 Tan Mosque (2017).	166
5.15	Views of the 72 Tan Mosque showing formal 'innovations' made possible by CAD design (2017).	167
5.16	Bust of Pourfathi in the Shahyad Museum (2017).	168
5.17	View upon entry in the main exhibition hall underneath the tower (2017).	169
5.18	General layout of a gallery with exhibits about development (2017).	169
5.19	Detail of exhibits showcasing (clockwise from top-left) education, the Persian Gulf, the environment, and culture and the arts. The exhibits pertain to aspects of the White Revolution and projects envisioned therein. Thus, the cases for education and culture and the arts have been emptied after the Revolution of 1979, presumably due to ideological incompatibilities (2017).	170
5.20	Under the watchful eyes of Khomeini and Khamenei, the amphitheatre was being prepared for an 'endorsed' weekend rock concert (2017).	171
5.21	Remains from a different time: exhibits in the Iranology gallery depicting the development and industrial projects that were meant to happen in each province (2017).	171
5.22	Fish tanks at the end of a travelator, leading to history of revolution in the back room (2017).	172
5.23	Tourism posters poorly mounted and lit at the end of the travelator at the Iranology gallery (2017).	173
5.24	Artwork about history of the Islamic Revolution (2017).	173

5.25	History of the Islamic Revolution depicted through prints (2017).	174
6.1	Louis Kahn project for Shahestān (source: *Art and Architecture* 1976, 8 (34), p. 6).	182
6.2	Kenzo Tange project for Shahestān (photo by Osamu Murai, 1974, reproduced in *The Japan Architect* 1976, 51 (8–9)).	183
6.3	The joint Kahn-Tange Shahestan Pahlavi Master Plan 1974. Legend: 1. National Historical Archive; 2. Mosque; 3. Museum; 4. Theatre; 5. Cultural Centre; 6. Outdoor Theatre; 7. "Piazza"; 8. Ministries and City Hall; 9. Artificial Lake; 10. Hotel and International Conference Centre; 11. Business and Financial Centre; 12. Gateway; 13. Parkland; 14. High-rise apartments; 15. Medium-rise apartments; 16. Horizontally bridging apartments (derived from first Tange scheme) (Nigel Westbrook after Arata Isozaki plan reproduced in *The Japan Architect*, 1976, 51 (8–9), p. 109).	185
6.4	The LDI scheme (source: *Art and Architecture* 1976, 8 (34), p. 6).	186
6.5	Reconstruction of area of Shah and Nation Square with City Hall scheme by Kenzo Tange and winning national library scheme by von Gerkan and Partners (collage by Nigel Westbrook, based upon model by LDI and Jaquelin Robertson, 1975, and projects published in *Art and Architecture* 1976, 45–6).	188
6.6	Aerial view of Abbās Ābād and Mosallā (based on Google Earth, 2017).	190
6.7	Aerial view of the realized Abbās Ābād plan superimposed on the LDI model (base images: *Art and Architecture* 1976, 8 (34), p. 6, and Google Earth (2017), superimposed by Nigel Westbrook).	191
6.8	The Tehran Book Garden (2017).	192
6.9	General view (above and below) of the bridge over the Art Lake passing by the Art Garden (not in the picture) connecting the Book Garden to the Sacred Defence Museum structure in the background (2017), and view along the main landscape axis (north–south) adjacent to the Art Garden in the form of a stepped promenade leading to the Art Lake (2010). The landscape and the museum were designed as part of the same project.	193
6.10	The promenade adjacent to the museum structure (2017).	194
6.11	Meinhard von Gerkan and partners, National Library competition entry, site plan (1977) (drawn by Nigel Westbrook after project published in *Art and Architecture* 1976, 45–6, 1978).	196
6.12	Yousef Shariatzadeh and Pirraz Consulting Engineers, National Library (2013).	197
6.13	The Chogha-Zanbil archaeological site, Khuzestan, southern Iran (2018).	197
6.14	Kerman, Shahid Bahonar University, by Yousef Shariatzadeh, Pirraz Architects: (above) the mosque with brickwork relief and	

xii　　　　　　　　　　　　*Figures and plates*

	(below) a general view into the courtyards with the amphitheatre at the right of the image (2004).	199
6.15	Cover of *Abadi* 12 depicting the winning scheme for the Islamic Republic Academies showing the competition winning entry by Mirmiran's office, Naqsh-e Jahan-Pars.	201
6.16	Another view of the winning competition entry by Mirmiran (source: *Abadi* 3 (12), p. 49).	202
6.17	Tajeer Architects (Ali Akbar Saremi and Taghi Radmard), entry for the Academies competition (source: *Abadi* 3 (12), p. 49).	203
6.18	Ivan Hasht-Behesht (Darab Diba), entry for the Academies competition (source: *Abadi* 3 (12), p. 49).	203
6.19	Competition entry by Bavand (source: *Abadi* 3 (12), p. 50).	204
6.20	Competition entry by Memar-Naqsh (source: *Abadi* 3 (12), p. 50).	205
6.21	Memar-Naqsh design for the Academies as constructed. Top row showing peripheral internal courtyards (2010) and bottom row showing the general massing of the project (2017).	205
6.22	Plan of Imam Khomeini Grand Mosallā in its urban context (drawn by Nigel Westbrook, base image Google Earth, 2019).	207
6.23	Moayyed-Ahd's winning scheme (artwork in public domain, source: Mosallā website history).	209
6.24	Two views of the central courtyard of the Mosallā under construction (2017).	211
6.25	Sports exhibition at the Mosallā (2017).	212

Plates

Plates appear between pages 179 and 180.

1 Kamran Diba, Shushtar Now (2015). User interventions in apartments and houses show the original ideas were undermined by the need to adapt the design to cars and to expanding spatial requirements of residents.
2 Kamran Diba, Jondishapur Academic staff residences (2017). Similar user adaptations are apparent in closing off balconies, blocking windows, and other spaces. Photos courtesy of Bakhtyar Lotfi.
3 Hossein Amanat, the Shahyad monument (2017), view from the platform looking west and general view of the entrance gallery with the bust of Mohammad Pourfathi at the centre-right of the picture.
4 Hossein Amanat, the Shahyad monument (2007), view of the minor arch from the platform looking south.
5 General landscape of the Abbās Ābād development (2017) (courtesy of Mohammad Shahhosseini, © Mohammad Shahhosseini 2017).
6 Kambiz Navaei an Kambiz Haji-Ghassemi, the main central courtyard of the Iranian Academies complex in Tehran (above) (2013); Jila Norouzi and Naqsh-e Jahan Pars architects, Sacred Defence Museum and Art Lake

Figures and plates xiii

   (2013), partial view of the Art Lake and its stepped garden adjacent and parallel to the museum structure (below).
7 Entry to the Sacred Defence Museum marking the graves of seven unknown martyrs (top-left) (view from the Tāleqāni Park, 2017); Parviz Moayyed-Ahd and others, the Grand Mosallā (2017), a colonnade adjacent to the main courtyard (top-right) (note how both edifices utilize the same symbolic arches also used in the Shahyad); interior of the main prayer hall of the Grand Mosallā during a sports exhibition (bottom).
8 General view of Bam citadel, a medieval fortified town in south-eastern Iran, prior to its devastation by an earthquake in 2003. This was a source of inspiration for Kalantari's competition entry for the Iranian Academies (copyright: Tibor Bognar/Alamy Stock Photo, original file name and address: Iran Bam Citadel – Image ID: AJX0E2, available from http://bit.ly/2OHOWIi).

Note on copyright

- Unless otherwise stated, all photographs belong to the personal archive of Ali Mozaffari.
- Images sourced from Iranian sources are either out of copyright or in the public domain.
- In other instances, all reasonable efforts were made in contacting the publishers to obtain clarification on copyright owners.

Acknowledgements

The production of this book was made possible through the generous institutional and financial support of the Alfred Deakin Institute for Citizenship and Globalisation, Deakin University, and the Australian Research Council, whose grant, awarded to Ali Mozaffari (ARC-DECRA, #DE170100104), facilitated financial and intellectual work for this project. We also acknowledge the institutional support of the University of Western Australia. Some of the basic ideas that inspired this volume were first presented in 2016, upon a generous invitation by Associate Professor Trinidad Rico to the international workshop she had organised at Texas A&M University at Qatar. Exploring the notion of heritage and design was encouraged by conversations with Professor Rodney Harrison. Our insights into development and its transformations were augmented by the generous contribution of Kieran D. Way. We also especially acknowledge Bakhtyar Lotfi's assistance in collecting and digitizing archival and field data, photography, and conducting photo elicitation interviews; Joely-Kym Sobot, for her tireless work in copy-editing various drafts of the manuscript; Mohammad Nazari, for his meticulous assistance with our fieldwork in Shushtar Now; Ali Javid, for assisting with some interview transcripts; and Hamidreza Mahboubi Soufiani, for helping with some of the translations of our material. Afshin Taslimi was instrumental in sourcing and digitizing some of our research archive. Professors Tim Winter and Anoma Pieris commented on the early drafts of our proposal. Tim's encouragement and friendship helped us through hard writing periods. Dr James Barry read parts of the final manuscript and Associate Professor Tod Jones and Dr Antonio Gonzalez-Zarandona lent their collegial support.

We also acknowledge our Iranian colleagues who agreed to be interviewed or provided other forms of assistance for this book including (but not limited to): Hossein Amanat, Pejman Akbarzadeh, Reza Daneshmir, Darab Diba, Farhad Diba, the late Abdolhamid Eshraq, Mohmmadreza Haeri, Kambiz Haji-Ghassemi, Seyyed Reza Hashemi, Iradj Kalantari, Hossein Sheikh Zeineddin, Hamed Mazaherian, Mohammad Moghaddam, Jila Norouzi, Hamid Nourkeyhani, Ali Novinpour, Bijan Shafei, Bahram Shokouhian, and the late Aligholi Ziaei.

The *Architecture of Changing Times in Iran* group, the National Library and Archives of Iran, the archives of the Ministry of Roads and Urban Development, the Library of Iran's Heritage, Handicrafts, and Tourism Organization, and the Statistics Centre of Iran granted Ali Mozaffari and Bakhtyar Lotfi access to their archives. We thank Emma Brennan, Robert Byron (who was particularly supportive of the idea of this book), Lucy Burns, and Humairaa Dudhwala of Manchester University Press for assisting us along the way with the production process, as well as Muhammad Ridwaan for his careful and efficient copyediting and Alan Rutter for indexing. Our anonymous reviewers benefited us with their intellectual generosity and helpful comments.

But above all, this work would have been impossible without the patience, support, and understanding of our families. Thank you, Minoo, Sepanta, Frida, Sarah, Hannah, and Charlotte.

Note on transliteration

We have used the simplified Persian transliteration standards as proposed by the Association for Iranian Studies, available online at: https://association foriranianstudies.org/journal/transliteration.

Other rules

- The *ezafeh* is written as -*e* after consonants, e.g. *ketab-e* and as -*ye* after vowels (and silent final *h*), e.g. *darya-ye* and *khaneh-ye*.
- The silent final *h* is written, e.g. *Dowleh*.
- The *tashdid* is represented by a doubling of the letter, e.g. *takhassos*.
- The plural *ha* should be added to the singular as in *dast-ha*.

Iranian Studies transliteration scheme

Consonants

z	ض	b	ب
t	ط	p	پ
z	ظ	t	ت
'	ع	s	ث
gh	غ	j	ج
f	ف	ch	چ
q	ق	h	ح
k	ک	kh	خ
g	گ	d	د
l	ل	z	ذ
m	م	r	ر
n	ن	z	ز
h	ه	zh	ژ
v	و	s	س
y	ی	sh	ش
'	ء	s	ص

Vowels

short	long	diphthongs
a (as in *ashk*)	a or ā (as in *ensan* or *āb*)	-
e (as in *fekr*)	i (as in *melli*)	ey (as in *Teymur*)
o (as in *pol*)	u (as in *Tus*)	ow (as in *rowshan*)

We have deviated from this standard on the following occasions:
1. common spelling of names of individuals established in literature or as used by themselves;
2. common or established spelling of some place names, e.g. 'Valiasr' Avenue (خیابان ولیعصر) (*not* Vli'asr) and Isfahan (*not* Esfahān).

Introduction
Development, architecture, and heritage: The formation of a collective imagination

This book examines the relationship between development, architecture, and the (re)production of the past through architectural design in Iran, from the early 1970s to the 1990s. It will show that this relationship is entangled in larger historico-cultural processes, many of which originated from outside Iran in European Enlightenment and post-Enlightenment intellectual discourses. This relationship between architectural design and the production of the past in the present, generally understood as heritage, is of ongoing concern in countries around the Persian Gulf, and in the wider, so-called Islamic world, which bestows the book with currency and relevance.

The book advances the argument that significant trends in the architecture of this period are driven by attempts to articulate a relationship between development and culture, and that this relationship continues to reshape both the production of, and theoretical debates about, the built environment within and beyond Iran. A growing body of scholarship in development studies suggests that the mutual interaction between development and culture, an interaction that induces tangible cultural change, gives rise to new forms of historical consciousness.[1] In architecture, such new consciousness becomes visually and spatially palpable through the process of design, producing repertoires of collective architectural heritages. Here, architecture, and more broadly the built environment, illustrate wider processes, the treatment of which in both heritage theory and architectural history requires a study beyond the usual power- and class-based analyses. This book takes a multidisciplinary approach, driven by discursive and empirical analysis, in order to theorize the engagement of architecture with a past that is vital for the production of a culturally situated future in a developmental context. This approach allows us to revisit well-known Iranian architectural projects in a new light, which maintains a critical distance from recently dominant positions, and situates architecture in relation to both heritage and development processes.[2]

Signs of the times: Thinking about architecture and culture in the 1970s

Iranian architectural discourse of the 1970s was enmeshed with Western developments in the field at the time. Indeed, the period of the 1960s to 1970s appears, in hindsight, to have been one of great change, when many of the official and unofficial, or so-called critical, theoretical approaches to architecture and heritage were first formulated. In both Iran and the West, one central strand was environmentalism. Growing out of the uncertainty of the Cold War, with its ever-present threat of nuclear annihilation, an intensifying apprehension of environmental collapse prompted a turn in architectural education and research away from development-led technology towards what became known as 'environmental design'. The shift was international, beginning at the University of California, Berkeley,[3] and by the end of the 1970s, many undergraduate design degrees in the US, Canada, and Australia had adopted this title. Environmental design was multidisciplinary, introducing perspectives of sociology, anthropology, and psychology to architecture. Stemming from this multidisciplinarity, which had a focus at UCLA, ethnologically based publications on vernacular buildings such as those of Bernard Rudofsky, Amos Rapoport, and Oliver were gaining currency.[4]

These trends in American and British architectural education, criticism, and research impacted upon Iran through publications, the return of foreign-trained Iranian architects, organizing international forums for exchange of ideas, specifically the architectural congresses of the 1970s (see Chapter 2), and through changes in architectural curricula. Among many returning foreign graduates, architect Kamran Diba, a graduate of the predominantly African American Howard University in Washington DC, declared himself an 'environmental designer', naming his short-lived first practice as the Office for Environmental Design. It is tempting to associate Diba's concern for a re-evaluation of traditional Iranian architecture with the turn to a more culturally grounded design process at Berkeley and elsewhere.

Architectural scholarship in 1970s Iran, or at least that of the minority not engaged in a slavish imitation of partially understood Western models,[5] was dominated by a similar conception of environmental design, manifested in particular by an approach grounded in the detailed study of traditional vernacular buildings, an emerging appreciation and study of how people actually occupied and created space,[6] a desire for the identification of cultural continuities, both within the Islamic and pre-Islamic eras, and an anxiety that the desired educational and technological modernization should not overwhelm and render redundant the cultural specificities of Iranian society. UNESCO would later express such concerns in relation to the dangers of cultural homogenization resulting from globalization.[7]

The terrain of thought on Iranian architecture and built environment

Recent architectural scholarship has re-evaluated several significant examples of the translation of modernist ideas of architecture to the Third World.[8] The example of twentieth-century Iran has been explored through a number of significant studies, some of which are noted below. Here, through a selective survey we will discern the broad themes and major theoretical leanings that have informed these studies in order to critically position the content of the forthcoming chapters.

The discontinuity between the intellectual environment of 1970s Iran and the context of recent anglophone scholarship on the Iranian architecture and planning of that period is striking. In the scholarship of 1970s Iran, diverse, sometimes contradictory, ambitions prevailed. The discursive threads included an unresolved amalgam of Western ideas of technological modernization, a desire for Iran to catch up with the international avant-garde, an opposing impulse to reject such Western ideas – an impulse which possessed both leftist and religious revolutionary aspects – and finally and related to the latter, a romantic valorization of premodern architectural culture. In the latter trend, a shift is seen towards the study of the vernacular and the aforementioned 'environmental design'.

Recent scholarship on 1970s Iranian architecture by Western-based Iranian authors draws upon Western critical theory from the early 1970s onwards, notably the critiques of postcolonialism and power. However, as Wright and Stieber have suggested, applying social theory within architectural history and theory yields variable and occasionally shallow results.[9] To make sense of the social and cultural milieu that constituted 1970s Iranian architectural culture, it is necessary to avoid falling into the trap of preconceived positions that seem to be present to various degrees in the scholarship addressing this period. It is, nevertheless, noteworthy that the question of power is bound up with the critical readings of memory and remembrance, for which heritage, especially in its objective monumental form, serves as a *lieu de mémoire*.[10] We shall return to this issue throughout the book.

The scholarship from within the field of architectural history and theory focusing on Iran has gradually proliferated since the late 1980s in Western European and North American institutions. This growing body of scholarship may be divided into two broad groups: field- and archive-based case studies and attempts to relate architectural production to larger cultural and political contexts. The first group comprises traditional works of architectural history. Mina Marefat's 1988 dissertation, 'Building to Power: Architecture of Tehran 1921–1941', is a good example.[11] In comparison with more recent studies, Marefat benefited from relatively unrestricted access to documentary archives, access to buildings, and interviews of both residents and architects in the period immediately prior to the Islamic Revolution. The study is grounded in empirical research, arguing that Westernizing processes really began with the modernizing programme of Reza Shah. There is a conscious avoidance of theoretical abstraction – in fact, the only theoretical text is Edward Said's *Orientalism* (1978, prior to the Revolution). In many respects, it represents a pre-Revolution scholarly perspective, emphasizing typological analysis of individual buildings, supplemented by interviews.[12]

Later scholarship on modern Iranian architecture has, inevitably, been affected by the 1979 Revolution. Many leading architects and academics either emigrated or were unable to continue working. Home-based Iranian scholarship under the Islamic Republic has been restricted through governmental controls and limited access to outside publications and intellectual networks. Foreign-based scholarship has, to a certain extent, taken on the perspective of the diaspora. A survey of this scholarship reveals certain predominant thematic areas: housing and culturally appropriate habitat, urban planning and design, public architecture and monuments, and, to a lesser extent, public open spaces, education-related projects, and the development of the architecture profession. Very little has otherwise been written on architectural competitions, architecture and modernity, and architectural patronage, despite these topics having clearly been important in the development and transformation of architectural culture pre- and post-Revolution.[13]

Arguably, Talinn Grigor has made the most substantial contribution to scholarship on modern Iranian architecture, viewed in relation to representations of national identity. Her work, much of which appears to be framed by postcolonial studies, engages with some modern Iranian monuments and heritage, especially the monumental architecture of the Reza Shah period, architectural heritage of the recent past, which in turn drew upon ancient heritage, while erasing a considerable amount of that of the Qajar period (1796–1925).[14] A critique of power informs her analysis of public representational architecture and modernization during the reign of Reza Shah (r. 1925–41), and of the later Shahyad monument.[15] Zahra Pamela Karimi examines the position of women and in particular the Pahlavi state's modernization programmes, through the lens of domesticity and interiority. Her research surveys Iranian expressions of 'home', reconfigured by the White Revolution (discussed below) and the Cold War, as well as subsequent official Islamist, gender-based constructions of social space.[16] Rana Habibi has researched modernist housing projects, both the estates designed by early post-war modern architects in Tehran, and later industrial housing and new towns,[17] arguing that the early projects adapt modernist principles to local cultural forms. Hamed Khosravi has speculated on post-war group housing from a Marxian perspective in which the latter projects are posited as integral to the *Tudeh* (Masses) Party's revolutionary agenda of creating a collective class-consciousness.[18] Shawhin Roudbari, in his dissertation focusing on the development of the architectural profession in Iran, effectively disproved Khosravi's thesis. Meticulously examining the roles and backgrounds of the founders of AIAD,[19] many of whom were well connected to the government, Roudbari is particularly convincing in his account of the development of the architectural profession in Iran.[20] Finally, Shirazi has examined pre-Revolution Iranian architecture from the standpoint of a supposed 'space in between', within which competing imperatives of tradition and modernity are negotiated in Iranian architecture. The rationality of Western culture is characterized, after Ricoeur (1965), as universalizing, a perspective which, while imparting benefits, is also destructive of cultural difference. To sustain the shock of this encounter, a culture must be both 'faithful to its origins' and open to cultural exchange.[21]

Of the case study-based research on housing, Kamran Diba's internationally recognized design for the new town Shushtar Now has attracted the greatest attention.[22] However, none of these studies, other than the recent book by Shirazi,[23] places the project in relation to its international context, which would become implicated in the cultural agenda of the Aga Khan Foundation, and the 'Critical Regionalism' debate. Two other Iranian housing projects, both in Tehran, have attracted scholarly attention: the American-designed Ekbatan complex[24] and the later Navāb development.[25] In both cases, the issue of housing has been conflated with larger issues of urban form and structure, as well as cultural representation.

Significant attention has been paid to the planning of the new Pahlavi governmental and cultural centre in Tehran, 'Shahestān', located in Abbās Ābād in northern Tehran, which was planned before the Revolution, and has been the subject of recent studies.[26] This area was intended as a new cultural and administrative centre for Tehran planned in the Pahlavi period (see Chapter 6). In relation to this state project, Shima Mohajeri has characterized what she claims to have been rival camps of patronage involved in the planning of the project for Shahestān. However, her scholarship does not articulate how the networks within these camps worked on the ground in material terms. Like Emami, Mohajeri draws a contrast between the 'culturalist' policies of the Queen's circle, and the technological and Westernizing approach of the Shah and his advisors, as reflected in the very different approaches of the Louis Kahn–Kenzo Tange team, and the selected Robertson–Llewellyn Davies International (LDI) project. The site of Shahestān was transformed after the Revolution through a number of competitions including one for a new Mosallā, recently discussed by the geographer Ehsani.[27] However, the ideologies, contestations of power, and machinations that have transformed and, in some respects, deformed Tehran in the post-revolutionary period have received little attention, with the exception of studies made into the development of the north–south corridor Navāb development in the 1990s through to the 2000s.[28]

This considerable, and expanding, body of literature often mentions, and at times analyzes, the relationship between architecture and social change. With the notable exception of Grigor's work, which addresses a form of heritage, what is missing from this body is a perspective that theorizes the relation between architecture, development, and heritage. While Grigor has discussed the work of the Society for National Heritage (SNH) in the early decades of the twentieth century, and Karimi discusses the Truman Point Four plan in relation to modernization and the transmission of domestic technologies in Iran,[29] the fields of architecture, heritage, and development have been treated largely independently from each other, despite their interconnections.

Examining the nexus between development and architecture, on the one hand, and the formation of heritage based on a specific historical consciousness, on the other, requires a particular theoretical approach. In this approach, nostalgia plays a key role in the context of development, and in relation to a search for authenticity, the attempted return to tradition, and references to civilization. Avoiding an ideologically driven position, this book explores the multiple interconnections between architecture, development, and heritage, and furthermore theorizes how architectural design may produce heritage through a syncretism of past traditions. The book contributes new insights into the rationale of architectural production, on the one hand, and the process of heritage- and identity-making through architecture in contemporary Iran, on the other – questions that are relevant for the wider context of Muslim societies.

Heritage and design

The following chapters critically reflect on a significant period of Iranian and global history, both in relation to the rise of various architectural discourses and their concomitant regionalisms, from within the field of architecture. The argument advanced here is straightforward but somewhat neglected: development and concomitant modernization processes result in cultural shifts that in turn complicate the experience of time.[30] Temporal slippages give rise to different perceptions of the past that are imbricated in and produce different cultural productions. In broad terms, many of these perceptions may be described as nostalgic. However, the very process of transformation also opens the past to be reimagined, redeployed, and mobilized, and from this process, new notions of heritage are born. It is true that historic precedents often inform future realizations, especially public architecture of the period. Still, in a process akin to a feedback loop, heritage is at once concretized as, and designed into being, through architecture through an imagined continuity with the past – the past is retrieved, syncretized, and projected towards a future. This function of 'heritagization' suggests that architecture takes various forms of political import, and an active, and yet often unpredictable, presence in remaking the past, and future. To assert that heritage can be produced through design is to propose that elements of the past may be appropriated through citations, and incorporated into new constructions, through which novel collective imaginations of the past may be engendered and hence encountered in everyday lives.[31]

With an examination of the use of heritage in mind, we draw case studies from both public, representational architecture, and from housing settlements. Almost all the projects discussed in the following chapters began in the 1970s but continued to be planned, re-planned, and eventually constructed in an 'afterlife' subsequent to the Revolution. It is precisely this double life that makes them interesting reference points for historical change. Examining these works produces insights into the enduring and mutable aspects of historical imagination in Iran, as well as the multifaceted and ever-surprising outcomes of global exchanges. Within the field of architecture, this book reveals the disjuncture between architecture and ideological polemic; that as a disciplinary practice and in material terms, architecture resists any enduring ascription of symbolic meaning.

As indicated above, in the face of unprecedented socio-historical changes, Iranians were not merely passive recipients; they also exercised agency in various ways and at different scales. While there were convergences in some of the broader ideas and occasionally a dominant rhetoric, it would be erroneous to assume the persistent presence of a cultural programme that produced a singular cultural, architectural, and artistic outcome. This aside, we are suggesting that in the process of exercising agency, and in engaging with these changes and with other actors, there was a desire on the part of Iranian intellectuals to reimagine a specific Iranian identity. Various organically developing precepts had been tested since the beginning of the twentieth century as paths to modernization; ironically, the latest such formula sought a path to modernization through an engagement with, and reimagining of, the past and its traditions. This reflexive and conscious concern for the import of the past in the present was, in retrospect, a heritage process, the vehicles for which were various modes of image-making, citations, and cultural practices exercised through spatial choreography and ritual, which are in various ways discussed throughout the chapters of this volume. Architecture functioned as a medium and facilitator of this process and, as such, it produced a critical engagement with, and interpretations of, the past and at the same time, a series of material spatial objects that came to constitute a contemporary heritage in their own right. This arguably nostalgic engagement ultimately also formed part of Iran's 'detraditionalization', which may be broadly understood as 'the decline of the belief in pre-given or natural orders of things',[32] a process that was neither purely imposed from outside nor solely the product of Iranian developments inside the country. It was, rather, a product of the interaction between transnational transformations, which included, but were not limited to, geopolitical machinations of a bipolar world, and internal cultural, historical, political, social, and technological specificities.

A proliferating cultural modernity, increasing rates of exchange of raw and processed materials, people's movement across multiple scales – from localities to metropolises, from hometowns to 'abroad' – and the creation of international and transnational institutions and alliances such as the UN (est. 1945), World Bank (est. 1945), and the CENTO Pact (1955–79), imposed various demands on the circulation of goods, people, and ideas, and of course, knowledge. These forms of globalization[33] had already begun to destabilize both smaller-scale localities, from the singular state down, and fixed identities and senses of belonging, yielding a certain degree of hybridization,[34] fusion, and liminality, as noted in recent scholarship. Here, attention needs to be paid to notions such as the relationship of the local to the global, useful in explaining heritage processes involved in and produced through acts of architectural design.

Anna Tsing articulates a useful perspective on the mutual relations between the local and the global, noting that even the term 'globalization' has a history, and was born of capitalist networks of exchange: 'the awkward, unequal, unstable, and creative qualities of interconnection across difference'.[35] Globality is imagined and made through specific projects, modernization constituting one example.[36] Problematizing the division between local and global, Tsing suggests that both are co-produced at various scales. More importantly, culture is formed through long-distance, transnational exchanges, the outcome of which, at a local level, contains 'messy and surprising features'.[37] Such hybridity and syncretism occurs in diverse modes of cultural production, including in the making of architecture. Tsing asks, 'How are people, cultures, and things remade as they travel?'[38] Friction is not to be mistaken for resistance, the term that has characterized some aspects of writing on the architecture of the peripheries, including in Iran. It is, rather, the process through which universals are engaged in historically, culturally, and locationally specific actions, thus becoming materially and locally embedded. Such 'engaged universals' move across different scales and places (across 'difference') and this circulation transforms them in diverse ways.[39] Culture is thus not autochthonous, but rather formed out of encounters.

Considering the concept of friction then, heritage may be seen as a perpetual project of 'networking and building lines of support' at multiple scales and, at times, with contradictory or conflicting directions.[40] It is also in this process that practices of architecture, including its international exchanges, its education, and its professional techniques of design, are operationalized. The definitions of these scales – local, regional, national, and global – comprise part of the cultural production, and their claims and contestations should be critically examined. Furthermore, it is possible to see the architecture of Iran in the period between the 1970s and 1990s, which is concerned with identity, time, past, and heritage, as a global project, and thus a topic worthy of re-examination.

Negotiating development and tradition

In examining a developmental context such as Iran, much of the critical perspective on development is informed by 'dependency theory', which posits an asymmetrical relationship between Third World and Western economies,[41] and involves, correctly, a critique of modernization and its place in the colonial enterprise. Aside from ideological fascinations, current critiques of the instrumental rationalization typical of 1950s approaches to modernization are inspired by a Foucauldian critique of power. While such critiques retain validity, it should be noted that universalist modernization and development theories had already been called into question during the 1950s.[42] 'Neo-populist', Third World-focused development theories,[43] such as Schumacher's new emphasis on sustainable development and appropriate use of technology in his book *Small Is Beautiful* (1973), are indicative of such critiques, which gathered pace since the early 1970s, and further clarified the distinction between modernization – defined as Enlightenment-inspired, Eurocentric policies and practices predicated 'on rational action and efficient institutions'[44] and socially beneficial development. But as Peet and Hartwick note, modernization continues to persist in theories, policies, and practices of development.[45] In other words, it is difficult to posit categorical and epochal divisions in development theories.[46]

The processes of modernization have been usefully categorized by Cowen and Shenton, who propose to distinguish between immanent and intentional forms of development.[47] Immanent development can be understood as the operation of the processes of globalized capitalism, where no specific agency can be identified. Intentional development, on the other hand, can be understood as deliberate, often state-led doctrines of development. In many developing contexts, including 1970s Iran under Pahlavi rule (1925–79), this was the preferred mode of development. Significantly, in the context of Iran, intentional development in the last decades of the second Pahlavi regime (1941–79) was enacted through forward-looking, modernist initiatives that in certain respects also relied on, and sought to validate, the present by referencing the past. It is this aspect of development that focuses attention on the valorization and deployment of heritage, as we shall see below and throughout this book.

Concurrently, development also involves destruction: inevitably, the old, or aspects of it, is destroyed to make way for the new.[48] Intentional development in the context of Iran was also an attempt to control what Cowen and Shenton have referred to as 'the disordered movement of population', a movement that, arguably, contributed to the downfall of the Pahlavi regime.[49] Through this framing, development in Iran can be understood as not only the product of the state's ambition to join the ranks of developed nations, and to restore due respect to Iranian civilization, but also as the attempt to exercise control over processes of modernization, and their consequent disruptions. Such attempts to restore or impose order invoked Iranian cultural specificities, and thus a renewed consciousness of the past, which operated in the present as heritage. Past traditions were drawn upon to validate present-day policies, which in turn – as we shall discuss in Chapter 1 – set the limits of experience and of meaning, by maintaining a sense of continuity. Furthermore, the forms of development in Iran over the period covered in this book, and the popular responses to them, were not mere consequences of Western manipulation. Instead, they were primarily the outcome of multiple agencies and interests responding to Western and Soviet-bloc influences and pressures and produced by friction in the Iranian setting. In Iran, this friction occurred precisely when the nation's culture was most exposed, even vulnerable, to global interconnection, and in the form of a nostalgic embrace of the vernacular, the authentic, and the traditional; an approach which was also common to Western attempts to introduce modernizing processes in a colonial or Third World context.[50]

The processes of development are clearly manifested in the built environment through various forms of construction, including architecture, which is thus a valid vehicle for reflecting on those processes and their historical effects.[51] Architectural and heritage discourses imbricated in projects of intentional development were codified within the framework of successive state 'development plans', and were redirected and transformed by multiple forces, those produced by globalization and tensions inherent to Iranian society – expressions of resistance from sections of society threatened by cultural and economic transformations and multiple forms of modernization. The relationship between culture and development, while causing concern in various arenas, would not be theorized and formally acknowledged until the 1990s.[52] Furthermore, the linkages between development and transformations in architectural discourses have not yet been articulated, which makes the explorations in the following chapters all the more timely.

Both development projects and their critiques have influenced attitudes towards past and currently existing cultural traditions. Especially in Third World contexts,[53] the ad hoc endeavours of individuals and groups on the ground acted as mitigating, experiential (and experimental) responses to development-induced sociocultural transformations. The result of those activities was a reassessment of the past and of traditions, with the reappraisal and deployment of their symbolic content in contemporary projects. This book attempts to read these processes in relation to an engagement with, and the design of, heritage. Critically, on the rare occasions when the term 'heritage' is used in scholarship on the built environment, as is the case mentioned above with Grigor and the Reza Shah period,[54] it is either deployed in lieu of a specific type of nostalgia, one that is reductive, reactionary, and chauvinistic, or is used in the technical sense associated with the preservation and conservation of building fabric and landscapes. The studies on Iranian modern architecture noted above, with the exception of Grigor's work, miss the productive potentials that a multidisciplinary approach to both heritage and architecture can bring to bear, most importantly in rewriting the histories of modernity, and the transformations that modernization has brought to traditions in developing countries like Iran.

The relationship between heritage and the built environment thus deserves further critical scrutiny. Architecture, in its monumental form, is often taken to constitute a symbolic site of memory. However, the material role of architecture in influencing the formation of heritage, through bodily immersion, rather than just symbolic representation, is often ignored or discounted. The objectification of heritage – its reduction to mere monuments and things at the expense of sociocultural processes that form heritage – is rightly questioned by critical heritage theorists.[55] However, the role of architecture and urbanism in post-1979 Iranian architectural studies has been characterized as little more than representative of an oppressive Pahlavi hegemony. One lacuna in the scholarship is the lack of examination of the role of architectural design in creating heritage in a developmental context. Here, following Harrison, Smith, and Harvey, among others, we recognize that heritage is a cultural process,[56] pertaining to the perception, role, and uses of the past for the purposes of the present.[57] While we agree that heritage has an inherently political component, and is subject to constant 'dissonance'[58] and inevitable contestation, and that one could discern official and unofficial forms of heritage, given the multiplicity of players and issues involved in heritage at any given time,[59] we do not believe that the state, no matter how powerful, can impose a singular idea of heritage for any sustainable period.[60] Specifically in the case of Iran's architectural heritage, there is more scope for interpretation of the complexities of architectural symbolism than in asserting some hegemonic cultural policy, racial ideology, or monarchic grandiosity and hubris. The production of the built environment, and the meanings it assumes post-production, are thus seen as a constant negotiation, the intentions underlying works of architecture being situational and fluid. Arguably, then, the relationship between these two fields of architectural history and theory, on the one hand, and heritage studies, on the other, and the intricacies of their interrelation within the context of 'developing' countries such as Iran, requires further theorization.

A local response to global processes: The White Revolution

Revisiting the decades of the 1970s to 1990s in Iran reveals the period's significance for its lasting transformations, in both the microcosm of Iranian cultural life and the macrocosm of transnational cultural and economic change. At the beginning of the 1970s, Iran reaped the benefits, albeit short-lived, of reform and the official 'development plans' of the Pahlavi administration. These plans were born of the White Revolution, a wide-ranging economic and social programme, primarily funded through the sale of oil, the value of which substantially appreciated after the 1973 Yom Kippur War.[61]

The White Revolution offers an example of transnational, globalizing processes. This socio-economic programme of the Pahlavi government, undertaken from 1963 to 1979, impacted many areas of national life, including industrialization, education (primary, secondary, and tertiary), health services, and the acknowledgement of women's rights.[62] The programme also occasioned negative consequences, notably the social disruption caused by agricultural land redistribution, compelling many of the poorest rural workers to migrate to the cities in search of work. The White Revolution is best understood through the lens of modernization theory, the prevailing theoretical framework that underlay the operation of the American Agency for International Development (AID) programme, created in 1961, at the height of the Cold War, by US President John F. Kennedy. A central aim of AID was to provide technical assistance to developing nations, and in so doing, to encourage political liberalization and tie countries like Iran into a global market.[63] AID, like the Truman-initiated

Point Four programme that preceded it, and the Shah's White Revolution, was informed by modernization theory, according to which traditional societies[64] could develop through 'progress in technology, military and bureaucratic institutions, and the political and social structure'.[65] These programmes were, in their basis, political, and should be seen in the light of the Cold War contestation. Because of its strategic geopolitical location and oil resources, Iran was, literally, a starting point of the Cold War,[66] and subsequently took on the role of a declared Western ally against its expansionist Communist neighbour, the Soviet Union, and received Western development aid.[67] Ironically, however, one can see similarities between some aspects of the White Revolution programmes and Soviet policies during the occupation of Iran in the Second World War.

Significantly for the Iranian example, a considerable part of the AID programme's agenda was the funding of widespread literacy programmes, and the expansion and improvement of the university sector.[68] This tied in with the Iranian government's own economic development priorities in the areas of agriculture and veterinary science.[69] The connection of new university planning with AID, American universities, the Ford Foundation, and MIT's Centre for International Studies (a think tank substantially funded by the CIA and the Pentagon) indicates the extent to which such support was intimately related to American containment policy in relation to the Soviet Union and China. However, it would be a mistake to reduce the ideas of development, their corollary manifestations in architecture, and the production of heritage to outcomes of an American agenda in Iran, or to explain them away in simplistic political (ideological) terms. Instead, we endeavour to reveal the entanglement of development and culture in architecture as a result of both international and domestic exchanges and machinations and how this has produced heritage as well as having had a lasting impact on schools of architectural thought and practice in Iran.

By the beginning of the 1970s, with the industrial and land reforms of the White Revolution having largely been implemented by the end of the previous decade, and with the general (albeit uneven) growth that the country experienced at the time in accordance with the government's Third and Fourth Development Plans (1962–68, 1968–73), previous efforts could now be expected to bear fruit.[70] Indeed, the decade of 1966–76 witnessed such significant economic growth[71] that by late 1967, Iran no longer required American aid.[72] Thus, by the usual development standards, the society was prospering. Under the Pahlavis, the country had modernized at a rapid pace, concomitantly with massive social, cultural, and economic repercussions. There were, however, clear concerns about inflationary pressures in the economy stemming from the capacity to absorb the generated wealth, and the growth of inequality, reflected in the development programmes' recommended income redistribution and equity.[73] Concerns, moreover, redoubled around the influence of development on Iranian cultural life. Here, the impact of modernization prompted increased support from the government for cultural projects, especially from the

Queen's Special Office. Indeed, the Sixth Development Plan recognized the necessity for preservation of, research into, and education in cultural heritage and the arts in general, together with the 'establishment of facilities for art, literature, creativity and expansion of cultural relations'.[74] It further noted the conflict between the imperatives of modernization and traditional cultural perspectives, a conflict which was exacerbated by the internal migration of provincial and rural populations to the cities, which had created shortfalls and unevenness in the provision of adequate housing and social and health services.[75]

The policies contained within the Sixth Development Plan for addressing the antimonies between modernization and culture were, however, never implemented because of the advent of the 1979 Revolution. Thus, the 1970s contained both the peak of this modernizing transformation and its end, with the demise of the Pahlavi regime. At the start of the decade, the Shah himself, increasingly confident and assertive on a national and international stage, projected a more independent stance in relation to the West, initiating commercial and expertise importation links with the Soviet Union.[76] Alongside other actors within the establishment, he showed interest in cultivating and strengthening a sense of collective national identity, aspects of which existed in the intellectual ferment independent of the monarchy's interests. The built environment in general, and architecture in particular, concurrently reflected both ideas of development and the prevailing cultural mood. There was, furthermore, a sense of urgency driven by Iran's circumstances: rapid population displacement resulting from industrialization, equally rapid growth on the peri-urban fringes, appeals for growth and development, and an increasing global engagement, to name but a few challenges that demanded responses.[77] However, beyond logistical and technological difficulties, Iran witnessed cultural transformations, the weight of which, for better or worse, was felt by both the establishment's intellectual elite and the general populace, with differing levels of reflection and understanding. Here, Iranian anxiety over the destabilization of its native culture and traditions also reflects a global condition, in which localities were perceived as being destabilized by modernity.

Appadurai, in his discussion on global cultural flows, notes the inherent fragility of 'locality' – which in modern societies is 'under siege'.[78] Iran was thus caught between the poles of technologically driven modernization and the diminishing relevance of its traditions, serving at once as a market for foreign expertise, a testing ground for novel ideas and for the adaptation of old ideas to a new context, and a site in which experimental practices could yield innovation. However, rather than being passive recipients of foreign influences, as we shall see in the forthcoming chapters of this book, Iranians themselves played an active role in their adaptation.[79] Both in the broader cultural and social scene and in architecture, this interaction with global expertise led to contradictory and paradoxical outcomes. Within architectural circles, and among the intellectual and political elite more generally, concern grew over the threat to Iranian traditions and authentic practices, in the face of the onslaught of development and concomitant modernization. But such a concern did not originate in Iran, nor would it remain confined there, despite expressions of Iranian exceptionalism. As we shall see below, this could be ascribed to the operation of globalization processes that, in turn, gave rise to a consciousness of local specificities.

While there are a number of narratives constructed out of the history of this period, the end of it is well known. The oil boom of the first half of the 1970s gave way to increasing economic instability in the latter part of the decade, in part induced by a fall in the price of oil. Bearish markets combined with various cultural and political problems precipitated a sudden implosion of the power of the monarchy in 1979.[80] By 1980, the Islamic Republic, a new political system based upon the principle of rule by Islamic jurists, was ratified through a public referendum. The new state system claimed to represent a comprehensive cultural, and religious, response to the monarchy, and sought to achieve a kind of Islamic utopia.[81] However, as we have previously observed, this ideological discourse did not produce a dramatic shift in the post-Revolution period in aspects of architectural thinking, debates, and production.[82] Instead, within the field of architecture, it perpetuated formal aspects that could be labelled as vernacularist or romantic. Nevertheless, at least for the first decade and a half after 1979, both the Islamic authorities and members of the academy did, implicitly or otherwise, discourage tendencies and design approaches that could be perceived as 'Western', both in architectural practice and education.[83] Persistence of the vernacular, a characteristic also of some pre-Revolution architecture supported by the Queen (notably the work of Nader Ardalan and Kamran Diba), is itself worthy of critical interrogation. With this in mind, we argue that, whether in built forms, or in unrealized building and landscape projects, architecture offers a valid register of possibilities and outlooks – the cultural mood – at any historical moment. Architecture is both born of a socio-historical setting, and gives form to it, thus containing what are often utopian projections for possible and alternative futures. Indeed, these forms, and the critical positions that give rise to them, are inherently projective, revealing much about ideological aspirations as well as other conditions underlying material production at any given time.

But architecture is also inextricably implicated in economic processes. Global movements of ideas, expertise, and capital, new development projects in Iran, and exponential economic growth,[84] led to burgeoning cultural activity including in architecture.[85] This was further stimulated by the rising number of Iranian architectural graduates from universities both within and outside Iran, notably in Italy, France, the UK, Germany, and the US.[86] The outcome was an exceptionally vibrant period in Iranian architectural development, in which the country briefly became one of the world centres for new architectural production. Iranian architecture of the 1970s needs to be understood in relation to this context, characterized by a major peak in state building projects. The bulk of construction and design activity focused on and within the capital city of Tehran, which is why the city and its architecture occupy a considerable amount of space in this book.[87]

In the following chapters, we will expand on the relation between development and heritage in discussing categories of architectural production, and this necessarily involves examining pertinent aspects of tradition, and how these relate to culture as a dynamic phenomenon and to development processes. As noted above, a central theoretical issue in this relationship is that of nostalgia; we acknowledge, however, that during the 1970s the issue of cultural nostalgia was only beginning to be recognized and was not yet formulated in any concrete manner. In the Pahlavi period, nostalgia was indeed institutionalized in cultural programmes, the creation of museums, and the use of heritage to showcase the nation and the regime through curated heritage sites and the mass media. Integral to this institutionalized nostalgia was the valorization of tradition and the vernacular, precisely at a time when the same modernization processes discussed above rendered vernacular forms and practices anachronistic. This was not just a governmental agenda, but also a concern of intellectuals, poets, and artists for a return to origins embodied in the vernacular. We will see that what we now know as heritage was central to the question of development at this time, and architecture was one of the vehicles that expressed this relation tangibly, symbolically, and in the everyday life of the nation.

The structure of this book

This book proposes a nexus between development, design, and heritage. Development induces palpable historical change giving rise to shifts in perceptions of time and reappraisals of the past.[88] It also involves the circulation and exchange of ideas and concepts. This condition is apt for various forms of nostalgia and is a basis for perceptions of heritage. In developmental contexts like Iran, forms of nostalgia have been expressed through discourses of authenticity, civilization, and tradition, a constellation of leitmotifs of intellectual cultural production that existed in late Pahlavi Iran and continued after the Revolution. This constellation cut across scale and time, meaning it manifested locally and in social time as well as trans-locally on a monumental time.[89] As such, and indicating particular and at times contradictory attitudes towards the past, these leitmotifs bore concrete manifestations in design and architecture. The structure of the book follows the logic of this proposition by developing the necessary analytical discussions (Chapter 1), tracing them in concepts and ideas that circulated at multiple scales heavily informing architectural debates and production (Chapter 2), and a detailed analysis of case studies as registers of development functioning at social and monumental times and spaces. These case studies focus on culturally appropriate housing in Chapters 3 and 4, and monumental edifices within urban ensembles in Chapters 5 and 6. This is followed by the Conclusion, which brings together the insights gained from the book. The significant point about the case studies is that they straddle pre- and post-Revolution eras, which yield further insights into the contextual shifts that took place in Iran.

Following this logic, Chapter 1 teases out theoretical aspects of the discussion considering the specificities of the Iranian context. It expounds the working of nostalgia, an essentially modern phenomenon, and tradition, within the Iranian context and focuses on the constellation mentioned above. While discussing authenticity and its manifestations, the chapter also elaborates on the nuances of the notion of tradition, all of which are necessary to situate the position and designs of various actors in the architectural scene. The chapter includes a concrete example where the analytical utility of its concepts is demonstrated.

Chapter 2 presents some of the major international flows of ideas in Iran through international congresses of architecture held in the country in the early to mid-1970s, and their subsequent impact on the field. These congresses are analyzed in relation to development and the production of heritage. Between 1970 and 1976, the Iranian government organized three international congresses of architecture, the last one held in conjunction with the fourth congress of the *Union Internationale des Femmes Architectes*, as well as the first two congresses of earthen architecture. These congresses addressed issues pertaining to development and the White Revolution. The delegates to these congresses included many of the leading international figures of the time and the presentations and sessions focused on pressing issues arising from developmentalism in the Iranian context. These included the complex relation of tradition and modernization, and the crisis of cultural identity in the face of the globalization of knowledge and media, but also, more generally, upon alternatives to existing normative models of modernist architecture, housing, and urbanism.[90] The congresses evidenced a turn to the vernacular by emphasizing the traditional village and focusing upon cities like Safavid Isfahan as models of organically holistic design, in which the collective subsumes individual expression. This interest in tradition is explored in relation to a more general cultural turn in the West towards regional authenticity. These regionalist alternatives to cultural homogeneity came to inform not only UNESCO's policies on culturally appropriate habitat, but also, arguably, the ensuing theory of Critical Regionalism. For Iranian architects, the congresses were an opportunity to theorize a specifically Iranian 'lifeworld', a contextually specific pattern of everyday life, in which architecture and urbanism were imbricated. The ideas that were to inform architectural thought and practice for the next two decades were the product firstly of the demands for development, and secondly, of an international engagement and exchange that resulted in both the creation of heritage through design, and design thinking processes that persisted – in some instances to the present – in the practice and jargon of Iranian architecture.

The production of heritage in the design of culturally appropriate housing before and after the Revolution is examined in Chapters 3 and 4 respectively. We will show how ideas that emerged in international discussions, especially the congresses, were activated in reimagining the past, a process that led to the creation of architectural heritage at a domestic level, in mass housing. Together, the chapters illustrate dominant approaches to reconceptualizations of the past in the architecture of the everyday, through the forms and spatial structures of housing.

In Chapter 3, we explore the design of culturally appropriate housing environments, or habitats, in the period before the Revolution. Mass housing had begun as a key instrument for the modernization of the Iranian economy, and in modern form was first constructed as company housing, and housing commissioned to accommodate public servants in government ministries, such as the mid-century Tehran housing estates for Chāhārsad Dastgāh, Kuy-e Nārmak, and Nāzi Ābād.[91] We argue that in Iran, the trajectory of ideas for culturally appropriate mass housing can be traced back to models developed by European colonial authorities for what they termed 'housing for the indigenous populations',[92] and at home for the provision of housing for post-war reconstruction and for new industries. The forms and spatial layouts for these new housing estates responded to the need for culturally and socially appropriate forms of housing for both local and foreign workers, but also for different classes – the middle-class professional and managerial echelons and the families of factory workers relocated from traditional towns and villages. International influences continued throughout the 1960s and 1970s, with the projects designed by Jane Drew, of Fry, Drew, and Partners, London, for workers' housing in the oil towns of Masjed-e Soleymān and Gachsārān. As in the public housing in French North Africa by Écochard and *ATBAT Afrique*, Drew adapted her essentially modernist planning and house typologies to local cultural norms and climatic conditions. These international projects, together with the cultural exchanges at the 1970s architectural congresses, formed the stimulus for significant, home-grown experiments in housing, by Kamran Diba at Shushtar Now in Khuzestan (1976 onwards), and other similar projects, in which both traditional Iranian forms, spaces, and motifs were syncretized with then-contemporary international housing projects. Both pre- and post-Revolution mass housing deploy interpretations of vernacular housing and urban form, presumably because of their familiarity to partly modernized populations.

But not all housing was referencing tradition. Contemporary with Shushtar Now is the enormous complex of Ekbatan, in north-western Tehran, an essentially private development. Here, there are no concessions to tradition – the complex was designed and built by a New York firm with experience in public 'projects' and mixed public–private complexes. As a vehicle for the transnational exchange of advanced housing technologies, the project is highly significant, but also serves as evidence for the cultural schizophrenia that characterizes Iranian architecture before and after the Revolution. While Ekbatan targeted educated, Westernized middle-class residents, Shushtar Now accommodated the rural poor who formed much of the workforce of the new industries such as agribusiness.

In Chapter 4, we examine the continuation of some of the heritage–design discourses after the 1979 Revolution. The Islamic Revolution stands as the first in modern times where a traditional, clerical elite, joining forces with various leftist groups, mustered enough popular support to overthrow a powerful and modernizing monarchy. The agenda of mass housing, however, did not change. In this chapter, we analyse the brief for, and selected projects entered in, nationwide housing competitions held by the Iranian Ministry for Housing in 1985. Here we examine the relationship between the submitted designs and the overtly Islamist agenda underlying the competition, with its anti-Western and traditionalist rhetoric. Drawing upon architectural precedents held to constitute 'Islamic architectural heritage', a few designs resembled Diba's project. We argue that this process of citing the past in new projects – the refashioning fragments of past traditions into new configurations – constitutes heritage by design. As yet another example of friction at work, these designs show novel, syncretic approaches derived from a Western context but responding to the specifics of the Iranian setting at the time. The analysis also shows the underlying continuities between the architecture produced in the pre- and post-Revolution regimes. This suggests a certain consistency in production of architectural heritage, perhaps as a result of economic embargoes and internally and externally imposed isolation.

In Chapters 5 and 6, we examine the relationship between public spaces and architecture and the design of heritage, and their role before and after the Revolution as projections of ideas of national identity. An important aspect of these projects was that the past and its motifs were reimagined or even reinvented in new contexts and scales as a form of vernacular representing a supposed authenticity. The difference with the housing examples is that here, these motifs were explicit and played a clear representational role, while the experiential aspects too were included and reimagined in designs.

In Chapter 5, we discuss a project that is perhaps one of the most recognizable symbols of modern Iran, the Shahyad (since 1979, 'Azadi' or freedom) monument in Western Tehran. From the 1960s, a form of public architecture was promoted by the Iranian state, which while utilizing the latest technologies, cited elements of pre-Islamic and Islamic period architecture in its quest for identity and engagement with the past. Such architecture expressed a utopian faith in the future, while largely rejecting the materialism of Western architectural culture. The iconic Shahyad cites historical sources but also constitutes a liminal zone, both in a physical sense – marking a threshold in the transition from the airport and new suburbs to the west – and metaphorically, by mediating between a certain past, the present, and future. In this chapter, in addition to architectural analyses, the monument is examined in relation to the relevant architectural scholarship on the edifice as well as the anecdotal evidence gathered through photo elicitations from those encountering it in the urban context.

In Chapter 6, we focus upon the project for a new governmental centre at Ābbās Ābād, in northern Tehran, which was planned in the Pahlavi period as the site for a new governmental centre, Shahestān. This project is significant for its role in projecting a Westernizing image of the city. As noted earlier in this

Introduction, Emami and Mohajeri have analyzed the Shahestān as a Pahlavi urban project. The existing critiques reveal as much about the authors' theoretical positions as they do about the motivations of the clients and architects. Departing from these analyses, the project is examined as an attempt to design a representational space, one which draws upon the past in a heritage process. The chapter traces the evolution of the project before and after the Revolution, culminating in the use of a significant portion of the area associated with this zone as the setting for the Mosallā, a gigantic Friday mosque intended to form a new religious centre for the city. The built Mosallā project shifts from the city's north–south orientation to one aligned with Mecca, thus effectively severing the site from the everyday time and space of the city. The erasure of a sense of public space within this zone has been reinforced by subsequent competitions and projects for public buildings in Ābbās Ābād, namely, the competitions for the Iranian Academies (1993–94), the National Library (1995), and later projects for a book fair and the Sacred Defence Museum (a museum commemorating the Iran–Iraq War) and associated parks, which in totality erase the clear spatial structure of the Robertson–Llewelyn Davies project. Tracing the continuities and discontinuities before and after the Revolution, we reflect on the evolving cultural agendas of the Islamic Republic.

For a brief period, Iran had appeared as a centre for world architecture, through the publicity engendered by its International Congresses of Architecture, its sponsoring of transnational collaborations between Iranian and international architects, its active participation in global cultural organizations like UNESCO and UN-Habitat, and through the extensive coverage of Iranian architecture and heritage via world media. Iranian oil wealth funded an explosion of new projects in every sector of society. We can see, after Tsing, that through friction, development led to new forms and themes. For a few decades, the vocabulary for discussing these new forms and themes pertained to the attempts to reconcile technological development and Iranian cultural traditions. These were explorations that anticipated the later international critique of globalized culture manifested in Critical Regionalism, and the Aga Khan awards programme. Just as suddenly, this dynamic transformation was ended by the Islamic Revolution, and the closing of cultural links between Iran and the Western world. And yet the architecture of this time evidences a cultural continuity that bridged these periods, in which designers drew upon the past, and upon memory and nostalgia, in fabricating a national heritage in the present, an imagination of place in which strands of collective identity are inscribed in material objects and spaces.

Notes

1 S. A. Radcliffe (ed.), *Culture and Development in a Globalizing World: Geographies, Actors and Paradigms* (Abingdon: Routledge, 2006); S. Schech and J. Haggis, *Culture and Development: A Critical Introduction* (Oxford: Wiley-Blackwell, 2000).

2 On scholarship of development studies, see J. M. Hodge, 'Writing the History of Development (Part 1: The First Wave)', *Humanity: An International Journal of Human Rights, Humanitarianism and Development*, 6:3 (Winter, 2015), pp. 429–63; J. M. Hodge, 'Writing the History of Development (Part 2: Longer, Deeper, Wider)', *Humanity: An International Journal of Human Rights, Humanitarianism and Development*, 7:1 (Spring, 2016), pp. 125–74. On development and culture, see A. Sen, 'How Does Culture Matter?', in M. Walton and V. Rao (eds), *Culture and Public Action: A Cross-disciplinary Dialogue on Development Policy* (Washington, DC: World Bank Publications, 2004), pp. 37–58; A. Sen, *Development as Freedom* (Oxford: Oxford University Press, 2001), pp. 227–48; A. Escobar, *Territories of Difference: Place, Movements, Life, Redes* (Durham, NC, and London: Duke University Press, 2008), 200–54; S. Schech, 'Culture and Development', in V. Desai and R. B. Potter (eds), *The Companion to Development Studies*, 3rd edn (London and New York: Routledge, 2014), pp. 50–54. On development and governmentality, see M. P. Cowen and R. W. Shenton, *Doctrines of Development* (London and New York: Routledge, 1996); T. M. Li, *The Will to Improve: Governmentality, Development, and the Practice of Politics* (Durham, NC: Duke University Press, 2007); T. M. Li, *Land's End: Capitalist Relations on an Indigenous Frontier* (Durham, NC: Duke University Press, 2014). On cultural studies, see J. Nederveen Pieterse, *Globalization and Culture: Global Melange*, 2nd edn (Blue Ridge Summit, PA: Rowman & Littlefield Publishing, 2009). For trends related to modernity, see D. Harvey, *The Condition of Postmodernity: An Enquiry into the Origins of Cultural Change* (New York: Wiley, 1992); A. Giddens, *Consequences of Modernity* (Cambridge and Malden, MA: Polity Press, 2012).

3 Diba's studies in America included a year of sociology. Diba in R. Dānishvar, *A Garden between Two Streets* (Persian) (Paris: Alborz, 2010), 115; K. T. Diba, *Kamran Diba: Buildings and Projects* (Berlin: Verlag Gerd Hatje, 1981), p. 8. On the beginnings of the pedagogy of environmental design, see S. Woodbridge, '"Reflections of the Founding" Wurster Hall and the College of Environmental Design [Two Place Tales]', *Places*, 1:4 (1984), pp. 47–58.

4 B. Rudofsky, *Architecture without Architects: A Short Introduction to Non-pedigreed Architecture* (Albuquerque, NM: University of New Mexico Press, 1964); F. Scott, 'Bernard Rudofsky: Allegories of Nomadism and Dwelling', in S. W. Goldhagen and R. Legault (eds), *Anxious Modernisms: Experimentation in Postwar Architectural Culture* (Cambridge, MA: MIT Press, 2000), pp. 215–37; A. Rapoport, *House Form and Culture* (Eaglewood Cliffs, NJ: Prentice-Hall, 1969), translated into Persian as A. Rapoport, *The Cultural Origin of Residential Complexes*, trans. R. Zadeh (Tehran: Tehran University of Science and Technology, 1366/1987): (1366) راپاپورت، آمس، ;P. Oliver منشاء فرهنگی مجتمع های زیستی، رضازاده، راضیه، جهاد دانشگاهی علم و صنعت ایران، تهران (ed.), *Shelter and Society* (New York: Praeger, 1969).

5 Diba cited in L. Bakhtiar (ed.), *Towards a Quality of Life: The Role of Industrialization in the Architecture and Urban Planning of Developing Countries: Report of the Proceedings of the Second International Congress of Architects, Persepolis, Iran, 1974* (Tehran: Ministry of Housing and Development, 1974), 95.

6 Diba cited in L. Farhad and L. Bakhtiar (eds), *The Interaction of Tradition and Technology: Report of the Proceedings of the First International Congress of Architects, Isfahan, 1970* (Tehran: Ministry of Housing and Development, 1970), 193.

7 UNESCO, *The 2005 Convention on the Protection and Promotion of the Diversity of*

Cultural Expressions (Paris: UNESCO and Diversity of Cultural Expressions, 20 October 2005), http://en.unesco.org/creativity/sites/creativity/files/passeport-convention2005-web2.pdf (accessed 2 February 2019).

8 J.-L. Cohen and M. Eleb, *Casablanca: Colonial Myths and Architectural Ventures* (New York: Monacelli Press, 2003); T. Avermaete, 'Coda: The Reflexivity of Cold War Architectural Modernism', *The Journal of Architecture*, 17:3 (2012), pp. 475–7; T. Avermaete et al. (eds), *Colonial Modern: Aesthetics of the Past, Rebellions for the Future* (London: Black Dog Publishing, 2010).

9 N. Stieber, 'Architecture between Disciplines', *Journal of the Society of Architectural Historians*, 62:2 (2003), pp. 176–7; G. Wright, 'Cultural History: Europeans, Americans, and the Meanings of Space', *Journal of the Society of Architectural Historians*, 64:4 (2005), pp. 436–40.

10 A. Herscher, 'In Ruins: Architecture, Memory, Countermemory', *Journal of the Society of Architectural Historians*, 73:4 (2014), p. 467.

11 M. Marefat, 'Building to Power: Architecture of Tehran 1921–1941' (PhD diss., Massachusetts Institute of Technology, 1988).

12 Before the Revolution, Marefat was already prominent in the Iranian architectural scene. She had been a keynote speaker at the 1976 Ramsar congress of women architects, and had worked for Diba's DAZ practice on projects including the new towns at Jondi-Shāpur and Ahvāz, Khuzestan, and participated in the 1976 UN Conference on Human Settlements in Vancouver.

13 Out of an, admittedly incomplete, survey of ninety-one articles and PhDs published since 1988, 36 per cent were urban related, 32 per cent concerned housing, 20 per cent concerned public architecture, while other topics only comprised 12 per cent between them.

14 T. Grigor, *Building Iran: Modernism, Architecture, and National Heritage under the Pahlavi Monarchs* (New York: Periscope Publishing, 2009).

15 T. Grigor, 'Of Metamorphosis: Meaning on Iranian Terms', *Third Text*, 17:3 (2003), pp. 207–25; T. Grigor, 'Recultivating "Good Taste": The Early Pahlavi Modernists and Their Society for National Heritage', *Iranian Studies*, 37:1 (March, 2004), pp. 17–45; Grigor, *Building Iran*, pp. 203–22.

16 P. Karimi, 'Westoxification', *Perspecta: The Yale Archiectural Journal*, 43 (2010), pp. 191–9; P. Karimi, *Domesticity and Consumer Culture in Iran: Interior Revolutions of the Modern Era* (London and New York: Routledge, 2013); P. Karimi, 'Architecture, Matter, and Mediation in the Middle East', *Traditional Dwellings and Settlements Review*, 25:1 (Fall, 2013), pp. 45–53; P. Karimi, 'Old Sites, New Frontiers: Contemporary Architecture in Iran', in E. G. Haddad and D. Rifkind (eds), *A Critical History of Contemporary Architecture, 1960–2010* (Abingdon: Ashgate, 2014), pp. 339–58.

17 See most recently, R. Habibi, 'Unveiled Middle-Class Housing in Tehran, 1945–1979', in A. Staub (ed.), *The Routledge Companion to Modernity, Space and Gender* (Abingdon: Routledge, 2018), pp. 253–69; see also R. Habibi, 'Modern Mass Housing in Tehran: Episodes of Urbanism 1945–1979' (PhD diss., Katholieke Universiteit Leuven, 2015), https://lirias.kuleuven.be/handle/123456789/497502 (accessed 25 January 2019); R. Habibi with B. de Meulder, 'Architects and "Architecture without Architects": Modernization of Iranian Housing and the Birth of a New Urban Form Narmak (Tehran, 1952)', *Cities*, 45 (2015), pp. 29–40; R. Habibi et

al., 'Re-visiting Three Neighbourhoods of Modern Tehran: Chaharsad-Dastgah, Narmak and Nazi-Abad', in F. F. Arefian and S. H. I. Moeini (eds), *Urban Change in Iran: Stories of Rooted Histories and Ever-accelerating Developments* (Basel: Springer, 2015), pp. 31–46; R. Habibi, 'The Institutionalization of Modern Middle Class Neighborhoods in 1940s Tehran – Case of Chaharsad Dastgah', *Cities*, 60 (2017), pp. 37–49.

18 H. Khosravi, 'Planning a Revolution: Labour Movements and Housing Projects in Tehran, 1943–1963', in C. Hein (ed.), *History – Urbanism – Resilience, Volume 2: 'The Urban Fabric, Housing and Neighbourhoods', Proceedings of the 17th IPHS Conference, Delft, 17–21 July 2016*, 17:2 (Delft: International Planning History Society, 2016), pp. 43–52; H. Khosravi, 'Politics of DeMonst(e)ration', *San Rocco*, 6, Collaboration (Spring, 2013), pp. 28–37, www.tehranprojects.com/Politics-of-DeMonst-e-ration (accessed 4 March 2019).

19 Association of Iranian Architects, Diplomate.

20 S. Roudbari, 'Instituting Architecture: A History of Transnationalism in Iran's architecture Profession, 1945–95', in M. Gharipour (ed.), *The Historiography of Persian Architecture* (London and New York: Routledge, 2015), pp. 287–332.

21 M. R. Shirazi, *Contemporary Architecture and Urbanism: Tradition, Modernity and the 'Space-in-Between'* (Cham: Springer, 2018), pp. 2–3. Shirazi's reference to Ricoeur derives from his reading of K. Frampton's Critical Regionalism thesis, notably 'Towards a Critical Regionalism: Six Points for an Architecture of Resistance', in H. Foster (ed.), *The Anti-aesthetic: Essays on Postmodern Culture* (Seattle, WA: Bay Press, 1983), pp. 16–30.

22 M. R. Shirazi, 'From Utopia to Dystopia: Shushtar-e-No, Endeavour Towards Paradigmatic Shift', in F. F. Arefian and S. H. I. Moeini (eds), *Urban Change in Iran: Stories of Rooted Histories and Ever-Accelerating Developments* (Cham: Springer, 2016), pp. 121–36.

23 Shirazi, *Contemporary Architecture*.

24 N. Forouzandeh and S. Motallebi, 'The Role of Open Spaces in Neighborhood Attachment (Case Study: Ekbatan Town in Tehran Metropolis)', *International Journal of Architecture and Urban Development*, 2:1 (2012), pp. 11–20; H. Haji Molana, 'Sense of Community and Residential Neighborhoods in Tehran, Iran' (master's thesis, Kent State University, 2016).

25 H. Bahrainy and B. Aminzadeh, 'Autocratic Urban Design: The Case of the Navab Regeneration Project in Central Tehran', *International Development Planning Review*, 29:2 (2007), pp. 241–70.

26 F. Emami, '"Civic Visions", National Politics, and International Designs: Three Proposals for a New Urban Center in Tehran (1966–1976)' (master's thesis, Massachusetts Institute of Technology, 2011); F. Emami, 'Urbanism of Grandiosity: Planning a New Urban Centre for Tehran (1973–76)', *International Journal of Islamic Architecture*, 3:1 (2014), pp. 69–102; Khosravi, 'Politics of DeMonst(e)ration'; S. Mohajeri, 'Louis Kahn's Silent Space of Critique in Tehran, 1973–74', *Journal of Society of Architectural Historians*, 74:4 (2015), pp. 485–504; S. Mohajeri, 'The Shahestan Blueprint: The Vestigial Site of Modernity in Iran', in M. Ghairpour (ed.), *The Historiography of Persian Architecture* (Abingdon and New York: Routledge, 2016), pp. 147–72.

27 K. Ehsani, 'The Cultural Politics of Public Space in Tehran's Book Fair', in H. Chehabi

et al. (eds), *Iran in the Middle East: Transnational Encounters And Social History* (London: I.B. Tauris, 2015), pp. 213–31.
28 H. Bahrainy and B. Aminzadeh, 'Evaluation of Navab Regeneration Project in Central Tehran, Iran', *International Journal of Environmental Research*, 1:2 (2007), pp. 114–27; N. Azizi-Matr, 'Regeneration Process in Tehran: The Ineffectiveness of Regeneration of Deteriorated Parts of Tehran' (Master's thesis, Politecnico Di Milano, 2014).
29 Grigor, *Building Iran*, pp. 17–45; P. Karimi, 'Policymaking and Housekeeping: President Truman's Point IV Program and the Making of the Modern Iranian House', *Thresholds*, 30 (2005), pp. 28–37.
30 Harvey, *Condition of Postmodernity*, pp. 201–307.
31 Harrison refers to the notion of heritage *as* design. See R. Harrison, 'What Is Heritage?', in R. Harrison (ed.), *Understanding the Politics of Heritage* (Manchester: Manchester University Press, 2010), pp. 4–42.
32 P. Heelas, 'Introduction: Detraditionalization and Its Rivals', in P. Heelas et al. (eds), *Detraditionalization: Critical Reflections on Authority and Identity* (Cambridge, MA: Blackwell, 1996), p. 2.
33 Nederveen Pieterse, *Globalization and Culture*.
34 P. Burke, *Cultural Hybridity* (Cambridge: Polity Press, 2009).
35 A. L. Tsing, *Friction: An Ethnography of Global Connection* (Princeton, NJ: Princeton University Press, 2005).
36 A. L. Tsing, 'The Global Situation', *Cultural Anthropology*, 15:3 (2000), p. 329. Tsing defines projects as 'relatively coherent bundles of ideas and practices as realized in particular times and places' (p. 347).
37 Tsing, *Friction*, pp. 18, 19.
38 Tsing, 'Global Situation', p. 347.
39 Tsing, *Friction*, p. 23.
40 Tsing, 'Global Situation', p. 331.
41 V. Ferraro, 'Dependency Theory: An Introduction', in G. Secondi (ed.), *The Development Economics Reader* (London: Routledge, 2008), pp. 58–64; N. Smith, *Uneven Development: Nature, Capital, and the Production of Space* (Athens, GA, and London: University of Georgia Press, 2008); R. Kiely, 'Dependency and World-Systems Perspectives on Development', *Oxford Research Encyclopedia of International Studies* (November, 2017), https://doi.org/10.1093/acrefore/9780190846626.013.142.
42 R. Peet and E. Hartwick, *Theories of Development: Contentions, Arguments, Alternatives* (New York: The Guildford Press, 2009), p. 132; D. C. Tipps, 'Modernization Theory and the Comparative Study of Societies: A Critical Perspective', *Comparative Studies in Society and History*, 15:2 (1973), pp. 199–226.
43 G. N. Kitching, *Development and Underdevelopment in Historical Perspective: Populism, Nationalism and Industrialisation* (Abingdon: Routledge, 2010), ch. 4.
44 Peet and Hartwick, *Theories of Development*, p. 16.
45 Peet and Hartwick, *Theories of Development*, p. 1.
46 U. Kothari, 'Introduction', in U. Kothari (ed.), *A Radical History of Development Studies: Individuals, Institutions and Ideologies* (London: Zed Books, 2016), pp. 7–8.
47 Cowen and Shenton, *Doctrines of Development*; T. H. Erikson, 'Between Universalism and Relativism: A Critique of the UNESCO Concept of Culture', in J. K. Cowan et

al. (eds), *Culture and Rights: Anthropological Perspectives* (Cambridge: Cambridge University Press, 2001), pp. 127–48.
48 Cowen and Shenton, *Doctrines of Development*, p. viii.
49 Cowen and Shenton, *Doctrines of Development*, p. 441.
50 M. von Osten, 'In Colonial Modern Worlds', in Avermaete et al. (eds), *Colonial Modern*, pp. 19–37.
51 R. Craggs, 'Development in a Global-Historical Context', in Desai and Potter (eds), *Companion to Development Studies*, pp. 5–10.
52 Schech, 'Culture and Development', pp. 42–46.
53 N. Dados and R. Connell, 'The Global South', *Contexts*, Taking on the Issues, 11:1 (Winter, 2012), pp. 12–13.
54 Grigor, 'Recultivating "Good Taste"'; Grigor, *Building Iran*, pp. 17–45.
55 See L. Smith, *Uses of Heritage* (London and New York: Routledge, 2006).
56 Harrison, 'What Is Heritage?'; R. Harrison, *Heritage: Critical Approaches* (London and New York: Routledge, 2012); Smith, *Uses of Heritage*; D. C. Harvey, 'Heritage Pasts and Heritage Presents: Temporality, Meaning and the Scope of Heritage Studies', *International Journal of Heritage Studies*, 7:4 (2001), pp. 319–38.
57 G. J. Ashworth et al., *Pluralising Pasts: Heritage, Identity and Place in Multicultural Societies* (London and Ann Arbor, MI: Pluto Press, 2007).
58 J. E. Tunbridge and G. J. Ashworth, *Dissonant Heritage: The Management of the Past as a Resource in Conflict* (New York: John Wiley, 1996).
59 Harrison, *Heritage*.
60 On 'authorized heritage discourse', see Smith, *Uses of Heritage*, pp. 29–34. On heritage contestation, see A. Mozaffari, 'The Heritage "NGO": A Case Study on the Role of Grass Roots Heritage Societies in Iran and Their Perception of Cultural Heritage', *International Journal of Heritage Studies*, 21:9 (2015), pp. 845–61, https://doi.org/10.1080/13527258.2015.1028961; E. Shamoradi and E. Abdollahzadeh, 'Antinomies of Development: Heritage, Media and the Sivand Dam Controversy', in A. Mozaffari (ed.), *World Heritage in Iran: Perspectives on Pasargadae* (Surrey: Ashgate, 2014), pp. 225–54; T. Jones et al., 'Heritage Contests: What Can We Learn from Social Movements?', *Heritage & Society*, 10:1 (2018), pp. 1–25, https://doi.org/10.1080/2159032X.2018.1428445.
61 A. M. Ansari, 'The Myth of the White Revolution: Mohammad Reza Shah, "Modernization" and the Consolidation of Power', *Middle Eastern Studies*, 37:3 (2001), pp. 1–24, https://doi.org/10.1080/714004408.
62 M. R. Pahlavi, *The White Revolution* (Tehran: Imperial Pahlavi Library, 1967).
63 R. Garlitz, 'U.S. University Advisors and Education Modernization in Iran, 1951–1967', in R. Garlitz and L. Jarvinen (eds), *Teaching America to the World and the World to America* (New York: Palgrave Macmillan, 2012), p. 41.
64 R. Popp, 'An Application of Modernization Theory during the Cold War? The Case of Pahlavi Iran', *The International History Review*, 30:1 (2008), p. 81.
65 N. Gilman, *Mandarins of the Future: Modernization Theory in Cold-War America*, New Studies in American Intellectual and Cultural History (Baltimore, MD, and London: Johns Hopkins University Press, 2003), pp. 3–4.
66 S. L. McFarland, 'A Peripheral View of the Origins of the Cold War: The Crises in Iran, 1941–47', *Diplomatic History*, 4:4 (Fall, 1980), pp. 333–51.

67 J. P. C. Carey and A. G. Carey, 'Industrial Growth and Development Planning in Iran', *Middle East Journal*, 29:1 (Winter, 1975), pp. 9–10.
68 T. J. La Belle, 'Inter-institutional Cooperation: A Case Study of UCLA (U.S.) and UTE (Iran)', *UCLA Educator*, 22:1 (1981), pp. 60–7.
69 Garlitz, 'U.S. University Advisors', p. 43.
70 F. Daftary, 'Development Planning in Iran: A Historical Survey', *Iranian Studies*, 6:4 (1973), pp. 176–228; N. R. Keddie, 'The Midas Touch: Black Gold, Economics and Politics in Iran Today', *Iranian Studies*, 10:4 (Autumn, 1977), pp. 243–66; M. Parvin and A. N. Zamani, 'Political Economy of Growth and Destruction: A Statistical Interpretation of the Iranian Case', *Iranian Studies*, 12:1/2 (Winter/Spring, 1979), pp. 43–78.
71 M. Kamiar, 'Changes in Spatial and Temporal Patterns of Development in Iran', *Political Geography Quarterly*, 7:4 (1988), p. 327.
72 E. I. Sadr, 'To Whisper in the King's Ear: Economists in Pahlavi and Islamic Iran' (PhD diss., Graduate School of the University of Maryland, 2013), p. 70, https://drum.lib.umd.edu/bitstream/handle/1903/13977/Sadr_umd_0117E_13985.pdf?sequence=1&isAllowed=y (accessed 8 December 2018).
73 Sixth Development Plan, Plan Organization, Tehran, 1978, pp. 10–11.
74 Sixth Development Plan, p. 29.
75 Sixth Development Plan, p. 20.
76 For example, his use of the oil revenue to massively increase expenditure of the armed forces attracted the criticism of the then-head of the Plan Organization, Abol Hassan Ebtehaj. See F. Bostock and G. Jones, *Planning and Power in Iran: Ebtehaj and Economic Development under the Shah* (London: Frank Cass, 1989), p. 157.
77 S. T. Hunter, 'Islamic Reformist Discourse in Iran: Proponents and Prospects', in S. T. Hunter (ed.), *Reformist Voices of Islam: Mediating Islam and Modernity* (London and New York: Routledge, 2009), p. 38.
78 A. Appadurai, *Modernity at Large: Cultural Dimensions of Globalization* (Minneapolis, MN: University of Minnesota Press, 1996), p. 179.
79 Within architectural practice, there was a shift from the domination of national projects by foreign experts to a transnational collaboration. See S. Roudbari, 'The Transnational Transformation of Archiecture Practice: Iranian Architects in the New Geography of Professional Authority, 1945–2012' (Phd diss., University of California, Berkeley, 2013), http://search.proquest.com.dbgw.lis.curtin.edu.au/docview/1526494875/abstract/AE714019B149437DPQ/1?accountid=10382 (accessed 1 April 2018); Roudbari, 'Instituting Architecture'; S. Roudbari, 'Renegade Cosmopolitans: Iranian Architects, Professional Power, and the State', *Iranian Studies*, 51:6 (2018), pp. 1–26.
80 H. Katouzian, *Iranian History and Politics: The Dialectic of State and Society* (London: Routledge, 2003), part I, ch. 1, considers the sudden implosion a characteristic of change in dictatorial monarchies which, he theorizes in relation to Iran, under the notion of 'arbitrary rule'.
81 See Constitution of Islamic Republic of Iran, 'Preamble' (Iran Chamber Society, 1980), www.iranchamber.com/government/laws/constitution.php (accessed 12 February 2019).
82 A. Mozaffari. and N. Westbrook, 'Designing a Revolutionary Habitat: Tradition,

Heritage and Housing in the Immediate Aftermath of the Iranian Revolution – Continuities and Disruptions', *Fabrications*, 28:2 (2018), pp. 185–211.
83 This is from the personal experience of Ali Mozaffari, who was educated in Iran at the time.
84 J. Amuzegar, 'The Iranian Economy before and after the Revolution', *Middle East Journal*, 46:3 (Summer, 1992), pp. 413–25; H. S. Esfahani and M. H. Pesaran, 'The Iranian Economy in the Twentieth Century: A Global Perspective', *Iranian Studies*, 42:2 (2009), pp. 177–211, https://doi.org/10.1080/00210860902764896.
85 R. Gluck, 'The Shiraz Arts Festival: Western Avant-Garde Arts in 1970s Iran', *Leonardo*, 40:1 (2007), pp. 20–28.
86 A. Naseriazar and A. Badrian, 'Iran', in B. Vlaardingerbroek and N. Taylor (eds), *Getting into Varsity: Comparability, Convergence and Congruence* (Amherst, NY: Cambria Press, 2010), pp. 169–83.
87 A. Mashayekhi, 'The 1968 Tehran Master Plan and the Politics of Planning Development in Iran (1945–1979)', *Planning Perspectives*, 34:5 (2018), pp. 849–76, https://doi.org/10.1080/02665433.2018.1468805.
88 In relation to development and built environment we have focused on the reception of the past and its projection towards the future – the idea of historical change – which is discussed in disciplines of architecture, political sociology, anthropology, and the field of heritage studies.
89 Following Michael Herzfeld, social time is taken to refer to the complex and unpredictable experience of the everyday and monumental time to more generic categories of the past, usually invoked in official discourses. See M. Herzfeld, *A Place in History: Social and Monumental Time in a Cretan Town* (Princeton, NJ: Princeton University Press, 1991).
90 For more on cities of modernist architecture, see Chapter 2.
91 Habibi, 'Unveiled Middle-Class Housing'.
92 M. Eleb, 'An Alternative to Functionalist Universalism: Écochard, Candilis, and ATBAT-Afrique', in Goldhagen and Legault (eds), *Anxious Modernisms*, pp. 55–73; Cohen and Eleb, *Casablanca*, pp. 324–55.

1

A vital past: Engaging nostalgia

ایران در سال‌های دهه‌های چهل و پنجاه داشت جهش می‌کرد. ما از آسیای جنوب شرقی آن موقع جلوتر بودیم. علت عدم موفقیت ما ته نظر من این است که ما شتاب تغییرات را تحمل نکردیم. حالا چرا؟ نمیدانم ... ما روشنفکران آن دوره هم پرتئودیم و تحلیل درستی از جایگاه خود در جامعه و جامعه ی خودمان در جهان نداشتیم ... ما روشنفکران جایگاه خود را ندانستیم و جامعه را خراب کردیم ... باید اعتراف کنم شرمنده‌ام که نسل ما گند زد![1]

Dariush Shayegan, Iranian Indophile philosopher

Introduction

In the Introduction, we argued that development transformed perceptions of time, resulting in a reassessment and recasting of relationships with the past. It amplified the distinction between the past and the present. However, rather than eliminating one in favour of the other, such a recognition posited the past–present–future in an interrelated context, a trajectory.[2] This process had romantic, nostalgic characteristics. Arguably, understanding the relationship between development and heritage, seen through or actualized in architecture, demands recognition and theorization of the function of nostalgia. Scholars of Iran in other fields are recognizing nostalgia, assessing its social and historical impact negatively in general. Ali Mirsepassi recently published a critique of authenticity discourse[3] – which he characterized as nostalgic – and its destructive political consequences in late twentieth-century Iran. In the context of rapid social change, various forms of nostalgia drove overlapping and confused notions of tradition, authenticity, culture, and civilization. By the 1970s, both the Pahlavi establishment and its opposition were fascinated by forms of nostalgic authenticity, as evidenced in the growing interest in (primarily Shi'ite) tradition: festivals, folklore[4] (recognized in 1971 by UNESCO, which recommended its protection),[5] traditional arts, and architecture,[6] paralleled by and reinforcing a rising religious sentiment among the general public.[7]

Indeed

> for both the elite and the youth of the time, religion provided a space for combining material values of life such as welfare and comfort with spiritual values. A wish for a return to religious identity ... had a profound influence among the elite.[8]

This desire to reinstate the past – nostalgia – was symptomatic of an insecure sense of identity created in large part by significant sociocultural changes imparted by development. In a futurology project conducted in 1974 that surveyed a group of youths, the researchers, Tehranian and Assadi, noted, among other issues, problems arising from rapid development and mass migration from villages to cities, rising income levels and GDP, proliferation of education bringing religious youth to cities and universities, combined with living, housing, and transport standards that were failing to keep up with the pace of economic growth, were creating a sense of confusion, uncertainty, and insecurity, particularly among the young, who sought a secure and stable sense of identity.[9] Their research also suggests that, contrary to the common assertion as to the existence and implementation of an 'establishment' cultural policy, there was neither sufficient attention given to broad-based cultural planning, nor a clear and consistent national cultural policy.[10] The popularity of nostalgia for an authentic culture in this context is thus not surprising – this, in turn, reinforced Islamist sentiments, contributing to the subsequent upheavals of 1978–79.[11] In such a volatile and confused context, overlapping notions of tradition, authenticity, and civilization (Islamic or otherwise) drove nostalgic ideas of culture, and were also expressed in forms of heritage and architecture. However, in the Iranian context, nostalgia's role in the re-engagement with tradition and the past remains unexplored. This chapter will elaborate civilizational discourses and tradition, but in order to understand their implications for design, it is imperative to first grasp the meaning of nostalgia beyond its usual, negative interpretations, and the critical potentials that such a broader understanding brings to bear.

Nostalgia

> The literature of the [60]s [which contained the essence of] its intellectual works was a melange of progress and the desire to progress, the nostalgia for progress and the nostalgia for social justice.[12]

It is fair to assume that nostalgia is at work whenever there is a romantic impulse, glorification of 'the masses', the purported authenticity of the local and the traditional community, or attraction to the indigenous and the vernacular in the arts and architecture.[13] Indeed, the search for the authentic in various modes of nativism, traditionalism, culturalism, and environmentalism is driven in large part by nostalgic impulses.[14] All such impulses and emotions have been present in significant strands of Iranian architectural and artistic expressions since the late 1960s. But the problem remains how to situate nostalgia as a useful critical lens beyond such generalities.

To begin with, nostalgia is elusive; it is a multifaceted, complex 'structure of feeling',[15] pertaining to authenticity.[16] This emotion has temporal dimensions (longing for times past, or a sense of historical decline[17]), spatial dimensions (longing for lost places, home), moral dimensions[18] (loss of moral certainty and the social codes that secured that certainty), social dimensions (breakdown of genuine social relations and the desire for their reinstatement), and political dimensions, to name but a few.[19] It is a universal emotional experience that produces various culturally specific imaginations.[20] Thus, while it is felt individually, it has collective roots (both home and the past are shared with others)[21] and is ultimately a social experience, at once 'melancholic and utopian'.[22] Nostalgia is inextricably linked to change and displacement. It results from recognizing the difference between what has been experienced in the past and what is anticipated, expected, and thus projected into the future, a difference that is produced and amplified by modernity.[23] As already suggested, this difference is experienced by people in social, cultural, physical, and epochal change,[24] resulting in re-signifying meanings and practices. This process re-forges identities,[25] and produces divergent views of the past and thus of heritage.[26] In such a context, nostalgia represents a reaction against uncertainty and ambiguity, or in Bryant's succinct definition, a 'longing for essentialism [...] for clearly defined identity with its clearly defined boundaries'.[27] But because nostalgia is polysemic, it cannot assume a sustained, unitary, and fixed meaning.[28]

While the classic modernist approach, exemplified by Adorno and Harvey,[29] has been dismissive of nostalgia, a nuanced and critical deployment of nostalgia recognizes its multiplicity[30] and that it plays different, ambiguous, and perhaps contradictory social and political roles.[31] The difficulty and polysemy of the concept is clear in its multiple, context-specific deployments.[32] It has been employed strategically as a discursive device[33] with variously colonialist or revolutionary undertones,[34] a commodified style or set of practices,[35] or to signify a 'moral direction' in periods of epochal change.[36] As Berliner notes, such descriptors also attempt to capture the complexity of the phenomenon arising from the 'intersection between the individual, the social and the political'.[37] It is precisely this constitutional ambiguity that bestows nostalgia with critical potentials, which can lead to a fruitful approach to understanding architectural and spatial production. The key is to recognize nostalgia as a desire to maintain a dialectic between the past and the present, continuity and fragmentation, the stable and the fleeting.[38]

Facets of nostalgia

Nostalgia straddles individual and collective structures of emotion and memories.[39] It performs a sociocultural function by producing meanings in the present through selective readings of the past.[40] It can be invoked – as it was in Iran – to activate, or construct, memories of the past either in service of, or resistance to, forms of social and political authority, morally legitimated through references to traditions.⁴¹ The experience of nostalgia links us to a past that remains distanced from the present.⁴² But it can mediate our relationship with that past in forming collective identities.⁴³ Such reflexivity may defamiliarize and displace everyday objects and motifs, such as architectural spaces, which can become re-signified as objects of contemplation and symbols of experience.⁴⁴ While nostalgia is not an essential part of a cultural product, such as a design or a text, that product may nonetheless lend itself to nostalgic experiences, depending on the time and place within which it is used and contemplated.

In light of this complexity, deploying nostalgia without nuance carries little analytical purchase. Rather, it is useful to defer judgement,⁴⁵ and instead to examine the place and use of nostalgia in the production and consumption of cultural products, like architecture, and its role in their production of heritage.⁴⁶ Irreducible to a single ideological stance, nostalgia's connotations depend on who mobilizes it, where and when.⁴⁷ Nostalgia can be deployed strategically to mobilize social groups or whole nations through essentialized self-definitions.⁴⁸ Animated by an imagined continuity with a past,⁴⁹ it is closely related to identity and tradition. As noted, it is a contradictory phenomenon, driven by 'utopian impulses', and plays an ambivalent role in social criticism, at once masking and exposing ideological aspects in modernity,⁵⁰ while disruptively transgressing perceived political and ideological boundaries, including the boundaries between the authentic and the invented.⁵¹

The deception of nostalgia is that it facilitates the persistence of ambiguity and disruption of certainties in the present, while at the same time perpetuating and projecting utopian imaginations of a secure future. It arises as the gulf between present and past widens in the face of progress, evoking a sense of loss – time's irreversible distancing from the past.⁵² In this respect, it is very much akin to heritage, in projecting a particular 'politics of the future'.⁵³ Just as it is a feeling which mediates between the local specificities and the universal,⁵⁴ nostalgia can allow the temporal and reflexive space in which the past and present can be compared, promoting an imagination of the past in the present and thus, the possible imagination of a different present and future emanating from that past.⁵⁵ If its object is that which is lost, then it is fruitful to consider what that object – time, place, home, a dream or myth – refers to, and what the political import of that referent may be. From this aspect, analysis of nostalgia provides insights into the modalities of friction and their affective responses within social contexts, by teasing out the complexities and multiplicities of the context wherein nostalgia occurs, and the actors who put it into practice. The imagination of the past in the present, and its use to assert a putative continuity, directly links nostalgia with the experience of authenticity as well as the formation and practices of tradition.

The mirage of authenticity

The nostalgia-driven discourse of authenticity was a significant driver of cultural and political debates in Iran before and after the Revolution. Ultimately deriving from the Western Romantic movement,[56] this discourse grew out of a sense of ethical crisis and dilution of identity, both of which elicited a desire for the establishment of what Taylor has termed a 'moral community'.[57] This Romantic impulse was associated with a nostalgia for the folk, an organic and holistic community that supposedly existed prior to encountering Western cultures and belief systems, scientific rationality, and attendant processes of globalization and modernity.[58] Particularly since the 1960s, debates around culture in Iran were politicized by interrelated domestic and international factors, the Pahlavi establishment and opposition groups competing over claims to authenticity and its cultural representation,[59] while sharing ideas generated by nostalgic-authentic intellectuals within and outside Iran.[60] At the time, the main concerns centred upon notions of the authentic native[61] (the latter being more a trope, an allegory with fluid meanings), and teleological notions of Iranian historical destiny. For opposition groups, utilization and propagation of the politics of authenticity, employing the Third Worldist nativist,[62] and anti-imperialist perspectives of Fanon, Cesaire, and others, was a means of indirectly criticizing the monarchy, in the face of Pahlavi curbs on political expression.[63] Competing claims to authenticity pertained to religious origins, and were expressed through ideas of civilizational conflicts, anti-Westernism, and anti-globalization.[64] These ideas were championed inside Iran by various intellectuals, both Iranian and foreign-born, notably Henri Corbin and his protege Dariush Shayegan.[65] But there were also contesting appeals to the legacy of Iranian tradition. Nabavi relates the position of the Iranian leftist intellectual Mehdi Parham in the 1970s, according to whom authentic culture could be found in Iranian's religion and myth, which – he stated ironically – once refined and purged of superstition could be exported to the West along with Iran's oil. Accordingly, Iranian mysticism needed to be an instrument through which a fairer society, freed from secular and religious authority, might come into existence.[66]

For proponents of this politics of authenticity, revisiting and animating cultural pasts provided a path to independence, emancipation, and restoration of the people's dignity.[67] As mentioned above, this process of resurgence, reimagination, or else complete reinvention and thus fabrication of the past, pertains to the political function of nostalgia. However, more importantly and beyond nostalgia, to the extent that the past was envisaged in programmes and plans, or indeed in the built environment, it suggests heritage in operation. Through heritage, authentic existence, one that enabled a free and dignified coexistence with other nations, would be substantiated and reaffirmed.[68] The nativist and xenophobic potentials of this tendency are self-evident, as notions of Westernization, modernization, and 'Westoxification' were at times collapsed into one another, and identified as the enemy of authentic local culture, a line of thinking subsequently taken up by ideologues of the Islamic Republic.[69]

Although dissenting voices existed, the dominant discourse of nostalgic authenticity[70] was, in the late Pahlavi period, championed by Ahmad Fardid (1909–94), a lecturer in philosophy at the University of Tehran with dubious academic credentials, whose ideas were a melange of the Islamic esotericism of Ibn Arabi, and a decontextualized reading of Heidegger's counter-Enlightenment and anti-modern thought.[71] Fardid dismissed the Western mind as 'incapable of representing "authentic" knowledge'[72] – it was rational, scientific, empirical, and constitutionally Orientalist. For Fardid, a significant part of Islamic thought was 'Westoxified', contaminated by this Western mindset. He privileged localized language and intuition as the representation of the locally authentic.[73] His concern with localizing language, and adducing specific meanings from it, was, perhaps in a more superficial and benign manner, also apparent in the search by architectural theorists and practitioners like Nader Ardalan for trans-historical motifs and signification. As Mirsepassi astutely and courageously observes, in many ways Fardid anticipated Said's *Orientalism*, some of the driving ideas behind postcolonial discourses in academia, as well as Foucault's political spirituality, with the difference that unlike them, he was happy to see the ideas through into action and celebrated their socially disastrous consequences as political realities.[74] Mirsepassi wryly argues that '[r]ough, rabble-rousing Fardid stated explicitly what fashionable, university-nurtured postcolonial theory very often prefers to leave darkly unspoken'.[75] In this light, the reproduction of traditional motifs and typologies in architecture, some of which had clear religious affiliations, and the heritage they produced through design processes, has to be read with extra care. From a critical perspective, what they signified at the time of inception and the latent ideological possibilities they contained in their afterlife, in the wake of the Islamic Revolution, are likely to be related but different. Indeed, we can see in some of the architectural productions of the 1970s in Iran, such as the Shahyad monument (Chapter 5), the Pasargadae site museum, both by Amanat (Figure 1.1), and the Tehran Centre for the Appreciation of Music by Ardalan, strongly intuitive, backward-looking, yet simultaneously highly innovative conceptual approaches, which evoke the past and an idealized Iranian place in a diffused yet Romantic manner.

Civilizational discourse and anti-Westernism

Another facet of the nostalgic discourse that underpinned cultural production in developing Iran was a concern for civilization, which in its various interpretations was often conflated with culture and, perhaps influenced by Soviet-inspired ideologies, came with a healthy dose of anti-Westernism.[76] Attention to Iranian culture and civilization – the perceived imperative to preserve Iranian culture, and to maintain a critical perspective on Western modernity – had been

1.1 Hossein Amanat, Pasargadae site museum (1973–ongoing).

articulated by early twentieth-century statesmen and cultural commentators. Redeploying the Western idea of civilization, Iranian, and other non-Western intellectuals and nationalists alike, proposed the multiplicity and equal legitimacy of cultures.[77] That civilizational outlook, perpetuating an essentializing 'myth of homogeneity' of both Western and non-Western civilizations, gave rise to anti-Western rhetoric, conflated with nativism,[78] which dominated 1970s Iran and continued after the Islamic Revolution. Such ideologies in Asian civilizational discourse were inspired by, but not limited to, romanticism and contained a 'narcissistic and nostalgic' impulse.[79] This cultural reaction was not a specifically Iranian 'malaise', but a by-product of friction. It was born out of broader historical conditions arising from the interaction between Western powers and Asian and Muslim societies since the mid-nineteenth century.[80] Aydin has identified the roots of anti-Westernism in Asia as a reaction to the 'legitimacy crisis of a single, globalized, international system ... [rooted in] nineteenth-century globalization, imperialism, and decolonization', in response to which strands of pan-Asian and pan-Islamic thought were formulated.[81] Driven by a desire for development, and membership of a global and equitable modern community of nations, the intellectual forerunners of these ideas attempted to expand and universalize conceptions both of the Enlightenment and civilization,[82] such that they transcended the national and ethno-religious

1.2 Shiraz Arts Festival, Karlheinz Stockhausen performing at Persepolis, Iran (3 September 1972).

boundaries imagined in the West. Civilization was invoked as the instrument of a critique of Western colonialist ideas and their semblance of a civilizing mission, a critique which subsequently gave rise to anti-Westernism.

Ideas of civilization and cultural exchange between East and West loomed large in the latter part of the Pahlavi period, as the use of the phrase 'Great Civilization' exemplified,[83] and were apparent in its international cultural programmes, especially art festivals such as the Arts Festival of Shiraz, funded by the government and patronized by the Queen (Figure 1.2).[84] Such programmes were intended to elevate Iran to the family of world cultures and thus to establish for it the prestige that their proponents thought it deserved. The confusions between culture and civilization notwithstanding, there was a strong attention here to aspects of heritage, at least in the official discourse.

The content and stated intention of various art festivals initiated by the Pahlavi government indicated the establishment's awareness and deployment of heritage for the future of Iran, and the drive to make cultural practices reflect back on the nation itself.[85] This intention was also apparent in the formation of the Iranian Centre for the Study of Cultures, under the direct patronage of the Queen and headed by Dariush Shayegan, Seyyed Hossein Nasr, and Ahmad Fardid,[86] and whose thinking would retain its currency and influence after the Islamic Revolution. The Centre, the driving agenda of which was 'to introduce Iran's real cultural stature in the context of other cultures',[87] outlined its objective as

[t]he study and research in gaining knowledge of cultures and civilizations, and introducing [them] and their relationships to one another, and establishing a productive dialogue among world cultures with a specific emphasis on the role and place of Iranian culture.[88]

In what seems to have been a marriage of pan-Islamist and pan-Asianist precedents, and cognizant of the geopolitics of the 1970s, the Centre's primary focus rested upon what it called 'the four great poles of Asian civilization': Iran and Islam, India, China, and Japan.[89] It sought to both promote the understanding of cultural heritage and the clash of cultures and civilizations, producing projects on art and architecture, including Arthur Upham Pope's archive, exhibitions of art and culture, and examination of architectural heritage and settlements in Iran, along with a visual archive.[90] The broad interest held by intellectuals for the presumed deep histories of local Iranian and Asian culture was propelled by the search for a greater Islamic or Asian identity, a kind of nostalgia that could be characterized as 'continental' or 'geopolitical',[91] in the face of modernizing processes.[92] It would, however, be simplistic to reduce such attempts to either an establishment 'plot' to pacify dissidents,[93] or to the self-glorification of a monarch. Indeed, the discourses were shaped by, and thus responded to, cultural forces inside and outside Iran.[94] The above constellation of movements and ideas, then, was prompted by a nostalgic reassessment of the past, its remembrance and restitution, sought in different approaches to tradition. In this process, symbols and forms of tradition were reimagined as raw material, vehicles for engaging with, and constructing, a relationship with the past. The process produced different forms of heritage, which is better understood by recognizing the various possibilities and approaches to tradition.

Engaging tradition

In Iran, debates around a return to, or resurrection of, tradition, especially pertaining to religion, predominated in intellectual and cultural concerns in the decade leading up to the 1979 Revolution. This turn to tradition was approached from different positions, all of which were part of a larger, nostalgic quest for authenticity.[95] Although in the end the discourse of Traditionalism, with its universalist reading of tradition, became dominant, the notion of tradition itself remained contested and is worth elaborating.

Tradition is a much used but elusive concept which, in its various definitions, has formed a basis for often nostalgic debates and critiques of the relationship between development, modernity, and identity. For example, critics of the Pahlavis sought to reinterpret traditions in order to effect change in the present, utilizing tradition as a basis for political ideology.[96] This is also apparent in debates in Iranian heritage and architecture but which, arguably, take place without critically examining its meaning and implications. Such an examination, however, is essential for understanding how tradition serves as a repository for novel interpretations of the past that produce heritage in a developing context.

Traditions are temporal, action-oriented processes within social settings.[97] They function as a repository of collective experiences handed down through time,[98] conveying a sense of continuity with a past that renders the present meaningful.[99] They construct social realities, and delimit the significance and scope of permissible experience.[100] As such, their change, demise, or weakening causes their adherents concern over the loss of organic societal unity.[101] Invocation of traditions, a frequent process in a nostalgic outlook, is the act of embedding a 'specific present in an equally specific past' that lends a patrimonial authority to actions within the present.[102] Various definitions of tradition address the above aspects, although there are differences around the sources of traditional authority – mundane or divine – which may be contested. Secondly, they are mutable – their encounter with modernity causes them to change, adapt, or disappear. Thus, the relation between tradition, continuity, and change is a significant issue for heritage and architecture, to which we shall return through a concrete architectural example at the end of this chapter. There are three major approaches to the dialectic traditional continuity and change, all of which inform spatial responses in Iran: traditions as mutable, as invented, and as static and thus bound to disappear.

Mutable traditions

From this perspective, traditions are temporal and, like any other sociocultural phenomena, are mutable.[103] The main issue is the rate and extent of mutability and change affecting traditions, their institutions, and constituents. In the encounter between traditional societies and modernity, Lerner's classic (albeit now largely discredited) theory has been that the encounter will obliterate traditions. Others, however, have couched the effect of such encounters as a qualitative change, within which traditions continue to exist 'by adapting to new realities'[104] wherein residues of past institutions, practices, and socialities mutate into new formations, resulting in a hybrid. Such disembedding of tradition from its customary communal and spatial settings has repercussions for collective identities, legitimacy of authority structures, and social order, which Heelas designates as 'detraditionalization', the posthumous experience of tradition.[105]

In their original settings, traditions function within a localized domain and are experienced directly, in an unmediated, processual fashion. But in encountering modernity and development, they become displaced from localities, surviving only if re-embedded in new geographical contexts.[106] It is this process of re-mooring, re-contextualization, and concomitant mediation that elicits creative responses to traditions.[107] In a developing society, habitational traditions for a displaced population can only be preserved if its symbols, spatial configurations, and social practices are reintroduced into new settings.

This re-embedding can also happen once a localized collective symbolism is transposed to the scale of the nation-state though various forms of mediation, including architecture.[108]

We can discern various forms of engagement with tradition in Iranian responses to social and technological development in the 1970s – modes of managing change, as well as maintaining, creating, and propagating a sense of collective identity, shared place (at both local and national scales), and social cohesion. These forms were, however, challenged by the nation's encounter with the bi-polar world of the Cold War, the rise of globalization and American hegemony, but also, from within, by the genuine need to change and the establishment's desire to enable it. If, after Schochet, we might consider tradition as 'a solution […] to the problem of social cohesion',[109] then the growing focus on tradition in this period was indicative of Iranians' perceived need for cohesion at a time of rapid flux.

Clearly, invocations of traditions and their institutions inevitably perform cultural and indeed political functions. These functions are, however, context specific, at times even progressive and dynamic, as when traditions become vehicles for resistance to unwanted change,[110] or are invoked in support of culturally sensitive change[111] that resonates with people's daily lives.[112] However, when invoked as a living element confronting modernity, as was evident in the Iranian context since the 1960s, tradition is activated as a means for a revivalist and conservative political project.[113] In such cases, multiple forms of nostalgia were at work, some providing a reflexive vehicle for contemplating and re-contextualizing traditions of the past in the present, others providing a kind of intellectual relief, a phantasmic dream, away from the realities of a modern, globalizing world, for a return to the warmth and safety of a world that could be controlled and imaginatively mastered.[114] Both forms drove an identity politics of 'resistance', apparent in Shayegan's statement opening this chapter. In response to this invocation of tradition, 'critical constructionists' have utilized Hobsbawm's well-known invented traditions thesis.

The conflicted in-between: The invention of tradition thesis

Broadly speaking, one could suggest that whenever traditions or customs are named and reified, then a process akin to invention is occurring. Hobsbawm and others have critiqued ideologically motivated turns to tradition, where a continuity with a specific past is asserted through repetition.[115] Such an assertion, which Hobsbawm termed 'invented traditions' – distinguished by being highly ritualized, symbolic, unchanging, and explicit, in contrast to 'authentic' customs that are variable and implicit – is made to mask actual discontinuities.[116] Their objective is to confer legitimacy to authority structures, and to reinforce a sense of social cohesion and community membership.[117] Such inventions are more frequent in times of rapid change, commonly in the modern era, and are linked with the establishment of the nation-state.[118]

While the concept of 'invented traditions' has its critics,[119] it focuses attention on the role of human agency in cultural processes of engaging with and transforming social structures.[120] 'Invention' is a conscious response on the part of actors – both those in power and sometimes those contesting dominant powers – to a set of historical circumstances. Thus, communities coalescing around certain traditions may sometimes feel that they need to consciously resuscitate traditions, and this cannot be dismissed out of hand as falsehood.[121] From this perspective, invention and construction per se are not reason enough to dismiss imaginative social engagements with the past; to do so risks falling into the undifferentiated view that they are all deliberate misinterpretations serving vested interests.[122] While the past and tradition might indeed be used for ideological or even sinister reasons, the authenticity of an invention is determined based on how, or whether, it is experienced as authentic, a point we address in the following chapters.[123]

Inventions are also responses to specific encounters with 'Others' – it is through such encounters that some turns to tradition may be explained as 'reactive identification'.[124] The central point here is that cultural forms and traditions should also be interpreted as products of larger, cross-cultural exchanges, such as globalization, thus as products of friction. This is, however, not necessarily reactionary and negative. Objectification has a certain dynamic as to what is being objectified, to what end and how, and similarly, to what external stimuli the process responds. Thus, in providing a nuanced reading of architecture and heritage within a developing context, it is important to note how the past and its traditional symbols are taken up, and how the meaning of the same design will change with a contextual shift.

Tradition characterized as static

The third characterization of tradition consists of a spectrum at one end of which are classic modernization theorists such as Daniel Lerner, who advocated for Western-style liberal capitalism in the Cold War context. These theorists also conveyed the desirability and inevitability for traditional Middle Eastern societies to transform in the image of the West, through the cultural impacts of changes in technology, economy, governance, lifestyle, and the media.[125] In this process, such traditional societies enter into a state of transition towards becoming modern, and in the process dispense with traditional customs. From this perspective, 'backward' societies undergoing development could change to attain the virtues of modernity and progress only if they overcame the 'barrier' of tradition.[126] At the other end of the spectrum, Lerner's position, and the broader modernization school to which he belonged, which was trenchantly criticized by anti-colonialists from the time of publication of his book in 1958, was also criticized by Traditionalists, such as the Iranian scholar Nasr. Given the significance of the Traditionalist discourse in politics and culture, both before and after the 1979 Revolution, which had direct architectural corollaries, it would be useful to consider some of its precepts. The Nasrian position comes close to exemplifying what Hobsbawm characterized as the invention of tradition.

Following Sedgwick, 'Traditionalism' designates an intellectual spiritual movement rooted in the affective response of some Western intellectuals to the horrors of the First World War, which they saw as evidence of the spiritual crisis caused by modernity's disruption of tradition. To remedy the resultant sense of alienation and unstable identity, Traditionalism posited a single universal origin to all traditions; a common essence. By the inter-war period, Traditionalists became involved in politics – fascism in the West and anti-imperialism in the East – and later in the 1960s, their ideas merged into general culture.[127] But Traditionalism continued to have political traction afterwards, especially in Muslim societies and significantly in Iran. In the Iranian context, Traditionalism merged with the living heritage of Sufism, which it elevated as the manifestation of an authentic Iranian culture, expressed in cultural forms such as architecture. Ironically, it found sympathy in both the Pahlavi establishment and its opposition. Nasr, its major Iranian exponent, claims that both the Pahlavi court and high-profile clerical figures, some of whom like Morteza Motahhari turned into opposition leaders, thought of Traditionalism as the only movement that could maintain the relationship between 'Islamic movements and state views', and thus prevent the 'threat of a communist takeover'.[128] Furthermore, modernization and rapid development created a sense of urgency and receptivity to Traditionalist positions among the broader populace. Here, nostalgia was at work, but with an ideological inflection.

Nasr's Traditionalism is fundamentally counter-Enlightenment and anti-modernist[129] and harbours strong ideological potentials. Traditionalist exhortations to preserve or rescue traditions suggest a political intention, in addition to, or perhaps instead of, a cultural one. This is not to deny that explicit knowledge of a past tradition – its memory – can strongly influence identity construction in the present. However, what is thus remembered is not in itself part of an active tradition. It does not necessarily change power structures, legitimation, and other issues pertaining to living traditions, unless the process of remembering involves traditional activity in its own right.[130] Here, the Traditionalist position resonates with the invented traditions thesis. Schochet is surely right in suggesting that aspects of tradition that are promoted as integrating, and thus officialized, are closely related to power and represent the interests of the powerful.[131] However, in the case of Iran, the locus of power shifts in unpredictable directions, also exposing the weakness of claims that there was a coherent cultural policy, uniformly enforced by the monarchy. Rediscovery or reconstruction of traditions can thus be a progressive (or regressive) vehicle for forging collective memories and identities.[132]

For the purposes of analysis, it is useful to note two aspects. Firstly, Traditionalism espouses a particular relationship with temporality, suspending both the past and the future in favour of the present. Nasr emphasizes the importance of the present as the portal, the life in the moment that he sees as the hallmark of traditional Iranian society.[133] As such, from his perspective, it would appear that both past and present become times of nostalgia, and that intuition, spontaneity, and some kind of vitality remaining within the 'norms' of tradition are of prime importance. Secondly, there is a civilizational dimension involved in the emergence and spread of Traditionalism,[134] in its quest for 'an appropriate traditional civilization'.[135] Nasr universalizes traditional civilization deploying the term in the singular, citing its function as creating a world of certainty oriented by the sacred, and divested of nihilism.[136] For him, modernity and tradition, represented by the West and non-West respectively, are essentially incompatible on civilizational grounds, while there is, however, the necessity for a robust dialogue among civilizations and religions, based upon their spiritual and traditional aspects.[137] Here, Nasr risks foreclosure of dialogues, a position close to that of the anti-Western perspectives espoused by Fardid and many other late twentieth-century intellectuals in Iran.[138]

In summary, the three-pronged (mutable, invented, or static) discourse of tradition in its varied interpretations has possessed cultural and political aspects, which in turn, influenced Iranian architecture. Those invoking tradition perpetually imagine and seek unrealizable utopias, and yet this harking back to tradition has persisted in national politics and culture, despite considerable changes in both arenas over the past fifty years. In architecture, recourse to tradition has been expressed through heightened attention paid to supposedly immutable native styles. Such architectural Traditionalism attracted renewed interest in the late 1980s and early 1990s with Persian translations of Bakhtiar and Ardalan's book, *The Sense of Unity* (see below). The book was underpinned by the intellectual project of Traditionalism espoused by Nasr which, as discussed above, transcends valorization of the past, and of cultural continuities, and in so doing becomes a (proto-)ideological project.[139]

The nostalgic search for cultural and civilizational authenticity involved paying close attention to the vernacular, the folk, the 'masses', and the traditions and symbols and rituals that stood for them. But it was also one aspect of an international drive for the recognition of what would later become classified as 'intangible heritage'.[140] Such an embrace of the folkloric also had an inevitable political function, one which collapsed the mundane and the sacred into one another, such that around every phenomenon there would be an aura of sacredness. The result was form without content, ritual without transformation, tradition without constituents. In his attack on Heideggerian essentialism, Adorno had argued that the Traditionalist 'jargon of authenticity' obfuscates realities, giving the appearance of a presence and actuality that does not exist; hence, the symbolic gestures in this language of authenticity refer to abstractions rather than to any grounded social context.[141] Arguably, this abstraction also characterized the assertion of legitimacy in architecture both before and after the Revolution, a utopia based on the reification of tradition.

Designing heritage through engagement with tradition: Nader Ardalan and the Iran Centre for Management Studies (ICMS)

> While the jargon overflows with the pretence of deep human emotion, it is just as standardized as the world that it officially negates.[142]

To illustrate Traditionalism's architectural import, we turn to Nader Ardalan's design for the Iran Centre for Management Studies (ICMS), an institutional building that, in a developmental sense, was an instrument of modernization. This project embodied aspects of development policies, including transnational exchanges of professional expertise (see Chapters 2 and 3). It also involved the deployment of formal and spatial traditional architectural typologies, in the design of a novel, and in the Iranian context experimental, form of tertiary institution, based upon American models of organizational structure and management training.[143] The American-educated architect Ardalan is representative of a generation of foreign-trained Iranians who returned to the country to participate in and benefit from its development projects, drawn by the Pahlavi government's appeals to expatriates to help develop the country's technology, management, and construction. Ardalan himself returned to a senior design position with the National Iranian Oil Company.[144] In 1966, he was invited by the University of Chicago's Oriental Institute to write a monograph on Iranian traditional architecture,[145] on the recommendation of Nasr, himself a doctoral graduate of Harvard University who had returned to Iran to teach at the University of Tehran.[146] The book, co-written with his then-wife, the American-Iranian Laleh Bakhtiar, and which was published in 1973 as *The Sense of Unity: The Sufi Tradition in Persian Architecture*, cemented the authors' reputations as experts on Islamic heritage. By the time of its publication, Ardalan had established his own architectural office in Tehran, the Mandala Collaborative,[147] after a period working for the leading Iranian firm of Abdolaziz Farmanfarmaian, and having gained the commission for the second stage of the ICMS.[148] At this time, he also maintained a strong link with the American firm Skidmore Owings and Merrill, in which he had been an associate in America. Again, it would appear that Nasr had been influential in introducing Ardalan to powerful figures in the Pahlavi establishment.[149]

Ardalan has claimed that it was in the project for the ICMS, designed and constructed between 1972 and 1975,[150] that his ideas for an 'authentic' Iranian architecture first crystallized, through what he described as an appearance of place, in which the essence or inner meaning was made manifest.[151] This 'authenticity' was based upon his formulation of 'universal', atemporal principles for Iranian architecture in the book, principles which drew upon the Sufi scholarship of Nasr and Corbin.[152] In the design of the project, an example of the interplay between economic development, exchange of expertise, and cultural representation in Iran,[153] Ardalan manufactured a semblance of tradition, 'Islamic' expression, and cultural specificity. The ICMS project is replete with nostalgic invocations of 'sites of origin' which Ardalan, as an Iranian who had been 'exiled' by providence, appears to have taken to be essences of authenticity.[154] The central argument Ardalan has posited for his choices of reference was that the history that the Iranians actually remember is that of the Islamic period and not the pre-Islamic, an argument previously made by another exponent of Islamic authenticity, Ali Shariati.[155] However, in his search for authenticity and a return to origins he may have also been reinforced by the concern for regional character expressed by the American landscape architect Ian McHarg, whom he would have known from his American studies and practice, and with whom he later worked on the design for Pardisān Park in Tehran of 1975, but even more so by the influence of the American architect Louis Kahn.[156]

The master plan of the ICMS (Figure 1.3) was based upon the reinterpretation of the *chāhār-bāgh*, or fourfold garden, a form that dates back to Achaemenid and even to pre-Islamic Sasanian origins.[157] Like historic *chāhār-bāgh*s, the

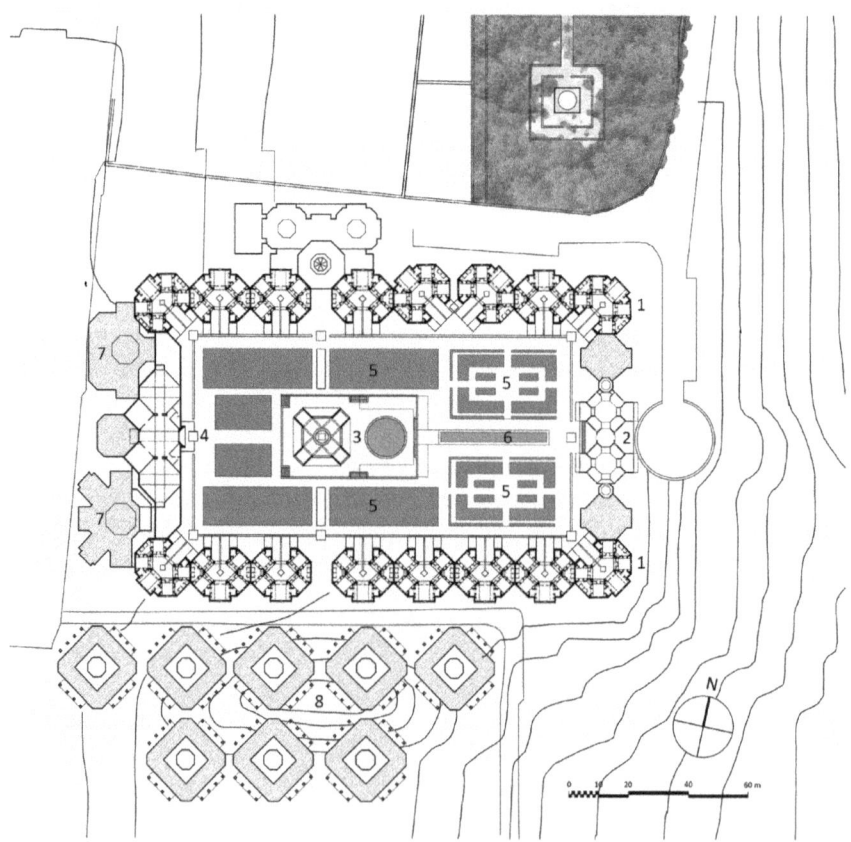

1.3 Nader Ardalan, Iran Centre for Management Studies (ICMS)/Imam Sādegh University (1978). Later phases shown in grey tone.

ICMS was laid out with a central pavilion – the library – axially aligned with the 'gatehouse' entrance and administration building, and the terminating pavilion which, in its location, resembles the layout of a garden pavilion in a Safavid palace, but here functions as a complex of lecture halls and seminar rooms. Running east–west along the centre spine of the garden is a water channel, resembling traditional gardens such as Bāgh-e Fin in Kāshān and Shāzdeh in Māhān, and several courtyards, flanked by cypress and poplar-lined orchards. Lining the central garden are eight student dormitory clusters on either side, forming a perimeter, enclosing a large garden area. Internally, the dormitories are formed of cells radiating from an octagonal courtyard – intimate 'communities', which mediate between the individual cell and the unified whole, and which Ardalan himself related to the layout of the traditional Iranian madrasa.[158] While Ardalan's project overtly references historical Iranian heritage sites, madrasas, and princely gardens, the traditional forms conceal a modern educational programme, while also conveying an overt elitism. The school was intended to train the new generation of economic managers to drive the White Revolution, but after the Islamic Revolution it became the Imam Sādegh University, one of the strategic universities in the Islamic system, bringing together clerical training and modern humanities for the regime's future political and administrative leaders. It has, since the Revolution, been under the direct supervision of powerful clerical authorities within the Islamic Republic.

The ICMS was also an example of the interaction of local and international influences in forging a semblance of cultural identity through the image of a community. Despite the Iranian references provided by Ardalan for the ICMS, the mandala form of the *Hasht Behesht*, the Pavilion of Eight Paradises in Isfahan, the pavilions and gardens of the Bagh-e Fin, and the *chāhār-bāgh*, Isfahan,[159] his design concept arguably derives equally from his experience in America, and the example of the teaching and work of the architect he appears to have taken as his mentor, Louis Kahn. Although he didn't use the metaphor of the garden, Kahn had designed his Indian School of Management (1961–74) with a similar concept of a central forum focused on the library and courtyard, which he defined as '[t]he meeting place of the mind, as well as the physical meeting place',[160] and a similar clustering of dormitory 'communities' – an interpretation of the madrasa type – and indeed used the same *parti* for the central court and scholars' offices of the Salk Laboratories at La Jolla California (1959–65), in which the court takes on the abstracted typology of a garden, with its central water channel, and the dormitories and study cells conveying the image of a scholarly community.[161] Kahn's Indian project, like the Iranian one, was an initiative undertaken in collaboration with the Harvard Business School. Materially, the two projects are also similar in their use of load-bearing brickwork for the most part, with limited use of structural concrete.

Ardalan was open in his admiration for Louis Kahn: '[Kahn] had an idea about architecture which dealt with the measurable and the unmeasurable [which] triggered in my mind to look for the unmeasurable in Persian architecture.'[162] The 'unmeasurable' pertained to architectural typologies that underlay particular forms, but beyond this geometrical dimension, also to a historical perspective that permitted connections to the monumental architecture of the distant past, re-mythologizing architecture in reaction to the instrumentalism of mid-century American architecture. For Kahn the transcendent value of geometry was a phenomenological given – indeed, what he called 'Form', some ethereal, ineffable matter waiting to be ordered, seems suspiciously like Platonic geometry in phenomenological cloth.[163] One can see certain parallels between Kahn's interest in 'archetypal' forms and their relation to places,[164] and Ardalan's emphasis upon architectural archetypes, which appears to be indebted to the Traditionalist philosophy of Nasr.[165] What is of relevance here is the question of was 'received' by Ardalan from both Kahn and Nasr – what he understood of Nasr's Traditionalist philosophy and Kahn's historicist ideas, and the uses to which he put them. There is much in this project that deserves historical examination, but here we must confine ourselves to the impact of Western influence on Iranian conceptions of authenticity as they pertain to tradition.

In his 1991 interview, Ardalan referred to certain universal architectural ideas, or archetypes, one of which he stated to be the Paradise Garden.[166] In his approach to the design of a 'meaningful' architecture, Ardalan used what he appears to have taken to be universal symbols that supposedly underly traditional forms. In his conception, place is an essential quality or 'being' that is associated with an underlying form and geometric structure, and is intrinsic to the production of a sense of place.[167] In a 2018 interview, Ardalan agreed that part of the discontent of people leading up to the Revolution derived from their sense of being displaced, an unease produced by the processes of cultural Westernization, technical transformation, and internal migration.[168] He considered that the Iranian 'experts', having returned from their foreign training, tended to apply foreign models without mediating and adjusting those models to accommodate local cultural specificities. Ardalan adopted a similar critical position to this feeling of estrangement from Iranian architectural traditions, in advocating the creation of modern architecture that incorporates and embodies Iranian heritage.[169] He characterized this approach as 'space-positive architecture', the 'seamless garment',[170] where the built form becomes the formative background that enables space to be perceived as the 'figure' – in an urban conception, as evident in the drawings of *The Idea of Unity*, that was seen as a *unicum*. Ardalan's approach, embodied in projects like the ICMS, consciously contrasted with the object-based architecture that he claimed to characterize Western culture.[171]

Such differentiation between Western architectural approaches and Ardalan's own culturally rooted approach raises a problem. Firstly, did not Ardalan 'displace' elements in his own work? Secondly, if there was to be no displacement, then there could be no transformation and thus no adaptation to modernity, which is of course ostensibly in line with Traditionalist thinking, although it lands Ardalan's position in a paradox. Not to adapt traditional forms and ideas to modern circumstances was to consign them to the museum, which is to say, to cultural death. Ardalan's ICMS 'garden madrasa' shares a nostalgic quest for community with Kahn's Ahmedabad project. Ardalan's utilization of nostalgia, however, possesses dangerous social connotations as it references the most backward-looking and patriarchal aspects of tradition. The school's *chāhār-bāgh*-derived plan, the embodied 'archetype', is no modern reinterpretation of a familiar typology but could, arguably, be seen as an example of what Boym has defined as 'restorative nostalgia', in which the synthesis focuses on reconstruction and unification, a reinstatement of the premodern hierarchical regime.[172] Ironically, Ardalan's approach to design, focusing on types and archetypes that were supposedly immutable, was still bound to a formalist conception of architectural significance, an approach that is Western in origin – as was the Traditionalist framework of his mentor Nasr for whom, as we have discussed above, there was at the heart of all world religions a common esoteric truth rooted in tradition.[173] Similarly, in the same 1991 interview, Ardalan noted the similarities between Quranic 'admonitions' and Zoroastrian expressions in the Avestā.[174] It was in the attempt to return Iranian architecture to an engagement with its spiritual origins, also reflected in his *Sense of Unity* research, that Ardalan and his like-minded fellow architects sought an alternative to their perceived cultural dependence on the West.

Conclusion

In setting out our theoretical approach, it is apparent that developmentalism gave rise to questions of authenticity, tradition, and civilization, all of which pertain to the past and are underpinned by nostalgia. However, we also emphasize that not all nostalgic impulses are retrograde and, despite familiar critiques, not all inventions of tradition are regressive. More importantly, the readings of things – material culture – will change with the changing context in time; what used to be progressive may cease to deliver its progressive function. It is this relationship to a past, underpinned with nostalgia, that through the process of design yields particular forms of heritage. Recalling Clifford's remark, we argue that the hallmark of tradition is its processuality and mutability, a mutability that can come from within as it can from without.[175] Neither of these processes is abrupt, and even when a tradition is transformed or completely discontinued, when embedded within a traditional culture such processes of mutation tend to be gradual. As societies change and modernize, traditions may lose their organic relation to society, becoming 'unmoored'.[176] Nonetheless, in the example of Iran, it is apparent that tradition continued in this period to supply the basis for identity and for interpreting and understanding the world in an hermeneutic process.[177] It was transformed rather than losing its significance outright.

Perhaps it is inevitable that development unmoors traditions, but if society accepts change, the question remains as to how far it can transform its traditions.

There are three possible social and critical responses to this detraditionalization process. The first position embraces the current unmooring of traditions and their displacement by modernizing programmes as sufficient and liberating. The second argues that the process of detraditionalization needs to go further in casting society adrift from its foundations. The third position, exemplified by Ardalan and Nasr's attitudes to architecture and heritage, is that replacement of traditional customs and practices has gone too far, that modernity has unsettled social life, and that there should be a return to the traditions; for example, to the vernacular.[178] This third position was strongly influential on Iran's 1970s architecture. It was in part a reaction to modernization, in part an attempt to redefine and reorient social institutions to shift towards a different group in power, and in part a reaction to outside influences. Those influences from within Iran came from different factions, and it was here that the Islamists in the Revolution, with the help of most of the left-leaning political groups, would eventually win the day, while the Pahlavi establishment fell, despite its stated concerns for tradition. As Hutton notes, after Aries, 'Political parties may rise and fall ... but popular traditions survive by adapting to new realities.'[179]

As we will see throughout this book, the work of Ardalan and others before the Revolution, and the state-sanctioned works of architecture after it, share a common characteristic with regard to their use of tradition. Such deployment is far from passive but is, instead, 'explicit and purposive' rather than culturally embedded. In the example of the ICMS, Ardalan engaged with tradition through the design of a contemporary institution, and through typological studies of canonical examples of historical architecture, identification of particular patterns and motifs, and by reference to the contemporary traditionalist philosophy of Nasr, relating forms and geometries to symbolic meanings that could be found in both Islam and older religions. Thus, the idealized image of architectural forms and spaces predominates in these essentially modern projects. From the 'library' of traditional Iranian architecture, the architect intentionally deploys motifs in order to conjure specific memories or haptic responses. The outcome is a form of mediated experience, the representational architecture standing for the past world that gave rise to it. In such purposive historicization, the modern subject is presented with an experience that links him or her to a past, with which the project purports to constitute a continuum. Here, the past is displaced and transformed into a form of heritage through the process of design and the conscious engagement with tradition.

This urge to engage tradition was put into action in the 1970s architectural congresses in Iran. In their organization of the 1970 International Congress of Architecture at Isfahan, Nader Ardalan, his then-wife, Laleh Bakhtiar, and like-minded Iranian architects, had sought to present this return to history and traditions with the intellectual support of leading international architectural figures. Architecture was to be situated in the context of Iran's Islamic and (perhaps to a lesser extent) pre-Islamic architectural heritage. The following chapter explores these congresses, which served as a vital nexus for the exchange of transnational ideas on architecture and cultural identity, which contributed to the production of a series of significant attempts to engage with the past and its traditions in architecture and urban environments.

Notes

1 'Iran was taking off [in the 1960s and 1970s]. We were then ahead of Southeast Asia, but later on they got ahead and became more successful. In my opinion, the reason for our failure is we did not tolerate the pace of change. But why is that? I do not know. Also, we intellectuals of the time were [...] confused and didn't have a proper analysis of our place within society and our society within the world. [...] I can confess that we, the intellectuals, did not understand our place and wrecked the society [...] I have to confess, I am embarrassed, that our generation stuffed up!' D. Shayegan cited in:

'مروری کوتاه بر دیروز و امروز داریوش شایگان: فکر در ساحت نامتناهی ذکر'، هفته نامه صدا، سال ۱۸، ۱۴ بهمن ۱۳۹۶: ۱۴۸.

2 M. Pickering and E. Keightley, 'The Modalities of Nostalgia', *Current Sociology*, 54:6 (2006), p. 927.
3 A. Mirsepassi, *Transnationalism in Iranian Political Thought: The Life and Times of Ahmad Fardid*, Volume 1 (Cambridge: Cambridge University Press, 2017), p. 58.
4 M. Merhavi, '"True Muslims Must Always Be Tidy and Clean": Exoticism of the Countryside in Late Pahlavi Iran', in M. Litvak (ed.), *Constructing Nationalism in Iran* (Abingdon: Routledge, 2017), pp. 158–72.
5 K. Kuutma, 'From Folklore to Intangible Heritage', in W. Logan et al. (eds), *A Companion to Heritage Studies* (Chichester, UK, and Malden, MA: Wiley-Blackwell, 2015), pp. 41–54.
6 'Islamic architecture' was seen as coterminous with traditional architecture.
7 Mirsepassi, *Transnationalism*; N. Nabavi, 'The Discourse of "Authentic Culture" in Iran in the 1960s and 1970s', in N. Nabavi (ed.), *Intellectual Trends in Twentieth-Century Iran: A Critical Survey* (Gainesville, FL: University Press of Florida, 2003), pp. 91–108; A. Matin-Asgari, *Both Eastern and Western: An Intellectual History of Iranian Modernity* (Cambridge: Cambridge University Press, 2018), ch. 6.
8 اسدی، ع.، تهرانیان، م.، ع. عبدی و م. گودرزی (eds)، صدایی که شنیده نشد: نگرش‌های اجتماعی- فرهنگی و توسعه‌ی نامتوازن در ایران گزارشی از یافته‌های طرح 'آینده نگری'، (تهران: نشر نی، ۱۳۹۵)، ص ۶.
9 اسدی و تهرانیان، صدایی که شنیده نشد، صص. ۲۳–۲۵.
10 اسدی و تهرانیان، صدایی که شنیده نشد، ص. ۲۷.
11 In 1974, religious texts were most popular among the youth:
اسدی و تهرانیان، صدایی که شنیده نشد، ص. ۱۷.
12 H. Sheikh Zeineddin, interview with A. Mozaffari, Tehran, September 2013.
13 Pickering and Keightley, 'Modalities of Nostalgia', p. 935; Scott, 'Bernard Rudofsky'; M. Sabatino, 'The Primitive in Modern Architecture and Urbanism', *The Journal of Architecture*, 13:4 (2008), pp. 355–64; N. Dames, 'Nostalgia and Its Disciplines', *Memory Studies*, 3:3 (2010), pp. 269–75.
14 A. Bonnett, *The Geography of Nostalgia: Global and Local Perspectives on Modernity and Loss* (London and New York: Routledge, 2016), p. 41.
15 Pickering and Keightley, 'Modalities of Nostalgia', p. 932, citing P. Grainge,

Monochrome Memories: Nostalgia and Style in Retro America (Westport, CT: Praeger, 2002).
16 G. Campbell et al., 'Nostalgia and Heritage: Potentials, Mobilisations and Effects', *International Journal of Heritage Studies*, 23:7 (2017), p. 609, https://doi.org/10.1080/13527258.2017.1324558.
17 R. Cashman, 'Critical Nostalgia and Material Culture in Northern Ireland', *The Journal of American Folklore*, 119:472 (Spring, 2006), p. 141, citing S. Tannock, 'Nostalgia Critique', *Culture Studies*, 9:3 (1995), p. 456.
18 R. Bryant, 'Nostalgia and the Discovery of Loss: Essentializing the Turkish Cypriot Past', in O. Angé and D. Berliner (eds), *Anthropology and Nostalgia* (New York and Oxford: Berghahn Books, 2015), pp. 165, 170.
19 B. S. Turner, 'A Note on Nostalgia', *Theory, Culture & Society*, 4 (1987), pp. 150–1.
20 Bonnett, *Geography of Nostalgia*, p. 48; O. Angé and D. Berliner, 'Introduction: Athropology of Nostalgia – Anthropology as Nostalgia', in Angé and Berliner (eds), *Anthropology and Nostalgia*, pp. 5, 7; Cashman, 'Critical Nostalgia', p. 140. On nostalgia's connotations, see Pickering and Keightley, 'Modalities of Nostalgia', p. 934; B. Mesquita et al., 'The Cultural Regulation of Emotions', in J. J. Gross (ed.), *Handbook of Emotion Regulation* (New York: The Guilford Press), pp. 284–301.
21 R. Bartoletti, 'Memory Tourism and Commodification of Nostalgia', in P. Burns et al. (eds), *Tourism and Visual Culture: Volume 1: Theories and Concepts* (Wallingford: CABI, 2010), pp. 24–25, cited in Bonnett, *Geography of Nostalgia*, p. 17.
22 Pickering and Keightley, 'Modalities of Nostalgia', p. 921.
23 D. Berliner, 'Multiple Nostalgias: The Fabric of Heritage in Luang Prabang (Lao PDR)', *The Journal of the Royal Anthropological Institute*, 18:4 (2012), pp. 769–86; Pickering and Keightley, 'Modalities of Nostalgia,' p. 924; R. Koselleck, *Futures Past: On the Semantics of Historical Time*, trans. K. Tribe (Cambridge, MA: MIT Press, 1985).
24 Bryant, 'Nostalgia and Discovery', pp. 163, 170.
25 On liminal nostalgia, see Bryant, 'Nostalgia and Discovery', pp. 170–2, after N. S. Tulbure, 'Drinking and Nostalgia: Social Imagination in Postsocialist Romania', *Anthropology of East Europe Review*, 24:1 (Spring, 2006), pp. 85–93; V. Turner, *The Ritual Process: Structure and Anti-structure* (New York: Aladine de Gruyter, 1969).
26 Angé and Berliner, 'Introduction', p. 5.
27 Bryant, 'Nostalgia and Discovery', pp. 156, 171.
28 Pickering and Keightley, 'Modalities of Nostalgia', p. 929.
29 Bonnett, *Geography of Nostalgia*, pp. 28–30.
30 Bonnett, *Geography of Nostalgia*, pp. 9–11; Angé and Berliner, 'Introduction', p. 10.
31 Pickering and Keightley, 'Modalities of Nostalgia', p. 928.
32 Berliner, 'Multiple Nostalgias', pp. 781–2; S. Boym, *The Future of Nostalgia* (New York: Basic Books, 2001), pp. 83, 89–90.
33 O. Angé, 'Social and Economic Performativity of Nostalgic Narratives in Andean Barter Fairs', in Angé and Berliner (eds), *Anthropology and Nostalgia*, pp. 178–97.
34 W. C. Bissel, 'Engaging Colonial Nostalgia', *Cultural Anthropology*, 20:2 (2005), pp. 215–48, cited in Berliner, 'Multiple Nostalgias', p. 770.
35 Pickering and Keightley, 'Modalities of Nostalgia', p. 932, after Grainge, *Monochrome Memories*.

36 Tulbure, 'Drinking and Nostalgia,' p. 85, cited in Bryant, 'Nostalgia and Discovery', p. 170.
37 Berliner, 'Multiple Nostalgias', p. 769.
38 Pickering and Keightley, 'Modalities of Nostalgia', p. 923.
39 Cashman, 'Critical Nostalgia', pp. 138, 140, 154.
40 Cashman, 'Critical Nostalgia', p. 138; Bonnett, *Geography of Nostalgia*, p. 48.
41 Angé and Berliner, 'Introduction', p. 5.
42 Angé and Berliner, 'Introduction', p. 11; Bonnett, *Geography of Nostalgia*, p. 33.
43 Pickering and Keightley, 'Modalities of Nostalgia', p. 925.
44 Cashman, 'Critical Nostalgia', p. 148.
45 Bonnett, *Geography of Nostalgia*, p. 87.
46 Pickering and Keightley, 'Modalities of Nostalgia', p. 925.
47 Angé and Berliner, 'Introduction', p. 7.
48 Bryant, 'Nostalgia and Discovery', p. 166.
49 Cashman, 'Critical Nostalgia', p. 136, citing F. Davis, *Yearning for Yesterday: A Sociology of Nostalgia* (New York: Free Press, 1979), p. 35; N. Atia and J. Davis, 'Nostalgia and the Shapes of History: Editorial', *Memory Studies*, 3:3 (2010), p. 184, cited in Angé and Berliner, 'Introduction', p. 12.
50 Turner, 'Note on Nostalgia', p. 154; Pickering and Keightley, 'Modalities of Nostalgia', p. 936.
51 Bonnett, *Geography of Nostalgia*, pp. 25, 33.
52 Boym, *Future of Nostalgia*, p. 34.
53 Angé and Berliner, 'Introduction', p. 11, citing D. Boyer, 'From Algos to Autonomos: Nostalgic Eastern Europe as Postimperial Mania', in M. Todorova and Z. Gille (eds), *Postcommunist Nostalgia* (Oxford: Berghahn Books, 2012), p. 25; Bryant, 'Nostalgia and Discovery', p. 164.
54 Boym, *Future of Nostalgia*, pp. 37–8.
55 Bonnett, *Geography of Nostalgia*, p. 34.
56 C. Taylor, *Sources of the Self: The Making of the Modern Identity* (Cambridge: Cambridge University Press, 1989), p. 25.
57 Taylor, *Sources of the Self*, p. 36.
58 H. Katouzian, *Sadeq Hedayat: The Life and Legend of an Iranian Writer* (London and New York: I.B. Tauris, 2002), pp. 67–71; R. D. Abrahams, 'Phantoms of Romantic Nationalism in Folkloristics', *American Folklore*, 106:419 (1993), pp. 3–37; A. Babadzan, 'Anthropology, Nationalism and "the Invention of Tradition"', *Anthropological Forum*, 10:2 (2000), pp. 131–55.
59 N. Nabavi, *Intellectuals and the State in Iran: Politics, Discourse, and the Dilemma of Authenticity* (Gainesville, FL: University Press of Florida, 2003), p. 92.
60 Nabavi, *Intellectuals and the State*, pp. 92–4.
61 N. Nabavi, 'The Changing Concept of the "Intellectual" in Iran of the 1960s', *Iranian Studies*, 32:3 (Summer, 1999), p. 348; Nabavi, *Intellectuals and the State*, p. 95.
62 M. Boroujerdi, *Iranian Intellectuals and the West: The Tormented Triumph of Nativism* (New York: Syracuse University Press, 1996); A. Milani, *The Men and Women Who Made Modern Iran, 1941–1979, Volume 1* (New York: Syracuse University Press and Persian World Press, 2008), pp. 298–304.
63 Nabavi, *Intellectuals and the State*, pp. 92–4.

64 Mirsepassi, *Transnationalism*, pp. 147–65; see also Nabavi, 'Discourse of "Authentic Culture"'.
65 Nabavi, *Intellectuals and the State*, pp. 102–3; see also D. Shayegan, 'Corbin, Henri', *Encyclopaedia Iranica*, Volume VI, Fasc. 3, 2011 [1993], pp. 268–72, www.iranicaonline.org/articles/corbin-henry-b (accessed 9 October 2018).
66 Parham cited in Nabavi, 'Discourse of "Authentic Culture"', pp. 92, 102–4.
67 Nabavi, *Intellectuals and the State*, p. 100.
68 Smith, *Uses of Heritage*, pp. 12, 29.
69 Nabavi, *Intellectuals and the State*, p. 94.
70 Mirsepassi, *Transnationalism*, pp. 61, 143.
71 هاشمی، م. م.، هویت اندیشان و میراث فکری احمد فردید، (تهران: کویر، ۱۳۸۳)، صص. 84–98
72 D. Ashuri, 'Fardid Was Not Very Religious', in A. Mirsepassi (ed.), *Iran's Troubled Modernity: Debating Ahmad Fardid's Legacy* (Cambridge: Cambridge University Press, 2019), p. 95; S. Mansouri-Zeyni and S. Sami, 'The History of Ressentiment in Iran and the Emerging Ressentiment-less Mindset', *Iranian Studies*, 47:1 (2014), pp. 49–64.
73 Mirsepassi, *Transnationalism*, p. 166.
74 Mirsepassi, *Transnationalism*, pp. 263–73.
75 Mirsepassi, *Transnationalism*, p. 23.
76 Here, Khalil Maliki's political conception of a 'Third Force', neither East nor West, was an attempt to think beyond the polarization of the Cold War, See H. Katouzian, 'Of the Sins of Khalil Maleki', *Iran Namag*, 2:1 (2017), p. 54.
77 C. Aydin, *The Politics of Anti-Westernism in Asia: Visions of World Order in Pan-Islamic and Pan-Asian Thought* (New York: Columbia University Press, 2007), pp. 9, 191–2.
78 Aydin, *Politics of Anti-Westernism*, p. 344.
79 C. Aydin, 'Japan's Pan-Asianism and the Legitimacy of Imperial World Order, 1931–1945', *The Asia-Pacific Journal* 6:3 (2008), p. 24; Aydin, *Politics of Anti-Westernism*, p. 189.
80 Aydin, *Politics of Anti-Westernism*, p. 28.
81 Aydin, *Politics of Anti-Westernism*, pp. 28, 349.
82 On European origins of the concept of civilization, see A. Pagden, 'The "Defence of Civilization" in Eighteenth-Century Social Theory', *History of the Social Sciences*, 1:1 (1988), pp. 33–45; Ali Mirsepassi, *Intellectual Discourse and the Politics of Modernization: Negotiating Modernity in Iran* (Cambridge: Cambridge University Press, 2000), pp. 18–24.
83 م. پهلوی، بسوی تمدن بزرگ (تهران: کتابخانه پهلوی، ۱۳۵۵).
84 Nabavi, *Intellectuals and the State*, p. 96.
85 Nabavi, *Intellectuals and the State*, pp. 95–6.
86 Matin-Asgari, *Both Eastern and Western*, ch. 6.
87 ع. ملایی توانی، ل. ملکی، س. م. ح. محمدی (eds)، مقدمه، اسنادی از مرکز ایرانی مطالعه فرهنگ‌ها، 5 جلد (تهران: پژوهشگاه علوم انسانی و مطالعات فرهنگی، ۱۳۹۶)، ص. م.
88 ملایی توانی وسایرین، اسنادی از اساسنامه مرکز ایرانی مطالعه فرهنگ‌ها-ماده ۱-هدف، ص. ۳.
89 ملایی توانی وسایرین، اسنادی از، صص. ۳–۴.
90 Nabavi, *Intellectuals and the State*, p. 100; د. ۱۵۱، ص، اسنادی از، ملایی توانی وسایرین آشوری، شرق و غرب
91 Bonnett, *Geography of Nostalgia*, p. 142.

92 Mirsepassi, *Transnationalism*, p. 24.
93 Religious groups were nevertheless perceived as natural allies of the monarchy and compared to other groups, enjoyed a considerable amount of freedom in their activities, and Traditionalist and counter-Enlightenment forces within the establishment (such as Nasr and Shayegan) played a de facto supporting role.
94 Abdi and Goudarzi recommended a national unity policy based upon cultural continuity:

اسدی و تهرانیان، صدایی که شنیده نشد، صص. ۲۸-۲۷.

95 Nabavi, *Intellectuals and the State*, pp. 94–8.
96 Nabavi, *Intellectuals and the State*, p. 99.
97 J. Clifford, 'Traditional Futures', in M. S. Phillips and G. Schochet (eds), *Questions of Tradition* (Toronto: University of Toronto Press, 2004), p. 152.
98 E. Shils, *Tradition* (Chicago, IL: The University of Chicago Press, 1981), p. 12; E. Shils, 'Tradition', *Comparative Studies in Society and History*, 13:2, Special Issue on Tradition and Modernity (1971), pp. 122–59.
99 G. Schochet, 'Tradition as Politics and the Politics of Tradition', in Phillips and Schochet (eds), *Questions of Tradition*, pp. 303–4.
100 S. N. Eisenstadt, 'Intellectuals and Tradition', *Daedalus*, 101:2 (Spring, 1972), pp. 3–5.
101 Z. Bauman, 'Morality in the Age of Contigency', in Heelas et al. (eds), *Detraditionalization*, p. 49.
102 Schochet, 'Tradition as Politics', p. 296.
103 Schochet, 'Tradition as Politics', p. 305.
104 P. H. Hutton, 'Ideas about Tradition in the Life and Work of Phillipe Ariès', in Phillips and Schochet (eds), *Questions of Tradition*, p. 276.
105 Heelas, 'Introduction', p. 8.
106 J. B. Thompson, 'Tradition and Self in a Mediated World', in Heelas et al. (eds), *Detraditionalization*, p. 94.
107 Bauman, 'Morality', p. 49.
108 Thompson, 'Tradition and Self', p. 99.
109 Schochet, 'Tradition as Politics', p. 302.
110 Eisenstadt, 'Intellectuals and Tradition', p. 6.
111 Eisenstadt, 'Intellectuals and Tradition', p. 3.
112 T. W. Luke, 'Identity, Meaning and Globalization: Detraditionalization in Postmodern Space-Time Compression', in Heelas et al. (eds), *Detraditionalization*, p. 116.
113 Bonnett, *Geography of Nostalgia*, p. 163.
114 Bonnett, *Geography of Nostalgia*, pp. 165–6.
115 E. Hobsbawm, 'Introduction: Inventing Traditions', in E. Hobsbawm and T. Ranger (eds), *The Invention of Tradition* (Cambridge: Cambridge University Press, 1983), p. 2.
116 Hobsbawm, 'Introduction', pp. 1–3.
117 T. Otto and P. Pedersen, 'Disentangling Traditions: Culture, Agency and Power', in T. Otto and P. Pedersen (eds), *Tradition and Agency: Tracing Cultural Continuity and Invention* (Aarhus: Aarhus University Press, 2005), pp. 14, 31.
118 Otto and Pedersen, 'Disentangling Traditions', p. 30.
119 M. S. Phillips, 'Introduction: What Is Tradition When It Is Not Invented? A

Historiographical Introduction', in Phillips and Schochet (eds), *Questions of Tradition*, pp. 4–5; C. L. Briggs, 'The Politics of Discursive Authority in Research on the "Invention of Tradition"', *Cultural Anthropology*, 11:4 (1996), p. 438; T. Ranger, 'The Invention of Tradition Revisited: The Case of Colonial Africa', in T. Ranger and O. Vaughan (eds), *Legitimacy and the State in Twentieth-Century Africa* (New York: Springer, 1993), pp. 80–1.
120 Otto and Pedersen, 'Disentangling Traditions', p. 21.
121 Phillips, 'Introduction', pp. 6–8; Ranger, 'Invention of Tradition', pp. 63, 77–8; Otto and Pedersen, 'Disentangling Traditions', pp. 12, 31, 35.
122 J. Friedman, 'The Past in the Future: History and the Politics of Identity', *American Anthropologist*, 94:4 (1992), p. 850.
123 Friedman, 'The Past in the Future', p. 846.
124 N. Thomas, 'The Inversion of Tradition', *American Ethnologist*, 19:2 (1992), pp. 213–14.
125 D. Lerner, *The Passing of Traditional Society: Modernizing the Middle East* (New York: Free Press of Glencoe, 1958), pp. 19–42; R. Bendix, 'Tradition and Modernity Reconsidered', *Comparative Studies in Society and History*, 9:3 (1967), pp. 292–346; H. Shah, *The Production of Modernization: Daniel Lerner, Mass Media, and the Passing of Traditional Society* (Pennsylvania: Temple University Press, 2011).
126 Tipps, 'Modernization Theory', pp. 206–7.
127 M. Sedgwick, *Against the Modern World: Traditionalism and the Secret Intellectual History of the Twentieth Century* (Oxford: Oxford University Press, 2004), p. 21.
128 H. Zareh, *The Horizons of Wisdom in the Sphere of Tradition: A Conversation between Hamed Zare and Seyyed Hossein Nasr* (Tehran: Qoqnus Publishers: 2014), p. 92 (ebook).
129 S. H. Nasr, *Knowledge and the Sacred: Revisioning Academic Accountability* (New York: SUNY Press, 1989), p. 99; Zareh, *Horizons of Wisdom*, p. 96.
130 Schochet, 'Tradition as Politics', p. 303.
131 J. Assmann and J. Czaplicka, 'Collective Memory and Cultural Identity', *New German Critique*, 65 (Spring–Summer, 1995), pp. 125–33.
132 Sedgwick, *Against the Modern World*, pp. 153–9; A. Mozaffari, *Forming National Identity in Iran: The Idea of Homeland Derived from Ancient Persian and Islamic Imaginations of Place* (London: I.B. Tauris, 2014), pp. 87–8.
133 Nasr, *Knowledge and the Sacred*, p. 194.
134 Sedgwick, *Against the Modern World*, pp. 25–6.
135 Sedgwick, *Against the Modern World*, p. 69.
136 Nasr cited in Zareh, *Horizons of Wisdom*, p. 76.
137 Nasr cited in Zareh, *Horizons of Wisdom*, pp. 78–9.
138 Nabavi, *Intellectuals and the State*, p. 99; Nasr cited in Zareh, *Horizons of Wisdom*, p. 92.
139 Sedgwick, *Against the Modern World*, pp. 251–2; Nasr, *Knowledge and the Sacred*, p. 194.
140 Kuutma, 'From Folklore to Intangible Heritage', pp. 41–54.
141 T. Adorno, *The Jargon of Authenticity*, trans. K. Tarnowski and F. Will (Evanston, IL: Northwestern University Press, 1973), p. 51.
142 Adorno, *Jargon of Authenticity*, p. 6.
143 J. B. Kassarjian and Nader Ardalan, 'The Center for Management Studies, Tehran',

in M. B. Sevçenko (ed.), *Higher-Education Facilities* (Cambridge, MA: Aga Khan Program for Islamic Architecture, 1982).
144 Haeri, S., 'Ardalan, Nader', Oral History interview (Boston, MA: Foundation for Iranian Studies, 21 July 1991), p. 27, https://fis-iran.org/en/content/ardalan-nader (accessed 11 September 2017).
145 Haeri, 'Ardalan', p. 17.
146 Nasr cited in W. C. Chittick (ed.), *The Essential Seyyed Hossein Nasr* (Bloomington, IN: World Wisdom Inc., 2007), p. xi.
147 Haeri, 'Ardalan', pp. 14, 18.
148 H. A. Rad, 'A Study of the Architecture of Nader Ardalan in Terms of Tradition and Modernity in the Islamic Context' (PhD diss., University of New South Wales, 2015), p. 72.
149 H. Ziya'i, 'Nasr, Seyyed Hossein', Oral History interview (Newton, MA: Foundation for Iranian Studies, 1982–83), p. 75, https://fis-iran.org/en/content/nasr-seyyed-hossein (accessed 14 January 2018); M. Afkhami, 'Pahlbod, Mehrdad', Oral History interview (Los Angeles, CA: Foundation for Iranian Studies, 25 and 30 May 1984), https://fis-iran.org/en/content/pahlbod-mehrdad (accessed 14 January 2018).
150 Haeri, 'Ardalan', p. 24.
151 Haeri, 'Ardalan', p. 18; M. A. Amir-Moezzi and C. Jambet, *What Is Shia Islam? An Introduction* (Abingdon: Routledge, 2018), pp. 15–16.
152 Sedgwick, *Against the Modern World*, pp. 153–9; Ardalan cited in Shirazi, *Contemporary Architecture*, p. 133.
153 R. Garlitz, 'Academic Ambassadors in the Middle East: The University Contract Program in Turkey and Iran, 1950–1970' (PhD diss., Ohio University, 2008), p. 43.
154 Haeri, 'Ardalan', p. 21.
155 E. Abrahamian, 'Ali Shariati: Ideologue of the Iranian Revolution', in E. Burke and I. Lapidus (eds), *Islam, Politics, and Social Movements* (Los Angeles, CA: University of California Press, 1993), pp. 56–63.
156 K. John-Alder, 'Paradise Reconsidered: The Early History of Pardisan Park in Tehran', in M. Gharipour (ed.), *Contemporary Urban Landscapes of the Middle East* (London and New York: Routledge, 2016), pp. 120–48.
157 R. P. Wilson, 'The Persian Garden: Bagh and Chahar Bagh', in E. B. MacDougall and R. Ettinghausen (eds), *The Islamic Garden* (Washington, DC: Dumbarton Oaks, 1976), pp. 69–86.
158 N. Ardalan, 'Places of Public Gathering', in L. Safran (ed.), *Places of Public Gathering in Islam* (Philadelphia, PA: The Aga Khan Award for Architecture, 1980), p. 14.
159 Kassarjian and Ardalan, 'Center for Management Studies', pp. 25–6.
160 A. P. Mohler and P. Papademetriou, *Louis I. Kahn: Conversations with Students* (New York: Princeton Archiectural Press, 1998), p. 40.
161 S. W. Goldhagen, *Louis Kahn's Situated Modernism* (New Haven, CT: Yale University Press, 2001), pp. 1–2; R. McCarter, *Louis Kahn* (New York: Phaedon, 2005), p. 183.
162 Haeri, 'Ardalan', p. 27.
163 R. Sommer, 'Four Stops along an Architecture of Postwar America', *Perspecta*, Resurfacing Modernism (2001), p. 79.

164 Haeri, 'Ardalan', p. 27.
165 Sedgwick, *Against the Modern World*, p. 154.
166 Haeri, 'Ardalan', pp. 27, 31; Ardalan, 'Places of Public Gathering', p. 16; Ardalan cited in Shirazi, *Contemporary Architecture*, pp. 72, 128–9.
167 Ardalan cited in Shirazi, *Contemporary Architecture*, p. 137.
168 Haeri, 'Ardalan', p. 19.
169 Amanat cited in Shirazi, *Contemporary Architecture*, p. 162.
170 Haeri, 'Ardalan', p. 35.
171 Haeri, 'Ardalan', pp. 36–7.
172 Boym, *Future of Nostalgia*, pp. 83, 89–90.
173 Nasr, *Knowledge and the Sacred*, endnote 140, pp. 6–61.
174 Haeri, 'Ardalan', p. 61.
175 Clifford, 'Traditional Futures', p. 152.
176 Thompson, 'Tradition and Self', pp. 92–4.
177 J. B. Thompson, *Media and Modernity: A Social Theory of the Media* (Stanford, CA: Stanford University Press, 1995), p. 185.
178 Heelas, 'Introduction', pp. 17–18.
179 Hutton, 'Ideas about Tradition', p. 276.

2

Canvassing a future: The international congresses of architecture in Iran and the transnational search for identity

Introduction

An important aspect of development is the flow of expertise and ideas that transforms localities. In relation to the built environment, the conduit for such flow in 1970s Iran was a series of five international congresses, organized between 1970 and 1976 by the Iranian government, of which three concerned architectural issues; the first two (Isfahan 1970, Persepolis 1974) addressed issues of development, impacts of advanced technology, and appropriate housing, while the third (Ramsar 1976) focused on women in architecture.[1] These congresses were driven by a concern for the destabilizing effect of development on cultural values and traditions, and a belief that architecture should be a vehicle for culturally sensitive modernization, particularly in the areas of housing and urban development. In hindsight, they reflected an official attempt to bridge development and culture. The delegates included leading international architectural figures of the time, who participated across multiple international forums, circulating ideas, concepts, and technical information. Delegates not only focused on pressing issues in Iran, such as the complex relation of tradition and modernization, cultural identity, and transnational exchanges of knowledge, but also on alternatives to existing normative models of modernist architecture, housing, and urbanism, which would subsequently inform UNESCO's Habitat articles and, arguably, the architectural theory of Critical Regionalism. From the perspective of Iranian architects, these congresses were an opportunity both to theorize a specifically Iranian lifeworld, a contextually specific pattern of everyday life, in which architecture and urbanism were imbricated, and to gain international validation for their ideas.[2] These exchanges, which informed architectural thought and practice for the next two decades, grew out of the larger context of rapid national development associated with the White Revolution.[3]

In the previous chapters we noted, following Tsing, that culture is formed through long-distance, transnational exchanges, the outcome of which takes on specific characteristics and produces surprising results in each locality – a process that she identifies as friction. Heritage, we noted, is one outcome of friction, augmented by the circulation and exchange of materials, ideas and knowledge, technologies, and expertise (and at times, the experts themselves). Tsing's notion of friction was at work during the congresses. In Iran's developmental context, elements within the government concurred with some influential architects on the necessity to employ tradition reflexively in furnishing a response to modernity in an Iranian context. The past was invoked, reimagined, and utilized in the process of developing new heritage formations. The congresses also facilitated a co-production of notions of architectural heritage in Iran;[4] heritage and its concomitant ideas of tradition, the vernacular and the local, were the outcome of discussions rather than pre-existing realities on the ground, but also the product of a global project of development interpreted in an Iranian context. From this vantage point, we will examine the themes that dominated these congresses, which have been briefly discussed in several recent architectural studies.[5] Here, we consider them in relation to the emergence of Iranian architectural heritage discourse.

Social and historical context of the congresses

As mentioned previously, rapid development in the country both ignited critical concerns about national cultural identity and a nostalgic search for authenticity that was also reflected in the art festivals and other cultural events in 1970s Iran, and may also be understood in relation to the Cold War ideological contentions.[6] The sudden growth in wealth generated by escalating oil revenues, averaging 10.5 per cent between 1963 and 1977,[7] enabled a rapid rise both in the standard of living and in government-funded development projects. However, major population displacement, resulting from industrialization, precipitated tangible socio-economic changes that revealed cultural schisms within the society, and highlighted the inadequacy of infrastructure and planning to mitigate the rapidly unfolding situation.[8] Population displacement continued, ad hoc or semi-planned settlements were built, and in response, especially in the capital, satellite cities were proposed and realized through master plans.[9] Architecturally, there was an attempt to include in some planned settlements symbolic expressions, images, and experiences by which a common ground of memory and identity could be cultivated between various groups within the society. The congresses took place in the context of this highly fluid socio-economic change. As discussed below, the debates among various domestic factions and their international counterparts revolved around appropriate cultural responses that might mitigate the effects of change. This was raised in the context of debating regional and national identities, developing versus first-world economies and societies, and differential rates of modernization. The central theme of the congresses was how Iran could address the challenges of modernization associated with development, while remaining true to its own cultural traditions, a theme which we can now retrospectively interpret as one of heritage.

A key area for discussion was housing, where previous developments of modern public housing and urban design from the late 1940s onwards had produced mixed results.[10] This was in part because the architects' designs had departed from traditional forms and were unfamiliar to the Iranian user, but also because economic realities encouraged the new owner-occupiers of the projects to engage in property speculation rather than residing in the developments.[11] Instances of the Iranian government engaging in international collaboration and technical assistance in the field of housing had taken place, including with Israel in the 1960s and 1970s,[12] whereby the government had faced the necessity of developing systems to supply housing following its own massive wave of immigration in the wake of the Six-Day War in 1967. By the 1970s, it had become clear that both technical and cultural aspects of housing and urbanism had to be addressed to accommodate the changing social and economic conditions of the country.

Also by the 1970s, and especially in the wake of the 1973 oil crisis, some Western architects were turning away from formal concerns towards environmentalism, and even towards the adoption of an anti-building ethos. There was, however, in the very different context of Iran's booming economy, a focus on development and infrastructural reform in the areas of new industries, tertiary education, and cultural institutions. After a decade of consistent growth, the monarchy was able to assert Iranian national identity through various development projects, especially a repertoire of symbolic public monuments. Despite the multiplicity of opinions and circles of influence within the royal court,[13] there was a degree of consensus that rapid socio-economic change had exacerbated existing cultural schisms.

Precedents for the Iran congresses

The congresses were significant for Iran as the first major meetings to be held there focused upon modern architecture and heritage. They were also internationally significant as sequels to the meetings and exhibitions held by the CIAM (*Congrés internationaux d'architecture moderne*) (1928 to 1959), the less formal meetings of its successor group Team Ten (1960 to 1981), and the *Union internationale des architectes* (1948 to present), and because they anticipated the formation of the Aga Khan Award for Islamic Architecture (1977 to present). In the immediate aftermath of the Second World War, CIAM delegates had introduced new cultural issues in response to the destruction of cultural heritage and social dislocation – there was a growing awareness of the need to compensate for the widespread sense of loss, alienation, and nostalgia for the way of life of the pre-war city.

In this cultural climate, the focus shifted to the connectivity between dwelling and community. At the 1949 CIAM 7 meeting,[14] Le Corbusier introduced the new term 'habitat' to replace 'minimum dwelling', without defining what it might mean.[15] At the 1951 CIAM 8 congress at Hoddesden, Jaap Bakema and the Dutch Opbouw group – then engaged in the post-war rebuilding of Rotterdam – returned to the idea of habitat and proposed a habitat charter, which was debated at the 1953 CIAM 9 congress at Aix-en-Provence. There, opinions polarized around two tendencies: on the one hand, applications of the Athens Charter (1933) supported by the older generation of modernists, proposing the separation of urban functions, and on the other hand, sociologically and anthropologically informed models that sought to base modern housing proposals upon the study of the way people actually lived. In these debates, there was a divergence of viewpoints based on very different conceptions of the relation between architecture, culture, and the city: was the city best described through Le Corbusier's conception of *urbanisme*, or Aldo van Eyck's 'settlement'? Similarly, should a conception of appropriate habitat be based around the anthropologically informed idea of dwelling or the functionalist idea of housing?

Concurrently, there had been a growing focus on ways of living in cities and neighbourhoods. At Aix-en-Provence, the delegates from French-administered Algiers and Morocco presented the *Habitat du Plus Grand Nombre* Grid (Écochard and ATBAT, Casablanca) and the *Bidonville Mahieddine* Grid (GAMMA, Algiers). The project panels offered anthropological and sociological studies of the way that local populations actually lived, both in their traditional villages and in the slums or *bidonvilles* that had sprung up on the outskirts of cities. This paralleled contemporary approaches used by the Italian architects Ridolfi, Quaroni, and Libera for immigrant housing in post-war Italian cities, in which the study of the fabric and social life of traditional towns formed the basis for new settlements. Starting at CIAM 9, a younger generation of architects had appealed to the example of the historic city in rejecting the functionalist model of urbanization associated with the modern industrial city and propagated through the Athens Charter and formulated by CIAM 4.[16] Alongside this new historicism, there was an engagement with anthropology; a younger generation of architects had come to associate the functionalist model of the Athens Charter with a culturally homogenizing and colonialist orthodoxy.[17] For these Western critics, and their Third World associates, contemporary culture was to be reconnected to local traditions through a rediscovery of what Dutch architect van Eyck termed the 'archaic principles of human nature',[18] and significantly, through an emphasis on the inclusive notion of habitat rather than the reductive notion of dwelling that had been developed within the CIAM.[19] In 1959, Jaap Bakema created what he called the 'Post Box for the Creation of Habitat'.

The Iran congresses and global exchanges

By the 1970s, the establishment's cultural interests and support and promotion of the fine arts and architecture had evolved. Beyond the individual agency of the Queen, these transformations and developments were the result of a series of transnational social and professional networks,[20] which (as mentioned in the Introduction) were fostered by the foreign training, work experience, and the intercultural roles of Iranian architects such as Kamran Diba, Nader Ardalan, Laleh Bakhtiar, Nasrin Faghih, and others. Such circles of expertise within transnational networks drove domestic discourses. For the Iranian organizers of the congresses, appropriate housing pertained to cultural identity, the identification with a national group within which local differences could be subsumed, and a common heritage. This process of cultural reimagination involved both remembering and forgetting.[21] It paralleled European modernizing contexts, which were seen to be transferable and informative to the Iranian condition.

The central themes of the 1970s Iran congresses continued the debates on habitat and regional identity that took place in Europe in the 1950s and 1960s. The delegates included many of the participants in those earlier CIAM and Team Ten meetings, such as Quaroni, Bakema, Sert, Alison Smithson, Jane Drew, Candilis, and Écochard, but also architects and experts from other predominantly Islamic countries. However, at these congresses, delegates addressed new problems: the impacts of globalization upon traditional societies and their cultures, the need to develop culturally appropriate alternatives to normative models of modernist architecture, housing, and urbanism, and in this decolonizing period, the need to recognize the validity of multiple forms of modernity.[22]

The Iran congresses, therefore, form a missing link connecting the CIAM and Team Ten debates over the meaning of 'habitat' to the Vancouver Declaration on Human Settlements at the 1976 United Nations Conference on Human Settlements, in Vancouver, Canada.[23] A core contribution to this declaration was a document prepared by delegates from the 1974 Persepolis congress (discussed later). Iran was also developing frameworks for the preservation and documentation of areas of historical heritage, such as the city of Isfahan – the venue for the first of the congresses, reflecting a new regard for the vernacular, both for inspiration and as valuable heritage. Traditional cities like Isfahan and Yazd served as models for the design of aesthetically and culturally harmonious social habitats. Significantly, this valorizing of regional difference was a precursor to the later discourse of regionalism as a form of resistance to cultural homogenization – the so-called 'Critical Regionalism' of Alexander Tzonis, Liane Lefaivre, and Kenneth Frampton, the 'authentic regionalism' of William Curtis (1985), and the 'modern regionalism' of Suha Özkan (1985).[24]

For Iranian architects, the congresses were an opportunity to exchange perspectives with international delegates in theorizing a specifically Iranian approach. The emerging ideas, which informed architectural thought and practice for the next two decades, were the product firstly of the demands for development, and secondly, of an international engagement and exchange that resulted in both the creation of heritage through design and design thinking processes that persisted – in some instances to the present – in the practice and jargon of Iranian architecture.

The three congresses, while exploring somewhat different themes, were connected by three persistent strands, which coincided at the question of tradition: firstly, there was a critique of modernist, technocratic approaches to housing and urban planning, and a re-evaluation of local cultural traditions with reference to traditional settlements; secondly, probing the idea of a contextually specific Iranian architecture, expressive of a local cultural identity, and the viability of traditional building techniques and settlements in the face of homogenizing global developmental processes;[25] and thirdly, the rejection of culturally homogenizing architectural projects associated with the local imitation of Western forms. All three strands pertain to the desire to forge an authentic identity, the need for which would have been felt through the global exchanges of expertise, ideas, and funds. But they also had international resonance and salience where processes of urban development were associated with alienation, discontinuity, and loss of social memory associated with the destruction of familiar environments. The debates around these questions also reveal underlying ideological differences in approaches to the past and its utilization in the present – heritage – between leftist critiques of 'capitalist hegemony' and the Traditionalist rejection of Western culture en bloc.

The Isfahan congress, 1970

The international congress of architects in 1970, entitled 'The Interaction of Tradition and Technology', was held over four days in the historic former Safavid capital of Isfahan. The central theme of the congress was the investigation of 'the mutual impact of tradition and technology'.[26] The sub-themes included: technology, tradition, the interaction between tradition and technology, and education and the profession. Through the discussions of these themes, the congress articulated strategies for reconciling modernization with cultural traditions.

The location of the congress in Isfahan was significant, given the status of Isfahan's old core at the time as a substantially intact, traditional Iranian city that possessed many exquisite examples of Islamic art and architectural heritage, and was characterized by an organic unity of building construction, urban structure, and architectural forms.[27] It is possible that the setting of the congress influenced delegates' perspectives and impressed upon them the genuine concern for developing local traditions on the part of the administration.[28] Isfahan thus served as a demonstration of the ideal, expressed by the conference title, of reconciling modern techniques with regionally authentic cultural forms. Delegates were also given a tour of Persepolis,[29] the exemplary pre-Islamic monument in the province of Fars,[30] which would be the location of the 1974 congress, but also the principal site for the celebrations of the 2,500th anniversary of Persian kingship in 1971 (Figure 2.1).

In the 1970 congress, delegates exchanged perspectives on architectural identity, the value and authenticity of traditional settlements, and the social

2.1 Delegates exploring site of Persepolis (1970).

and ultimately political context of architecture. The questions raised strongly suggest that the Iranian side recognized the need for a cultural basis for development. Indeed, the congresses represents an attempt to establish such a basis. The congress was opened by the Queen (Figure 2.2), who, in her opening speech, declared the importance of reconciling local traditions with progress, and noted the potential of technological developments to benefit the human living environment. But she added a caveat: 'What is of utmost importance to us, and all nations with ancient heritage, is finding a solution to reconcile traditions with rapid advances.'[31] In pursuing the congress theme, the organizers – Chairman Mohsen Foroughi, the American Deputy Chairman Buckminster Fuller, Secretary General Naser Badi', and Rapporteur-General Aptullah Kuran – invited contributions from the delegates, which took the form of several focused workshops.[32] The international composition of the organizing committee and the round-table discussions indicated the desire for a truly global exchange, which was extensively reported on in the prominent architectural journal at the time, *Honar va Memari* (هنر و معماری = *Art and Architecture*), indicating a desire on the part of domestic actors to leverage legitimacy for their opinions from the international support.

One could further assume that this legitimization assisted local architects to enhance their professional credibility and intellectual capital as much as it facilitated potential transfer of knowledge and expertise in the future.[33] The choice of international delegates reflected the organizers' desire to discuss heritage and

2.2 The Queen opening the 1970 congress.

identity in relation to processes of modernization in overwhelmingly Muslim Iran. One delegate, the celebrated American architect Louis Kahn, was the author of influential projects in India and then-East Pakistan (now Bangladesh), and was known for his teaching on the symbolic basis of architecture. Another keynote speaker, Aptullah Kuran, was a Turkish modernist architect, founding president of Boğaziçi University, and an expert on Ottoman architectural history. Kuran promoted the regionalist architecture of Sedad Hakki Eldem in Istanbul.[34] Two other keynote speakers, Georges Candilis and Michel Écochard, were well known for their urban and housing projects in Africa and the Middle East, notably in Casablanca and Damascus, as well as then-current planning, housing, and institutional projects in Iran. Oswald Matthias Ungers had risen to prominence through his investigation into the formal structure of urban districts in Berlin and elsewhere. Ludovico Quaroni had designed a master plan and new governmental centre for the medina of Tunis in 1962–69, while Paul Rudolph, after Lewis Mumford, was one of the first consciously regionalist modernist architects and theorists in America.[35]

As reflected by the Queen's address, the 1970 congress was intended as a response to the destabilizing effect of rapid development on Iranian cultural traditions. It was, as Minister for Development and Housing Kourosh Amouzegar remarked at the congress, an attempt to address problems born of liberal (and modernizing) economic and educational policies, and their repercussions for the field of architecture. He outlined several key questions:

> Can we identify basic principles distinguishing tradition and modern technology?
>
> Can traditional forms, methods of construction, traditional materials and handicraft techniques be replaced with modern materials and techniques to give the same usefulness and effect?
>
> What is the impact of advanced systems of construction on traditional architecture?
>
> And, how can the needs of [a rapidly growing] population for housing and working places be solved using modern technology [and through] a consideration of traditional buildings?[36]

In retrospect, Amouzegar was attempting to locate the cultural component in development and modernization, an element lacking (or less pronounced) in many development projects that had been implemented following the American model in the wake of the Second World War.[37] His remarks reflect an identity crisis in Iran, to which a subsequent governmental response was the exponential growth in the share of spending on culture in the overall budget at the time.[38] Approaches to the main theme, 'the mutual impact of tradition and technology', reveal the entanglements of developmentalist programmes with tradition and the past.[39] Echoing the Queen's introduction, and focusing on the relevance and maintenance of traditional continuity in the present,[40] the congress president, Mohsen Foroughi – a prominent architect, Honorary Chair of the Iranian Architects' Institute, and the former dean of the Faculty of Fine Arts – proclaimed:

> since the continuity [consistency] between traditional and contemporary architecture is now gone, we do not know to what extent we can be inspired by the form and spirit of past art.[41]

This resonated with the views of some international participants, notably Quaroni, who saw tradition as a thing of the past, a trace of a dead or dying culture. Others, especially from the developing world, took a nuanced approach. Kuran recognized that traditions helped construct a sense of social identity, noting that they were endowed with a processual character and mutability while remaining 'a continuous process [... that] cannot be turned off like a tap of water'.[42] But, he argued, some of the remedies for countering the effects of developmental change – such as identity confusion, cultural inauthenticity, and placelessness – may be sought from within tradition itself.

A further, unequivocal position regarding tradition was represented by the Iranian architect Nader Ardalan, who ascribed a timeless and immutable quality to it. Following Nasr, Ardalan saw Islamic tradition as the most direct manifestation of Iranian culture. Geometry, spatial organization, orientation, and place, he argued, conveyed the unity of the esoteric and exoteric, and material and spiritual meanings of this culture,[43] and were reflected in authentic

Iranian architecture and urban formations.[44] Geometry also ensured spiritual unity between architecture, nature, and culture.[45] In *The Sense of Unity*, and in his contributions to the congresses, Ardalan appealed to architects to return to, or more specifically learn from, tradition as the guarantor of civic and cultural continuity and communal spirituality. Ardalan advocated that architects should search for such unity by reconnecting with tradition. This effectively entailed the creation of works imbued with a distinct Iranian character, through selective juxtapositions of the past forms and geometric relations. Such architectural engagements, as evidenced in the design for the ICMS (Chapter 1), play nostalgically upon real and invented memories, in what was essentially a heritage process, but one in which the past is objectified and muted.[46] Theoretically, tradition denoted esoteric truths rather than human life – it was a source of emulation. Ardalan's prominent position at the first two congresses, and his overt equation of Iranian culture with an Islamic identity, is indicative of one strand of the complex and arguably conflicted cultural outlook, at the time common between those within and outside officialdom.[47]

Ardalan's colleague Badi' took a similar stance, calling in his presentation for a contextually specific Iranian architecture, and rejecting international modernism as unsuitable for Iran's local, climatic, and ethnic characteristics, thus mixing a kind of cultural essentialism with a Lamarckian evolutionism.[48] Resonating with Ardalan's turn to tradition, his reactive emphasis on continuity and Islamic tradition rested on highlighting the emblematic role of traditional architectural heritage in the face of a perceived homogenizing globalism. For both, architectural authenticity was bound to immutable, place-based traditions. Paradoxically, however, a design subscribing to this position must enforce a lifeworld that is already superseded.

An ostensibly similar position to those of Ardalan and Badi' was presented by the eminent American architect and educator Louis Kahn, who called on delegates to look for inspiration for future architecture in the architecture of the past, mediated by the individual intuition of the designer, in effect drawing upon and at the same time constructing an architectural heritage. In his approach, the past was accessed through a nostalgic hermeneutic poetics expressed through formal archetypes. In his subcontinental projects, Kahn pursued the ideal of reconciling the individual and the universal through the abstraction of historical forms and spatial typologies.[49] In a 1991 interview,[50] Ardalan would acknowledge the debt in his practice and writing to Kahn and particularly his concept of the measurable and immeasurable.[51] Kahn's words at the congress buttressed the anti-modernist position of those Iranians like Ardalan and Badi' who sought a return to the security of familiar traditions.[52] Kahn, in his discussion on the nature of inspiration, defended an intuitive approach to understanding relationships in nature, humanity, and architecture. In engaging with tradition, inspiration should emerge from this individual intuition rather than from a top-down, religious, or political process. Kahn's approach found fertile ground in Iran, in the context of the prevalent nativist discourse. Through the Sufi concept of spirit apprehended by the mind via mathematical and geometrical abstractions of the material world,[53] Ardalan and others seem to have appropriated Kahn's universalist message as a formula for a more authentic Iranian architecture.[54]

In partial agreement with Kahn's historicist approach, Quaroni, who had witnessed the profound change in attitudes towards heritage and in the fabric of traditional Italian cities, was more ambivalent about the position of tradition, noting its weakening and labile nature. For tradition to survive, he argued, both the conveyer and the recipient must willingly embrace it.[55] But the modern context was unstable and discontinuous and could not sustain traditions as such, so it fell upon the individual creative architect to establish meaningful connections in their work, through poetic imagination. The hitherto missing link to establish that connection was the integration of architectural and urban thinking, where cultural identity was emphasized:

> Our cities are growing by the day but the concept [meaning] of a city as a tangible expression of a tangible cultural heritage is weakened by the day ... Today it is hard to speak of tradition ... this is the first time that anyone has had the courage to discuss this issue, which is so difficult.[56]

Here Quaroni would appear to refer to tangible heritage, in the sense of urban fabric and monuments, the preservation of which was the mission of the International Council on Monuments and Sites (ICOMOS) – formed from the Venice Charter (1964), itself building on the Athens Charter (1931). From his statement, it is apparent that the relationship between tradition, heritage, and daily life was yet to be theorized. But it also reflects the ambition of the Team Ten generation to reconnect architectural projects with urban structures and systems, captured in van Eyck's aphorism 'a house must be like a small city if it's to be a real house; a city like a large house if it's to be a real city.'[57] Similar to Quaroni, Ungers, another architect associated with Team Ten, considered tradition to be in a dialectical, and therefore dynamic, relationship with the present, connected through memory and trace, or impression, the evocation of what is absent.[58]

But these speculative positions presented a sharp contrast to that of Ardalan, Badi', and even Kahn. Quaroni, for example, recognized that modernity disrupted traditional continuities, and instead of inventing tradition through eclectic historicism,[59] he advocated creative approaches to internalizing the essence or spirit of the past and its spatio-cultural relationships, and establishing a poetic relationship with the city rather than emulation of past forms.[60] His approach treated the past as a resource and repository, as cultural heritage, in what could be interpreted as a rejection of semiotically based representational regimes in architecture.[61] However, a return to symbolism was precisely the approach of Traditionalists like Ardalan and Badi', who advocated a creative embrace of Islamic traditions, while Kahn employed a universalist symbolism. Compared to Quaroni, who retained a forward-looking, reflective nostalgia, Ardalan's approach was inclined to restorative nostalgia.[62]

Other Iranians recognized the inevitably destabilizing effects of development. Ali Sardar-Afkhami, a prominent Iranian practitioner and designer,[63] rebuffed the Traditionalist position, arguing that modernity had caused a crisis in tradition resulting in both social and spiritual discontent. The problem of contemporary architecture in Iran was but a symptom of that crisis, one that was not precipitated by new technology, but rather through the increase of scale, which made the solutions of the past untenable:

> It is [...] necessary that tradition reply in each instant to the practical as well as the spiritual needs of the moment. It is thus illogical and without consequence to strive to perpetuate at all costs, in spite of the exigencies of time, traditions out of tune with present events, which answer no rational needs.[64]

That is to say, while traditional means and methods were no longer sufficient for today's problems, architecture could not be seen as an autonomous field, siloed from social, economic, and cultural vagaries.[65]

In summary, the congress's focus upon the relation of tradition and technology indicates a concern for how Iran, with its traditional but evolving culture, could engage with technological modernization and its imbrication in global processes,[66] as well as influencing the tenor of architectural tendencies in the coming decades. In relation to reconciling tradition and modernity, or development and culture, three approaches emerged: firstly, a radical modernity which considered traditions and its forms to have become obsolete by modernity (Quaroni); secondly, a critical and reflexive engagement with tradition, wherein traditional architecture is abstracted and thematized within a formalist semiotics (Ungers); and thirdly, an ambiguous and perhaps internally inconsistent reconciliation of tradition and modernity (Ardalan), characterized by an assumed unity and immutability of traditions. The latter position foreclosed the possibility of gradual (dialectical) change in traditional practices, resulting in the construction of utopias, a criticism that has also been levelled at Louis Kahn.[67]

This global engagement had two other effects. Firstly, it consolidated a traditionally inclined position, of Ardalan and others, about Iran's architecture, which critiqued technocratic approaches, pursued local identity, and rejected generic global trends. Secondly, through statements recognizing the dynamics of tradition, such as Aptullah Kuran's call on architects to combine their local cultural understandings and intuitions with advances in materials and new technologies, it prefigured the later regionalist critiques of modernism.[68] In the end, the understanding of tradition as a dynamic process, rather than a set of immutable representations and practices, underlay the congress resolutions, namely:

> Tradition is valuable in assuring the identity, the material and human particularities of man, region, country, place, and universe. [...] To respect tradition is to build the dwellings, the cities and the environment in the total condition of our epoch and at the same time anticipat[e] the future.[69]

While nostalgia underpinned the discussions at the congress, the approach in its final resolution historicized tradition, using the past as a repository for the present and future; in other words, as heritage.

The Persepolis congress, 1974: Traditional towns as models

The second international congress of architects in Iran was held at the ancient Achaemenid heritage site of Persepolis and entitled 'Towards a Quality of Life – The Role of Industrialization in the Architecture and Urban Planning of Developing Countries'. It addressed the following general themes:

- continuity and change;
- ecology and the man-made environment;
- methods and materials of expression; and
- appropriate habitat, which delegates identified as the central question.

The issue of appropriate housing was clearly perceived with urgency in the Iranian context. Houshang Ansari, the Minister for Housing and Urban Development, noted that '[s]ocieties grow and change, yet seek to maintain relevance, continuity and a sense of cultural identity'.[70] This statement recognized that Iranian society was evolving, but called for maintaining links with traditions. Indeed, through its cultural policies, the government paid considerable attention to its Islamic period heritage. Among the delegates, there were distinctive universalist and particularist views, separated not by categorical irreconcilability – the views were connected after all – but in most cases by their often-nostalgic appeal to the past or tradition. Among delegates from developing countries were strong advocates for the latter group. There was a consensus that as well as meeting specific technical standards, the CIAM goal, mass housing should also be culturally appropriate. Reflecting the conditions, delegates argued that unlike the generic industrially fabricated housing estates, which had become widespread in the post-war period, Iranian housing should be based upon an understanding of the traditional house, village, and city.[71]

The traditional city or village was the central trope for nostalgic appeals to the past, as well as the point of difference between universalist and particularist approaches. Tradition-focused discourses found their architectural, and thus heritage, dimension in that trope as the carrier of memory, cultural practice, and expression of the past.[72] For the Egyptian Hassan Fathy, who came of age during the national liberation movement in Egypt, the village was the symbol of authentic nationalist and native architecture, hence his emphasis on the folk and the vernacular. Like many other societies in the developing world, in his society traditional life persisted, albeit in a fragmentary fashion. Along with the Egyptian artists with whom he associated,[73] Fathy was an Islamic modernizer attempting to forge a link between modern architecture and authentic Egyptian heritage, which he interpreted in terms of an Islamic architecture and its iconography.[74]

68 *Development, architecture, and the formation of heritage*

From a more nationalistic position, Iranian delegate Badi' hailed Iranian culture and architecture as authentic to its place and closely related to the land, containing the genius of the people and a superiority that enabled it to prevail over invading influences.[75] Ironically, he also bemoaned the fact that foreign influences were destroying Iranian culture. This linkage of Iranian cultural continuity to place resonated with contemporaneous phenomenological writings on *genius loci*,[76] as well as with the environmental psychology texts of Lynch and others, which were being translated into Persian. [77] From a more universalist position in relation to tradition, Ardalan argued that new housing should be based upon an understanding and adaptation of authentic traditional settlements, recalling the 1969 statement by Louis Kahn that

> [t]raditions are just mounds of golden dust, not circumstance, not the shapes which have resulted as an expression in time. I believe ... [man] learns today from this golden dust, free of circumstance, nature-man. And if you can just put your fingers through this golden dust, you can have the powers of anticipation.[78]

Among the Western delegates, too, there were appeals to the traditions and architecture of the past. Their intent, however, was different to the particularist positions of delegates from developing countries, especially Iran. The Western architects' reference to the village seemed like a nostalgia for the passing of tradition, a destabilization and loss of the senses of identification and place created by the instrumental rationality of modernization. In both views, heritage is substantially important; in the first case, native traditions are invoked in seeking to forge a national identity through the appeal to, and operation of, nostalgia; in the other, it is about making a future inclusive of humanity rooted in history. [79] But far from just reflecting an Iranian point of view, such arguments resonated with the pronouncements of Team Ten members Bakema, van Eyck, and the Smithsons, who advocated for a high degree of reflexivity between dwelling and urban structure in support of a unitary, and ultimately abstract, conception of habitat as integrated network. However, the same notion of coherence applied to the traditional settlement implies the existence of an atemporal cultural and aesthetic unity. Here, Georges Candilis declared that a house had to be seen 'in a total environment',[80] an idea that was in vogue in international architectural discourses at the time and was espoused by both international and local speakers at the conference.

Candilis was essentially arguing that architecture needs a socio-economic context and cannot be understood merely in terms of technique or form. Going beyond the traditional settlement, he envisioned a modern equivalent, in fact a megastructure, of the kind which he and others, notably Rudolph and Tange, were advocating for European, Japanese, and American cities. This shifted the focus from housing to habitat, a whole, integrated social environment, which reflects the Smithsons' 'Hierarchy of Associations' – individual–village–town–city and house–street–district–city[81] – and ideas of Spanish architect and former president of the CIAM, José Luis Sert, who considered the provision of appropriate housing as a universal problem.[82] But for the most part at the conference, the idea of a total environment was constructed around (once again) the structure and image of the traditional organically growing village. The trope of the village thus played multiple roles: it affirmed the need to reproduce cultural forms, in effect to produce heritage; it played an aesthetic role as an organicist reference point, in contrast to mechanical- or systems-based conceptions of settlement; and as we have seen, it enabled certain parallels with international Metabolist[83] and megastructural conceptions – the city as a unified building.[84]

The apparent similarity between such Iranian perspectives and those of Western delegates concealed actual difference. Underlying the Western viewpoint was not an embrace of traditional urban structures but rather anthropologically informed theories of designing habitats for premodern or partially modernizing populations, as seen in the French North African projects, as well as an emerging discourse of regionalism, which probably stemmed from the latter. These two sides of the same debate illustrate how a universal project – the quest for appropriate housing that remains universal, even today – gave rise to and amplified specific concerns for local manifestations and characteristics related to authentic architecture in housing, a subject which we discuss in Chapters 3 and 4. These cross-purpose exchanges, however, proved fruitful at a global level.

Outcomes of the 1974 congress

From the Persepolis congress a partial consensus emerged through which Sert, Ardalan, Diba, and others developed a set of principles for human dwelling, the Habitat Bill of Rights, presented to the 1976 UN Conference on Human Settlements, and which was developed into the Vancouver Declaration. It was based upon the calls by Diba, Ardalan, and Sert for the codification of urban human rights, a development on the housing aspect of the Universal Declaration of Human Rights, Article 25.[85] The Bill of Rights explicitly valued the vernacular and the traditional as containing 'valuable truths' which provide 'a solid base from which to learn' (Figure 2.3).[86]

In its introduction to Iran as a case study, the Habitat Bill of Rights refers to fundamental, timeless principles pertaining to humankind's way of dwelling in its environment. Engagement with this supposedly timeless way of living is not to be effected through mimicry of traditional styles, but rather through interpretation of this supposedly immutable quality underlying indigenous architecture.[87] Authentic modern architecture is only achievable by a hermeneutic enquiry into these principles. In a section entitled 'Progressive Standards: Dwelling Observations', comparisons were made between the environmentally and culturally sustainable traditional habitat, and the 'exposed,' 'alien', and 'de-humanized' contemporary habitat – only the issue of technology was weighted in favour of the contemporary Iranian domestic and urban environment.[88]

2.3 Habitat Bill of Rights, image of traditional and modern habitat.

At a neighbourhood and urban scale, the study draws upon the traditional habitat to propose that new settlements should be centred upon communal facilities such as the mosque, bazaar, schools, clinics, and gardens, and defined by thresholds or gateways. Paralleling then-contemporary Western cluster-housing principles, it stated that cars should not conflict with these neighbourhoods, but rather should be kept to the periphery. Housing should be protected from public space, be aggregated in clusters, and focused upon the courtyard, with correct solar orientation of openings. There should be a network of covered or shaded pedestrian streets and lanes, and a clear spatial hierarchy from private to public, with thresholds marked by portals. Pathways should cross each other, creating nodal points, which, the document reminds the reader, recall the *chāhār-bāgh* (fourfold garden) or *chār-sough* (four paths bazaar). At a more detailed level, the Persepolis Declaration advocated the use of platforms to separate public and private areas, people and cars, porches and porticos as transitional spaces, landmarks 'which respect the cultural values of the area'.[89] In each case, traditional and modern equivalents were provided as illustrations.

The Habitat Bill of Rights grew out of the revision of modernist thinking on housing informed by anthropological and sociological research, and of the regionalisms advocated by intellectuals in Iran, Turkey, and other developing societies. It is also traceable to planning and settlement experiments in Israel and North African French colonies, as noted above and in Chapter 4. This convergence of Western and Eastern viewpoints would result in several later outcomes, not least in the anti-universalizing stance of Critical Regionalism. Underlying the latter was a dichotomous pairing of authentic and inauthentic, in which globalization was seen to have a displacing effect, and which argued for an architecture based upon an understanding of culture, climate, and locality. Such an architecture, it was assumed, might provide the scaffolding for authentic forms of social life to develop.[90] Social housing was to be the constructive material out of which emplaced communities could evolve. Inherent to this project was the projection of images of authenticity and national identity, an ambition evident in the Iranian projects of Hossein Amanat and Kamran Diba, among others.[91]

Here was a theme that would resurface in the post-Revolution period – elements of the past put to use in new ways through the syncretic assemblage of old and new. Tradition was not to be slavishly imitated, but learned from, and its principles, however interpreted, were emulated where appropriate. Later, under the Islamic Republic, recourse was made to a timeless eternal present of archetypal principles and essences, but concurrently and paradoxically, the past was mastered, put into the service of the present and future as heritage.[92]

The Ramsar congress, 1976: The crisis of identity in architecture[93]

The third of the international congresses of architecture in Iran, entitled 'The Crisis of Identity in Architecture', with all-female delegates, was held on behalf of the *Union Internationale des Femmes Architectes*,[94] in the northern Iranian resort town of Ramsar. Its focus was on women's professional challenges in the industry. Nonetheless, several key exchanges reinforce the debates of the first two congresses.

The major issues addressed by the congress were:

- identity: its nature and expression;
- the role of women in architecture and planning;
- education and raising the level of awareness of good architecture;
- popular culture and high culture: debate over whether architects or the people should set the agenda for architecture, resulting in a kind of architectural populism; and
- architects' impact in architecture and planning upon society and decision-making processes.

Beyond promoting equal opportunities for female architects, a developmental goal pursued in the White Revolution,[95] the congress addressed topics relating to the issue of Iranian urban heritage as reflected by the title, 'The Crisis of Identity in Architecture'. Of special interest were discussions around the questions of identity, tradition, and social engagement in architecture.

Iranian delegates Laleh Bakhtiar's and Nasrin Faghih's references to questions of cultural identity diverged from those of their prominent Western counterparts. Bakhtiar appealed directly to divine inspiration and drew upon her study of geometry in Iranian architecture to which she attributed a 'participation mystique',[96] suggesting a connection between traditional creativity and the sacred in 'a state of oneness with nature'. This unity between nature and human creation, she argued, was disrupted by the rationalizing, secularizing conditions of the Enlightenment, resulting in a loss of cultural identity.[97] Denying the existence of an identity crisis in tradition itself, she rejected the modernists' imperative of truth to materials as materialist superficiality. While Bakhtiar ascribed a divine basis to geometry, Louis Kahn's former partner and collaborator, Anne Tyng, advanced an intuitive reading of geometry, focused on 'the evolution of natural forms'.[98] The challenge for architecture and urban design in Iran, she argued, was to embody this traditional natural and human order, which facilitated symbolic, social, and ecological dimensions, in new projects with appropriate technology.[99] The similarity, and at the same time difference, between Tyng's discussion of geometry, and that of Ardalan and Bakhtiar, highlights the selective interpretation of Western ideas by Iranian architects at the time, and their modification and incorporation into a local identity discourse.

In contrast to these essentialist presentations, Jane Drew, a veteran of the Chandigarh project in India along with Maxwell Fry and Le Corbusier, presented a modernist perspective. Rejecting the return to past forms, she instead proposed 'scientific' studies and objective environmental responses like the housing settlements she designed in Southern Iran.[100] Drew referred to the Shahyad monument by Hossein Amanat in the new western district of Tehran (see Chapter 5) as 'the arch in Tehran where a masonry form has been contorted into reinforced concrete in a misguided attempt to give it Iranian identity'.[101] Similarly, the Team Ten member Alison Smithson argued that social conservatism, consisting of fear of the unknown, of change, and the perceived need for continuity, could overwhelm the adaptive and progressive potential of people for high-quality social engagement, which, she argued, could be facilitated through design 'quality'. But who could determine this quality – experts, or the people?[102]

In response, a populist group – Iranian delegates Laleh Bakhtiar, Leila Farhad, Mina Marefat, and Nasrin Faghih – supported by European speakers Gae Aulenti and Marie-Christine Gangneaux, advocated a non-elitist architectural habitat. They all seem to have had in mind something like Rudofsky's *Architecture without Architects*, then very 'current'.[103] Discussing public housing provision, Farhad called for a cultural re-awakening. What she described as the 'showpiece towns' such as Yazd were not, she argued, static museums – dead heritage – but rather the products of continuous growth and adaptation deriving from communal life. In this reference to 'showpieces' there was a strong conservation and museification impulse that ignored the necessity for such settlements to evolve in response to modern social and economic factors. She argued that rather than a top-down supply process driven by the authorities and experts, housing design should include residents' participation, and employ local materials and traditional building processes.[104] In their summary resolutions, the delegates emphasized '[i]dentity as unity and persistence of character',[105] and meaningful urban environments based upon knowledge of indigenous examples: 'buildings should transmit their identity in respect of climate, culture, geography and location [...] connections to natural truths that speak of the integrity and consistency of indigenous buildings which supported and identified their inhabitants.'[106] As we shall see in the next chapter, these ambitions would form the central principles for Kamran Diba's housing complex at Shushtar Now.

Conclusion: Heritage and the tropes of tradition

The 1970s international congresses of architecture in Iran were driven by forms of nostalgia for traditional authenticity, expressed through tropes such as 'the village'. Two streams of discourse were apparent in the rhetoric of the congresses. On the one hand, the cultural crisis of late Western modernism is painfully evident in the embryonic regionalist counter-discourse, which emphasized the authentic in environmental response, use of appropriate materials, and cultural rootedness. Architecture was seen as a communicative language with a transformative power. On the Iranian side, strong voices critiqued earlier modernist projects and programmes, in a romantic-nostalgic turn to the Rudovskian embrace of the vernacular and the traditional settlement. In hindsight, this search for authenticity was syncretic, combining aspects from the pre-Islamic and Islamic past into a nativist synthesis.[107] Such tendencies were evident in Kamran Diba's comparison between the unity of the traditional Iranian village and the individualism and disharmony of Iranian cities: 'It is about some contemporary ways of thinking which destroys those general harmonies ... we will not have an integrated form as a result.'[108]

In Diba's nostalgic formulation, residents in traditional towns came to a consensus over time, and their settlements' spatial and aesthetic unity reflects this consensus.[109] This position echoed the Egyptian architect Hassan Fathy's romantic nativist advocacy of traditional construction techniques, forms, and symbolism.[110] However, the foreign and Iranian delegates did not share a uniform approach to the question of tradition. While Diba, Ardalan, and other Iranians held vernacular forms and practices to be in harmony with traditional culture and religious beliefs, the more critical position of European delegates

Quaroni and Candilis placed architecture in the context of the global flow of ideas, capital, and goods. They sought to place the issue of tradition, vernacular architecture, and crafts in a wider political context that would examine the effects of modernity and international capitalism upon such structures, and to engage with the displacing and culturally fragmenting consequences of economic migration upon traditional culture.

The multiple perspectives of architects from developing countries were presented as exemplars within the context of the congresses. Through the promotion of the traditional village as a putative site of cultural origin, of the vernacular and 'Mediterranean'[111] sub-stream within modernism, and the re-evaluation of traditional spatial and material practices, heritage was effectively drawn upon as a vehicle to inform the design of appropriate habitat, through which cultural problems associated with development might be ameliorated or overcome. Thus, heritage was being constituted from a rediscovered past, employed in design processes, and with practical outcomes – Iranian heritage was imagined and popularized through architecture. This retrospection brings out our contemporary relationship with the historicity of architectural objects. What emerged at the 1970s congresses was also a discrepancy of ideal and praxis, between, on the one hand, an appeal to the social and aesthetic unity of traditional settlements, and on the other, the reality that the villagers were migrating to the Iranian cities in large numbers. This crisis of urbanization, and the need for provision of mass housing to accommodate displaced villagers, appears in hindsight to have been one of the driving forces behind the discourse of Critical Regionalism. In all three congresses, the issue of tradition was always there in the background, reflected in one of the final declarations in 1974:

> To create a dynamic document in which the sense of continuity and the quality of life aims are pursued while responding to the desirable diversity of perceptions and means inherent in the particular circumstances of time and place.[112]

Beyond Iran, the congresses left their mark internationally in several significant ways and this highlights the nature of circulation of ideas and the place of specific encounters in producing larger, universal concepts. First, the congresses constituted a forum where the ideas regarding regionalist architecture of the 1980s – Critical Regionalism – found their initial synthesis.

Second, they contributed to the initiation and development of debates around human habitat. As noted above, the respective positions at the 1970 and 1974 congresses were later accommodated in and presented as the Habitat Bill of Rights by the Iran delegates to the 1976 UN Conference on Human Settlements in Vancouver. The ethos of the Bill of Rights is indeed at the core of the UN-Habitat conferences. In this way too the congresses left their own mark on the field.

Finally, they reinvigorated the conception of an intrinsically Islamic heritage. In the congresses, delegates called for architecture to have both global and local characteristics, a position that implied a certain licence in interpreting the past, and its adaptation to accommodate present and future needs. In response to a homogenizing globalization, they called for activating cultural processes of emplacement, which in Iran and its neighbouring states would be interpreted in terms of Islamic heritage. Thus, the congresses series was a direct predecessor of the Aga Khan Award programme of Islamic architecture and heritage, and various more-or-less chauvinist appeals to national identity expressed through architectural populism.

In the congresses, culturally appropriate housing became a key topic for discussion because of its significance for the questions of identity. In practice and following on from the discussions there, Kamran Diba proposed an exemplary design for company housing at Shushtar in Khuzestan, Southern Iran. This project, the Shushtar Now (New Shushtar), which grew directly out of the government's development agenda, and served as a kind of benchmark for future culturally sensitive housing projects, creatively interpreting architectural heritage, is the focus of the following chapter.

Notes

1 Shahbānu (Queen) Farah and the Ministry of Housing and Development supported the architectural congresses. Additionally, the first two congresses of earthen architecture, held in association with ICOMOS, focusing on methods for the conservation of built heritage, were held in Yazd, Iran. Concurrently, there were also efforts in the fields of archaeology and art history to preserve, present, and promote Iranian culture and arts to both a domestic and international audience through a range of media. It is noteworthy that these efforts, which had begun under Reza Shah, and his son's government, expanded and received more financial support. See A. U. Pope, *Introducing Iranian Architecture* (Oxford: Oxford University Press, 1969); R. Beny, *Persia: Bridge of Turquoise* (Toronto: McClelland and Stewart, 1975); R. Beny, *Iran: Elements of Destiny* (Toronto: McClelland and Stewart, 1978); Y. Kadoi, 'Persia through the Lens: Poetics and Politics of Architectural Photographs in Pahlavi Iran', *Iranian Studies*, 50:6 (2017), pp. 873–93, https://doi.org/10.1080/00210862.2017.1293374.
2 On the concept of lifeworld, see A. Schutz and T. Luckmann, *The Structures of the Life World*, trans. R. M. Zaner and H. T. Engelhardt (London: Heinemann, 1973), pp. 3–4; A. Buttimer, 'Grasping the Dynamism of Lifeworld', *Annals of the Association of American Geographers*, 66:2 (1976), pp. 277–92; D. Seamon, *A Geography of the Lifeworld: Movement, Rest and Encounter* (London: Croom Helm, 1979), p. 20.
3 The arguments in the chapter are supported by archival material pertaining to the congresses as well as interviews by Ali Mozaffari with some of those present at the events.
4 M. Gravari-Barbas et al., 'World Heritage and Tourism, from Opposition to Co-production', in L. Bordeau et al. (eds), *World Heritage, Tourism and Identity: Inscription and Co-production* (Abingdon: Ashgate, 2016), pp. 1–24; A. Clarke, 'World Heritage, Tourism and Identity: Inscription and Co-production', *Journal of Heritage Tourism*, 12:2 (2017), pp. 220–1.
5 Roudbari, 'Transnational Transformation'; Roudbari, 'Instituting Architecture';

Karimi, *Domesticity and Consumer Culture*, pp. 149–53; Mohajeri, 'Shahestan Blueprint'.

6 K. Blake, *The U.S.–Soviet Confrontation in Iran 1945–1962: A Case in the Annals of the Cold War* (Lanham, MD, and Plymouth: University Press of America, 2009), pp. 28–61.

7 R. Alvandi, 'Introduction: Iran in the Age of Aryamehr', in R. Alvandi (ed.), *The Age of Aryamehr: Late Pahlavi Iran and Its Global Entanglements* (London: Gingko Library, 2018), p. 19.

8 The government's Plan Organization had proven inadequate in addressing the sociocultural issues of development. See Bostock and Jones, *Planning and Power*; H. Amirahmadi, 'Regional Planning in Iran: A Survey of Problems and Policies', *The Journal of Developing Areas*, 20:4 (1986), pp. 501–30; T. H. McLeod, *National Planning in Iran: A Report Based upon the Experiences of the Harvard Advisory Group in Iran* (Regina, Saskatchewan: The Library and Archive of the Plan Organization of Iran, 23/07.1978 no. 2261, 31 December 1964).

9 V. F. Costello, 'Planning Problems and Policies in Tehran', in H. Amirahmadi and S. S. El-Shakhs (eds), *Urban Development in the Muslim World* (New Brunswick, NJ: Rutgers University Press, 1993 [2012]), pp. 157–61. On population displacement, see F. Kazemi, 'Urban Migrants and the Revolution', *Iranian Studies*, 13:1–4 (1980), pp. 257–77; L. Beck, 'Revolutionary Iran and Its Tribal Peoples', in T. Asad and R. Owen (eds), *The Middle East* (London: Palgrave, 1983), pp. 115–26; M. J. M. Tilaki et al., 'Challenges of the Informal Settlements in Developing Countries' Cities: A Case Study of Iran', *World Applied Sciences Journal*, 12 (2001), pp. 160–9; A. Bayat, 'Squatters and the State: Back Street Politics in the Islamic Republic', *Middle East Report*, 191 (1994), pp. 10–14; M. Parsa, *Social Origins of the Iranian Revolution* (New Brunswick, NJ, and London: Rutgers University Press, 1989); M. M. Azizi, 'Evaluation of Urban Land Supply Policy in Iran', *International Journal of Urban and Regional Research*, 22:1 (1998), pp. 94–105.

10 See, most recently, R. Habibi, 'Unveiled Middle-Class Housing'. On Drew and Fry's housing for the Anglo-Iranian Oil Corporation (later BP) at Gachsaran, see I. Jackson and J. Holland, *The Architecture of Edwin Maxwell Fry and Jane Drew: Twentieth-Century Architecture, Pioneer Modernism and the Tropics* (London and New York: Routledge, 2014). The leading Iranian architect Nader Ardalan also began his career in working on housing for the Iranian oil industry.

11 مشهودی، س.، نگرشی بر کارکردها و نارسایی های کوی نهم آبان، مقاله شماره ۴۲، مرداد ۱۳۵۵، http://bit.ly/2WqCUFN (accessed 10 May 2018).

12 N. Feniger and R. Kallus, 'Building a "New Middle East": Israeli Architects in Iran in the 1970s', *The Journal of Architecture*, 22:4 (May, 2017), pp. 765–85, https://doi.org/10.1080/13602365.2016.1204073.

13 L. Diba, interview with T. Farmanfarmaian, 1984.

14 Congrès international d'architecture moderne (CIAM), *Documents: 7 CIAM, Bergamo, 1949* (Nendeln: Kraus Reprint, 1979).

15 E. P. Mumford, *The CIAM Discourse on Urbanism 1928–1960* (Cambridge, MA: MIT Press, 2000), p. 192.

16 Congrès international d'architecture moderne (CIAM), *La Charte d'Athenes or The Athens Charter, 1933*, trans J. Tyrwhitt (Paris: Library of the Graduate School of Design, Harvard University, 1946).

17 A. Pedret, *Team 10: An Archival History* (Abingdon: Routledge, 2013), pp. 166–212.
18 Mozaffari recalls a conversation in the early 1990s in Tehran with the late professor Mozayyeni, who was present in the congresses and noted that in his presentation, the Dutch architect Aldo van Eyck severely criticized Ardalan for all the 'nonsense' that was presented. These comments were not included in the proceedings volume, suggesting an editorial policy of shaping views for posterity, a fact confirmed in A.-H. Eshragh, interview with A. Mozaffari, Paris, 2011; Eshragh was the editor of the journal *Honar va Memari* (هنر و معماری = *Art and Architecture*), which covered the congresses.
19 Pedret, *Team 10*, p. 81 ff.
20 Roudbari, 'Transnational Transformation'.
21 P. Connerton, *How Societies Remember* (Cambridge: Cambridge University Press, 1989), pp. 6–13.
22 Delegates with connections to Team Ten included Kahn, Smithson, Bakema, van Eyck, Candilis, Soltan, Ungers, Voelcker, and Tange. See A. Smithson, *Team 10 Primer* (Cambridge, MA: MIT Press, 1968). Jose Luis Sert was former president of CIAM, while Ludovico Quaroni and Bruno Zevi were trenchant critics of CIAM orthodoxy.
23 The Vancouver conference took place between 31 May and 11 June 1976. Its declaration led to the UN General Assembly resolution 31/109: 'Habitat'. See United Nations Conference on Human Settlements, 'UN Documents: Gathering a Body of Global Agreements', www.un-documents.net/a31r109.htm (accessed 2 May 2019).
24 A. Tzonis and L. Lefaivre, 'The Grid and the Pathway', *Architecture in Greece*, 15 (1981), pp. 164–78;. Frampton, 'Towards a Critical Regionalism'; W. Curtis, 'Towards an Authentic Regionalism', in H.-U. Khan (ed.), *Mimar 19: Architecture in Development* (Singapore: Concept Media, 1986), pp. 24–31; S. Özkan, 'Introduction: Regionalism within Modernism', in R. Powell (ed.), *Regionalism in Architecture* (Singapore: Concept Media/The Aga Khan Award for Architecture, 1985), pp. 8–16.
25 Tsing, *Friction*, pp. 1–6.
26 Farhad and Bakhtiar, *Interaction of Tradition and Technology*, p. 5.
27 Isfahan also formed the primary example in Ardalan and Bakhtiar's book, *The Sense of Unity*. At the time of the 1970 congress, Ardalan was, together with his then-wife and congress proceedings editor Laleh Bakhtiar, in the process of writing this book, with an introduction by Seyyed Hossein Nasr.
28 The city's central square complex, Naqsh-e Jahan, was inscribed as a World Heritage site in 1979. As arguably the most notable example of living heritage in Iran, it suggested the touristic potentials of the land and offered to foreign delegates an introduction to Iranian architectural traditions.
29 Persepolis was registered as a World Heritage site in 1979.
30 Farhad and Bakhtiar, *Interaction of Tradition and Technology*, p. 23.
31 Farhad and Bakhtiar, *Interaction of Tradition and Technology*, p. 13.
32 For the names of participants, see Farhad and Bakhtiar, *Interaction of Tradition and Technology*.
33 Roudbari, 'Transnational Transformation', pp. 54–8; Roudbari, 'Instituting Architecture', pp. 299, 302–3.

34 On Sedad Hakki Eldem, see N. Ozaslan and A. Akalin, 'Architecture and Image: The Example of Turkey', *Middle Eastern Studies*, 47:6 (2011), p. 914; S. Bozdogan, *Sedad Eldem* (Istanbul: Literatür Yayınları, 2005).
35 P. Rudolph, 'Regionalism in Architecture', *Perspecta*, 4 (1957), pp. 12–19; L. Mumford, *Sticks and Stones: A Study of American Architecture and Civilization* (New York: Bonui and Liveright, 1924); L. Mumford, 'Regionalism and Irregionalism', *The Sociological Review*, 19 (October, 1927), pp. 277–8; L. Mumford, *The Brown Decades: A Study of the Arts in America 1865–1895* (New York: Harcourt Brace and Co., 1931); L. Mumford, *Technics and Civilization* (New York: Harcourt Brace and Co., 1934).
36 Farhad and Bakhtiar, *Interaction of Tradition and Technology*, p. 16.
37 R. Nassehi, 'Domesticating Cold War Economic Ideas: The Rise of Iranian Developmentalism in the 1950s and 1960s', in Alvandi (ed.), *The Age of Aryamehr*, pp. 77–139.
38 A. Gholipour, *Cultivation of Popular Taste in the Pahlavi Era: The Nation's Aesthetic Training in the Government's Cultural Policies* (Tehran: Nazar Publications, 2019), pp. 137–142 (particularly diagram 1 on p. 139).
39 Farhad and Bakhtiar, *Interaction of Tradition and Technology*, p. 5.
40 Shils, *Tradition*, p. 12.
41 Farhad and Bakhtiar, *Interaction of Tradition and Technology*, p. 20.
42 Farhad and Bakhtiar, *Interaction of Tradition and Technology*, p. xiv.
43 Farhad and Bakhtiar, *Interaction of Tradition and Technology*, p. 31.
44 Ardalan cited in Farhad and Bakhtiar, *Interaction of Tradition and Technology*, pp. 34–7.
45 N. Ardalan and L. Bakhtiar, *The Sense of Unity: The Sufi Tradition in Persian Architecture*, with a foreword by S. H. Nasr (Chicago: The University of Chicago Press, 1973).
46 Here, we refer to the embedding of elements of the past in the present in the process of making cultural identity.
47 Emami, '"Civic Visions"', p. 51.
48 Farhad and Bakhtiar, *Interaction of Tradition and Technology*, p. 24.
49 D. Brownlee and D. de Long, *Louis Kahn: In the Realm of Architecture* (Los Angeles, CA: Museum of Contemporary Art, and New York: Rizzoli, 1991), pp. 78–87.
50 Haeri, 'Ardalan', p. 27.
51 Ardalan collaborated with Kahn on pre-Revolution projects, notably the project for Shahestan (see Chapter 6). Beny, *Elements of Destiny*, p. 352. Ardalan's architectural practice, the Mandala Collaborative, also collaborated with the French office of Josic, Candilis, and Woods on the design of the Bu Ali Sina University in Hamedan.
52 Farhad and Bakhtiar, *Interaction of Tradition and Technology*, pp. 6–7; Kahn cited in R. S. Wurman, *What Will Be Has Always Been: The Words of Louis I. Kahn* (New York: Rizzoli, 1986), p. 57.
53 Ardalan and Bakhtiar, *Sense of Unity*, pp. 21–31.
54 Kahn's former student, Ali-Akbar Saremi, later compared the 'loose order' of traditional Iranian architecture with a similar quality in Kahn's work; he saw Kahn's work and writing as a lens through which to discern a more authentic Iranian architecture and noted Kahn's influence on Ardalan. See F. J.

Javaherian-Mehrjui, 'Ali-Akbar Saremi in Conversation with Faryar Javaheriyan Mehrjui', *Environmental Design: Journal of the Islamic Environmental Design Research Centre*, 1 (1996), pp. 94–7.
55 Farhad and Bakhtiar, *Interaction of Tradition and Technology*, p. 54. On Quaroni, see M. Tafuri, *History of Italian Architecture, 1944–1985*, trans. J. Levine (Cambridge, MA, and London: MIT Press, 1989), pp. 62–5.
56 Farhad and Bakhtiar, *Interaction of Tradition and Technology*, p. 60.
57 A. van Eyck, 'Is Architecture Going to Reconcile Basic Values?', in O. Newman (ed.), *CIAM '59 in Otterloo* (Stuttgart: Kramer Verlag, 1961), pp. 26–35.
58 O.M. Ungers, *Die Thematisierung der Architektur* (Dortmund: Technische Universität Dortmund and Walter A. Noebel, Niggli Verlag, 2009).
59 Hobsbawm, 'Introduction', p. 1.
60 Farhad and Bakhtiar, *Interaction of Tradition and Technology*, p. 75.
61 M. Tafuri, *The Sphere and the Labyrinth: Avant-Gardes and Architecture from Piranesi to the 1970s*, trans. P. d'Acierno and R. Connolly (Cambridge, MA: MIT Press, 1987), pp. 293–5.
62 Boym, 'Nostalgia and Its Discontents', *Hedgehog Review*, 9:2 (2007), pp. 7–18.
63 Among Sardar-Afkhami's significant works is the iconic building of the Tehran Civic Theatre (completed 1972).
64 Farhad and Bakhtiar, *Interaction of Tradition and Technology*, p. 60.
65 Farhad and Bakhtiar, *Interaction of Tradition and Technology*, p. 66.
66 Indeed, global thinking had been the mantra of the congress deputy chairman, Buckminster Fuller, an American autodidact then riding a wave of popularity through his unitary and technologically utopian writings. He had called on the use of technology in the service of the sustainability of humans on earth. See R. B. Fuller, *Utopia or Oblivion: The Prospects for Humanity* (Toronto and New York: Bantam Books, 1969).
67 Tafuri, *Sphere and Labyrinth*, pp. 293–4.
68 Farhad and Bakhtiar, *Interaction of Tradition and Technology*, p. 52; Frampton, 'Towards a Critical Regionalism', pp. 16–30.
69 Farhad and Bakhtiar, *Interaction of Tradition and Technology*, pp. 247–8 (summary of deliberations (1)).
70 Bakhtiar (ed.), *Towards a Quality of Life*, p. ix.
71 Bakhtiar (ed.), *Towards a Quality of Life*, p. xvii.
72 Cohen and Eleb, *Casablanca*; Eleb, 'Alternative to Functionalist Universalism'; L. Mumford, 'l'Oeuvre d'Artur Glikson', *Le Carré Bleu*, 4 (1966), www.lecarrebleu.eu/PDF_INTERA%20COLLEZIONE%20LCB/FRAPN02_CARR_1966_004.pdf (accessed 3 December 2017).
73 A.-A. M. El-shorbagy, 'The Architecture of Hassan Fathy: Between Western and Non-Western Perspectives' (PhD diss., University of Canterbury, 2001), pp. 35–6.
74 But here was a pragmatic economic argument too. The delegates Fathy and Hartman (Mexico) argued that industrialization and standardization would not solve the problem of housing the poor in their countries. Bakhtiar (ed.), *Towards a Quality of Life*, pp. 273–4, 303–6, 351–6. See also N. Radwan, 'Hassan Fathy and the Arts', Hassan Fathy seminar on the occasion of the fifth anniversary of the Bibliotheca Alexandrina, Alexandria, 25 October 2007, https://doc.rero.ch/record/8381/files/Bibalex.pdf (accessed 4 June 2018).

75 Bakhtiar (ed.), *Towards a Quality of Life*, p. 12. This is a familiar nationalist trope but also Lamarckian in its assumption of the role of geography in developments and evolution.
76 C. Norberg-Schulz, 'The Phenomenon of Place', in M. Larice and E. Macdonald (eds), *The Urban Design Reader* (Abingdon and New York: Routledge, 2013), pp. 125–37; Y.-F. Tuan, 'Topophilia: Personal Encounters with the Landscape', in P. W. English and R. C. Mayfield (eds), *Man, Space and Environment: Concepts in Contemporary Human Geography* (Oxford: Oxford University Press, 1972), pp. 534–8; Y.-F. Tuan, 'Place: An Experiential Perspective', *Geographical Review*, 65 (1975), pp. 151–65.
77 K. Lynch, *The Image of the City* (Cambridge, MA: MIT Press, 1960). The translation of Lynch's work into Persian was by the late professor Manutchehr Mozayyeni and was published in 1976.
78 Bakhtiar (ed.), *Towards a Quality of Life*, p. 38; Kahn cited in Wurman, *What Will Be*, p. 57.
79 These differences of perspective were productive. In the collaboration between Ardalan and Candilis on the Bu Ali Sina University, structuralist ideas of the matrix, web, and network and of liminal mediating spaces inherent to the megastructure idea would, arguably, be married to those of the authentic village. Bakhtiar (ed.), *Towards a Quality of Life*, p. 56.
80 Bakhtiar (ed.), *Towards a Quality of Life*, p. 237. Candilis was presumably invited to the 1974 congress on the basis of his co-design of the Casablanca housing projects 'for the indigenous', with ATBAT-Afrique.
81 The Smithsons' 'Hierarchy of Associations' was presented at CIAM 9, Aix-en-Provence.
82 After the Revolution of 1979, Fathy would become one of the exemplary architects for ideologically committed and traditionally inclined architects teaching at universities (Mozaffari's recollection of education at the University of Tehran).
83 On Metabolism (1959 onwards), see C. Wendelken, 'Putting Metabolism Back in Place: The Making of a Radically Decontextualised Architecture in Japan', in Goldhagen and Legault (eds), *Anxious Modernisms*, pp. 279–99.
84 Merhavi, '"True Muslims"'.
85 Bakhtiar (ed.), *Towards a Quality of Life*, p. 204.
86 Bakhtiar (ed.), *Towards a Quality of Life*, pp. xvii–xviii.
87 C. Alexander et al., *A Pattern Language: Towns, Buildings, Construction* (Oxford: Oxford University Press, 1977); C. Alexander, *The Timeless Way of Building* (Oxford: Oxford University Press, 1979).
88 N. Ardalan et al., *Habitat Bill of Rights: Presented by Iran* (Tehran: Hamdami Foundation, 1976), pp. 18–28.
89 Ardalan et al., *Habitat Bill of* Rights, pp. 164–65 (recommendations 4, 7, 8, 6, 10).
90 A. Mozaffari and N. Westbrook. 'Shushtar No'w: Urban Image and Fabrication of Place in an Iranian New Town, and Its Relation to the International Discourse on Regionalism', *Fusion Journal*, 6 (2015), pp. 1–15, www.fusion-journal.com/issue/006-fusion-the-rise-and-fall-of-social-housing-future-directions/shushtar-now-urban-image-and-fabrication-of-place-in-an-iranian-new-town-and-its-relation-to-the-international-discourse-on-regionalism/ (accessed 14 September 2017).
91 A. Mozaffari and N. Westbrook, 'The (Unfinished) Museum at Pasargadae', in

A. Mozaffari (ed.), *World Heritage in Iran: Perspectives on Pasargadae* (Surrey: Ashgate, 2014), pp. 197–224.
92 Ardalan et al., *Habitat Bill of Rights*, p. 417. This mastering and reuse of the past could be seen as an example of what Lash has described as 'detraditionalization'. See Chapter 1.
93 L. Bakhtiar (ed.), *The Crisis of Identity in Architecture: Report of the Proceedings of the International Congress of Women Architects, Ramsar Iran, 13–17 October 1976* (Tehran: Hamdami Foundation, 1976).
94 On UIFA and the international context of women architects, see M. Simon, 'Hungarian Women Architects in the UIFA: the Ambiguities of Women's Professional Internationalism', in M. Papchinski and M. Simon (eds), *Ideological Equals: Women Architects in Socialist Europe 1945–1989* (London and New York: Routledge, 2017), pp. 157–71.
95 The 1976 congress served a bigger agenda in relation to cultural development and international cultural relations, notably gender equality. See 'Declaration Presented by Princess Ashraf Pahlavi to the Secretary General of the U.N' (Tehran: Women's Organization of Iran, 10 December 10, 1974), p. 5, https://fis-iran.org/sites/fis/files/Princess%20Ashraf%20Declaration%20to%20UN%20P1.pdf (accessed 23 March 2018).
96 Bakhtiar (ed.), *Crisis of Identity*, p. 21.
97 Bakhtiar (ed.), *Crisis of Identity*, pp. 22–5.
98 Bakhtiar (ed.), *Crisis of Identity*, p. 116.
99 Bakhtiar (ed.), *Crisis of Identity*, p. 130.
100 Jackson and Holland, *Architecture of Fry*, p. 260.
101 Bakhtiar (ed.), *Crisis of Identity*, p. 32.
102 Bakhtiar (ed.), *Crisis of Identity*, p. 69.
103 Rudofsky, *Architecture without Architects*, preface.
104 Bakhtiar (ed.), *Crisis of Identity*, pp. 83–6.
105 Bakhtiar (ed.), *Crisis of Identity*, p. 235.
106 Bakhtiar (ed.), *Crisis of Identity*, p. 236.
107 Mozaffari, *Forming National Identity*, pp. 95–114.
108 Farhad and Bakhtiar, *Interaction of Tradition and Technology*, p. 86.
109 Farhad and Bakhtiar, *Interaction of Tradition and Technology*, p. 88.
110 H. Taragan, 'Architecture in Fact and Fiction: The Case of the New Gourna Village in Upper Egypt', *Muqarnas*, 16 (1999), pp. 169–78.
111 French and Italian references to the vernacular forms of architecture were frequently couched in terms of a supposed pan-Mediterranean culture, permeating a strand of twentieth-century European modernism. See J.-F. Lejeune and M. Sabatino (eds), *Modern Architecture and the Mediterranean: Vernacular Dialogues and Contested Identities* (London: Routledge, 2010); M. Fuller, 'Mediterraneanism: French and Italian Architects' Designs in 1930s North African Cities', in S. K. Jayyusi et al. (eds), *The City in the Islamic World, Volume 2* (Leiden and Boston, MA: Brill, 2008), pp. 977–92.
112 Bakhtiar (ed.), *Towards a Quality of Life*, p. viii.

3

Heritage in the everyday: Housing and collective identity before 1979

Introduction

One of the most tangible cases where heritage, place, and collective identity are construed and constructed on an everyday basis is in the design of collective housing. In this chapter we examine a particular case of engagement with the past through the architectural design of group housing, Shushtar Now (New Shushtar) by Kamran Diba, a project that arose out of the 1974 Persepolis congress as an exemplary model for future mass housing in Iran. Such mass housing fulfilled both practical and cultural functions. As we shall see, Diba's design was a vehicle for the workings of both nostalgia and memory – closely associated and yet distinguishable processes – and has been successful in creating a lasting sense of heritage and place. To expand on this proposition, for our purposes there is an intricate relationship between memory and nostalgia. Both have social roots and are activated through imagery and symbols (Figure 3.1).

Through the description and interpretation of Diba's project, we will demonstrate the role its design plays in framing and facilitating the occupants' experience of the past, constructing a perception of bounded place through the design of familiar dwelling environment, 'habitat'. Traditional motifs – forms, spaces, and details – are redeployed in activating personal and social memories. We will further reveal how nostalgia lingers on, inextricably connected to the experience of place, regardless of 'regime changes', and assumes multiple roles at different scales.

In discussing the operation of memory and nostalgia in the design of Shushtar Now, the engagement of residents with the complex is revealed through evidence from the field. Through various devices, from planning, to layouts and use of material, the design actively constructs memories – transforming the lived and experienced memory of the lifeworld into cultural memory, as *lieux de mémoire*.[1] From this perspective, the complex emplaces collective memories through material and spatial engagement with the architectural environment. Repeated bodily

3.1 Shushtar Now, view across rooftops (2015).

routines arguably create habit memories, which contribute to the configuration of customs, which are in turn validated by normative traditions. However, this created memory operates on two levels: in the outset, it is about creating a sense of belonging and identification in a new community.[2] Through time, however, the familiar environment and its memories give rise to nostalgic feelings among its residents – something that is clearly evident in our recent interviews with residents. On another level, this chapter will show that the design was driven by nostalgia, connecting the past to a future and this was, in the first place, a nostalgia experienced by the architect, Diba, himself. Nostalgia has allowed a sense of community and identification to take root in Shushtar Now. It appears that the project is driven by what Boym refers to as 'restorative nostalgia',[3] where memories are invoked in spatial contexts in support of an agenda for a future wholeness, to imagine a 'return' through design, one that is both backward- and forward-looking. It is this double gaze that creates heritage and the vehicle for that is a carefully crafted assemblage of architectural images.

The origins of the project

The project for a new town, Shushtar Now, across the Karun River from Old Shushtar, an ancient city of Sasanian origins, was a direct result of the

'Resolutions of the Second International Congress of Architects Persepolis 1974'.[4] The key resolutions were:

> 4. To develop, through a research study, a code of human habitat with such procedures and strategies necessary to enable the achievement of principles essential to the creation of a wholesome, balanced and equitable habitat [as ...] a working tool suitable for use by [...] the decision makers.

> 5. As a means to test and implement the above code, several prototype communities are recommended to be built and continuously evaluated [...] by a task force of international reputation in many different fields to achieve compact and balanced communities.

> 6. To develop an inventory of the indigenous adaptive strategies of the various regions of Iran. This inventory will allow a more quantifiable understanding and application of relevant building systems and technologies.

While these resolutions were couched in objective-sounding language, this belied the extensive debates that had been engaged in by the delegates on the issue of culturally appropriate habitat. One of the delegates, British architect James Stirling, reflected these preoccupations in his presentation, in which he argued that 'a building should indicate – perhaps display – the usage and way of life of its occupants' and is therefore 'likely to be rich and varied in appearance and [expression]'. He emphasized the need for housing to create popularly understood forms 'which the everyday public can associate with, be familiar with and identify with'. Stirling had previously participated in the PREVI housing competition of 1969 in Lima, Peru, which he presented to the 1974 congress.[5]

Iranian congress delegates James Stirling, Georges Candilis, and Aldo van Eyck had designed projects for the PREVI competition, and subsequently had a number of their schemes constructed.[6] In fact, Stirling's PREVI project bears some resemblance in its repetitive courtyard structure to Diba's Shushtar Now project, and combines a capacity for inhabitants' self-modification, a goal which had been stressed at the 1970 Isfahan congress, both by Iranians and European delegates.[7] At Persepolis in 1974, Candilis also insisted on the necessity of designing a total environment.[8] There was a need not just to build housing, but also to create a social habitat – this of course being the title of Safdie's Montreal Expo housing of 1967. These Western architects were, in essence, arguing that architecture needed a social context, and was necessarily bound to economic and indeed political conditions; it could not be understood merely in terms of technique or form. The question of what might constitute culturally appropriate habitat in Third World contexts can be traced back to late colonial experiences and European models developed both for the pacification and disciplining of 'indigenous' populations in the colonies[9] and at home for the provision of housing for post-war reconstruction and new industries. All were responses to the challenges of both post-war reconstruction and industrial development, and the perceived gap between popular and high culture, deploying nostalgic variants of the vernacular, arguably in order to produce settled, compliant populations.

In retrospect, we can identify the linkage between these debates and the context of the ambitious development plans in Iran. The 1974 congress delegates had been confronted by the pressing issue of housing for the internally displaced villagers in big cities, searching for work in the new industries through the country's development activities. In a significant seminar session, Sert and Ungers referred to the possibility of an 'Urban Bill of Rights' that would establish the basic standards for all urban dwellers and address the problems in housing associated with the internal migration of rural villagers to the outskirts of cities.[10] Here, Diba noted the current socio-economic transformations, rural migration to cities, and uncontrolled urbanization in Iran. One response to this problem, he argued, was the design of model communities that would form paradigmatic examples for future projects:

> [T]his [is] a unique opportunity for us to come up with a resolution of a primary body of people whose main objective would be urban human rights [...] a constructive result of the ideas of the experts of the professionals with experience from different parts of the world. If [...] the Iranian government gave us the necessary financial aid [...], *such an organization could implement some model communities*.[11]

Diba called on delegates to use the intellectual moral force of the congress to 'give force and direction to the future development of [habitat], towards a more positive response to ... human needs', in whose statement one can perceive a certain nostalgia for a lost humanity.[12] Indeed, it was Diba who would attempt to reconcile modern planning with this concern for organic unity in his project for company housing at Shushtar Now, surely a direct consequence of the resolutions of the 1974 congress. The housing complex, located to the north-west, and across the Karun River from the historic city of Shushtar in Khuzestan, was the most paradigmatic project within this context of government-funded model housing communities in Iran. A year after the Persepolis congress, its commission was awarded to the firm DAZ Architects, Planners, and Engineers, of which Kamran Diba was the design director, and which had already prepared planning schemes for Shushtar and nearby Dezful.[13]

The project that resulted from the awarding of this commission to Diba and his firm came to represent one of the exemplars of 'Islamic housing', as defined by the Aga Khan Award judges. Extensively published at the time, it featured on the cover of the 1988 Awards book on housing.[14] An Aga Khan commendation was awarded to the architects in 1986, by which time the first stage design had been approved (1977) and completed (1980), while further extensions had been undertaken in Diba's absence by other architects. By 1986, the project was associated with the theory of Critical Regionalism, one which, through its response to local place, climate, and culture, resisted globalizing trends in architecture.[15] This is understandable, as both Diba's appeal to the precedent of the Iranian traditional towns and villages, and direct interpretation of traditional architectural motifs in Khuzestan, resembles the call by critical regionalists for architects to learn from the local, but also to resist the commodification and reification of design through an understanding of the traditional formal typologies, material practices, and climatic responses of a region. But Kenneth Frampton, one of the proponents of Critical Regionalism, was at pains to distinguish his approach from that of an embrace of tradition:

> It is necessary to distinguish at the outset between Critical Regionalism and the simplistic evocation of a sentimental or ironic vernacular. I am referring, of course, to that nostalgia for the vernacular which is currently being conceived as an overdue return to the ethos of a popular culture.[16]

In contrast, Diba arguably, in his design, was consciously exploiting the potentials of nostalgia. In a brief outline of his design concepts, he asserted a continuity with traditional Iranian and Islamic architecture:

> The new town is sympathetic to the cultural values of Iranian society and also maintains *a traditional continuity*. Its outstanding characteristic is a tightly-knit fabric physically *reminiscent of Islamic vernacular architecture*; this encourages a high degree of social interaction and collectivity. The streets and spaces respond to the climatic conditions, with narrow streets and small courtyards to preserve the coolness of the night during the hot humid daytime [...]
>
> In older cities, streets often serve as a kind of playground or meeting place. In emulation of this, we created a number of dead-end streets which preserve privacy and identity [...]
>
> We felt that an attitude of 'total environmental control' could be positively incorporated into the architectural programme and design process; the community and social behaviour which is the final product of social and architectural endeavour was perhaps predictable. In other words, our goal was akin to writing a script for human interaction, anticipating all possible action and yet leaving room for spontaneous improvisation within the given architectural spaces.[17]

Diba is here explicit in his stated attempt to engender certain emotional responses in the residents through the employment of spaces and forms that mimic traditional ones. His reference to 'total environmental control' further suggests the production of certain social behaviours through the suggestiveness of the design – perhaps, to use Taylor's term, the fostering of an Islamic 'moral community'.[18] The intended population of residents was drawn from the region of Shushtar and its surrounding villages; the dense layout, narrow pedestrian streets, and intimate courtyards would have been experienced by them as familiar. In leaving their traditional environments, such new residents were invited to recall them through the design of New Shushtar, and furthermore to transplant their sense of 'home' to this new settlement, with its evocative forms and spaces.

Shushtar Now as a development project

We now turn to the place of the project in the state's development programmes. Shushtar Now was planned as an extension of Old Shushtar, an ancient settlement of pre-Islamic origin and the centre of an agricultural district situated on the Karun and Gargar Rivers, which possesses important surviving heritage structures, including remains of Achaemenid and Sasanian irrigation structures (recognized as World Heritage sites by UNESCO), as well as, together with the town of Dezful, distinctive regional masonry building traditions. The housing project for Shushtar Now was commissioned by the Pahlavi government to accommodate the workers of the Karun Agro Industry Inc., an entity that had been established to develop a mechanized sugar cane industry in the area, one of a number of centres throughout Iran which were identified for industrialization and modernization within the successive plans of the White Revolution. In fact, the project was one of the very first Iranian-designed and -executed company towns. As discussed in Chapter 2, the booming 1970s petro-economy of Iran had produced negative consequences, including the displacement of rural villagers to larger industrial cities and towns by the score, in what was effectively an internal migration of workers and their families in search of employment.[19] In response to this situation, new industries such as the Karun Agro Industry Inc. were established, in part to provide local employment and at the same time to fund the introduction of modern services, infrastructure, and institutions, through which the population might adapt to the modern world while avoiding the loss of its traditions.[20] Central to the establishment of a stable labour force was the provision of adequate housing. Construction of Shushtar Now was undertaken in concert with the Iran Housing Corporation, a government agency established to manage these issues of population displacement arising from industrialization.[21]

Diba's project for Shushtar Now, largely undertaken in accordance with the principles of habitat discussed at the 1974 Persepolis congress, operates both at the scale of the individual housing unit, the agglomeration of units structured around courtyard and laneway (the 'street' of houses), and at the scale of the urban assemblage, an organic unity that corresponds to the congress's call for the creation of a wholesome, balanced, and equitable habitat for studies of environmental impact; a balanced relationship between the quality of life and economic imperatives, and for regionally and climatically appropriate construction.[22] In this regard, Diba's project can be understood as representing the 'prototype community' called for by the congress.

Diba's design (Figures 3.2 and 3.3) is laid out along a pedestrian spine, linking the sports grounds to the south-west, the various nuclei of housing, the central shopping and services centre, and to the south-east, a Friday mosque and a large urban square, which although never constructed were intended to unite the two communities.[23] The employment of what could be construed as citations of historic monuments and spaces, a deeply nostalgic form of design, links the project

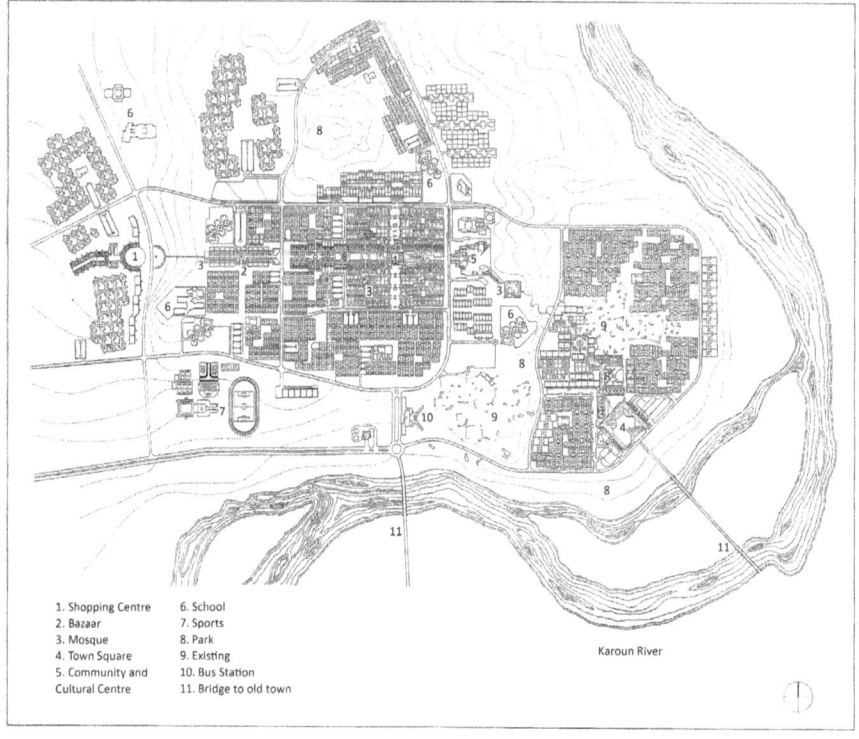

3.2 Kamran Diba, overall plan of Shushtar Now.

to Bairro Malagueira,[24] the near-contemporary project by the Portuguese architect Alvaro Siza on the outskirts of the historic town of Évora (1978 onwards), which was published alongside Shushtar Now as noted above. Both towns are deliberate attempts to 'learn from' the existing historical structures and spatial networks in developing a new outgrowth that 'talks' to the old one.[25] Shushtar Now, like Siza's project, can be understood as an attempt to create a familiar environment for its residents by subtly appropriating motifs and spatial types from historical urban environments, in this case the ancient settlements of Shushtar and Dezful. Thus, the housing units, predominantly laid out over two stories, were constructed around courtyards accessed from laneways, and in some cases apartments, which would share a common courtyard (Figure 3.4).

Staircases were designed to connect the ground floor to upper balconies and then up to a habitable roof which, like the local traditional houses, could be occupied by residents on hot summer nights, with privacy provided by perforated brick screen parapet walls. Furthermore, a *chāhār-bāgh* urban layout imposes a cruciform disposition of linear parks, lined with walls of higher housing, through which gates headed by perforated brickwork frame the entrances to semi-private residential streets (Figure 3.5).

Heritage in the everyday 89

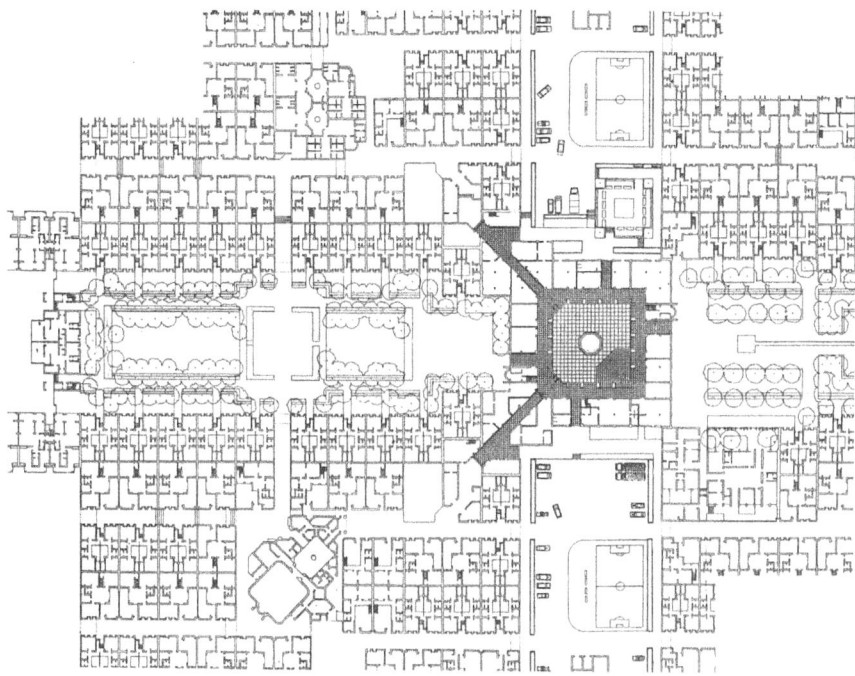

3.3 Kamran Diba, detail of Shushtar Now central area.

The new town was conceived by Diba not as a separate township to historic Shushtar, but instead as an outgrowth of it. His layout was designed to encourage residents of the old town to cross the bridge to attend the planned large mosque and the cultural centre, while the new residents would cross in the reverse direction to shop at the markets.[26] In the absence of a developed public transport system, and with few residents capable of affording private cars, this would enable a pedestrian or bicycle-based city, similar to the old town. The combined town was intended to grow by 25–30,000 people, or 6,500 family groups.[27] However, as we have noted elsewhere, the project was overtaken by subsequent events – the Islamic Revolution, soon followed by the Iran–Iraq War – leading to a change in the eventual population mix, from the intended community of company employees to a mix of employees, migrants, squatters, and war veterans.[28] Shushtar Now had been planned from the start as part of an attempt to deal with the internal displacement of populations attracted to the big cities, by establishing new regional industries in the various provinces of Iran. However, the catastrophic displacement ushered in by the war ironically prevented this from happening. This, then, was the situation on the ground at the time of the Aga Khan Award commendation.[29] Despite the impacts on the project by social disruption and inevitable economic constraints, and significantly the flight of the architect from Iran, the project was praised by the judges

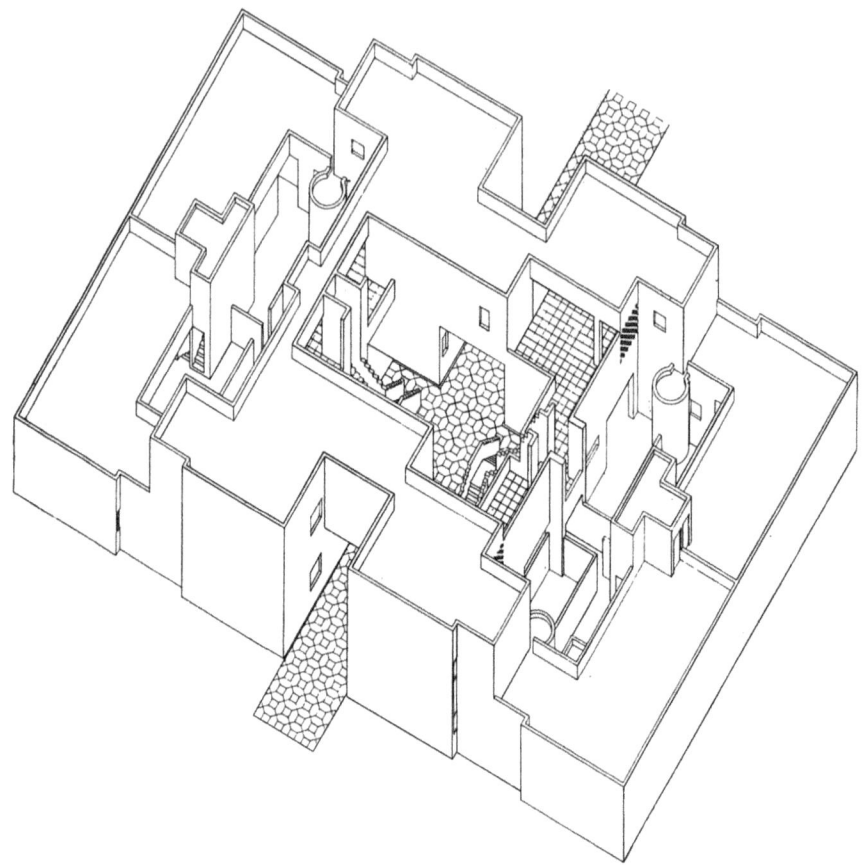

3.4 Axonometric view of group of courtyard apartments, Shushtar Now.

for its 'cultural expression', its 'continuity with the past', and its response to the local 'indigenous lifestyles', while facilitating industrial development.[30] Thus, from the perspective of so-called Islamic Architecture and the Aga Khan Award panel, the Shushtar Now project was understood in a very different way from the lens through which it was seen by Western admirers. And, as we have noted above and shall further expand below, the project was subsequently caught up in the project of Critical Regionalism. Of interest here is what this reception reveals about what the various critics wanted to see in it – an exemplary 'Rationalist' project, or a link back to authentic Islamic architecture.

This divergent reception is reflected in the way that subsequent writers have dealt with the project. Here there are two problematic aspects. Firstly, the discussion of the project has been unhelpfully complicated by a continuing attempt to understand it through the lens of Critical Regionalism,[31] rather than Diba's interest in environmental design, and learning from the vernacular. This is an

3.5 View of parkway, Shushtar Now (2015).

approach to the understanding and ordering of the built environment which we have above (see Introduction) associated with the turn to the vernacular of Rapoport, Oliver, and others. At the time, the approach from the perspective of environmental design promised a total control of the human environment, through the bringing together of the sciences of architecture, anthropology, and behavioural psychology.[32] Rather than constituting Critical Regionalism, we argue that the embrace of the vernacular in Diba's design for Shushtar Now, distilled through a personal poetics, is the result of the workings of universalizing projects of development and modernity rather than constituting 'resistance', albeit some may have found it expedient to categorize it as such after the fact.[33]

Keith Eggener has critiqued the way modernist preferences for structural integrity, abstraction, and simplicity of detailing were projected onto premodern and Third World vernacular architecture.[34] This construction of a self-justifying genealogy was, in a number of cases, reproduced by local modernizing architects. Alvaro Siza in the early 1970s made a similar study of Portuguese vernacular urban forms which he cited as validating precedents for his Malagueira project,[35] despite this project also exhibiting an evident debt to the social housing of Oud in the Netherlands,[36] the houses of the Viennese architect Adolf Loos, and significantly, the Italian Rationalism of the mid-1930s.[37] This selective modernist appropriation of the vernacular may be further associated with an embrace of the 'primitive' and vernacular in pre-war European modernism, notably in France, Italy, and Spain, an approach which was linked to the colonialist ambitions of these nations.[38] A similar process was evident in the embrace of Greek vernacular building by Doxiadis,[39] Konstantinidis,[40] and others, but here in support of an independent cultural stance, a tendency which led directly to the work of Dimitri and Susana Antonokakis, from which the first reference to Critical Regionalism by Alexander Tzonis and Liane Lefaivre emerged.[41] In Iran, these modernist attempts to learn from the vernacular influenced Diba who, like Ardalan, rejected the uncritical adoption of foreign cultural trends in architecture, and sought authenticity, with a nostalgic tendency, in traditional architecture. From this perspective, Diba's approach at Shushtar Now can be interpreted as an enthusiastic embrace of both modernist technologies and social science, and of the nostalgic recuperation of the past in new constructions, rather than fitting the mould of Critical Regionalism.[42]

A second problem resides in the judgements made of the Shushtar Now project with the benefit of hindsight, and from an unnecessarily ideological standpoint. Of course (as Amirjani has recently acknowledged), the project was conceived from above in accordance with national development plans,[43] and unlike at Siza's project, the residents had no agency in voicing their housing preferences. It is, furthermore, indisputable that the current state of the complex is rather sad, and reflects a mismatch between the architect's intentions and the cultural preferences of the residents. Yet critiques of Diba's project[44] arguably fail to take sufficiently into account the abnormal social, political, and economic conditions bedevilling the project: the Islamic Revolution that terminated Diba's supervision of the project, the Iran–Iraq War that led to an influx of displaced people, the resultant congested population that consisted of those from a lower socio-economic group than had been planned for, the products of neglect and mismanagement by the local authorities, selling off planned open spaces and failing to maintain the upkeep of the settlement,[45] and finally, the ongoing problem of residents flouting planning guidelines.[46] The productive conflict at Malagueira, which Siza has described as a designer–resident interaction,[47] is totally absent at Shushtar Now, and in its place is the evident failure of civic consensus.

The failure of will, or disinterest, on the part of the local authorities can be demonstrated in the fate of Diba's planned pedestrian street. The use of a street to structure a series of architectural and spatial 'events' was apparently a favourite device of the architect, used to different degrees at Jondishapur University, Ahvāz (1968–78), the *Namāz Khāneh* (prayer room) in Lāleh Park (Figure 3.6), Tehran, positioned in relation to tree-lined *allee*s (1977–78),[48] and even, arguably, the cultural centre and garden of Niāvarān (1970–78), in which a descending pedestrian promenade connects a series of cultural buildings and courtyards. The inspiration for such a device can be found in the great spatial set pieces of Safavid Iran, most notably the bazaar, Āli Qāpu Palace, and Naqsh-e Jahān Square of Isfahan. However, it was also a compositional device

Heritage in the everyday

3.6 Kamran Diba, Jondishapur University, Ahvāz, part of the sports facility (above); general internal space of a faculty (middle); and faculty courtyard (below) (2017).

3.7 Kamran Diba, primary school at Shushtar Now (2015).

used by leading international Rationalist architects of the early 1970s, including Aldo Rossi and Carlo Aymonino at the Gallaretese housing complex outside Milan (1973), and James Stirling's Derby Civic Centre project (1970) and Olivetti Headquarters project at Milton Keynes (1971), and would later form the armature of many later postmodernist 'analogous cities' such as Stirling's key project of the Neue Stadtsgalerie, Stuttgart (1984).

In this regard, Diba was 'of his time', syncretically combining modernist and nostalgic elements into inventive assemblages. At Shushtar Now, Diba threaded public buildings and spaces onto his armature like beads: Persian garden and public baths; houses and shops; an institute of technology; a primary school (Figure 3.7); a pedestrian bridge; a (high) school; bazaar (Figure 3.8); more houses; green vertical; commercial centre; more shops; civic centre; the Friday mosque; another public garden (Figure 3.9); yet more shops, houses, and another public garden; and finally an open space which was clearly intended as a major civic space linking across to the river and old city. As with his partially realized plan for Jondishapur, the buildings are partially figurative and space forming, a characteristic which is surely a product of his close study of the introverted spaces of traditional Iranian architecture, but also of his understanding of the then-current exploration of positive and negative urban space by Colin Rowe, James Stirling, and Louis Kahn. It is the local authorities' abandonment of the concept of this pedestrian street spine connecting to Old Shushtar that

Heritage in the everyday 95

3.8 Kamran Diba, view of Bazaar courtyard (2015).

3.9 Kamran Diba, general view of public garden (2015).

most clearly demonstrates the dissonance between Diba's vision and their ambivalence towards urban form. One could perhaps discern here a distrust of creating public spaces – in place of Diba's clear and emphatic articulation of residential and public spatial hierarchies, the later stages are fragmentary and incoherent, lacking any sense of a greater whole.

In hindsight, despite the many problems apparent in the realization of the project, most of which appear to be either circumstantial or the result of poor management, the design was, in many respects, responsive to its local context. Thus, the layout of apartments, rather than the modern functional programme of a house, was derived from a principle of spatial units of rooms, all of which were planned to be of a larger than typical size; a characteristic of traditional Iranian houses, in which rooms took on multiple functions, but had also been a strategy previously used in the French colonial housing project for the 'indigenous' *Carrières Centrales* in Casablanca, and in the housing typologies developed by the Doxiadis firm for master plans in Iranian cities.[49] The Shushtar housing typologies permitted functional flexibility, as well as consisting of two zones separating private family areas from external and socializing areas.[50] At an urban scale, the complex has a hierarchy of courtyards, from individual, to communal and to public spaces, as in Old Shushtar. The internally oriented openings shield against the harsh sunlight and privilege the courtyard gardens, reminiscent of traditional courtyard houses, while providing a culturally appropriate social seclusion. Finally, the design was consciously based upon a study of the way in which people in nearby towns interacted in public and private space.[51] The construction also reflects a modification of traditional construction – thus, the thick walls are labour intensively constructed of local brickwork, while the roofs are constructed of brick barrel vaults springing from the bottom flanges of steel beams, spanning between brick load-bearing walls spaced a maximum of 4–5 metres apart. While this hybrid resembles traditional structures, it provides additional resistance to earthquake damage. Brick is additionally used for pedestrian street paving and breeze block parapets.[52]

Shushtar Now as an assemblage of nostalgic images

Studies of Shushtar Now undertaken from an architectural perspective have, as noted above, focused upon its interpretation of traditional Iranian architecture,[53] its exemplification of critical regionalist principles,[54] its reinterpretation of Western ideas, and its response to place. Our aim here is to discuss the project in relation to an expanded understanding of place, and the relationship of its design thinking and heritage and development processes. This is to interrogate design as a vehicle that, in close correlation with culture and development, interprets and represents forms of the past in constructing a model town intended as a prototype for future developments, but also in so doing creating modern heritage. This process deploys memory and nostalgia, resulting in what could be described as an urbanism of desire. Here, 'desire' also reflects the horizon of possibilities, potentials for the future, but a horizon that is historically engaged, where a meeting between expectation and experience is suggested, or ideally actualized.[55] It is thus the projection through specific design enactments, of the promise of a certain sense of community.[56] Rather than viewing the project through abstract theorizations, then, it is more productive to explain the concrete mechanisms or processes through which there is an attempt to fashion, firstly, a spatial response and embodiment of a collective cultural identity, and secondly, to construct the 'local' in terms of place. Diba, himself, in a panel discussion on housing held in Indonesia, stated that he deplored the expression 'mass housing', as being devoid of cultural depth and 'totalitarian': 'We should stop thinking housing and start thinking and designing neighbourhoods, and perhaps towns.'[57]

Diba's statement suggests nostalgia for a lost community which, as if somehow, was at once more liberating and safe. This type of nostalgia, which appears to have been felt by the architect on behalf of other 'community members', pertains to perceptions of geographical loss: of place, with its boundedness and horizons, of social and historical loss of community and its sense of temporal grounding, and, with the latter in particular, the potential for a loss of a moral community.[58] Ultimately, the combined sense of loss prefigures anxiety about a weakening of identity. So, in proposing a shift from a focus on 'housing' to 'neighbourhood or town', Diba appears to be advocating some form of return to a holistic understanding of the collective (the urban expression of which is the opposite of the metropolis). There is a shift in focus away from the technicalities of mass housing such as prefabrication, construction, planning, formal typologies, and the attendant technical challenges. Thus, in both his statements and in his creative practice at Shushtar Now, Diba seems to have emphasized the creation of communities through the institution of place. Through emplacing communities, the neighbourhood, or town institutes' boundaries and group identities, formed through lived experience.

In his statement on housing, Diba, while clearly referring to the creation of place, does not, however, define what it might constitute. How then was 'place' discussed in architectural discourse at the time, and subsequently deployed in his projects? As discussed in the Introduction, a strong anthropological influence can be discerned in architectural discourse on place in the 1970s, an influence which permeated Diba's approach. Instrumental in the process he used to design such emplaced neighbourhoods and towns was an architectural mnemonic. The subtle use of familiar spatial, figurative, and motival elements enables mental connections to be made between a place, or multiple places, comprising buildings, spaces, and their urban and suburban contexts, but also the lives lived in and through them.[59] Thus, places constitute reservoirs of memory.[60] It is this aspect, so evident in Diba's own recollections of his projects, that has arguably been neglected in the scholarship on his work. Here we are interpreting a design process that is only evidenced by a posteriori deductions drawn from the immanent reality of work itself, and the often eloquent judgements in hindsight by the architect. At Shushtar Now, it would appear to us that Diba integrated both personal and cultural memory[61] in fabricating urban and domestic 'situations'[62] that might engender, through everyday habitual experiences, a nostalgia born of a sense of familiarity among the intended residents.[63] Crucial to this 'emplacement' is an architectural process that calls upon, and incorporates, *image*,[64] suggesting an architectural process through which certain spaces, forms, and motifs are configured so as to both mimetically cite the original, the 'authentic' so to speak, but also to construct a bounded place.[65] This horizon is not merely material, but is also constituted by a sociocultural consensus. It is the boundary that 'gives space ... to that which appears'. Thus, Diba's design for Shushtar Now, through its familiar materiality and spatial sequences, was, and perhaps still is, capable of engendering a sense of authenticity for its residents, within an experiential space that constructs its own horizon, a place.[66]

This authenticity perceived by the dweller could, with caution, be compared with the 'existential authenticity' proposed by various authors in relation to the (tourist) visitor's experience of certain places. Here, Zhu has distinguished between three forms of authenticity: 'objective authenticity, constructive authenticity and existential authenticity'.[67] The first pertains to a heritage that is objectively verifiable as authentic – real;[68] the second, constructivist authenticity[69] pertains to the position that authenticity is a social construct rather than an absolute, a projection[70]. Zhu argues that 'the constructive approach neglects the agency of the actors', in his case both tourists and performers, but arguably here the residents of Shushtar Now, who choose to adapt to and transform their environment.[71]

The question is raised here as to how Zhu's third, existential category of authenticity might apply to the situation of the Shushtar Now residents. Building on the work of others,[72] Zhu advances the notion of performativity, 'the transitional and transformative process inherent in the action of authentication where meanings and feelings are embodied through the ongoing interaction between individual agency and the external world'.[73] It is an idea that would appear to derive, among others, from Bourdieu's concept of 'habitus'[74] in which cultural practices, but also the physical reality of the material and spatial environment, are embodied in everyday life.[75] Applying this to the case of Shushtar Now, however, requires nuancing based upon fieldwork. As noted above, the majority of the existing population do not correspond with the originally intended users of the complex, and the effects of the influx of refugees and migrants, with ensuing problems of unemployment and underemployment, illegal activities such as drug dealing, and the weakening of civil structures, have undermined the application of the design principles upon which the town was based. Kemp notes that de-traditionalization, producing individualism in place of communal identity, '[lessens] the power of [...] habitus to determine social action as they once might have done'.[76]

The function of image

We have argued above that image was a constituent element in the construction of place at Shushtar Now. Such a tactile, rather than purely visual, image-ability[77] might be understood as giving rise to corporeal memory,[78] through immersion in a material 'body-space',[79] in which individuals might merge with their environment, mimetically identifying with it.[80] Without mimicking traditional local architecture, Diba was able to embed such images into what is otherwise a rational configuration of pedestrian streets. Whereas the traditional Iranian palaces, shrines, and gardens which Diba cited at Shushtar Now were visually and spatially unitary, his projects retain a somewhat playful and idiosyncratic personal interpretation of the sources. The places which he brings into being forestall a unitary vision. Instead, like James Stirling's 1970s museum projects,[81] he 'nests places within other places', to use Malpas's terminology.[82] The urban configuration of Shushtar Now is based, in Diba's words, on the concept of a fire temple courtyard occupying the highest part of the hill,[83] and forming an axial centre for two broad spines of open space at right angles to each other; thus, a similar configuration to traditional Safavid garden layouts like that at Qazvin, with quadripartite form (*chāhār-bāgh*) and cross axial paths (*khiyābān*). Now clearly there was no intention to create a spatial network equivalent to the *chāhār-bāgh*; however, the articulation of movement, through courtyards and linear passages and under thresholds formed by bridging structures, might be said to 'imagine' a familiar spatial sequence. Similarly, in the original design for Shushtar Now by Diba, the axial spines were extensively landscaped as a series of shady garden rooms. In each of the four resultant quadrants, narrow, shaded pedestrian streets were planned to connect to local neighbourhood courtyards, and were abutted by blocks of courtyard houses separated by lanes stepping down the hill (Figure 3.10).[84] Apparent in this ceaseless proliferation and reinterpretation of images through direct, tactile encounter with spatial sequences is the operation of memory and nostalgia.

Diba's housing design for Shushtar Now follows a process that, unlike postmodernism, does not collapse the past into the present. In preserving the distance between the two, it positions the triad of past–present–future as a trajectory within which the present is understood. Thus, a selection of what becomes heritage is in part a response to the needs of the present, and in part a response to social memories of the past. These memories are collected from a range of geographical scales that include, but are not limited by, the immediate proximity of the local. Finally, this 'imagination' is in part an attempt to foresee a future, akin to the utopian aspects of early twentieth-century workers' settlements. Shushtar Now is laid out in the image of an ideal Iranian town, recombining the imaginations of pre-Islamic and Islamic settlements in a vaguely familiar manner that still manages to appear strikingly contemporary.

Notwithstanding Diba's familiarity with key Western projects sharing similar qualities, the built project conveys an image of Middle Eastern and by implication 'Islamic' architecture. His lattice brickwork bridges, which frame the residential streets at points adjacent to neighbourhood courtyards, form an image that is reminiscent of the nearby towns of Shushtar and Dezful. At the same time, it also indirectly recalls similar bridges and shaded pedestrian streets in Kahn's Indian School of Management project. In both projects, unlike their vernacular

3.10 Shushtar Now, view of pedestrian street (2015).

analogues, the spatial composition of streets, courtyards, and bridges contrive a visual tableau, and form a network of courtyards and diagonal pathways which counteract the overall rectilinear geometry. Despite these similarities, several of Diba's former collaborators, while not discounting the possibility of a connection with Kahn, were unaware of any direct influence on the design of Shushtar Now.[85]

Shushtar Now followed Western garden suburb designs in separating cars and pedestrians. In the original plan, cars were kept to the periphery of the complex, and the public spaces were reserved for pedestrian traffic, as in a traditional town like Old Shushtar. However, in the realized settlement, following the Islamic Revolution and during the economic and social disruption of the Iran-Iraq War, the policy of separating cars and residential areas was abandoned through neglect, and as a result, the original design for the pedestrian precinct has been compromised (Figure 3.11 and Plate 1). This was to the considerable detriment of the complex – the original pedestrian network, as in Diba's design for the Jondishapur University campus in Ahvāz,[86] connects a pedestrian spine of rectilinear and oblique orientation with islands of dense built form. Both projects create an image of organic unity, but formed out of fragments, suggesting an incremental development over time. In Shushtar Now, however, the actual incremental development of the new town resulted

Heritage in the everyday 101

3.11 Residents' transformation of the original design in Shushtar Now: (above) a courtyard being covered, and entrance changed; (below) additions to forecourts and entries (2015).

in a failure to realize its potential – with the exception of the first stage, entirely constructed in brick, the realized new town lacked the rich synthesis of local and exotic influences evident in the master plan. Shirazi notes the distance in the project between the initial conception and the constructed reality[87] while the 1986 judging panel had noted 'the premature ageing and poor state of maintenance of the complex'.[88] A number of factors contributed to this – after the Revolution and the Iran–Iraq War, social disruption had prevented the creation of the intended landscape elements, and poor squatters and refugees had come to make up 20 per cent of the population, with a consequent lack of upkeep. Perhaps more significantly, Diba had to flee Iran for his life, and in his absence the subsequent additions did not live up to the ambitions of the master plan. The final indignity was the construction of a colony of Ahmadinejad-era 'Mehr housing' towers, entirely devoid of any reference to, or understanding of, the original conception, and in which there was expressed no interest in the role of heritage and the recollection of the past in the formation of contemporary social spaces.[89]

We have characterized the original plan as composed of tactile 'images' through which the past and present are brought into contact; however, rather than constituting a continuity with tradition, the project is a product of modern techniques and familiarity with advanced Western architectural concepts. In this respect, while Diba was American trained, the work presented at the 1970s architectural congresses was the most likely immediate influence upon the design of the project. Diba's former associate, Mr Kashanijoo, noted that the intention was to design a 'total environment', a notable theme of the 1970 and 1974 congresses, over which had hung the direct and indirect influence of Louis Kahn.[90] At the congresses, the call for an organic unity and continuity between the individual dwelling and the community as a whole was common to both Iranian and several of the leading Western modernist architects. Such calls can be associated with a similarly shared narrative of loss and estrangement characteristic of the modern city, which, Tafuri has noted, was common to both radical and conservative modernist and anti-modernist cultural commentators, in which the protagonists substitute order and universality for historical perspective, a charge he levelled at Louis Kahn.[91] Here the contradictory workings of nostalgia and the past are at play. Nostalgia is at once modern and looking to the past to reaffirm that modernity. Like Kahn's historicism, Diba's project is driven by a sense of nostalgia, but is arguably far more grounded in contemporary social realities than, for example, Kahn's Bangladeshi buildings. In other words, while Kahn was conjuring a fictional past, Diba engaged with traces of a past that existed in then-living memory. The latter thus had a claim to social grounding for his understanding of a 'moral community',[92] one based on a perceived and imagined tradition, which for Kahn existed in the realm of ethereal abstractions.

In modernity, there is both a sense of liberation and loss. Disenchantment strips culture of its grounding narrative, creating a 'crisis of values', in reaction to which the avant-garde and derrière-garde constructed their progressive and regressive utopias.[93] Benjamin famously argued that the past can only be comprehended as a fleeting image: 'The true picture of the past flits by. The past can be seized only as an image which flashes up at the instant when it can be recognized and is never seen again.'[94] This idea of the past returning as nostalgic memory may be juxtaposed with that of the citation of the past within a new construct. Here, the image is constructed in support of a projection into the future,[95] thus qualitatively different from the postmodernist surface flatness. Image as citation entails the construction of place through the recollection of fragment – such an imageability was distinguished by Benjamin from 'Phantasmagoria' – the distracting effect of modern mass media on the individual's capacity to connect in a meaningful way with society.[96] However, such an imageability is just as likely to refer to a collective that has already disappeared, or to anticipate a future that has yet to appear. It may also conceal the irrevocable rupture characterized by Hannah Arendt as a 'loss of tradition' – a 'gap between past and future' which seemed to her irreparable.[97]

The experience of Shushtar Now

The image of Shushtar appears to have been perceived by its residents as a place that recalls the urban heritage of Iran. Street and focus group interviews conducted in 2018 in Shushtar Now with residents who comprised a mix of people currently working for, or in the past had worked for, Karun Agro Inc., and had grown up in the town, and those who have moved there, mostly from Ahvāz, have revealed a surprising degree of unanimity in their understanding of the town as possessing a traditional appearance. Interviewees, it could be argued, had a grounding in traditional social relations of this region of Iran. While not 'authentically' traditional, they were neither Westernized individuals, especially in their cultural orientations, as revealed in general male–female relations and roles, occupation, socio-economic status, and even appearance and outfit. The traditional cultural basis of most of the interviewees is also reflected in their interests: most women brought up issues of whether or not Shushtar Now was safe to walk in, and the lack of mosques. The question of safety pertains to issues of sexual harassment: leering, catcalling, and other unwanted attention. The lack of mosques, we speculate, pertains to population growth in the area, which appears to be in excess of what Diba would have had in mind in his initial plans. Furthermore, with the official push for mosque building as a state propaganda mechanism over the past forty years, and in comparison to some other areas with a similar population, this area would appear to have fewer mosques. Additionally, mosques also provide an acceptable social environment for females in a male-dominated society, where chances of harassment are significantly diminished (as compared, for example, to the bazaar). The gendered nature of public space as dominated by men was also apparent in territorial behaviours of groups. Men were suspicious of outsiders coming into the area, despite many of them having come from somewhere else. There were various forms of aggressive, direct, and indirect checks of the interviewer by way of verbal interrogation by some men in the area, some for territorial concerns, others for concerns over drug turfs. The 'outsider' could find this intimidating, of course.

Some educated people had, in some cases, a surprising familiarity with the details of the architecture, indicating a certain sense of ownership and pride in residence at the place. To this extent, and for these people at least, Diba's efforts in making place has been a resounding success. Most female interviewees thought that the builders had been British (despite buildings resembling Iranian architecture) and in one instance, a female university graduate stated that 'the complex was designed by foreigners ... [to look] like a place in Italy'. Such comments appear to convey a sense of exoticism within the fabric, a defamiliarization of the familiar that, as discussed in Chapter 1, goes hand in hand with both nostalgia and de-traditionalization. The familiar structure, materially resembling some traditional place, must be a foreign interpretation of the original. The following two examples corroborate this interpretation:

> Its architecture is modern while resembling traditional cities;

> [Shushtar Now] was built by foreigners to resemble the traditional architecture of Shushtar with a big yard surrounded by rooms, two flower beds on two sides of the central water feature, and thick columns inside the rooms.

But for some, the resemblance is even closer to familiar places:

> [T]he architecture of the place resembles the traditional design of the houses in Shushtar ... It's like being in Old Shushtar when walking down the streets of Shushtar Now.

And as such, its recollection of the past makes it worthy of protection:

> Maybe the design of the [bazaar] was inspired by nature, the architect provided all facilities in the area like a beehive.

> [It is an] exceptional design (there is no dead-end alley, buildings in each part are similar in design, [the] traditional bazaar is spectacular with four main gates opening to the main four streets) ... [my] generation wanted to protect the traditional design of the area.

The past becomes embedded in the present, as suggested by the comments of one resident who referred to Diba's Shushtar Now as 'Old Shushtar'. This perception of Shushtar Now being a traditional setting seems to cut across class, gender, and occupation. For example, in our interviews a local salesman (a drug dealer) interviewed in the street thought the area was 'a traditional environment', echoing the sentiments of other residents.

The overall 'human scale' of the layout is also appreciated by the residents. Unlike larger cities, such as Ahvāz, the majority of units are limited in height, lending the overall layout a certain homogeneity and scale that can be appreciated at a walking pace:

> [T]he houses are at most two storeys and beautiful.

The 'beauty', however, is ascribed to the internal layout and materials of each lot, its houses being perceived as

> a faultless traditional design [with] authentic architecture.

A semblance of age is evinced through the layout as well as the choice of materials:

> [T]he entrance gates make the area look very old.

Both men and women liked the presence of courtyards with water features, and the visual privacy of the houses and roof terraces, noting that given the climatic conditions of this region, roof terraces are an extremely useful space and often utilized for sleeping in summer. As such, they also need to have certain degrees of visual privacy, which explains the high brick parapets.

However, with the disruptive changes in population mix and growth that have spiked due to deliberate policies after the Islamic Revolution and generational change, the original fabric has been forced to adapt. This can be seen at multiple scales: transformation of pedestrian streets to vehicular; transformation of courtyards to garages; and the transformation of the room-based housing layout to a more subdivided and air-conditioned layout. In many instances, balconies are covered or taken over, and in some cases, there is an additional structure built, so that there is a room to either rent out, or to accommodate the younger generation who would not otherwise be able to afford housing (Plates 1–2).

Some of these transformations are the inevitable result of economic change, or concern for protecting valuable assets like automobiles. In other cases, the transformations are more down to the changing inter-generational taste:

> [T]he young are tired of the traditional design of the houses because they don't have a hall.

> The traditional urban design, bazaar, streets and houses are old and are not attractive for the new generations ... [the] new generation demands [a] modern life style.

> Traditional houses were attractive for traditional people ... [The] new generation does not accept traditional houses with separated rooms.

Curiously though, such criticisms only highlight the fact that Shushtar Now is indeed experienced as 'traditional' by young and old alike. That experience may, however, elicit different responses, some of which are clearly nostalgic for the original design of Diba:

> The area was very beautiful before the recent changes ... residents should consider [the] original architecture of the place when making a change.

These are people with a background in the area, who feel nostalgia for the town's former appearance, their memories tied to old pedestrian streets, the initial structure of the bazaar, and the former design of the houses with a yard. They yearn for the former stone pavement of the street and the initial architecture of the place with clean traditional houses and big trees and flowers. And yet, there is still apparent a strong sense of bonding to the place, despite all the seemingly negative changes. Some residents hope that this place becomes registered as heritage! Others have clear social activities; for example, having recently succeeded in setting up a local football pitch for children after fighting a long battle with the municipality. In other words, there is a sense of civic community within the area. And interestingly enough, despite diversity of ethnic background, there is no ethnic strife, which is in itself a positive sign.

Some interviewees expressed sentimentality. A thirty-seven-year-old man noted, for example, that 'Shushtar Now is a beautiful but lost place that has nice winters and hard summers'. All these comments convey the sense that the architecture has not only recalled traditional urban environments, but indeed possesses an experiential authenticity. In other words, many but not all inhabitants experience Shushtar Now as a traditional place with all its positive and negative aspects.

Conclusion

AlSayyad argues that the notion of tradition, once understood as 'a repository of authentic and hence valuable ideas that have been handed down from one generation to another',[98] has now come to an end in the disciplines of architecture and urbanism, falling victim to a globally uneven capitalist economy. Traditions are commodified and their authentic-appearing image is exploited through reliance on tourism as an economic resource. The case of Shushtar Now can, however, provide an interesting insight into this analysis. At the time when Shushtar Now was conceived and constructed, this idea of an authentic repository was at its height while, arguably, local architects addressed a desire for the authentic through an eclectic appropriation of exotic architecture. Perhaps such work should be considered authentic in the sense of its embodying a specific cultural meaning through its 'experiential authenticity' – the perceived familiarity of its appearance, its tactility, its spatial sequences, but also of the forms of life that take place within it giving rise to a sense of a discrete place. The subsequent history of Shushtar Now has been one of conflict and neglect. But, as evidence on the ground shows, despite upheavals, Shushtar Now has a population for whom it constitutes a place with which to identify.

Against its interpretation as a construction based upon invented traditions, we have argued here that Shushtar Now may be better understood as being comprised of tactile images that can resonate with a population for whom they form part of a recent past. The attempt on the part of Diba and others of his generation to evoke the architectural image of a traditional community has been characterized here in relation to a sense of cultural loss and displacement. In a way, to project a sense of the authentic, architecture requires to be located, in the corporal, social, and cultural senses, and to be temporally oriented, meaning a sense of successive relationality. Such a cultural organicity was already impossible by the time of the inception of the Shushtar project. Millward, in 1971, had noted:

> Under present conditions, the moral ambivalence of the society is likely to continue and become more exacerbated. Secularism is advancing steadily with the spread of present educational facilities and the heavy stress on science and technology. No one expects a society facing the kind of change presently taking place in Iran to be able to maintain a stable value structure and a balanced moral climate ... Where those attempts to discuss the whole problem of changing values in a changing society, from whatever angle, are stifled or prohibited, where no forum for discussion and exchange of views on these implications of social change exists, tension and dislocation are bound to increase and the process of modernization curtailed accordingly.[99]

In summary, the contradictions resulting from the attempt to improve the human environment through public housing projects, without resolving the existing economic and political stresses and conflicts, can be discerned both in respect of the Shushtar project and the final resolutions of the 1974 Persepolis congress. At Persepolis, delegates had proposed that housing should no longer be considered at the scale of the individual dwelling but should extend to the community level, and that the process of reforming housing should be accelerated through the development of model communities, exemplified by Shushtar Now, in which individuals and cooperatives should work in concert. At Shushtar Now, the cooperation between various stakeholders was missing. Instead, there was a managed relationship between project sponsors. Nevertheless, the project architect Diba attempted to sow the seeds of a community through its planning scheme and, specifically, through a montage of tactile and reassuring images from a disappearing world. No doubt, there is an element of nostalgia in this process, but we would argue that the tactile and corporeal experience created by the architect through his linking of the past and present has proven successful at Shushtar Now. Indeed, the image of this project defies singular categorization. The place is now historicized. Although it ended up only housing a minority of the intended inhabitants and thus failed to fulfil its original role as a company town and model community, one might venture that, nonetheless, the image somehow works, in an ambivalent way, as a trace of something familiar and fleeting. In this respect, it recalls Ungers's statement, at the 1970 Isfahan congress, that tradition was a dialectical process. The contemporary architect might wish to embrace tradition but remains uncertain of it. Tradition contains an otherness – there is an inevitability of formal and theoretical transmutation.[100] Despite all the transformations imposed upon the project, the disruptions caused by political turmoil and war and population displacement, and the ideological displacements after the Revolution, Shushtar Now became a silent model, as well as an ideal type, for later urban developments in Iran. To many Iranian architects it showed a way of integrating a yearning for the past with regional and vernacular interpretations of being Iranian. It looked Islamic enough but also it looked Iranian.

Without him being often mentioning by name – Diba was persona non grata for well over two decades in Iran and still does not travel back – his ideas and designs were admired and borrowed by students and practitioners alike. There was, however, a closer connection too, and that came through the part-time academic engagement of the likes of Diba and Ardalan in studios which included site visits to traditional towns such as Old Shushtar; while they were influential in training a good many architects through their practices, some of the latter stayed in Iran after the Revolution, upped their ideas, and implemented them in the immediate aftermath of the Revolution in various public housing projects. The following chapter addresses these linkages and debates in tracing architectural approaches to the design of culturally appropriate housing and neighbourhoods.

Notes

1. P. Nora, 'Between Memory and History: Les Lieux de Mémoire', *Representations*, 26 (Spring, 1989), pp. 7–24; J. Assmann, 'Communicative and Cultural Memory', in A. Erll and A. Nünning (eds), *Cultural Memory Studies: An International and Interdisciplinary Handbook* (Berlin and New York: de Gruyter, 2008), pp. 109–18.
2. C. Lasch, 'Memory and Nostalgia, Gratitude and Pathos', *Salmagundi*, 85/86 (1990), pp. 18–19.
3. Boym, *Future of Nostalgia*.
4. Bakhtiar (ed.), *Towards a Quality of Life*, pp. 359–60.
5. Bakhtiar (ed.), *Towards a Quality of Life*, pp. 309–10. For complete visual documentation of Stirling's Previ housing, see http://socks-studio.com/2019/01/20/clusters-and-growth-previ-housing-project-by-james-stirling-1976/.
6. On the PREVI competition, see F. García-Huidobro et al. (eds), *¡El Tiempo Construye! Time Builds!* (Barcelona: Gustavo Gili, 2008).
7. Bakhtiar and Farhad, *Interaction of Tradition and Technology*, pp. 81–94.
8. Bakhtiar (ed.), *Towards a Quality of Life*, p. 237.
9. Eleb, 'Alternative to Functionalist Universalism'; Cohen and Eleb, *Casablanca*; Avermaete et al. (eds), *Colonial Modern*.
10. For a contemporary project to Shushtar Now that was probably also influenced by the example of Kahn, Anguri Bagh residential complex, in Lahore, Pakistan (1975), by Yasmeen Lari, see: N. Amini, 'Modern Architecture as an Agency of Political Competition: The Case of Iran and Pakistan', *Studies in History and Theory of Architecture*, 6 (2018), pp. 92–107.
11. Bakhtiar (ed.), *Towards a Quality of Life*, pp. 201, 204 (emphasis added).
12. Bakhtiar (ed.), *Towards a Quality of Life*, p. 204.
13. M. R. Shirazi, 'New Towns – Promises towards Sustainable Urban Form: From

"Shushtar-No" to "Shahre Javan Community"', Young Cities Research Paper Series, Volume 7 (Berlin: Universitätsverlag der TU Berlin, 2013); A. Kashanijoo, interview with A. Mozaffari, Skype, November 2014; H. Nourkeihani, interview with A. Mozaffari, Skype, November 2014; L. Micara and V. Salomone, 'Shushtar New Town: The Idea of a Community. Interview with Kamran Diba', *L'ADC L'architettura delle città. The Journal of the Scientific Society Ludovico Quaroni*, 8 (2016), p. 133.
14 R. Powell (ed.), *The Architecture of Housing* (Singapore: Aga Khan Awards, 1990). K. T. Diba, 'Shushtar New Town, a Company Town in Persia', *Lotus International*, 36 (1982), pp. 118–24.
15 Shirazi, 'New Towns', p. 24.
16 K. Frampton, 'Prospects for a Critical Regionalism', *Perspecta*, 20 (1983), p. 149.
17 K. Diba, 'A Case Study: Design Concepts of Shushtar New Town', in L. Safran (ed.), *Housing Process and Physical Form*, Proceedings of Seminar Two in the series Architectural Transformations in the Islamic World, Istanbul, Turkey, 26–28 September 1978 (Philadelphia, PA: The Aga Khan Award for Architecture, 1980), pp. 41–44 (emphasis added).
18 Taylor, *Sources of the Self*, p. 36.
19 H. Mahdavy, 'The Coming Crisis in Iran', *Foreign Affairs* (October, 1966), www.foreignaffairs.com/articles/iran/1965-10-01/coming-crisis-iran (accessed 8 August 2018).
20 E. Hooglund, *Land and Revolution: 1960–1980* (Austin, TX: University of Texas Press, 2014); R. K. Ramazani, 'Iran's "White Revolution": A Study in Political Development', *International Journal of Middle Eastern Studies*, 5 (1974), pp. 124–39; Ansari, 'Myth of the White Revolution'.
21 K. T. Diba, *Shushtar New Town* (Aga Khan Award for Architecture – Technical Report, 0117.IRA, 1986).
22 Bakhtiar (ed.), *Towards a Quality of Life*, p. 360.
23 Mozaffari and Westbrook, 'Shushtar No'w'.
24 Compare Shushtar Now with images of Malagueira found here: www.flickr.com/photos/27245899@N07/7778001114/in/photostream/.
25 J. Spencer and N. M. Seabra, 'Context, Identity and Architectural Design Thinking: Álvaro Siza's "Bairro da Malagueira"', in H. Casakin and F. Bernado (eds), *The Role of Place Identity in the Perception, Understanding, and Design of the Built Environment* (Sharjah, UAE: Bentham Science Publisher, 2012), pp. 194–208; N. Mota, 'Between Populism and Dogma: Álvaro Siza's Third Way', *Footprint*, 5:1 (Spring, 2011), pp. 35–58.
26 Diba cited in Micara and Salomone, 'Shushtar New Town', p. 133.
27 D. Diba, 'Architect's Design Report: Aga Khan Technical Review Summary' (Philadelphia PA: The Aga Khan Award for Architecture, 1986 [1980]), p. 41.
28 Diba, 'Architect's Design Report', pp. 10–12.
29 The 1986 Aga Khan Award jury comprised Soedjatmoko, Mahdi Elmandjra, Abdel Wahed El-Wakil, Hans Hollein, Zahir Ud-Deen Khwaja, Ronald Lewcock, Fumihiko Maki, Mehmet Doruk Pamir, and Robert Venturi.
30 I. Serageldin (ed.), *Space for Freedom: The Search for Architectural Excellence in Muslim Societies* (London: The Aga Khan Award for Architecture, Butterworth Architecture, 1989), p. 165.

31 Shirazi, 'New Towns'; Shirazi, *Contemporary Architecture*.
32 A. Rapoport, *Human Aspects of Urban Form: Towards a Man–Environment Approach to Urban Form and Design* (Oxford: Pergamon Press, 1977), p. 1.
33 Shirazi, *Contemporary Architecture*, pp. 27–39.
34 K. L. Eggener, 'Placing Resistance: A Critique of Critical Regionalism', *Journal of Architectural Education*, 55:4 (May, 2002), pp. 228–37.
35 Spencer and Seabra, 'Context, Identity and Architectural Design Thinking', p. 198.
36 These projects include Hoek van Holland (1924), and the row houses at the Stuttgart Weissenhof housing estate, 1927.
37 Mota, 'Between Populism and Dogma', p. 46.
38 J.-F. Lejeune and M. Sabatino, 'North versus South: Introduction', in Lejeune and Sabatino (eds), *Modern Architecture and the Mediterranean*, pp. 1–12.
39 I. Theocharopoulou, 'Nature and the People: The Vernacular and the Search for a *True* Greek Architecture', in Lejeune and Sabatino (eds), *Modern Architecture and the Mediterranean*, pp. 110–29.
40 P. Cofano et al., *Aris Konstantinidis, 1913–1993* (Milan: Electa Architettura, 2010); D. Leatherbarrow, *Uncommon Ground: Architecture, Technology and Topography* (Cambridge, MA: MIT Press, 2000), pp. 213–39; Theocharopoulou, 'Nature and the People'.
41 A. Tzonis et al., 'Die Frage des Regionalismus', in M. Andritsky et al. (eds), *Für Eine Andere Architektur* (Frankfurt am Main: Fisher, 1981), pp. 121–34.
42 Shirazi, *Contemporary Architecture*, pp. 27–42.
43 R. Amirjani, 'An Analogical Quotation', in J. Ting and G. Hartoonian (eds), *Quotation: What Does History Have in Store for Architecture Today?*, Proceedings of the 34th Annual Conference of the Society of Architectural Historians of Australia and New Zealand, 5–8 July 2017 (Canberra, ACT: Society of Architectural Historians, Australia and New Zealand, 2017), pp. 13–23.
44 Shirazi, 'New Towns', pp. 42–7; Shirazi, 'From Utopia to Dystopia'; Amirjani, 'An Analogical Quotation', pp. 13–23.
45 Shirazi, 'New Towns', pp. 131–2.
46 Shirazi, 'New Towns', pp. 43–4.
47 Amirjani, 'An Analogical Quotation', p. 17.
48 On Namaz Khaneh, see T. Der-Grigorian, 'Construction of History: Mohammad-Reza Shah Revivalism, Nationalism, and Monumental Architecture of Tehran, 1951–1979' (PhD diss., Massachusetts Institute of Technology, 1998), pp. 9–11, 168.
49 National Housing Five Year Development Plan by Doxiadis Associates, 1972–77.
50 Mozaffari and Westbrook, 'Shushtar No'w'; Diba, 'A Case Study', p. 42.
51 Shirazi, 'New Towns', p. 36.
52 Aga Khan Award for Architecture (ed.), 'Shushtar New Town On-site Review Report', 1980, http://bit.ly/35sPGHX (accessed 23 October 2017); see also H.-U. Khan (ed.), 'Shushtar New Town', *Mimar: Architecture in Development*, 17 (July–September, 1985), p. 52; I. Serageldin, 'Shushtar New Town', in Serageldin (ed.), *Space for Freedom*, p. 165.
53 Serageldin (ed.), *Space for Freedom*, pp. 161, 165.
54 Shirazi, *Contemporary Architecture*, pp. 41–42, 45 note 1.

55 Koselleck, *Futures Past*, pp. 255–75, cited in M. Pickering, 'Experience as Horizon: Koselleck, Expectation and Historical Time', *Cultural Studies*, 18: 2–3 (2004), pp. 271–89.
56 Koselleck, *Futures Past*, p. 259.
57 Kamran Diba in discussion on mass housing, Powell (ed.), *Architecture of Housing*, p. 142.
58 Bryant, 'Nostalgia and Discovery', p. 164.
59 A. Buttimer and D. Seamon (eds), *The Human Experience of Space and Place* (New York: St. Martin's Press, 1980); T. Cresswell, *In Place/Out of Place: Geography, Ideology and Transgression* (Minneapolis, MN: University of Minnesota Press, 1996); D. Massey, 'A Global Sense of Place', in T. Barnes and D. Gregory (eds), *Reading Human Geography: The Poetics and Politics of Inquiry* (London and New York: Arnold, 1997), pp. 315–23; D. Massey, *For* Space (London: Sage, 2005); J. Malpas, *Place and Experience: A Philosophical Topography* (Cambridge: Cambridge University Press, 1999), pp. 1–43 (introduction and ch. 1).
60 D. Trigg, *The Memory of Place: A Phenomenology of the Uncanny* (Athens, OH: Ohio University Press, 2012); E. W. Said, 'Invention, Memory and Place', *Critical Inquiry*, 26:2 (Winter, 2000), pp. 175–92.
61 Assmann, 'Communicative and Cultural Memory', p. 113.
62 J. D. Edgerton and L. W. Roberts, 'Cultural Capital or Habitus? Bourdieu and Beyond in the Explanation of Enduring Educational Inequality', *Theory and Research in Education*, 12:2 (2014), p. 195, citing P. Bourdieu, 'Habitus', in J. Hillier and E. Rooksby (eds), *Habitus: A Sense of Place* (Burlington, VT: Ashgate, 2002), p. 27.
63 Mozaffari and Westbrook, 'Shushtar No'w', pp. 1–16; R. B. Bechtel, 'Behaviour in the House: A Cross-cultural Comparison using Behaviour-Setting Methodology', in S. M. Low and E. Chambers (eds), *Housing, Culture and Design: A Comparative Perspective* (Philadelphia, PA: University of Pennsylvania Press, 1989), pp. 165–81.
64 M. Taussig, 'Tactility and Distraction', *Cultural Anthropology*, 6:2 (1991), pp. 147–53.
65 J. Malpas, 'Place, Space, and Modernity', lecture, 14 November 2016, International Studies Institute at the University of New Mexico, www.youtube.com/watch?v=mFqX6AA19T4 (accessed 29 May 2018).
66 E. Casey, *The Fate of Place* (Berkeley, CA: University of California Press, 1997); Malpas, *Place and Experience*.
67 N. B. Salazar and Y. Zhu, 'Heritage and Tourism', in L. Meskell (ed.), *Global Heritage: A Reader* (Oxford: Wiley-Blackwell, 2015), pp. 240–58.
68 E. Relph, *Place and Placelessness* (London: Pion, 1976); N. Wang, 'Rethinking Authenticity in Tourism Experience', *Annals of Tourism Research*, 26:2 (1999), pp. 349–70; D. MacCannell, 'Staged Authenticity: Arrangements of Social Space in Tourist Settings', *American Journal of Sociology* 79:3 (November, 1973), pp. 589–603.
69 Hobsbawm, 'Introduction'.
70 Wang, 'Rethinking Authenticity'.
71 Y. Zhu, 'Performing Heritage: Rethinking Authenticity in Tourism', *Annals of Tourism Research*, 39:3 (2012), p. 1497.
72 B. T. Knudsen and A. Marit Waade, *Performative Authenticity in Tourism and Spatial Experience: Rethinking the Relation between Travel, Place and Emotion in the Context*

of Cultural Economy and Emotional Geography (Leeds: Channel View Publications, 2010).

73 Zhu, 'Performing Heritage', p. 1498.
74 P. Bourdieu, *Outline of a Theory of Practice* (Cambridge: Cambridge University Press, 1977); N. Crossley, 'The Phenomenological Habitus and Its Construction', *Theory and Society*, 30:1 (2001), pp. 81–120; N. Crossley, *The Social Body: Habit, Identity and Desire* (London: SAGE Publications, 2001), pp. 91–119.
75 Bourdieu, *Outline of a Theory*.
76 C. Kemp, 'Building Bridges between Structure and Agency: Exploring the Theoretical Potential for a Synthesis between Habitus and Reflexivity', *Essex Graduate Journal of Sociology*, 10 (2010), p. 9.
77 On 'imageability', see Lynch, *Image of the City*; K. Lynch, *What Time Is This Place?* (Cambridge, MA: MIT Press, 1972).
78 E. Casey, *Remembering: A Phenomenological Study*, 2nd edn (Bloomington, IN: Indiana University Press, 2000 [1987]), pp. 149–50.
79 S. Weigel, *Body- and Image-Space: Re-reading Walter Benjamin*, trans. G. Paul et al. (London and New York: Routledge, 1996), pp. 8, 19–20.
80 T. W. Adorno and M. Horkheimer, *Dialectic of Enlightenment*, trans. E. Jephcott (Stanford, CA: Stanford University Press, 2002), p. 237.
81 P. Arnell et al. (eds), *James Stirling: Buildings and Projects, James Stirling and Michael Wilford and Associates* (London: Architectural Press, 1984); G. H. Baker, *The Architecture of James Stirling and His Partners James Gowan and Michael Wilford* (Surrey and Burlington, CT: Ashgate, 2011).
82 Malpas, *Place and Experience*, p. 23.
83 Diba, 'Architect's Design Report', p. 4.
84 R. L. Delevoy et al. (eds), *Architecture Rationelle: La Reconstruction de la Ville Europeenne* [Rational Architecture: The Reconstruction of the European City] (Brussels: AAM, 1978), pp. 64, 109.
85 S. H. Nourhkeihani, interview with A. Mozaffari, Tehran, 2017.
86 For an image of this footpath, see: https://s3.amazonaws.com/media.archnet.org/system/media_contents/contents/10641/original/IAA1429.jpg?1384691651.
87 Shirazi, 'New Towns', p. 46.
88 Serageldin (ed.), *Space for Freedom*, p. 165.
89 On the Mehr housing programme, see M. T. Kazerooni et al., 'Comparative Exploration of Social Housing in Iran', *MAGNT Research Report*, 2:7 (2014), pp. 28–49.
90 Kashanijoo, interview with Mozaffari, November 2014.
91 M. Tafuri, *Theories and History of Architecture* (New York: Harper and Row, 1980 [Italian 1st edn 1968]), pp. 7–8; A. Vidler, *Histories of the Immediate Present* (Cambridge, MA: MIT Press, 2008), pp. 180–3.
92 Taylor, *Sources of the Self*, p. 36.
93 M. Tafuri, *Architecture and Utopia: Design and Capitalist Development*, trans. B. L. La Penta (Cambridge, MA: MIT Press, 1976 [1973]), p. 51.
94 W. Benjamin, 'Theses on the Philosophy of History', in H. Arendt and H. Zohn (eds), *Illuminations: Essays and Reflections* (New York: Schocken Books, 1969 [1968]), p. 255.
95 W. Schenkluhn, 'Bermerkungen zum Begriff des Architektur-Zitats: Zur

Erinnerung an Hans-Joachim Kunst (1929–2007)' [Remarks on the Concept of the Architectural Citation: In Memory of Hans-Joachim Kunst (1929–2007)], *Ars*, 41:1 (2008), pp. 3–13.
96 G. H. Kester, 'Aesthetics after the End of Art: An Interview with Susan Buck-Morss', *Art Journal*, 56:1 (1997), p. 42.
97 H. Arendt, *Between Past and Future: Eight Exercises in Political Thought* (New York: Penguin Books, 1993 [1961]), pp. 191–2.
98 N. AlSayyad, 'Consuming Heritage or the End of Tradition: The New Challenges of Globalization', in Y. Kalay et al. (eds), *New Heritage: New Media and Cultural Heritage* (Abingdon: Routledge, 2007), p. 155.
99 W. Millward, 'Traditional Values and Social Change in Iran', *Iranian Studies*, 4 (1971), pp. 29–30.
100 Bakhtiar and Farhad, *Interaction of Tradition and Technology*, p. 63.

4

Forming a future from the past: Realizing an everyday Islamic identity

Introduction

In the Pahlavi period, rapid development brought problems of supply, typology, and quality of forms of habitation to larger Iranian cities. It had encouraged population displacement, uncontrolled peri-urban districts of shanty towns, and increased congestion in established districts and cultural conflicts between existing and recently arrived populations – problems that were similar to housing crises in French North African colonies, where the idea of culturally appropriate housing had originated. Internal rural–urban migrations, which pressurized major urban centres during this period, continued with the advent of the 1979 Islamic Revolution, spiking in 1976–86. This trend was exacerbated by the Iran–Iraq War (1980–88). The result was the temporary, and ultimately unsuccessful, implementation of policies restricting migration to large urban centres.[1] As such realities on the ground continued, the new Islamic establishment promoted the ideological rhetoric of a return to an authentic Islamic past (the very cultural logic of the Revolution), and the glorification of the 'oppressed' (*mosatzafin*), while concurrently militating against outside influences. As previously indicated, such discourses had begun decades before among establishment and anti-establishment intellectuals and artists alike and had a strong Islamist and leftist base as well.

In this context, where Iran was still grappling with the effects of state developmentalism as well as social upheavals, approaches to culturally appropriate housing are worthy of analysis as they reveal the intricacies of addressing an Islamic past through design under a new ideological regime. Despite the political rupture, however, there was a considerable degree of continuity between pre- and post-Revolution ideas for housing design, especially in the aspects of social memory and nostalgia embodied in references to selected signifiers of an Iranian past – traditional, vernacular (native), architectural and urban forms, motifs and spaces. In both periods, ostensibly traditional motifs facilitated the communication of the state's messages to significant sectors within the society. This continuity is significant, given the central importance of state-provided housing in Iran, as in other developing countries, as one of the primary instruments of modernization, cultural adjustment, and economic development.

The following analyses are based on the results of nine nationwide housing competitions held by the Iranian Ministry of Housing and Urban Planning between June and November 1985,[2] during the war. A selection of competition entries was subsequently published as a book in 1989. These competitions were among the first to be held since the Revolution.[3] Our analyses are also informed by interviews with authors of some of the entries as well as other Iranian academic architects. Our specific focus is on the relationship between the submitted designs and the expressed Islamist agenda underlying the competition. We also note that in drawing upon architectural precedents held to constitute 'Islamic architectural heritage', a few architects revealed the influence of Diba's project. We build on previous work that traces the ideas behind the designs to Iranian intellectuals and their European counterparts as well as to foreign architects and commentators. These interrelationships reveal both the highly syncretic and novel basis of the architecture, and the underlying streams of continuity connecting the architecture produced by the pre- and post-Revolution regimes. Within the constraints of economic embargoes, war, and internally and externally imposed isolation, architects lent a local significance to motifs in part derived from foreign influences, in the process reinscribing the past in the present. This process was nostalgic and employed various interpretations of tradition towards the creation of heritage.

The condition of housing after the Revolution

The Pahlavi establishment had initially adopted a modernizing, technocratic approach to housing provision by investigating the possibilities of industrial prefabrication. However, by the 1970s, its approach had divided into at least three major directions. The first direction continued with modern forms of housing, either mass produced or produced by private sector developers, such as the Ekbatan development.[4] This type of housing had a specific clientele in the emerging and growing urban educated and professional (or public service) class – the government remained one of the major employers at the time as it would through to the early 2000s. The second direction comprised one-off, architecturally designed houses for the aspiring cultural elite, designed in all forms ranging from neo-traditionalist to ultra-modern. The third direction addressed an emerging urban class, those more recent migrants to cities who had arrived subsequent to the reforms of the White Revolution, and who were still in the process of shifting from older modes of family structure and economic production to new industrial and urban modes of existence. It was particularly in reference to the latter sector that, in opposition to foreign acculturation, modernist models were replaced by interpretations of traditional domestic and urban fabric, as exemplified by Diba's Shushtar Now.[5] Nevertheless, all these efforts had been inadequate in addressing the problem of housing at a national scale. Indeed, the lack of adequate housing, impacted by the mass migrations following the White Revolution, had been a significant factor in galvanizing opposition to the previous regime.[6]

In the aftermath of the Islamic Revolution, the new constitution of the Islamic Republic of Iran stated that the nation had 'returned to the authentic Islamic worldview and intellectual positions ... and was determined to establish its exemplary model society [...] based on Islamic criteria'.[7] It also promised 'to create prosperity and eliminate poverty'[8] and fulfil its goal of housing the masses, among other essential needs.[9] Significantly for our analysis, Islamic criteria were also applied to the social spaces of housing and urban structure. In the context of significant housing shortage, growing the housing stock was essential for the economic development of the state as well as social stability. Furthermore, the housing industry was a necessary source of economic stimulus.[10] But in the context of the declared intention to create a model Islamic society, a necessary linkage was made between, on the one hand, state ideologies and their aestheticized representations, and on the other, the material forms and processes of housing.[11] The linkage paralleled the cases in both liberal democracies and in the Soviet Bloc.[12]

The Islamic Republic under Ruhollah Khomeini made pronouncements on the principles which should govern social norms, especially the behaviour and dress of women in public and private space.[13] These principles pertained both to the policing of social behaviour through, for example, compulsory hijab for women, enforcing restrained behaviour in public spaces, and promoting ideas of *mahramiyat* (female seclusion from the gaze of men who are not close family members) within the domestic environment.[14] One might then expect that under the nascent Republic, housing policy, funding for mass housing, the form of housing typologies, individual architectural designs, and their urban settings responded to this revivalist mood by spatially and materially embodying a return to the precepts of a 'pure Islam', reinterpreted in the present. Presumably, the realization of these precepts would fall under the remit of official housing bodies within the Islamic Republic, the Housing Foundation of [the] Islamic Revolution (inaugurated by a decree issued by the Supreme Leader Ayatollah Ruhollah Khomeini on 10 April 1979),[15] and the Ministry for Housing and Urban Development, under the auspices of which the competitions were organized.

The competitions were held for cities throughout Iran: Hamedan, Isfahan, Tehran, Shahr-e Kord, Garmsār, Khorram Abād, Rasht, Khuzestan, and Mashhad. Most sites were located on the periphery of the urban centres and the projects were directed towards the provision of adequate housing for the lower socio-economic classes (Figure 4.1). The land for these future housing estates was acquired through the Urban Land Organization[16] under Article 67 of the Urban Land Act,[17] which facilitates investment in developing low-cost housing by individuals and legal entities.[18] The timing of the competitions, held during

Forming a future from the past 117

4.1 Distribution of housing competitions sites in nine locations (1989).

a calamitous war with Iraq, which was draining national financial resources, is curious, and it is unclear which winning submissions, if any, led directly to an architectural commission, although several winning firms would later be awarded substantial government housing consultancies. The jury's choices in competitions were guided by 'the goals of the Islamic Republic establishment in relation to housing and Islamic culture'.[19] In other words, they reveal the impact of the dominant Islamist ideology upon the formulation and representation of 'ideal' Islamic habitat. The jury decided that out of the fifty-one submissions for the nine locations, fifteen projects merited a competitive ranking of first to third position. In four locations, submissions were not ranked.

The *Competitions* book cover indicates the underlying intention of the competitions (Figure 4.2). At the top, there is a panorama of traditional mud-brick

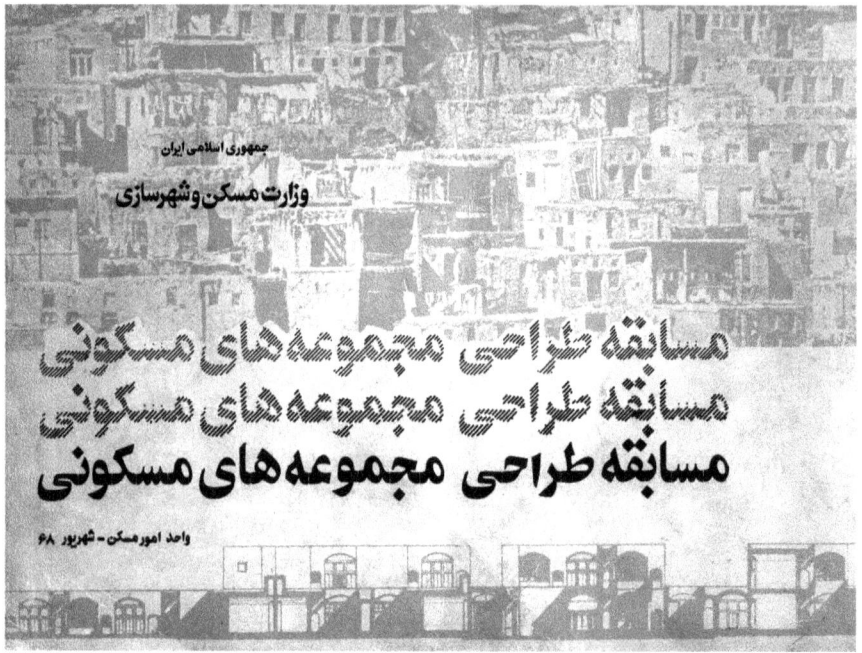

4.2 Cover of *Competitions* book (1989).

houses from a mountain village, possibly Ābyaneh in Isfahan province. The title is repeated three times, gradually solidifying from grey to black, as though the architecture at the base of the page, an elevation of one of the winning entries, is a concretization of the latent typologies represented by the ideal village, the past giving birth to the future. Thus here, as in the 1970–76 congresses, the traditional village is put forward as a model of essential Iranian (Islamic) habitat for the competition projects.

As we have noted elsewhere,[20] there are two aspects evident in many of the projects, and in the editors' narratives. Firstly, there is the assumed possibility of an intrinsically Islamic architecture; one that could embody in form and space 'culturally appropriate' responses to Islamic customs governing social norms, especially those around privacy and gender segregation.[21] Secondly, there is an invocation of traditional Iranian architecture and historical settlements such as Isfahan, Yazd, and Kashan, as a repository of appropriate design language and as models for attaining lofty spiritual goals, pertaining to a putative 'Islamic-Iranian' architectural character. While the Islamizing tendency was heightened after the Revolution, as we have seen in previous chapters, both aspects existed before the Revolution – in architectural education, in much of the architectural discourse at the Iranian congresses, in particular the turn to the traditional village as a source of inspiration by Ardalan and others – and were embodied in key architectural projects. This informed the way architecture was discussed and formulated in the Islamic Republic. Behind a veil of esoteric unity, Islamic heritage was formed out of a syncretic assembly of both international and local traditional and modern sources and signs. This repertoire of traditional iconography sustained its dynamism and vitality by responding to competing social interests with a multiplicity of ideological 'accents'.[22]

The competition projects reveal a dual origin. Domestically, they are inspired by the Islamic authenticity and traditionalism associated with the antimodernism of Shariati and Jalal Al-e Ahmad, and with the philosophy of Nasr and the architecture and writing of Ardalan. But just as those tendencies had syncretic origins, these too were compounded by the influence of contemporary Western writers in various disciplinary backgrounds, writing on popular vernacular building in traditional societies – notably among them, Bernard Rudofsky, Amos Rapoport, Christopher Alexander, and to a lesser extent Aldo van Eyck who, drawing upon the fields of environmental psychology, anthropology, heritage, and conservation, advocated the study of vernacular architecture as an 'authentic' counterbalance to the late modern architecture and urbanism of the West. The ideological roots of this discussion about human value and authenticity in post-revolutionary architectural discourse ironically derive, as we discussed in the Introduction and Chapter 1, from twentieth-century European thought.[23]

An example of this writing was Joseph Rykwert's essay 'The Idea of a Town' in van Eyck's magazine, *Forum*. The essay was subsequently expanded into the eponymous book – a survey of the symbolic basis of the ancient Roman city – but was also a thinly veiled attack on post-war modernist welfare state architecture and urbanism.[24] It is in the context of this cultural turn that Ardalan and Bakhtiar's book, *The Sense of Unity*, can be positioned and understood. This book, commissioned by the Oriental Institute of the University of Chicago on the recommendation of Nasr, continued to exert a significant influence upon the traditionalist discourse after the Islamic Revolution.[25]

A key characteristic of much of the Iranian architectural projects from the 1970s was a selective citation of forms, motifs, and spaces derived from traditional – Islamic and pre-Islamic – architecture. In the 1985 housing competitions, architects similarly laid claim to the principles of their projects as having derived from traditional, denoting Islamic, precedents. Rather than constituting a return to the past, however, these competition projects used aspects of the past to instil authentic experience and practice through the force of architecture. In this respect, they followed the references to vernacular building by regionalist Iranian architects in the decade before the Revolution. However, in the Islamist atmosphere in the wake of the Revolution, the fabrication of a supposedly authentic habitat took on new and ambiguous dimensions. On the one hand, authenticity was supposed to be projected – effectively this meant surfacing modern industrialized mass housing with traditional motifs. In line with pre-Revolution projects, such citations of the past were attempts to conjure or invent from scratch memories of a tradition through the 'design of heritage'.

On the other hand, much of the architectural production was contrived, with architects either becoming quasi-ideologues or, for purposes of survival, falling into the trap of self-censorship, or else, operating opportunistically. The relationship between architectural design and heritage must be understood in relation to the balancing by designers of economic and personal survival in the context of state ideology. Given that housing directly addressed the relationship of public and private space, it was an area where the demands of such a meeting of government policies, ideological rhetoric, pressing social demands, and professional survival came to the fore.[26]

In response to the pressures of war and the economy and echoing the efforts of their Italian counterparts in the aftermath of the Second World War,[27] Iranian architects attempted to create familiar environments in their mass housing designs. In this endeavour, they referred to pre-Revolution experiments with tradition, such as Diba's Shushtar Now, as design precedents. Despite the fact that in 1985, a year before this project's award from the Aga Khan Foundation, neither these awards nor Diba enjoyed any official endorsement or recognition in Iran.[28] Nonetheless, one of the competitions' architects, Amir Houshang Ardalan, who had previously worked for Diba, acknowledges the architect's influence on his design approach.[29]

The competitions

In the aftermath of the Revolution and particularly since the Cultural Revolution (1980–83),[30] there had been a purging of architectural journals,[31] dismissal of 'un-Islamic' lecturers and the appointment of ideologically sympathetic new staff,[32] and the rewriting of curricula in university architecture courses and the deletion of 'un-Islamic' subjects and their substitution with courses pertaining to Islamic and traditional architecture.[33] The recollection of one interviewee reflects a broadly shared sentiment:

> [With the advent of the Revolution] in our architectural mentality we hit something, as if a huge boulder had (suddenly) landed in the middle of a road. We tried to build another road and go around this boulder and we somehow did this. That boulder was the reactionaries, the religious, and their theoreticians who were students of the University of Tehran itself; the cliché[-minded] religious people.[34]

In such a climate, both the judges' and the architects' statements shared a common architectural discourse emphasizing authenticity, tradition, and adherence to Iranian cultural specificities.

In the 1989 *Competitions* book, three authors – Valiollah Pour-Keramati, Ali Ghaffari, and Hossein Sheikh Zeineddin, all academic architects – set out what they held to be the principles underlying Islamic habitat.[35] Pour-Keramati, who was additionally described in the text as the 'Vice President's Consultant',[36] articulated the purpose of the competitions: architecture, and in particular housing, had to be imbued with 'Islamic and cultural [i.e. authentic] values', as mandated by the Islamic Republic. However, here, architectural authenticity was not simply identified with traditional practices and customs or a call for the return to the practices of the premodern past. Instead, clearly illustrating the function of heritage, the past was to inform the present, and thereby 'retrofitted' to modern requirements. The question is, how would this aim inform a contemporary Islamic architecture? Pour-Keramati argued that tradition was in a constant state of evolution, changing and accommodating itself to the vagaries of the present. Concurrently, he rejected an architecture borne out of nihilistic consumerism and materialism[37] – architecture needed to be a transmitter and embodiment of both local culture and Islamic values. Evidently, Pour-Keramati believed in the mutability of tradition while invoking it in the present as a heritage resource and facilitator of resistance to a universalizing Western modernity and the global forces of capitalism. In this sense, he sat between the poles of the debates on tradition that occurred in the 1970s congresses. Following the paradigm of 'Islamic and cultural values', interpreted within the collectivist ethos of the Islamic Republic,[38] the ideal Islamic habitat was seen in terms of gendered domestic spaces, separating women's and men's quarters along the lines of the premodern society, where, particularly in the more affluent traditional houses, habitable spaces were divided into *biruni* (meaning 'of outside', for male guests) and *andaruni* (related to the 'inside or intimate' area, for women and family).[39] Similarly, in his essay in the *Competitions* book, Ali Ghaffari, an ideologically committed academic and member of the Cultural Revolution Curriculum Revision group, outlined some of the Islamic(ist) principles of Iranian culture and environment. These were primarily concerned with the protection of female privacy (*mahramiyat*), through differentiation of indoor and outdoor spaces, avoidance of overlooking (*eshrāf*), and norms of social interaction in the neighbourhood leading to the organization of 'brotherly' communities, facilitating Islamic hospitality without invading families' privacy.

This reimposed segregation was propounded despite a minority of the population not belonging to the Muslim religion, or indeed any religion, and a substantial but indeterminate percentage of the population not subscribing to the conservative attitudes imposing such gender separation.[40] But there was also a social collectivist aspect to the design of appropriate habitat, here interpreted as both the dwelling unit and its social environment. This kind of habitat was considered a guarantor of human dignity, as well as a preserver and manifestation of authentic Islamic values, through its use of the courtyard house – the spatial preserver of the *biruni–andaruni* separation as paradigm – and the *mahalleh* as a culturally specific setting focusing on the neighbourhood mosque. This was also the kind of ethos and discourse advanced by Diba and Ardalan, and then by many others prior to the Revolution – there was nothing new on offer under the Islamic Republic. Even the typology of the mosque as a neighbourhood centre was pre-revolutionary and perhaps even quasi-Orientalist. The discourse evident in the *Competitions* book painted a reductionist picture of purportedly Islamic urbanism, a kind of nationalist and self-orientalizing civilizational imagination in which the Islamic world was positioned in contradistinction to the Western world. So, rather than being the outcome of an attempt to return to traditional habitat, the principles articulated by Pour-Keramati may be said to possess, however ambivalently, an element of social engineering.

Despite the sinister implications of the term, such 'engineering' could, perhaps, be useful in mitigating the deleterious effects of development. In fact, the nascent state of Israel, like the French authorities in North Africa, had enacted similar policies to encourage the various groups of immigrants to identify themselves as a community, rather than as ethnic minorities.[41] It was anticipated that a design-induced sense of familiarity in place would, on the one hand, create a cohesive (and perhaps compliant) collective identity, while on the other hand, fostering difference (or evolution) by facilitating cultural transformation. This of course relied on the double role of mimesis – at once similar and different – in alterity. In the case of the competitions, an underlying assumption of the organizers, and perhaps some of the architects, seems to have been a behaviouralist belief that architecture and the material environment coaxes, perhaps even determines, certain authentic behaviours through a daily practice that resurrects, and reminds inhabitants of, an Islamic heritage.[42] This, however, discounts the inherent duplicity and ambivalence of mimesis,[43] as well as the fact that architectural typologies and their iconographical symbolisms have fleeting and multiple meanings (as Turner and others have shown).[44]

The apparently common ground created in these designs conceals divergent intentions between authorities, architects, and the end users – it is based on misapprehension and miscommunication rather than on an actual communion. But concurrently, such a social behaviouralist approach reflects and enacts a certain violence to living traditions, in that, through the essentializing of what it means to be Islamic, it reduces a pre-existing diversity of practices, multiple traditions, into a state-sanctioned normativity of both social relations, their spatial settings, and, in architecture, their symbolic configurations. Here, politics was cloaked in aesthetically based, and thinly veiled, ideology and nostalgia. Within the context of heritage studies, this normative process may, perhaps, be defined through Smith's concept of an 'authorised heritage discourse',[45] or Harrison's idea of an 'official' heritage.[46] These authors refer to an, often specifically object-oriented, understanding of heritage as something that can be governed by officialdom and validated by experts. Heritage thus operates as a mechanism for governing social and cultural identity. Subjects acquiesce and participate in the management of their own conduct by accepting, or being disciplined into, sanctioned social relations.[47]

The influences of Traditionalism are apparent in Pour-Keramati's statement in the introduction, which stresses the importance for Iranian housing design of cultural origin and authenticity. An awareness of cultural origins, which in the Iranian context is an ambiguous task, comprising both Islamic and pre-Islamic imaginations, as noted by Mozaffari,[48] is characterized by Pour-Keramati as being supportive of social stability and cohesion, presumably through its proffering of a common narrative of origin and identity. It is, therefore, through a connectivity and ostensible continuity with the past, despite the very real changes and disruptions caused by development, that one might supply an architectural legitimation.[49] While, from this viewpoint, there was a need to balance the cultural continuity of traditions with economic necessity and functional needs, from the perspective of the ideologues of the Islamic Republic, a (reinterpreted) tradition 'was an active force endowed with revolutionary potential in the present'.[50] In summary then, the statements in the *Competitions* book suggest the intention to use architecture as a mimetic device for engineering cultural change, and to make tangible and visible those supposedly authentic Islamic cultural values in the symbolic structures of the architecture and its urban setting.[51]

The social agenda of the competitions

Most of the published projects take inspiration from traditional patterns and spatial structures. The architects' statements and the design of the projects suggest a confluence of positions sympathetic to tradition but perhaps consonant with a widespread jargon of Traditionalism, which was also incorporated in the Islamic Republic's ideological rhetoric.[52] Thus while Pour-Keramati argued that traditions in Iran were context specific – advancing an essentially modern viewpoint, and suggesting the historicization of tradition in the service of the present – Traditionalists held that despite contextual variations, traditions descended from a universal, sacred basis, a common Islamic spiritual unity that exceeded the present. To them, the material manifestation of this sacred basis was the traditional house and village, a trope apparent at the Iranian congresses, as we noted in Chapter 2.[53] The traditional habitat continued to be seen as a cultural expression that was both tangible and transcendent. The jargon of spirituality could not, however, conceal a growing divergence of attitudes to the past in the present – in other words, a dissonant, if not contested, heritage.[54]

Referring to this heritage, Pour-Keramati listed four key objectives for the competitions. Firstly, it was imperative that Iranians should regain and recognize their authentic cultural identity. This identity should be recovered through the creation of an appropriate habitat that is based upon traditional Islamic values. Secondly, such Islamic values should be apparent in the architecture; in other words, Islamic values and identity should be manifested in the architectural forms, spaces, and urban layout. Here was a recognition of past failures to impose modern spatial solutions, materials, and technologies upon traditional populations without any measure of cultural adaptation. Thus Pour-Keramati called on architects to develop new construction strategies that utilize 'the facilities and people's creativity', and overcome the potential cultural gap between architects and the buildings' users.[55] He further opined the architects' responsibility '[to] safeguard against potentially devastating impacts on the environment'.[56] Pour-Keramati's statements, made in the context of war and economic sanctions, reveal the anxieties of Iranian intellectuals in confronting a globalized and modern world, before and after the Revolution. Such concerns had also been shared by Diba, who had tried to adapt traditional environments to modern practices and spatial regimes through techniques, materials, and planning – for example, by encouraging local masons to incorporate familiar patterns and motifs into the brickwork, a form of participatory design, as Fathy had encouraged in Egypt.[57]

In Shushtar Now, local know-how contributed to the embodiment of their cultural practices. Yet, participatory design had mixed origins, in part borne out of the interest in popular culture of Team Ten, and concurrently appropriated into the nativist advocacy of the Egyptian architect Hasan Fathy, and the cultural policies of the Aga Khan Foundation, despite the differences in their political and cultural origins and their objectives. However, the statements of the competition judges reveal a sense of nostalgia that defined a moral community,[58] which underpinned their collective identities with reference to an Islamic past and its mores, much as Nasr had done so in his pre-Revolution statements at the Aga Khan Award symposium.[59] Thus, beyond functional concerns (for adaptation), both the local and the traditional were designated as belonging to a (superior) moral order compared to the global, meaning the Western, which was projected as a lesser culture with flawed moral precepts. Rhetorically at least, this represents a basic difference to Diba's syncretic embrace of both Western ideas and local traditions, despite the apparent similarity of certain motifs in his work to the competition projects.

In his essay, Hossein Sheikh Zeineddin[60] also emphasized the need for Iranian architecture to be authentic to its society. He raised the issue of Iranian culture having been poisoned by foreign influences – what had before the Revolution been labelled 'Westoxification' by Al-Ahmad and picked up by other Iranian critics, as discussed in the Introduction.[61] In a similar vein, Sheikh Zeineddin claimed that the decadence of Iranian architecture derived from local architects having mimicked the residues of global trends in the absence of an adequate understanding of its technology. Iran had been subject to technological and cultural stagnation. Echoing Ardalan and Bakhtiar's *The Sense of Unity*, Sheikh Zeineddin argued that mimicry served only to further undermine cultural identity and transcendental aspects of architecture, and to attenuate the past generations' knowledge and experience, as embodied in the built environment.[62] Reference to, and incorporation of, elements of traditional architecture was seen to be at once a guarantor of cultural identity and stability, as well as also being environmentally sound *if* traditional building principles were understood and adapted.[63] Thus, instead of blindly following Western models, contemporary Iranian architects should respect Iran's cultural heritage and identity. Furthermore, he argued that there was a necessity for architects to communicate with their end users, by developing a design idiom or language that was understood by specialists and the public. Rather than expressing their individual 'genius', architects should subordinate their creativity to

Iranian culture and identity.⁶⁴ Much of this discourse, however, was presupposed by dogma and thus ideological in nature. Yet Sheikh Zeineddin's reference to 'shared language'⁶⁵ reflects the international interest at the time in the semiotics of architecture advanced by Venturi, Scott Brown, and Izenour's *Learning from Las Vegas* and Alexander's *A Pattern Language*, both published in 1977,⁶⁶ and thus having preceded the Revolution.⁶⁷ Here, Skurvida notes: 'Postmodernism bears a special meaning in relation to Iran [where] the Islamic Republic's cultural production displays tell-tale signs of neoconservative, revivalist postmodernist aesthetics, characterized by ornamentality, figuration, and ahistorical narrativity.'⁶⁸ Similarly, post-Revolution conservatives in the architectural establishment echoed Ardalan's previous exhortations for architects to learn from traditional environments in arguing that new designs should follow traditional patterns; indeed, *The Sense of Unity* was fast becoming the 'post-Revolution [architectural] gospel' and 'was doing the rounds along with a graduation thesis, *Khesht-o-Khiāl* (خشت و خیال = adobe and apparition), by two of his proteges, Kambiz Navaee and Kambiz Haji-Ghassemi.⁶⁹ This was restorative nostalgia in action.

The stated need for the subordination of architectural creativity to Iranian culture and Islamic identity articulated by the housing competitions judges was paralleled by the then-contemporary (late 1980s) architectural curriculum at Iranian universities. A description of the learning outcomes for a design studio unit stated that the various current international viewpoints will be discussed and 'analyzed with respect to the [fundamentals of Islamic beliefs] and in this way, it will be possible to achieve a unified and established idea on the basis of [them]'.⁷⁰ Thus, the goal was to pursue a revival of tradition in synthesis with modern techniques and appropriate modern concepts in architecture. Through both education and practice, this was a cultural process, in part introspection, in part reinvention, and in part commemoration, and thus heritagization, of a traditional past.

A survey of the competition entries

As we have seen from the judges' statements for the 1985 competitions, architects were encouraged to use figurations of the past, an idealized Islamic habitat. This was carried out in the recognized entries through several devices. As discussed above, there were, at a public scale, references to traditional *mahalleh* and typologies of the *chāhār-bāgh* and *meydān*, and, at a domestic scale, the designs incorporated, as had Diba's Shushtar Now project,⁷¹ reinterpretations of the traditional courtyard house (Nader Kazemi-Nejad, for Hamedan; Tajeer Architects, for Mashhad), and external staircases leading to roof terraces (Tajeer Architects, for Isfahan and Mashhad; Mandan Engineers, for Khuzestan).

Thus, for example, the project by Tajeer Architects, led by Ali Akbar Saremi for the historic cities of Isfahan (third place) and Mashhad (the same design

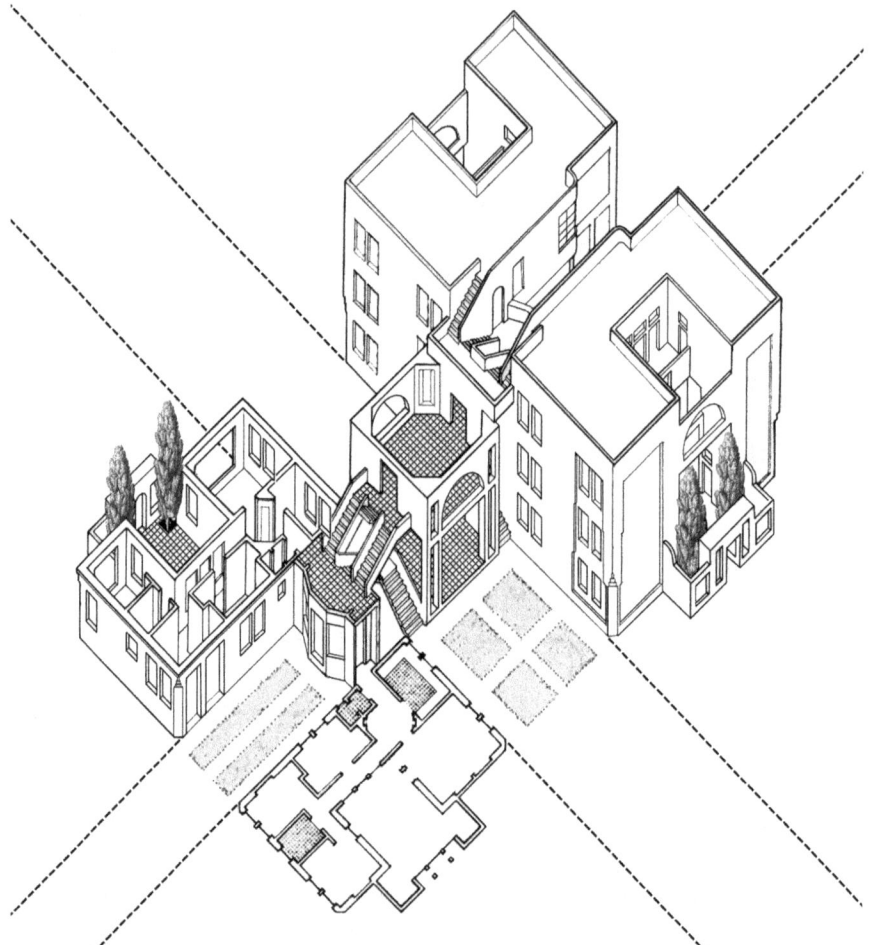

4.3 Saremi and Tajeer Architects, project for Isfahan (repeated for Mashhad).

was submitted for both), resembles Shushtar Now (Figure 4.3) in its structuring of dwellings around courtyards, covered and uncovered passageways, and pedestrian streets. Individual apartments are grouped into three-storey blocks, resembling traditional houses. Furthermore, like Shushtar Now, it evokes the traditional *chāhār-bāgh*, or fourfold garden structure, in its intersection of broad *meydān* (square) and principal pedestrian streets. The architectural details show evocations of tradition, especially nineteenth-century Qajar architecture.

In the Tajeer Architects' project, the geometrical division of the 'gateways' into each block are clearly inspired by Qajar architectural elements, probably the preserved gate on Sepah Avenue leading into the National Garden in Tehran, as is the plan of the lobbies bulging out towards the secondary

4.4 Bāgh-e Melli gate, Tehran (2008).

courtyards (Figure 4.4). The Tajeer design positions pairs of cypress trees either side of arches entrances into shared courtyards. This pairing, a symbolic visual element in Iranian folklore as well as miniature paintings, suggests an attempt to transpose the poetic space of such miniatures – the *Shahnameh* of Ferdowsi and the *Khamsa* of Nezami – into architecture. But the Tajeer project also reveals Western Rationalist influences in both the use of historicist citations and in its graphic style, deploying the axonometric view, as popularized by James Stirling and the Krier brothers.[72] This hybrid character is not surprising, given the foreign experience of the Tajeer partners during their university years (see Chapter 2).

The adoption of what is essentially a postmodernist classical style by Saremi was not an innovation of the post-Revolution period, but dates further back to the late phase of Iranian architecture under the monarchy. Here, comparison can be made with projects executed by Saremi with the University of Venice-educated Nasrin Faghih, and Taghy Radmard, and published in the 1978 issue of *L'Architecture d'Aujourd'hui* (Figure 4.5). In his description of the design

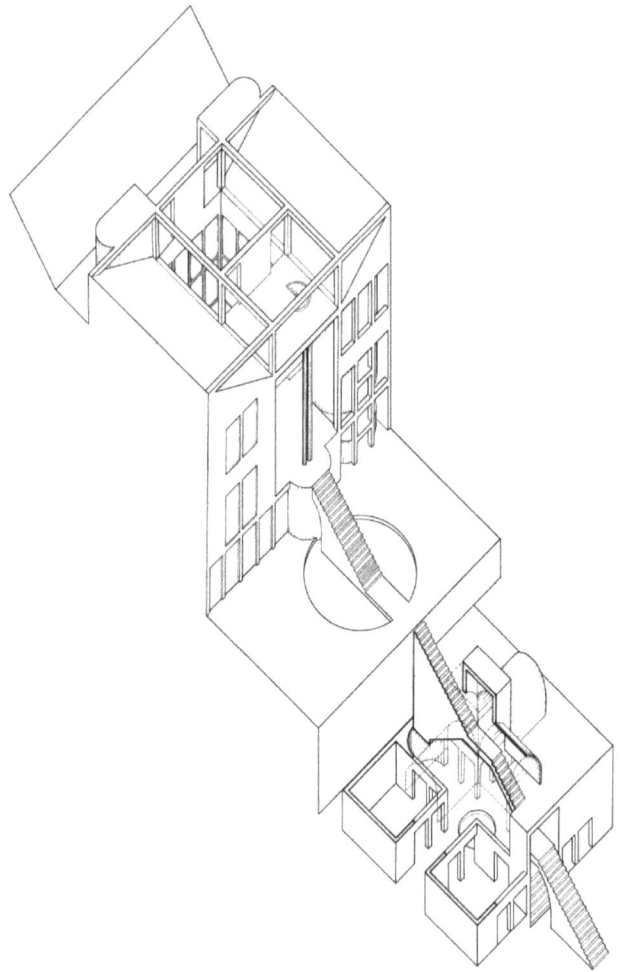

4.5 Arabshabi House, Tehran. Architects: Nasrin Faghih, Taghi Radmard (Bahram Hooshyar Yousefi), Ali Akbar Saremi.

rationale for Arabshabi House, a townhouse in Tehran he had designed in collaboration with Faghih and Radmard, Saremi wrote:

> This internal organization of space proves, moreover, that monumentality does not depend solely on the scale of a form, but on the remembrance which this form conveys by the use of certain elements and their arrangement in particular places. This space, intended to be functional, is considered as being also architectural and monumental.[73]

In their project for Arabshabi House, Saremi and his collaborators designed vaulted vestibules, arched staircases, courtyards with central pools, and an abstracted *iwan*, with slender columns presumably intended to recall Safavid precedents, such as the Chehel Sotoun Palace in Isfahan.

As in Tajeer's competition project for the two sites of Isfahan and Mashhad, these pre-Revolution Tehran houses, the Afshar House (constructed in 1976) and the unrealized Arabshabi House, evidence a familiarity with and a fluency in adapting then-contemporary Western fashions; for example, the modernist revival of Richard Meier, and the abstracted symbolism and semiotic focus of Agrest and Gandelsonas.[74] Demonstrating a concern for the semiotics of architectural composition, and a play between cartesian grid and defined volumes, combined with the citation of familiar traditional Iranian forms and motifs, these projects may also reflect Saremi's collaborator Nasrin Faghih's Venice and US East Coast training.[75] In the competition project for Mashhad and Isfahan, however, Saremi and his Tajeer Architects abandon semiotic play for direct historicism. There are references to what Saremi terms 'nostalgic space' – the traditional spaces of bazaar, *chāhār-bāgh*, gate, *hashti*, and courtyard, elements which were disappearing from Iranian cities through the transformative effects of modernization – and to the experiential qualities of harmony and introversion. He implies that these so-called nostalgic spaces will form children's mental images using elements of traditional architecture and will be maintained in their visual memory. Thus, a pre-Revolution formal and historicist tendency is re-couched in terms of the construction of cultural memory.[76]

There is, perhaps, a personal note in Saremi's appeal to the mnemonic significance of these traditional urban elements, a sense of the rapid loss of traditional practices, and the lifeworld that supported them. Saremi notes in his autobiographical work, *Weaving In and Out and Still: Architecture and My Life's Journey*, how his parents' house in Zanjan was traditional and based on extended family relations; he includes his sketches recollecting the house and his memories of moving as a student to Tehran.[77] For him, it would appear, even in one lifetime there was a rapid shift in the pattern of life, impacted by the processes of modernity.

In other competition entries, there is evidence of regional variations. Thus, in the project by Amir Houshang Ardalan and Mandan Consulting Engineers for Khuzestan, the same province as Diba's housing, the density and architectural grain of the residential units resembles the built fabric of traditional towns in the vicinity of the Persian Gulf, Bushehr in particular. The project is marked by flat roofs, deep, shaded courtyards and verandas. The presence of palm trees in the architect's renderings is suggestive of the design's locality (Figure 4.6). Whether or not it was a consequence of the competition, the Mandan office would be commissioned to design a realized project for housing workers' families of the National Petrochemical Company at Māhshahr, Khuzestan (1994). The latter project combines dense rows of free-standing housing with a social centre, recreational facilities, shops and mosque, all within a walkable distance.[78] The design architect, Amir Houshang Ardalan, had previously worked on the Shushtar Now project for the DAZ office, and in a recent interview confirmed that this

130 *Development, architecture, and the formation of heritage*

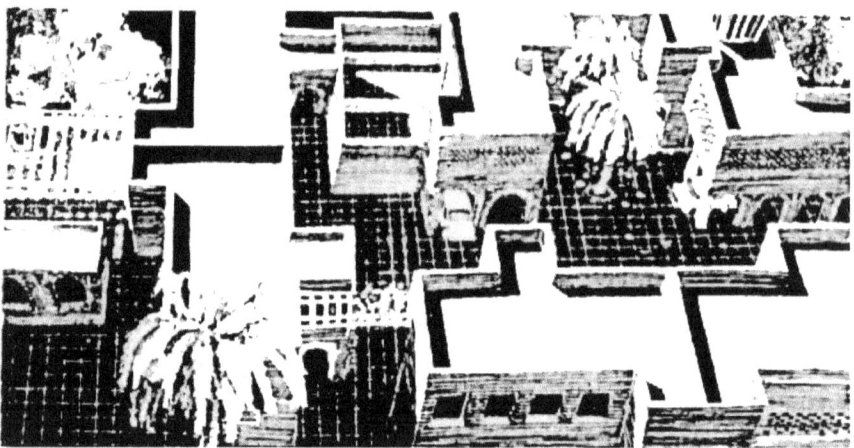

4.6 Amir Houshang Ardalan and Mandan Consulting Engineers, project for Khuzestan, *Competitions* book (1989).

project served as a precedent for the Mahshahr project.[79] The project, which was eventually constructed, was also based upon fieldwork in the region. Amir Houshang Ardalan described the design's objectives as consisting in economical construction, low upkeep, and functional in the severe climate. But beyond these aspects, he emphasized that the project had to respond to the local context:

> The structure of neighbourhoods, responding to light and topography and the heat and shade – all the stuff that has been in the south of Iran and a villager would build his house referring to them; we have been inspired by those very simply and considered movements, adjacencies, neighbourhoods, etc. but the luck we had was the possibility of horizontal movement.[80]

In Amir Houshang Ardalan's drawings, the intricate spatial network of a traditional town or village is evoked without deploying traditional motifs. He claimed that his design did not look to repeat past architectural forms, but instead addressed contemporary needs. Instead of being driven by technology, the design should subsume it, while serving its inhabitants.

Other projects, such as the first-prize winner for Hamedan, by Nader Kazemi-Nejad of Socnā Engineers, made explicit reference to the Islamic principles of seclusion of women in their justification: privacy (*harim*, *mahramiyat*) and prevention of overlooking (*eshrāf*). Kazemi-Nejad's scheme also emphasized the use of cul-de-sacs, presumably based on traditional *mahalleh* structures where such passages were often formed by only a few residences, sometimes one extended family. While the overall massing and planning is modern, a link to the past is supplied using masonry arches, walled courtyards, and habitable roof terraces (Figure 4.7).

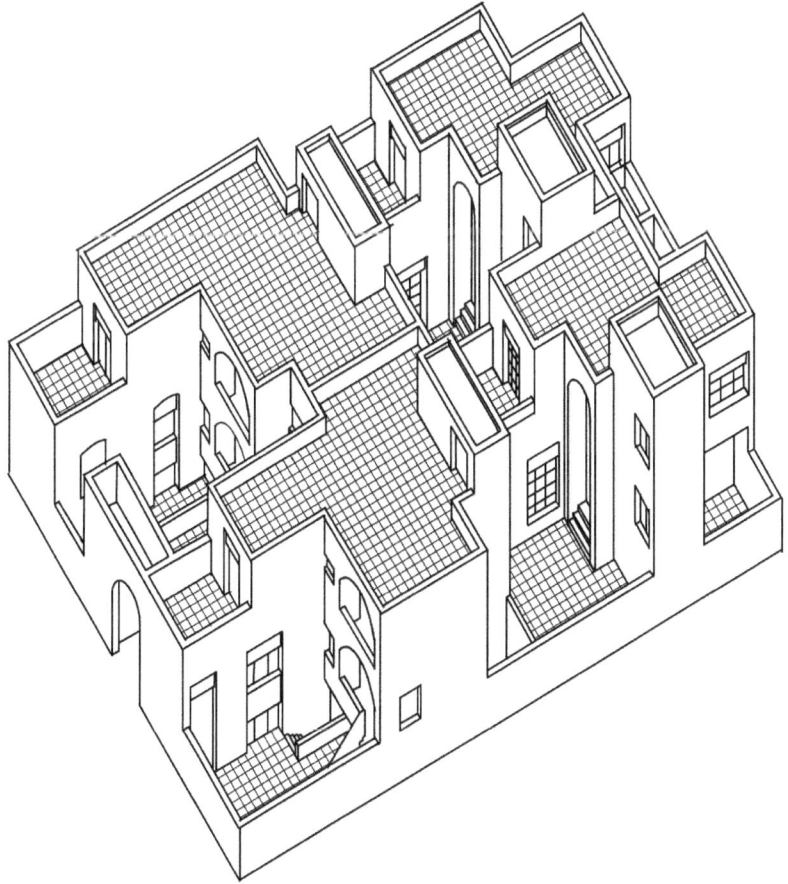

4.7 Nader Kazemi-Nejad of Socnā Engineers, first-prize winning project for Hamedan.

132   *Development, architecture, and the formation of heritage*

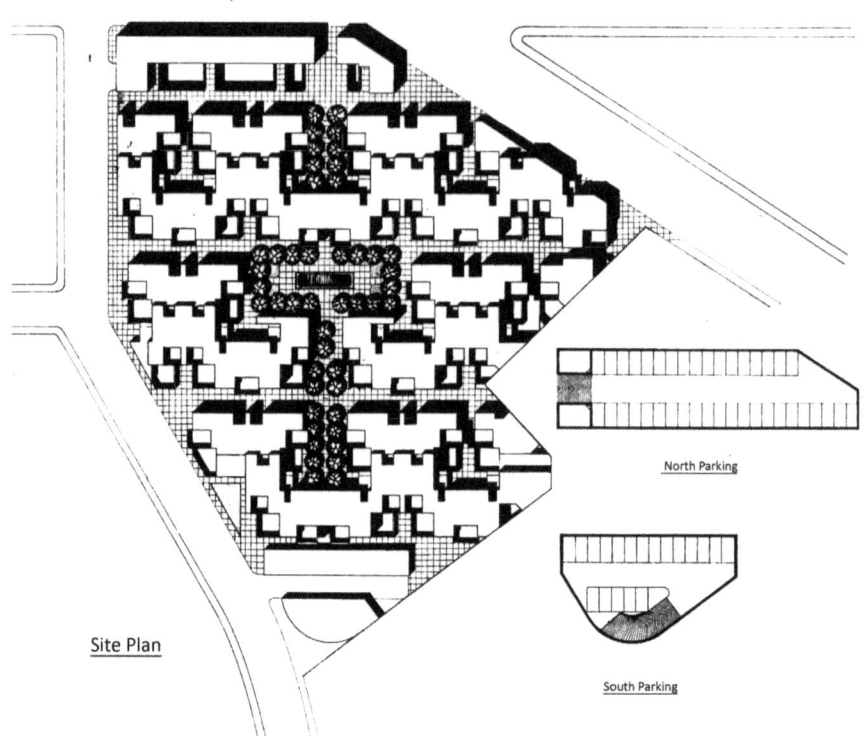

4.8 Giti Etemad, Tarh-va-Memari Architects and Planners, second-prize winning project for Hamedan.

Similarly, the second-place winner for Hamedan, Tarh Architects (Tarh-va-Memary Architects and Planners, founded by Giti Etemad in 1981), declared that '[the] urban design is inspired by traditional urban spaces ... eliminating their inadequacies', thus implying the adaptability of tradition and its operation as heritage. However, rather than aggrandizing tradition, the statement acknowledges its shortcomings (Figure 4.8).[81]

Sharestān Consulting Engineers, led by Behrouz Ahmadi (1946–2012),[82] in their third-place scheme for Hamedan, produced an interpretation of the pre-automobile city of narrow pedestrian streets and neighbourhood courtyards (Figure 4.9). This project represents a somewhat uneasy marriage of the fourfold garden with Western ideas of neighbourhood planning, the Iranian neighbourhood with the emergent principles of American new urbanism. Figuratively, the citations are clear and apparently the architects saw them as sufficient markers of 'Iranian-ness' in the design, its ambiguities notwithstanding. One wonders how the extended family-based *mahalleh* structure would function as a

Forming a future from the past 133

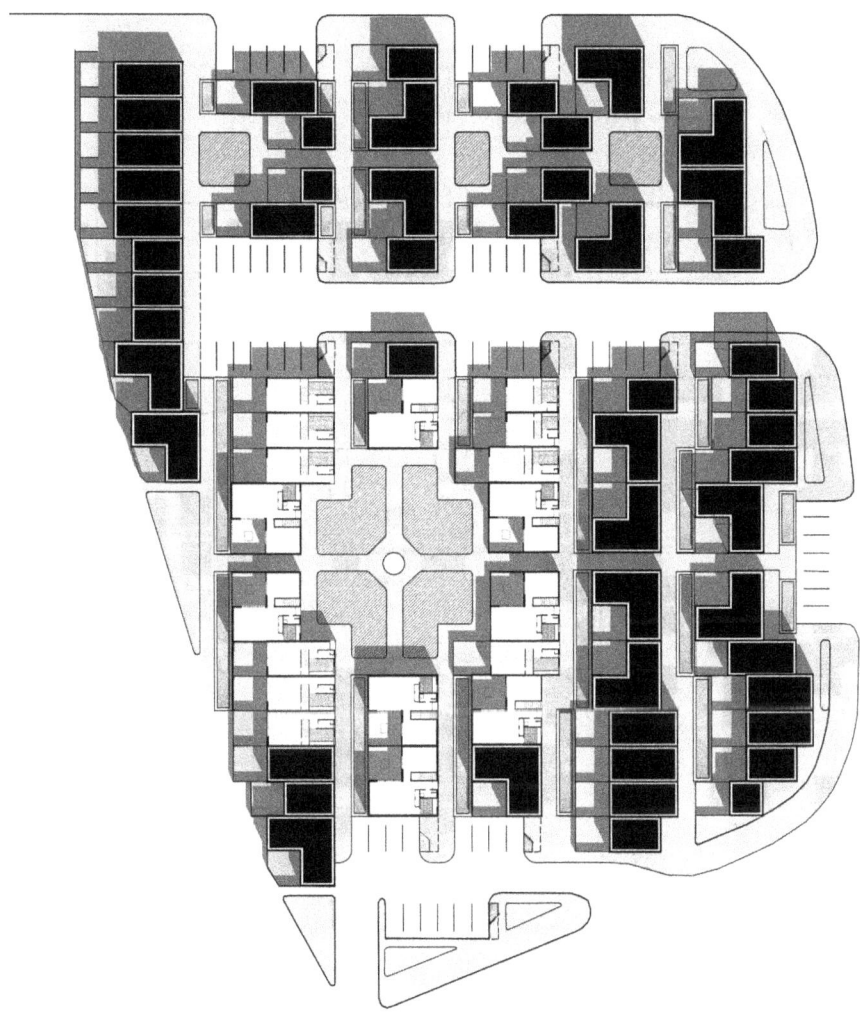

4.9 Behrouz Ahmadi, Sharestān Consulting Engineers, project for Hamedan.

neighbourhood for economic immigrants with little traditional association with the place.

In most of the entries, there is an overt intention, as Kazemi-Nejad expressed it, to satisfy spiritual and cultural needs as well as materialistic ones.[83] And yet, in most cases, the architect is presumptuous in ascribing to the end user a necessary set of preconceived spiritual inclinations. However, the overwhelming emphasis is rather upon tradition. A keyword search reveals that, of the nineteen published entries, twelve made reference to courtyards, ten to tradition, and seven to privacy, while there were many other references to traditional Iranian architectural elements.[84] Repeated citation of the elements that had constituted the traditional Iranian town seems incongruous for these projects, which were overwhelmingly proposed for satellite towns or suburbs of established industrializing towns and cities and where the housing typologies were essentially modern or modern interpretations.

This phenomenon may be explained in the context of three developments. Firstly, as discussed in Chapter 3, the vernacular, the traditional, and the village constituted fundamental tropes in the international search for authenticity in architecture and cities, a search that was inherently nostalgic. Secondly, this development occurred in the context of the burgeoning scholarship on environmental design and on traditional settlements, by Western scholars, some of whom were obsessed with authenticity.[85] Thirdly, authenticity and tradition also formed fundamental tropes in the Islamic Republic's ideology, as did the support for the 'oppressed', a group which was at times conflated and equated with traditional people. Therefore, such arguments found fertile ground in the Islamic Republic, which summoned particular and selective narratives of the past in its ideological programmes. The architectural corollary of these developments, which followed the pre-Revolution directions, was the attempt to mediate the social impacts upon displaced populations through design.

The housing designs published in the 1989 *Competitions* book reveal a hybrid discourse – a mixture of foreign theories and practices, local limitations, pervasive identity politics, and Iranian architectural practice – which weave in and out of each other to produce or reproduce approaches to housing that could also be interpreted by the Islamic Republic under the aegis of its ideological exhortations. But this hybridity, and its tenuous relationship with state ideology, is itself worthy of attention. The schemes are also responses to pressures of population settlement proceeding from the developmentalism of the Pahlavis and, as indicated, were forms of engagement with the past and the creation of heritage through design. They also signify the dominant, official mood in architectural production and education following the Revolution.

The heritage implications of Islamic identity discourses in architecture

According to the official explanation, the distribution of competition sites in nine cities indicated a national housing agenda by the Revolutionary state, the 'missing link' between master planning and housing resulting in controlling land speculation, serving vulnerable social groups, and creating economic activity independent of oil.[86] Alternatively, as an equally plausible explanation, it may have been a mixture of Pahlavi-era plans and happenstance, as has been the case in many developments since 1979. According to one participant, the publication of the book was in line with other developments in the country at the time:

Forming a future from the past 135

> [The general working conditions of the country as well as the intent behind conceiving the book] was a mess (chaos) and it [the situation] developed like an amoeba without well-conceived plan. The greatest talent of these people [those who took the reins of power in the field] was their opportunism [...] This book was one opportunity.[87]

Either way, as some of the first architectural competitions held since the Revolution, they constitute a useful body of evidence for the impact of the Islamic Republic upon architecture in its first and most radical phase, in wartime and under economic isolation. The rhetoric underlying the competitions reflected this, being couched in terms of a local resistance to globalization, and a nativist call for a circumscribed national and religious identity – the construction of a kind of modernity reflective of local traditions, and in the competition projects, conjuring an idealized past through design.

The competitions, despite references to the past, grew out of modernizing processes – industrialization, the construction of industrial and satellite cities, and the adoption of policies of regional development. Thus, the ambiguity at the heart of the competition projects lies in the question of whether they comprise the making, or merely imaging, of an authentic habitat, whose authenticity is derived from its connections with a past. To this end, the organizers and the jury pursued a nationwide policy of culturally appropriate housing in suburbs of historic cities, as well as in new towns, with only minor concessions to local differences. Thus, the competitions indicate that a particular relationship with a past – a version of official heritage[88] – was propagated by state apparatuses in the built environment and design. For the most part, the nostalgic pursuit of the authentic in the competitions' entries culminated in citations of ostensibly traditional Iranian architecture. Historical forms, such as the multi-generational courtyard house, bazaar, madrasa, caravanserai, and *chāhār-bāgh*, were deployed in new functional and social contexts – this nostalgic pursuit of authenticity transformed tradition into a set of tactics or actions in the world.[89] This strategy was modern in essence and moralizing in its intent – appeals for communal, consensual attitudes towards habitat were morally, rather than technically, based. In repeating rhetoric, in form and in language of justification, these projects produce an historicist semblance of authenticity, which shares in the alienating quality that Jameson identified in Western postmodernism, the reduction to image.[90] Nevertheless, this kind of nostalgic pursuit dominated the rhetoric and products of architectural practice and education alike for at least two decades after the Revolution.

But these efforts also indicated an ideological intention, the desire to effect social change through architectural form. In the citation of traditional architectural forms, spaces, and motifs in these projects, there was the attempt to create the semblance of the spatial, and by implication sociocultural, unity of traditional towns. The underlying presumption was that the design of places would instil, perpetuate, and sustain certain patterns of behaviour, which – given the intrusive nature of the Islamic establishment that dictated both public and private practices – was intended to lead to the cultural conditioning of citizens. In other words, this constituted architectural Islamization, an aspiration which has now been seen to have completely failed and is debunked in practice. As noted, this kind of Islamization was based on the production of a kind of architectural heritage that was interpreted in the service of the state, as a reified, congealed image of tradition. Here, the expertise of the architect was subservient to ideological domination, through the institution of official heritage, romanticizing traditional settlements, and forming nostalgic idealizations of the past, promoted by the state apparatus, which became entangled in the everyday life of the citizenry.

Pre- and post-Revolution continuities in architectural discourse

It is also possible to observe a continuum between pre- and post-Revolution periods in the emphasis upon a pursuit of authenticity and an engagement with tradition. This is apparent both in official rhetoric and in the practice of the architects, some of whom were trained or gained work experience under pre-Revolution figures such as Diba and Ardalan. There was a continuum, but with the difference that, here, diversity was stifled and silenced. And there was also an agenda of pacifying the fringe, meaning those who did not subscribe to the dominant interpretations of tradition, as well. In relation to the provision of culturally appropriate habitat, despite the shift in official rhetoric, there was little actual shift or evolution from the pre-Revolution discourses on culturally appropriate habitat, the likes of which had appeared in Diba's Shushtar Now project. Indeed, some of the more architecturally sophisticated projects, in their represented designs as well as in the authors' statements, appear to share similar concerns to those of Diba at Shushtar Now. Furthermore, the notion of a (partial) return to origins had also been a cultural policy of the monarchy, evidenced in the Shah's support of the appointment of the traditionalist Nasr as a university chancellor and advisor to the government on cultural matters.[91] But while Nasr extolled the virtues of a pure Islamic past and urged shedding the deleterious influence of Western secular customs,[92] from the time of Reza Shah a competing narrative persisted, one that turned upon an ancient Persian imagination of place. Attempts to combine and integrate the two would be apparent in various cultural productions, including in architecture – structures such as the Shahyad (now Azadi) monument in Tehran (see Chapter 5).[93] Indeed, the circle of intellectuals around the Queen had in the 1970s advocated for an indigenized modern architecture infused with the spirit of a 'timeless' Iranian culture, one that combined Islamic and pre-Islamic strands. The Islamic Republic maintained such a trajectory, but in so doing attempted to put historicist forms to work in support of a partial return to traditional practices and social codes. This endeavour was driven by an ideological understanding of religion that transcended the nation-state,[94] rather than asserting a patrimony, which, regardless of its Islamic or pre-Islamic emphasis, ultimately focused on nationhood.[95]

It is thus possible to say that both regimes attempted forms of heritage production through architectural design. There is, however, a small but significant difference between the policies of the Pahlavi monarchs and the Islamic Republic. Despite the official support for exploring relationships with tradition in general and perhaps Islamic tradition in particular, the Pahlavis did not circumscribe Iranian traditions and identity within an Islamic identity. Heritage was not construed in merely Islamic terms. The result was the possibility and potential for existence of multiple voices and strands in the design of both private and public buildings. By contrast, the Islamic Republic, especially in its early years, reduced and reified Iranian identity in official Islamic terms. There, official Islamic identity subsumed and silenced all difference.

The effects of the Islamic Revolution on the architecture of housing in Iran

Islamic identity discourses had practical consequences for design (and education, which falls outside the purview of this book). Within the practice of architectural design, and its representational techniques, interpretation of tradition inevitably necessitated a degree of abstraction and theorization, while the valorization of traditional techniques, and their incorporation into a personal design language risked, and still risks, fetishization of old motifs, again displacing them from a contextual continuity. Whereas 'materialist' elite culture architecture was seen to be bound to the vagaries of fashion, vernacular housing was, supposedly, timeless.[96] Again, this straight-jacketing of non-Western habitat as unchanging contains within it a profoundly objectifying position, another form of (self-)Orientalism. But it is also a nostalgic reaction to the loss of perceived continuity with the past, a quest for identity. Here, images of tradition play a double role – at once looking into the past but also projecting an ideal moral community into the future. This amounts to the employment of a heritage process, suggesting the desire for a historicist architecture that was transformational, but also rooted in an imagined, bygone golden age.[97] The commissioning authorities encouraged modern architects to learn from the past, ironically recalling the title of the international festival of postmodernism, Paolo Portoghesi's curated exhibition at the 1980 Venice Biennale: *The Presence of the Past*.[98]

How then did the published entries to these 1985 housing competitions reflect the evolving discourse of architecture after the Islamic Revolution, when from the perspective of the authorities, emphasis was placed upon the need to create an authentic habitat that would respect, and reinforce, local traditions, culture, and religious beliefs? The Revolution, and the creation of the Islamic Republic, exerted a profound effect upon both the opportunities for the creation of new forms of architecture, but also upon the representational modes, the visual and symbolic language of architecture, deployed for projects which had a public, or in the case of the housing competitions a social, character. The Revolution created a hiatus in contact between Iran and the West caused by trade embargoes and cultural isolation, which created the artificial situation of a cultural bubble.[99] As noted at the beginning of this chapter, there was a shortage of international publications such as books and magazines in the university architecture libraries. But this was not to say that currents occurring outside of Iran were not detected – there were furtive private attempts to import such publications, leading to the widespread distribution of photocopied versions, in a kind of *Samizdat* operation.[100] In this state of relative isolation, architects were, ironically, free to interpret the meagre resources in ways that suited their, and their clients', perspectives and requirements. The influence of the Revolution was felt both in the language of, and attitude towards, architecture. In the early years, it would appear that individualistic approaches ran the risk of being labelled 'materialist', just as the competitions judges had condemned what they called 'anti-values' and 'pretentious models which can lead to false values and standards in people's (social) life'.[101] In this climate, designers arguably became more circumspect and introspective in attempting innovation. Certainly, the inventive design approaches of the 1970s were missing. The discourse in architectural journals in the decade after the Revolution revealed little new material, instead focusing on non-controversial 'professional' issues, indicating the attempt to adapt to new, more difficult circumstances, and to fill a perceived gap between the Iranian reality and the world of architecture in the West. It was in this respect that one could perhaps see the efforts as representing a kind of regionalism. Within these constraints, Iranian architects creatively acted upon the diverse and fragmentary sources, reframing them – in a sense reinscribing them – with a local, and for some ideologically weighted significance, through which Iranian heritage and tradition was reinvented, that is, designed, in the present. The tensions embedded in this process, the shift from the rigid and fetishistic conception of tradition to a reflexive one, are evident in this statement by Hossein Sheikh Zeineddin:[102]

> After the Revolution we were all part of this massive wave of identitarianism and thought it is now time that we produce something ourselves rather than remaining disciples [of the West]. Everyone, from the late Mirmiran to Mr Ahmadi to myself and others, we all tried, and it was part of [...] our growth [...] our identity; [it] is what we build not what we inherit. What we inherit [heritage] is our treasure, we use this treasure to build our identity [...] Only at this late stage in my career I have learned how much I could use my treasure [for my designs rather] than [be] the person who only copies [the past].

Notes

1 H. Mahmoudiyan, 'Internal Migration and Urbanization in Iran: Status Quo, Challenges and Policy Guidelines', *Policy Papers: Emerging Population Issues in IR*

of Iran, 1:1 (2015), pp. 47–55; Z. Fanni, 'Cities and Urbanization in Iran after the Islamic Revolution', *Cities*, 23:6 (2006), pp. 407–11.
2 An earlier article erroneously identified this date as 1986. See Mozaffari and Westbrook, 'Designing a Revolutionary Habitat'.
3 Department of Housing and Development (Islamic Republic of Iran), *Housing Complexes Design Competition* (Department of Housing, September 1989) [مسکن های مجتمع طراحی مسابقه]; see also R. F. Farahani et al., 'The Impact of Architectural Competitions on the Improvement of the Post-Revolution Architecture in Iran', *International Journal of Architecture and Urban Development*, 2:2 (2012), pp. 35–44.
4 H. Akhavi-Pour, 'The Economy', in G. E. Curtis and E. Hooglund (eds), *Iran: A Country Study* (Washington, DC: Federal Research Division, Library of Congress, 2008), pp. 155–6.
5 Boroujerdi, *Iranian Intellectuals*, pp. 11–12.
6 H. Zanjani, 'Housing in Iran', *Encyclopædia Iranica*, Volume XII Fasc. 5, 2012 [2004], pp. 535–40, www.iranicaonline.org/articles/housing-in-iran (accessed 21 October 2018); N. R. Keddie, 'Iranian Revolutions in Comparative Perspective', *The American Historical Review*, 88:3 (1983), p. 588; Parsa, *Social Origins*, p. 77.
7 Constitution of the Islamic Republic of Iran 1979, 'The Form of Governance in Islam', World Intellectual Property Organization (WIPO), amended 28 July 1989, https://wipolex.wipo.int/en/text/332330 (accessed January 21, 2018).
8 Islamic Republic Constitution, art. III, cl. 12.
9 Islamic Republic Constitution, ch. IIII, art. XLIII, cl. 1.
10 A. K. Tibaijuka, *Building Prosperity: Housing and Economic Development* (Abingdon: Routledge, 2013), pp. 7–11; D. McCallum and S. Benjamin, 'Low-Income Urban Housing in the Third World: Broadening the Economic Perspective', *Urban Studies*, 22:4 (1985), pp. 277–287, https://doi.org/10.1080/00420988520080521.
11 On the relationship between ideology and material aesthetics, see D. Harvey, *Condition of Postmodernity*; D. Harvey, 'Die Postmoderne und die Verdichtung von Raum und Zeit (The Postmodern and the Compression of Space and Time)', in A. Kuhlmann (ed.), *Philosophische Ansichten der Kultur der Moderne* (Frankfurt: Fischer Taschenbuch Verlag, 1994), pp. 48–78; K. Goonewardena, 'The Urban Sensorium: Space, Ideology and the Aestheticization of Politics', *Antipode*, 37:1 (2005), pp. 46–71; M. Müller, 'Avant-Garde, Aestheticization and the Economy', *Footprint*, 5:11 (Spring, 2011), pp. 7–22, https://journals.open.tudelft.nl/index.php/footprint/article/view/729/905.
12 F. Urban, *Tower and Slab: Histories of Global Mass Housing* (Abingdon: Routledge, 2013), pp. 59–78.
13 A. Najmabadi, 'Hazards of Modernity and Morality: Women, State and Ideology in Contemporary Iran', in D. Kandiyoti (ed.), *Women, Islam and the State* (London: MacMillan Press, 1991), pp. 65–8; A. Najmabadi, 'Feminism in an Islamic Republic: Years of Hardship, Years of Growth', in Y. Haddad and J. L. Esposito (eds), *Islam, Gender, and Social Change* (New York: Oxford University Press, 1998), pp. 59–84; P. Paidar, 'Gender of Democracy: The Encounter between Feminism and Reformism in Contemporary Iran', UNRISD Democracy, Governance and Human Rights Programme Paper 6 (2001), p. 3; A. Kian, 'Gendered Occupation

and Women's Status in Post-revolutionary Iran', *Middle Eastern Studies*, 31:3 (1995), pp. 407–21.
14 M. Nafisi, 'Khamenei's Fight against "Un-Islamic" Architecture in Iran', *Your Middle East*, 12 December 2014, https://yourmiddleeast.com/2014/12/12/khameneis-fight-against-un-islamic-architecture-in-iran/ (accessed 26 May 2015).
15 The Housing Foundation of the Islamic Revolution (HFIR) came into existence on 11 April 1979 by order of Ayatollah Khomeini and was directed towards the provision of housing for the 'oppressed' and 'underprivileged': https://bonyadmaskan.ir [ا سلا می اذ قلاب مسکن بنیا د].
16 Since 6 August 1993, this organization was restructured into the National Organization for Land and Housing and remains under the aegis of the Ministry of Roads and Urban Development. For further information, see: www.nlho.ir/index.jsp?fkeyid=&siteid=1&pageid=132.
17 Department of Housing and Development, *Housing Complexes*, p. 9.
18 The Act is available through the web portal of the Islamic Parliament Research Center of the Islamic Republic of Iran: http://rc.majlis.ir/fa/law/show/110931.
19 Department of Housing and Development, *Housing Complexes*, p. 9.
20 Mozaffari and Westbrook, 'Designing a Revolutionary Habitat,' pp. 185–211.
21 G. Memarian and F. E. Brown, 'Climate, Culture, and Religion: Aspects of the Traditional Courtyard House in Iran', *Journal of Architectural and Planning Research*, 20:3 (2003), p. 190; see also M. Sadoughianzadeh, 'Gender Structure and Spatial Organization: Iranian Traditional Spaces', *SAGE Open*, 3:4 (2013), p. 5.
22 T. Eagleton, *Ideology: An Introduction* (London and New York: Verso, 1991), p. 195.
23 S. Akhavi, 'Islam, Politics and Society in the Thought of Ayatullah Khomeini Taliqani and Ali Shariati', *Middle Eastern Studies*, 24:4 (1988), pp. 404–31; Mirsepassi, *Intellectual Discourse*, p. 11.
24 J. Rykwert, 'The Idea of a Town', *Forum*, 3 (1963), pp. 99–148; J. Rykwert, *The Idea of a Town: The Anthropology of Urban Form in Rome, Italy and the Ancient World* (London: Faber and Faber, 1976); see also G. Teyssot, 'Aldo Van Eyck and the Rise of an Ethnographic Paradigm in the 1960s', *Joelho: Revista de Cultura Arquitectónica*, Intersecções: Antropologia e Arquitectura, 2 (April, 2011), pp. 50–67.
25 Mozaffari's recollection of architectural education at the University of Tehran.
26 Roudbari, 'Instituting Architecture', pp. 309–16.
27 F. Garofalo and L. Veresani, *Adalberto Libera* (New York: Princeton Architectural Press, 1992), pp. 39–47, 149–55; M. Casciato, 'Neorealism in Italian Architecture', in Goldhagen and Legault (eds), *Anxious Modernisms*, pp. 25–53; Tafuri, *History of Italian Architecture*, pp. 3–33, 41–8; S. Z. Pilat, *Reconstructing Italy: The Ina-Casa Neighborhoods of the Postwar Era* (Oxford and New York: Routledge, 2014).
28 Aga Khan is the leader of the Ismailis, a Shi'ite sect that, although originating in Iran, is different to the dominant Iranian sect of Twelver Shiism. The Ismaili leaders refer to themselves as Imam – the title of a religious leader for all Muslim masses – which put them in direct competition with Iran's revolutionary leader, Imam Khomeini. Diba had been proscribed by virtue of being the Queen's cousin, thus while his project was an obvious model for new housing projects referencing tradition, it was not cited by the competition judges.
29 Ardalan, interview with Mozaffari, 2017.
30 See R. Razav, 'The Cultural Revolution in Iran, with Close Regard to the

Forming a future from the past 141

Universities, and Its Impact on the Student Movement', *Middle Eastern Studies*, 45:1 (2009), pp. 1–17.
31 *Honar-o-memari* (*Art and Architecture*) was the leading Iranian architectural journal in the 1970s. See Roudbari, 'Instituting Architecture', pp. 287–332.
32 In the words of Shafe`i, 'it was fashionable to trail academics who were (seen to be related to) the previous regime'. B. Shafe`i, interview with A. Mozaffari, Tehran, 2017.
33 S. Golkar, 'Cultural Engineering under Authoritarian Regimes: Islamization of Universities in Postrevolutionary Iran', *DOMES: Digest of Middle East Studies*, 21:1 (2012), p. 2.
34 Ardalan, interview with Mozaffari, 2017.
35 Pour-Keramati and Ghaffari worked at the Shahid Beheshti (Melli) University. Sheikh Zeineddin was a prominent architect and also affiliated with the ultra-conservative Iran Science and Technology University in Tehran.
36 This may have been the vice president – head of the management and planning organization.
37 N. R. Nahad, *Cultural Revolution in Islamic Republic of Iran* [*Enghelabe Farhangi dar Jomhoorie Eslamie Iran*] (Tehran: Markaze Asnade Enghelabe Eslami [Centre for Islamic Revolution Documents], 2004), pp. 32–33.
38 A. Gheissari and V. Nasr, 'Iran's Democracy Debate', *Middle East Policy*, 11:2 (Summer, 2004), p. 94.
39 S. Mazumdar and Sh. Mazumdar, 'Societal Values and Architecture: A Socio-physical Model of the Inter-relationships', *Journal of Architectural and Planning Research*, 11:1 (1994), pp. 66–90.
40 Mazumdar and Mazumdar, 'Societal Values and Architecture', p. 83.
41 H. Shadar, 'Between East and West: Immigrants, Critical Regionalism and Public Housing', *The Journal of Architecture*, 9:1 (2004), pp. 23–48; A. Glikson, 'L'Unité d'Habitation Intégrale', *Le Carré Bleu*, 1 (1962), pp. 1–6; R. W. Marans, 'Neighborhood Planning: The Contributions of Artur Glikson', *Journal of Architectural and Planning Research*, 21:2 (2004), pp. 112–24; R. Kallus, 'Nation-Building Modernism and European Post-war Debates: Glikson's "Integral Habitational Unit" and Team 10 Discourse', *Architectural Research Quarterly*, 18 (2014), pp. 123–33.
42 Sheikh Zeineddin, interview with Mozaffari, 2013.
43 M. Taussig, *Mimesis and Alterity: A Particular History of the Senses* (London and New York: Routledge, 2018).
44 V. Turner, *The Forest of Symbols: Aspects of Ndembu Ritual* (Ithaca, NY, and London: Cornell University Press, 1970), especially ch. 2.
45 Smith, *Uses of Heritage*.
46 Harrison, *Heritage*, pp. 15–20.
47 M. Foucault, *The Foucault Effect: Studies in Governmentality* (Chicago, IL: The University of Chicago Press, 1991).
48 Mozaffari, *Forming National Identity*, pp. 8–10.
49 و. پور کرامتی، 'اهداف برگزاری مسابقات'، در وزارت مسکن و شهرسازی-واحد امور مسکن، مسابقه طراحی مجموعه های مسکونی (تهران: وزارت مسکن و شهرسازی، ۱۳۶۸)، ص. ۱۵.
50 Mozaffari and Westbrook, 'Designing a Revolutionary Habitat', pp. 185–211.
51 پور کرامتی، 'اهداف برگزاری مسابقات'، ص. ۱۵.

52 Mozaffari, *Forming National Identity*, pp. 173–4.
53 پور کرامتی، 'اهداف برگزاری مسابقات'، ص. ۱۵.
54 Tunbridge and Ashworth, *Dissonant Heritage*.
55 Here, parallels can be drawn, not just with Kamran Diba's interest in exploiting the local crafts of the Shushtar masons, but also the interest of Indian architects Charles Correa and Balkrishna Doshi in regional crafts and spatial patterns in the 1970s and 1980s. Doshi attended the 1974 Persepolis congress as a foreign delegate, while Correa visited Iran as a judge in the 1978 National Library competition.
56 پور کرامتی، 'اهداف برگزاری مسابقات'، ص. ۱۶.
57 H. Fathy, *Architecture for the Poor: An Experiment in Rural Egypt* (Chicago, IL: The University of Chicago Press, 1976 [1973]).
58 Bryant, 'Nostalgia and Discovery', pp. 155–77.
59 S. H. Nasr, 'The Contemporary Muslim, and the Architectural Transformation of the Islamic Urban Environment', in Renata Holod (ed.), *Towards an Architecture in the Spirit of Islam* (Aiglemont: The Aga Khan Award for Architecture, 1978), p. 3.
60 Hossein Sheikh Zeineddin is the managing director of Bavand Consulting Engineers, one of Iran's more significant architectural firms.
61 B. Hanson, 'The "Westoxication" of Iran: Depictions and Reactions of Behrangi, Āl-e Ahmad, and Shariati', *International Journal of Middle East Studies*, 15:1 (1983), pp. 1–23.
62 پور کرامتی، 'اهداف برگزاری مسابقات'، صص. ۱۲–۱۴.
63 S. H. Nasr, 'Islam, the Contemporary Islamic World, and the Environmental Crisis', in R. C. Foltz et al. (eds), *Islam and Ecology: A Bestowed Trust* (Cambridge, MA: Harvard University Press, 2003), pp. 85–105.
64 پور کرامتی، 'اهداف برگزاری مسابقات'، صص. ۱۱–۱۳.
65 پور کرامتی، 'اهداف برگزاری مسابقات'، صص. ۱۲–۱۳.
66 R. Venturi et al., *Learning From Las Vegas: The Forgotten Symbolism of Architectural Form* (Cambridge, MA: MIT Press, 1977); A. Vinegar and M. J. Golec, *Relearning from Las Vegas* (Minneapolis, MN: University of Minnesota Press, 2009), p. 10; Alexander et al., *A Pattern Language*.
67 Sheikh Zeineddin's approach to working with, and adapting, traditional architecture is seen in his Allameh Dehkhoda University in Qazvin, of 1989, with its mildly historicist references to Qajar portals, but more so in his Aga Khan Awards nominated Darolshefa Bazaar Bridge (1997–99) which, he argued, was based upon the precedents of the Safavid bridges over the Zayanderud in Isfahan.
68 S. Skurvida, 'Iranian or Not: DisLocations of Contemporary Art and Its Histories', *Art Journal*, 74:3 (2015), pp. 73–7, review of H. Keshmirshekan, *Contemporary Iranian Art: New Perspectives* (London: Saqi, 2013); T. Grigor, *Contemporary Iranian Art: From the Street to the Studio* (London: Reaktion, 2014).
69 Shafe`i, interview with Mozaffari, 2017.
70 Iranian Ministry for Higher Education, Curriculum for Master of Architecture course, Tehran, 1984 (translated).
71 K. T. Diba, 'The Recent Housing Boom in Iran – Lessons to Remember', in L. Safran (ed.), *Housing: Process and Physical Form*, Proceedings of Seminar Three in the series Architectural Transformations in the Islamic World, Jakarta, Indonesia, 26–29 March 1979 (Philadelphia, PA: The Aga Khan Award for Architecture,

1980); Khan (ed.), 'Shushtar New Town'; Serageldin, 'Shushtar New Town'; K. T. Diba, 'Aspects of a University Project and a New Town in Iran', in W. Reilly (ed.), *Sustainable Landscape Design in Arid Climates* (Geneva: Aga Khan Trust for Culture, 1989), pp. 34–7.
72 J. Stirling, *James Stirling: Buildings and Projects 1950–1974* (Oxford: Oxford University Press, 1974); see also Mozaffari and Westbrook, 'Designing a Revolutionary Habitat', p. 198.
73 A.-A. Saremi, 'Recherche d'un Nouveau Vocabulaire', *l'Architecture d'Aujourd'hui*, 195 (1978), p. 28.
74 See, for example, M. Gandelsonas and D. Morton, 'On Reading Architecture', *Progressive Architecture* (March, 1972), pp. 29–59.
75 Faghih obtained a doctorate at the IUAV (Istituto Universitario di Architettura di Venezia), Venice, in 1969, a town planning degree from E.P.H. Paris in 1971, and a master's in environmental design at Yale University in 1974.
76 Saremi cited in Mozaffari and Westbrook, 'Designing a Revolutionary Habitat', pp. 185–211.
77 صارمی، س.ع.ا.، تار و پود و هنوز ... سرگذشت من و معماری ما (تهران: هنر معماری قرن، ۱۳۸۹)، صص. ۱۹–۲۹.
78 For Mahshahr, see 'NPI Housing Mahshahr', *Archnet*, https://archnet.org/media_contents/16006 (accessed September 13, 2017).
79 Ardalan, interview with Mozaffari, 2017.
80 Ardalan, interview with Mozaffari, 2017.
81 In an interview with Ali Mozaffari in 2017, Etemad rejected the existence of an 'Islamic urbanism'.
82 Behrouz Ahmadi became a major figure in Iranian architecture post-Revolution. He was appointed project architect of the Quran Museum (1995–98), originally designed as the Negarestan Cultural Centre in 1976–78 by Manouchehr Iranpour for the Pahlavi government, the renovation of the Ferdowsi museum in Tus (2003–5), designed by Houshang Seyhoun, as well as the façade of the new Iranian Parliament House in central Tehran (2001), based upon the abstraction of a traditional Iranian tile pattern.
83 پور کرامتی، 'اهداف برگزاری مسابقات'، ص. ۴۳.
84 The most commonly used terms in the architects' descriptions of their projects are: courtyard (12 times); tradition (10); neighbourhood (8); privacy (7); overlooking (7); environment (7); religion/religious (6); region/regional (6); cultural (6); indigenous (6); bazaar (5); garden (5); introversion/introvert (5); mosque (3); Islam/Islamic (3); *eyvān* (3); harmony (3); identity (2); culture (2); *mahalla* (2); *harim* (2); boundaries/bounded (2); *chāhār-bāgh*/fourfold gardens (1); nostalgic (1); past ()1; alley (1); *caravansārāy* (1); spiritual (1); *hashti*/vestibule (1).
85 On Western scholarship on traditional settlements, see Rudofsky, *Architecture without Architects*; Scott, 'Bernard Rudofsky'; Rapoport, *House, Form and Culture*; Oliver (ed.), *Shelter and Society*. The title of Rapoport's book, *House, Form and Culture*, was published and translated into Persian by Razieh Rezazadeh in 1987 and published by the ideologically Islamist wing of the Student Association in Iran, *Jihad-e Daneshgahi*, at the University of Tehran; thus a year later than the competitions, the post-revolutionary architectural profession was familiar with Rapoport's book:

راپاپورت، آمس، (1366) ،منشاء فرهنگی مجتمع های زیستی، رضازاده، راضیه، جهاد دانشگاهی علم و صنعت ایران، تهران.

86 Department of Housing and Development, *Housing Complexes*, pp. 11–12.
87 Ardalan, interview with Mozaffari, 2017.
88 Harrison, *Heritage*.
89 M. de Certeau, *The Practice of Everyday Life*, trans. S. Rendall (Berkeley, CA: University of California Press, 1984), pp. 94–5.
90 F. Jameson, *Postmodernism or, the Cultural Logic of Late Capitalism* (Durham, NC: Duke University Press, 1991), pp. 98–99.
91 Ziya'i, 'Nasr'.
92 Nasr, 'The Contemporary Muslim'.
93 Mozaffari, *Forming National Identity*, pp. 34–43.
94 Mozaffari, *Forming National Identity*, pp. 214–15.
95 Nonetheless, in recent decades, there has been a return to the nationalist use of ancient monuments enlisted in support of contemporary political agendas. For example, then-president Ahmadinejad was officially photographed in 2006 making an acclamation in front of a pair of Achaemenid bull-man sculptures at the entrance of the Gate of All Nations in Persepolis. See: www.chinadaily.com.cn/world/2007–04/20/content_855319.htm.
96 M. Eliade, *Cosmos and History: The Myth of the Eternal Return* (New York: Harper Torchbooks, 1959), cited in Rapoport, *House, Form and Culture*, p. 15.
97 On heritage as a design process, see R. Harrison, 'Heritage and Globalization', in E. Waterton and S. Watson (eds), *The Palgrave Handbook of Contemporary Heritage Research* (New York: Palgrave, 2015), pp. 303–4.
98 G. Borsano and P. Portoghesi (eds), *The Presence of the Past: First International Exhibition of Architecture – The Corderia of the Asrsenale: la Bienale di Venezia* (London: Academy Editions, 1980).
99 Here, by 'West' we include other actors in the global architectural discourse, such as Japan, India, and the Soviet Union.
100 Roudbari, 'Instituting Architecture', pp. 314–15.
101 Ghaffari cited in:

پور کرامتی، 'اهداف برگزاری مسابقات'، ص. 20.

102 Sheikh Zeineddin, interview with Mozaffari, 2013.

5

Forming a national image through public projects: The Shahyad Arya-Mehr Tower

> The monument of Shahyad Ariamehr is being built near Teheran to celebrate the 25th centenary of the foundation of the Iranian Empire, and of the Declaration of Human Rights by Cyrus the Great. As is fitting for such an occasion, it is a monument to the past – its inspiration clearly coming from traditional design. But it has another purpose concerned very much with today.[1]

> I think one of the reasons that Persians feel so close to Shahyad Tower is that it is reminiscent of Ctesiphon [the capital of the Persian Sassanian Empire near Baghdad].[2]

Introduction

Perhaps the most obvious and readily available instances of design and heritage are found in public buildings and monuments intended to represent the nation. Through these edifices, competing notions of collective identity and memory as well as divergent senses of nostalgia are expressed and performed. Despite their static appearance, these edifices have multiple lives – they construct heritage and in time become objects of heritage in their own right. In this chapter we examine one such structure: the Shahyad Arya-Mehr (and since the Revolution, Azadi) Tower. We examine this edifice as the product of the development–culture relationship in Iran, in relation to its design and its implications for, and continuing relevance to, discourses of heritage.

The Shahyad Tower is still the most striking monument in the Iranian capital of Tehran. While serving as a new symbolic gateway into the city, it also comprises a public park and museum complex. But the fluidity of the monument's meanings arguably constitute its most interesting aspect, illustrating the role of design in the fabrication of national architectural heritage.[3] The Shahyad monument was evidently constructed both as a representation of power, and as a vehicle for the exercising of that power, as attested by the many occasions

146   *Development, architecture, and the formation of heritage*

5.1 Official opening ceremony of the Shahyad.

when it was used as a monumental backdrop for official photographs,[4] as well as by the presence of a museum of Iranian development located underneath it (Figures 5.1 and 5.2).

However, in time, the elements of the design created to effect these aims – the powerful archway forming both the centrepiece of a vast space and an intentional national symbol, and its citation and invocation of motifs from

Forming a national image through public projects   147

5.2 The opening of the Shahyad 6 Bahman Museum with the presence of Queen Farah (26 January 1971).

pre-Islamic and Islamic periods of Persian culture – produced an inverted effect as the monument became the potent symbol of the Islamic Revolution and other social upheavals in the following decades (Figure 5.3). At key historical moments, hegemonic powers have been contested by groups who have appropriated the monument and its setting for their own causes.[5] In this respect, the project demonstrates both the impossibility of constructing an immutable image of identity through architecture, and conversely the capacity of such architectural forms, and their reproduction in multiple images, to influence and engage with a national imagination that recognizes the presence of a collective past. Here, Bakhtyar Lotfi argues that monuments like the Shahyad-Azadi 'gate' possess 'spatial agency'. That is to say, they are part of a 'socially embedded network'.[6] But beyond this imbrication in more extensive networks of identification, implied significance, and power, the Shahyad-Azadi monument can also be understood as a mnemonic instrument. Through its syncretic incorporations, moments of the past are dragged into the present, in what Walter Benjamin described as a constellation, 'the "time of the now" which is shot through with chips of Messianic time'.[7]

5.3 The Shahyad during the uprisings of the Islamic Revolution.

Scholarship on the Shahyad monument

Despite the significance of the Shahyad-Azadi monument, the published scholarship about it is dominated by familiar tropes about Iran. Thus, in a retrospective critique of the monument, Talinn Grigor has approached it from the Foucauldian narrative of power, arguing that '[the] Shahyad allegorically evoked the image of the monarch, his absolute power, and his role in the destiny of the nation-state'.[8] Through such monuments, she notes, institutions construct 'figures of memory',[9] in service of the Shah's attempted imposition of a homogenous Iranian identity, which was 'official and unchanging'. Both this construction of identity through memory, as well as the disciplinary memory consisting of techniques, orders, and the like, partake of 'cultural memory'.[10] Memory intervenes in social flux through cultural formations and social performances. This intervention culminates in 'figures of history', which engender dissonance between the mutability of historical processes and the attempt to utilize monuments like the Shahyad to project a symbolic fixity.[11] According to Grigor, power thus creates social meaning and cultural memory.[12]

In short, the monument was intended by the Shah to monumentalize his legacy. Its syncretic design, which incorporates both pre-Islamic and Islamic citations, further serves to connect the Pahlavi monarch to the legitimizing past of both the Achaemenid founders of the Persian Empire and the Islamic golden era represented by the monuments of Isfahan, Yazd, Mashhad, Kerman, and other centres. There are, however, problems associated with such interpretations of historic monuments in Iran. To begin with, in the absence of sufficient fieldwork that might evaluate the reception of the monument by the public, propositions about reception of figures of memory and their effect on collective identity-making, including those posited here by Grigor, cannot be verified.

To assume that the spectators of the monument receive the exact meaning intended by the source of power (in this case the monarchy) is to discount their agency in ascribing meaning to it. And yet, the highly fluid historical engagement of this monument with its audience, its 'career', such as the appropriation of the monument both by revolutionary crowds in 1979, and by anti-regime protesters of the Green Movement in 2009, suggests otherwise.[13] Secondly, such an explanation fails to account for the complexity of the architectural design, and its role as part of an ensemble that forms connections with the surrounding district. The reception of its meaning by the public may also vary from the symbolic meanings intended for it by its architect Hossein Amanat, or the Pahlavi government. Thirdly, the explanation sidesteps heritage processes, which are concerned with fleeting and retrospective reimaginings of past–present–future trajectories. In any heritage process, the past is reconstituted in the present, a temporal designation that is, by definition, shifting, and to which things cannot be 'fixed', just as nostalgias represent different and shifting emotional structures in time. Finally, a fixation on the constructed nature of social and architectural phenomena as a point of critique distracts from the actual process of production of both architecture and heritage. Isn't everything constructed, after all? Explaining phenomena away as constructed may be less fruitful than seeking to understand how they are constructed, to what extent such constructions are stable or unstable, and what this might imply.

While Grigor correctly discerns dissonance in this monument, this is to be expected as a product of the convergence of multiple intentionalities upon the same site, concurrently or otherwise.[14] Here, through focusing on its heritage aspect, we will go beyond the monument's 'power critique' and examine how it is appropriated and received. For example, despite multiple ascriptions of meanings, are there references to ideas of collective heritage and culture that transcend political regime and persist through time? We argue that there is a particular kind of future-oriented nostalgia in the Shahyad that has to be understood in the larger urban context and, as such, the edifice constitutes or constructs a heritage that is constantly invoked and activated; social memories are constructed in action both by successive administrations and their detractors. The meanings of the monument are mutable (which Grigor does note), and subject to multiple reinscriptions. In the Shahyad, as discussed below, nostalgia and heritage are expressions of the condition of modernity and are closely connected to development.

Architectural analysis

The history of the monument's conception is well known.[15] The Shahyad monument was completed in 1971, after a competition held in 1966 for its design was won by the recently graduated architect Hossein Amanat, and a documentation and construction phase during which he collaborated with his mentor, the eminent Iranian architect Houshang Seyhoun, and the London engineering practice of Ove Arup.[16] It was thus a fusion of local cultural expression and global technology. Opened in 1971 as part of the commemorations celebrating the 2,500 years since the birth of the Persian Empire, the Shahyad monument's programme was, given the contested political situation of the time, ideological in origin.[17] In its commemoration of the Shah himself – its original title, Shahyad Arya-Mehr, translates as 'Monument of the Shah, Light of the Aryans [i.e. Iranians]' – Shahyad also served as the assertion of a national identity and unity. This was projected by its design, incorporating abstractions of motifs from the pre-Islamic and Islamic eras, the original curatorial programme housed in its museum, and the Cyrus Cylinder, loaned to Iran by the British Museum for the duration of the above commemorations. More than any other building of the pre-Revolution period, the Shahyad monument's material presence asserts a common heritage and identity. Amanat's highly syncretic design evokes both the past[18] and the future, and in so doing invokes what Herzfeld has termed 'monumental time', the official account of a nation's collective experience, objectified in architecture, which may be overtaken and muted by events.[19] These qualities were recognized by its listing as modern heritage on 17 March 1975 following Iranian legislation, which was itself inspired by international developments in recognition of contemporary (modern) architectural heritage (Figure 5.4).

However, the Shahyad cannot be understood purely in art historical terms – it also forms the central node of a greater urban project. The futuristic western gateway to the city was located near Tehran's Mehrabad International Airport, which had been used as an airstrip from the 1930s, but in 1972 was inaugurated as the national airport.[20] Postage stamps and tourist posters commemorated the commencement of direct flights to the USA in the 1970s, joining together the Shahyad and jet aeroplanes as a symbol of national progress. The monument's recollection of the past through its citations of national heritage, as well as its sweeping, futurist forms, created a powerful image, which was probably responsible for its adoption by Iran Air for their advertising in the mid-1970s.[21] The two sites of Shahyad and Mehrābād were also adjacent to the modernist and middle-class housing development of Ekbatan, Stage One.[22] The Ekbatan complex, with its stepped housing towers, extensive parks, and sporting facilities, forms a Westernized image contrasting with the formerly close-grained and introverted urban structure of Tehran. Together, these three construction projects, Shahyad, Mehrabad Airport, and Ekbatan, form a consciously modernistic, and modernizing, ensemble (Figure 5.5).

In addition to its sculptural form, the Shahyad houses a large museum at its base, an original concept incorporated by Amanat into his competition entry.[23] Above the sunken museum is a huge east–west aligned arched opening, framed by marble-clad piers in the centre of an oval plaza, and further

Forming a national image through public projects 151

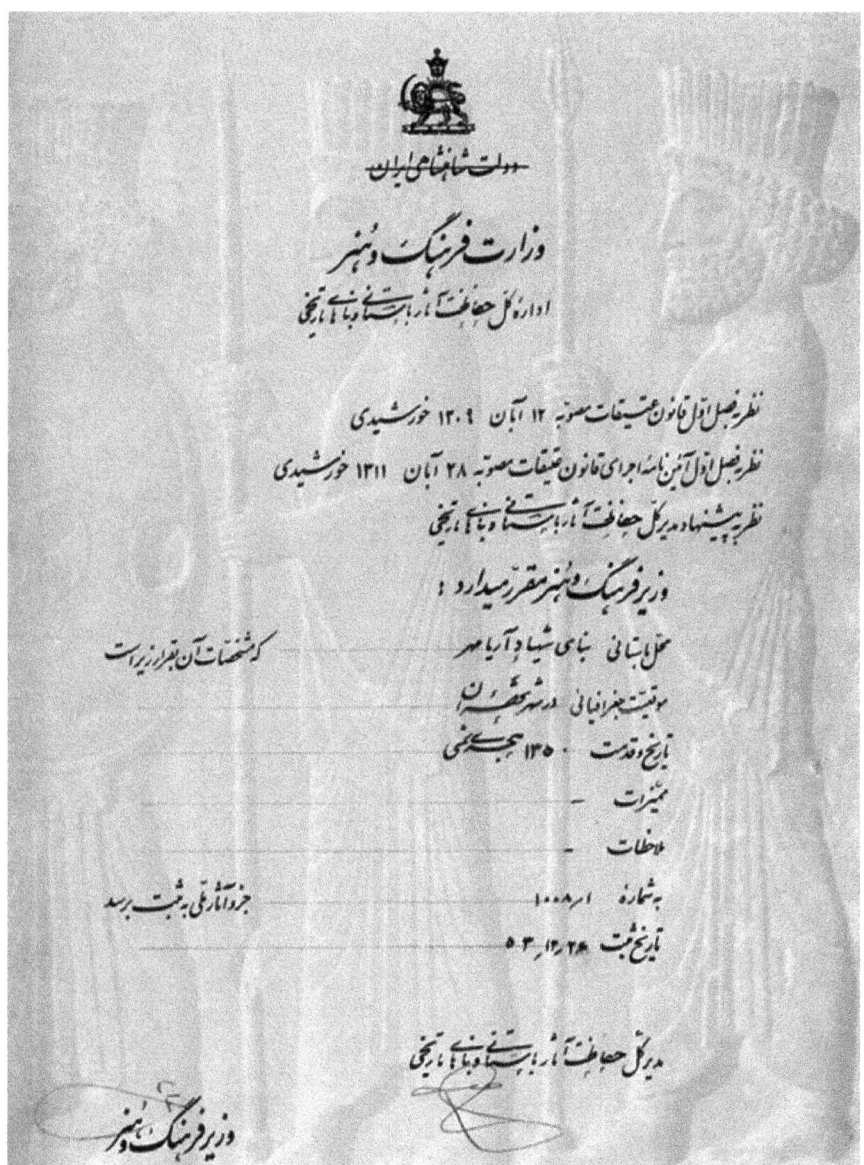

5.4 Shahyad heritage registration document.

exhibition spaces are located in the surmounting halls. The overall spatial sequence and curatorial narrative forms a progression from the past to the present and future, while the form expresses the sense of an organic growth, flowing in parabolic curves up to a tower-like form,[24] recalling present-day projects produced through parametric design, such as the work of Zaha Hadid.

5.5 Aerial view of the urban ensemble with Shahyad at its focal point.

It was, however, designed by manual methods, as had been the Sydney Opera House, supplemented by then-basic computer technology. In each case, the architect's intuitively derived forms were rationalized and systematized into expressions of static forces.

While referencing historic Iranian monuments, the Shahyad also brings to mind the ancient Roman *quadrifons* that marked significant road crossings and usually defined the route to a palace. But here the form is dramatically dynamic. Two sets of piers form transverse parabolas in plan which frame minor north and south arches and support a massive east–west arching vault directed towards the heart of the city (Figure 5.6 and Plates 3–4). The vault's underside is supported by criss-crossing ribs not dissimilar to the ribbed forms in Seyhoun's Omar Khayyám mausoleum in Nishāpur (Figure 5.7). In an interview, the architect Amanat compared the vaulted form to Sasanian arches, notably the great *eyvān* (a lofty portico enclosed on three sides) of the palace of Ctesiphon, the capital of the Sasanian Empire, but now located in the Arab state of Iraq.[25] The interpretation of a motif lying outside Iranian boundaries also possesses political import, implying perhaps a 'Greater Iran', a cultural and civilizational interpretation that transcends current geopolitical boundaries. The same arch had previously been cited in the National Archaeological Museum, designed by the French architect and archaeologist André Godard, and erected under the first Pahlavi monarch, Reza Shah, in 1931–39.[26]

Amanat attributes the design of the Shahyad monument to the influence

Forming a national image through public projects 153

5.6 The minor north–south arches in the Shahyad (left) and the major east–west arch (right) (2007).

5.7 Shayhad, the underside of the east–west arch (left) (2007); mausoleum of Omar Khayyám (right).

of his teacher, Houshang Seyhoun, who, he said, introduced the field study of traditional buildings and towns as part of the architectural curriculum:

> Many of us students would often travel with him to different cities, where we'd sketch a lot of buildings – sketch the bazaars and the beautiful textures of traditional Iran. There was a kind of hidden message in that, which we absorbed, about how you can use what you see in your modern interpretation of architecture. [...]
>
> For me, there are two significant periods in Iranian architecture: Iran before the invasion of Arabs – before accepting the Islamic culture – and the period after

it. They have a tremendous effect on each other, since old Iran has impacted all Islamic architecture, everywhere, since.[27]

Perhaps significantly, both Amanat and Seyhoun follow the Baha'i faith, which originated in nineteenth-century Persia, developing first as a movement from within Islam, and which syncretizes ideas from older faiths, emphasizing a unitary view of creation.[28] From this viewpoint, the combination of Islamic and non-Islamic motifs is perfectly understandable and legitimate. For Amanat, the design was made 'for the culture'; it was thus presumably intended to communicate through its vaguely familiar forms to the people on an intuitive, perceptual level. Here we are referring to the potential for affectivity in architecture, the connection between sensate experience, architectural production, and their role in contributing to cultural memory and hence to the construction and experience of heritage.[29] In this respect, the Shahyad's design functions analogously to Shushtar Now in affective and experiential terms: in both cases, the created images are 'tactile', encountered and appreciated in bodily movement.

The urban function of the monument

While there are undeniable references to an Iranian past, the urban function of the Shahyad also takes its cue from European and American precedents such as Napoleon's Arc de Triomphe (1806–36). In time, the symbolism of such monuments was often replaced by a more general topological significance as urban marker, demarcating the entrance into the city, and as generator of urban transformation. The resemblance was not lost on some of the public – indeed Grigor cites a report on the opening of the monument, describing it as 'Tehran's answer to the Arc de Triomphe and the landmarks of other great cities'.[30] Furthermore, the monument could also be seen in the context of other 'portals to the future' of the mid-twentieth century, such as the Gateway Arch (1963–65) in St. Louis, Missouri, designed by Eero Saarinen. This arch was surely in the collective consciousness when the Shahyad was designed. Here, however, it is useful to consider how the Shahyad is different from, and similar to, these Western examples.

The Arc de Triomphe, and its subsequent emulations, cited ancient Roman triumphal arches in asserting the commissioner's imperialist claim to be the inheritor of the legacy of that empire. There was, however, no tradition of monumental archways in open urban spaces in Iranian architecture, or of the grand *allees* leading to them, other than the linear gardens defined by avenues of trees in *jubs* (water canals), as at *Bāgh-e Shāzdeh* (The Garden of the Prince), Māhān, Kermān in the Qajar period, or *Chehel Sotun*, Isfahan, associated with Safavid palaces.[31] While there is an implicit triumphalism in the Shahyad, rather than seeing the fabrication of identity in the monument as a Foucauldian power-based 'construct', we interpret it as a genuine attempt on the part of the designer to bring together existing, and remembered, cultural threads. Through this weaving or imbrication, material and intangible elements, practices and memory, might operate around the monument, multiple heritages might be embraced, and a cultural continuity and identity posited. Perceived in movement from the vantage-point of traffic circulating around the plaza for which it forms the focus, the monument's form gradually transmutes from the semblance of a pre-Islamic Sasanian *eyvān* to that of a pointed arch, thus coming to resemble a familiar Islamic period form. This in itself implies the semblance of a symbolic and iconic continuity and fluidity consistent with the view of history promoted, even today, by many Iranians within and outside the state. As a gateway to Tehran, both from the east and the airport, but also in a sense from the outside world, the symbolic and urban function of the monument meant that it was inevitably a global edifice at one scale and one that also brought the local and the global together. Arguably, an impetus behind this expression of historical continuity, indeed the historical consciousness that made that expression possible, was the dynamic and changeable condition of the country under development.

From another perspective, the edifice exemplifies a co-production of heritage, the result of a dialogue between Iranian actors and their counterparts on multiple levels. Intellectually, it is situated within the debates about Iranian identity that were current at the time. In its design, the edifice engages in a dialogue through time and place with similar works as mentioned above. Technically, the construction was only feasible through the collaboration between Iranian architects and engineers and the Ove Arup firm's advanced technological capabilities. Its programmatic demands notwithstanding, the Shahyad arguably produces an architectural heritage which, as we shall see later, transcends the limits of a given ideology. As elaborated below, the urban space acts as a hub that brings multiple modes of transport together, and thus sets the edifice up as a pivotal point in the flow of various scales of movement. Despite its 'national' connotations, this suggests a cosmopolitan and global outlook, rendering its meaning at once ambivalent and fleeting.

The current state of the monument and its context

> [E]verything is in this. [The] Islamic period is here as is the period before it ... it has mixed all of it together well. [Referring to one of the lines of the building,] Persepolis is here too ... this showed the development of Iran.[32]

> It symbolizes Tehran ... I think it was built before revolution ... have seen it once up close ... there is only one of it ... it can possibly be the symbol of Iran. ... It looks historic ... [its motifs and design] predate Islam. ... It impresses me ... it will be lasting ... they cannot destroy it.[33]

Depending on the scale and purpose one considers, the function of the Shahyad monument is constant or fleeting. This ostensibly paradoxical claim becomes clear once we examine the structure in its urban context. Here, we will discuss its reception (albeit by a limited number of respondents), and its internal workings – the relationship between the museum and other subterranean spaces. In this manner, one might gain a deeper understanding of the nature of dissonance in the monument by bridging the gap between its social and monumental times,[34] its daily life and its official gestures. In other words, the meaning of the tower is constituted through a web of relations that operate on three, possibly four, interconnected scales: national, which is also implied in a global setting, urban (including regional), and local (meaning on the ground). These scales correspond to different temporalities: the national intersecting with monumental time, while the local mostly coincides with social time, and the urban or regional vacillates between the two. Thus, it is possible to simultaneously experience the monument as a symbol, as a local place, and as a landmark while navigating the city. There are no clear boundaries between these scales and the temporalities they pertain to, as one seeps into the other.

In the following section, we will attempt to navigate this web by examining examples of the above intersections of various scales. We will examine the structure and its settings firstly by reflecting on the experience of encountering it on the ground. Then, to provide a broader context for its symbolic function, we will present the results of a pilot study in photo elicitation. Finally, to shed light on the complexities of contested state discourses surrounding the edifice, we will examine the museum underneath the tower and the addition of a mosque to the space of the square.

Encountering the monument in its context[35]

How is the Shahyad-Azadi tower experienced and understood today? It is useful to approach this question by recounting its quotidian experience, on a day with a bearable level of pollution and clear skies, in conditions of the encounters of daily life, rather than just on the occasion of a protest or celebration. Functioning as the western gateway to the city, the monument is usually encountered, and indeed depicted, from its forecourt, located on its east–west axis (refer back to Figure 5.6). The north–south axis, however, is somewhat less 'majestic' (Figure 5.8).

Many Iranians have a memory of the monument through various forms of media, including television, newspapers, stamps, posters, and various other forms of virtual and published images in circulation, related to various events. As most scholars have observed, people recognize it concurrently as a gateway to the city, a national edifice, and a space for political spectacles of state and opposition.

Given the limited pedestrian accessibility, the tower being located on an island only accessible via several underpasses, the usual way to grasp the everyday experience of the tower is to approach it by vehicle. Furthermore, guardrails erected around the traffic lanes, presumably to protect the pedestrians from entering the flow of traffic willy-nilly, reinforce the idea that the place is, above

Forming a national image through public projects 157

5.8 View approximately from north to south (2017). This is the usual casual view of the edifice when one approaches it from the north.

all, a spectacle. From the outside, then, the image of this space is formed by the monument, traffic, and edges of pedestrian walkways and fences. Additionally, the place is circumscribed by peripheral flag-poles, the number of which has increased in recent years. People who hang out on the edges of the road are, for the most part, passengers awaiting a pick-up, or day labourers congregating in pockets at certain times throughout the day. There is often a significant amount of noise and, at times, atmospheric pollution in this space.

Once under the main platform of the tower, however, the space is open and impressive. The complex outline of masonry work and joints remains striking, despite signs of surface ageing. Colours and motifs appear familiar, without invoking a specific building, as is the case with the underbelly of the arch or the northern broken arch (Figure 5.9). The east–west axis is, however, clearly reminiscent of the iconography of Ctesiphon to viewers familiar with this palace's ruins. Equally interesting are the turquoise-ornamented ribs that run along the surface of the edifice and constitute a cross-ribbed web striating its underside. The colour scheme and the fine patterns on the tiles are reminiscent of Safavid architecture, such as the turquoise dome of the Shah mosque in Isfahan, though perhaps the patterns and convergence of lines is a stronger reminder of Seyhoun's work. But this is where figurative and concrete resemblance stops. Instead, the monument is a clear, almost surreal, example of what

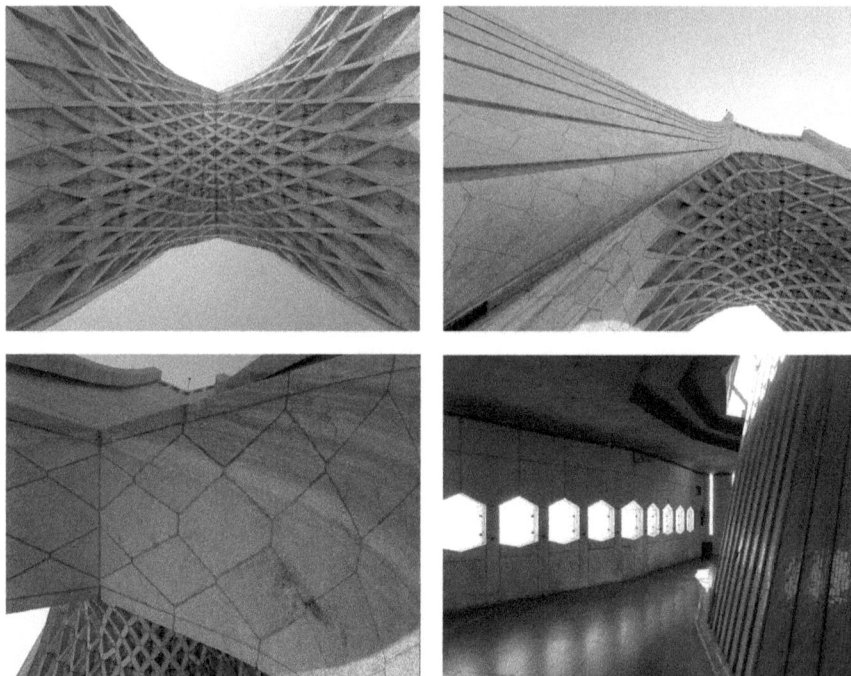

5.9 Decorative relief (ribs) that feature underneath the monument are integral to its spatial expression inside and outside (2017).

the creative reinterpretation of tradition can offer, at once majestic and intimate, the latter quality having been acquired over forty years of public life and massive representation through various media.

Here nostalgia plays a particular role in the conception of the design, which does not conceal its 'high-tech' construction techniques. Despite invoking dream-like motifs of the past, it is indeed future oriented. The motif of a gateway also operates as a metaphor for liminality and transition. Rather than harking back to a treasured past and indicating a regressive resistance to change, nostalgia in this design is utilized to imagine a different future. And here, far from manifesting a rigid set of rules, tradition supplies flexible raw material. Iconography and colour retain a sensuous link with a past. Regardless of changing political ideologies impacting upon the monument, the edifice creates heritage in suggesting a seamless past through representational motifs. It was in the 1970s, and still remains, a tangible testimony to the ideal of culturally specific development – at once technologically sophisticated and ultra-modern and historically connected. The museum underneath the tower once conveyed a strong developmental agenda coloured by ideology, one which is presently lost, and to which we shall return.

From the central platform, there is a remarkable contrast between outside

Forming a national image through public projects 159

5.10 The 72 Tan Mosque as seen from the upper levels of the Shahyad Tower (left) (2017) and the mosque facing the main avenue with the Shahyad in the background (right) (2017).

and inside. Here, the hustle and bustle of traffic and urban passengers gives way to open horizons and tidy greenery. The immediate horizon seems almost clear; except for the recent addition of a large white mosque and beyond that, the housing complexes, no structures rival the tower (Figure 5.10). The mosque and the displaced museum, with its lost curatorial narrative, bear out ongoing ideological battles over history and identity under the Islamic Republic. At this point, however, it is useful to explore the potential heritage and iconic role that the edifice plays as a public monument.

The platform

The platform itself is a place for respite, casual chats, and tourist hangouts. On the day of visit, there were tourists but also three or four photographers with their folios on display, offering to render an instant print service, as well as a good deal of 'selfie' takers, a practice officially acknowledged by a public artwork (Figure 5.11). Far from the reputation of the monument as an ideological site, either for the Pahlavis or for the Islamic Republic, on this ordinary day the place and its activities resembled any other tourist site. There were a few Iranians of different age groups 'hanging out' on the platform, including a few young couples on vacation or colleagues on a work trip from the provinces, taking selfies or occasionally engaging the on-site photographer for a snapshot (Figure 5.12). The man at the beverage stand, however, was not complimentary about local visitors to the site, referring to those taking photographs with the monument as 'village idiots' (ironically, he himself was a villager from one of the provinces!). There were also groups of foreign tourists on-site; from Hong Kong, from the Netherlands, and from Germany. They

160 *Development, architecture, and the formation of heritage*

5.11 A makeshift photo shoot and print shop on the Shahyad platform (left) and the selfie-take statue (right) (2017).

5.12 People on the platform; note the 72 Tan Mosque in the background dominating the skyline (2017).

were most interested in the structure and its internal spaces – the museum and other facilities.

The collective-symbolic function of Shahyad-Azadi

> A nostalgic [activity] among many in our country is to visit the Azadi Tower and take a snapshot for memory's sake.[36]

The tower evokes questions as to whether it constitutes a nostalgic national place, and if so, what the nature of nostalgia here might be. Does the tower convey any collective-symbolic meaning in the present, or are people, as Grigor asserts, indifferent to the monument and its connotations? Does it symbolize a dated ideology? Is the meaning simply nostalgic or just contingent upon power? These are important questions beyond theoretical ruminations about architecture. They refer back to the potential for a persistence of symbolism, its association with national identity, and thus to the place of heritage in relation to that identity.

To go beyond theoretical speculation, we staged a pilot study which, although anecdotal, delivers some insights into the above questions, as well as into the role of design in the creation of a recognizable national heritage. Towards such ends, we built a collection of eleven photographs (black and white, and colour), intended to be shown sequentially and depicting both details and overall views of the tower internally and externally (Figure 5.13). The collection was used as a device to engage ordinary people of different age groups from Tehran and from the provinces (the majority from Tabriz) in conversation about the monument, but away from the site of the edifice. Our main aim was to gauge the iconicity of the building, or more accurately, to see what it signified to this random group, whether it referred to a particular form of identity, a place, or time. Additionally, we hoped to obtain a sense of the structure's connotations at different scales. In total, we interviewed nineteen individuals for photo elicitation, and the results reflect a common ground in the following areas.

The tower's 'imageability'[37]

The absolute majority of people recognized the tower almost instantaneously, by the third detail picture, which depicts something of the outside of the building (the top row of images in Figure 5.13). This is surprising, because the most widely circulated images of the tower depict its external form, often in its totality and not its details. Such images are frequently broadcast on television, seen in relation to official ceremonies, as well as protests, and before the Revolution, circulated on the back of bank notes. However, the web of lines underneath the tower is clearly the key visual identifier of the building. While the pattern is abstract, and for some a reminder 'of the geometry exercises we did in maths classes at school',[38] it is nonetheless unique and, as we noted before, its combination with the inlaid tile work and the colour scheme is oddly familiar. This quality, a certain distanciation from tradition and its familiarity, is also apparent in other Iranian architectural productions of the 1970s and more recently. There was a double movement in this process – on the one hand, particular traditions and their symbols and patterns were removed from their context and universalized; on the other, they were vested with specific meanings to differentiate a larger cultural community, an Islamic civilization or the Iranian nation, from others. There is, in this process both a familiarity and a defamiliarization, and from tradition to 'detraditionalization'.[39] Through this reciprocity, the monument is abstracted from the purely familiar and traditional, and engages with a heritage process, in which elements of the past are abstracted and refashioned in the

5.13 Images selected for random analysis (2017). These were shown to participants in the numbered order here.

present, in support of a collective identity. Being in the public eye, the monument exposes the public to this process as well, mediating heritage.

The Shahyad's multiple connotations and its scalar iconicity

The second interesting quality is the scalarity of the monument.[40] By this we mean that the edifice assumes different meanings, or performs different functions, at different scales, pertaining to a sense of spatiality, or in other words, of place. While meanings and functions change over time, the question of scale in relation to place adds to the architectural understanding of the edifice. Here, some of the responses to images of the Shahyad-Azadi monument and the ruminations they prompt reinforce our descriptive encounter with the place. For individuals, the edifice seems to operate on four different scales, each with different but perhaps overlapping emotional and identity connotations, including individual encounter, regional (urban scale), national, and global. On an individual scale, the place instigates ambivalent meanings. For some, the place didn't invoke any particular sensation, in fact as one interviewee noted:

> [i]t was peculiar ... perhaps because the stairs [going down to the museum complex] were fenced off [this happened during a period in the first decade after the Revolution], the place was full of litter and we thought, so what? Did they go on parade during the Shah Period? No![41]

For others, the monument recalls a period in a personal history:

> Shahyad reminds me of my childhood [before the revolution of 1979]. I remember that they used to show it on television ... I also add that then [during the Shah period] its image was printed on the 20 Tuman bill.[42]

Clearly, this refers to multiple layers of the social and political construction of memories. The place signifies what is an intimate memory, that of a child at home watching television. Yet it also refers to the process of circulating the image as an icon by official and unofficial media.

For others still, the scale of its meaning (its signification) is ambivalent, entangled with layers of historically shifting power relations that do not operate, or replace one another, sequentially, but rather exist concurrently upon the site, which thus becomes an arena for different kinds of nostalgia. Reassessing multiple pasts, these nostalgias work with the edifice, assisting the comprehension of the monument, and through it, revealing the present mentalities of individuals, and the collectives with which they identify. It is in such delineations of the shifting boundaries of identity, through the inherent liminality of this process, that different official and unofficial heritage processes pertaining to different scales coexist and collide.[43] Indeed, the place provides the possibility for such productive and 'dissonant' collisions.[44] Here, individual statements about the connotation and iconicity of the monument are revealing:

> I think this place [Azadi] for Iranians symbolizes Tehran but for foreigners [it] symbolizes Iran. Of course, it is not a symbol of freedom ... of course, we don't have freedom in Iran ... what freedom?[45]

This is a clear statement of the scalar operation of the edifice, connoting different meanings at different scales, and is at the same time referring to the irony of the name Azadi, 'freedom', which 'we don't have'. This latter reference is also a negative, and somewhat nostalgic, acknowledgement that the edifice symbolizes a shift in the political system subsequent to the revolution of 1979.

Another Tabrizi respondent believes that

> [it symbolizes] Tehran. Usually Persepolis is the symbol of Iran, I mean when they want to show Iran, they show Persepolis.[46]

The respondent's comment suggests that the edifice has a stronger regional (Tehran-centric) connotation and that an historical depth, a certain heritage value, is necessary for a monument to symbolize a country:

> I believe what could be most expressive of Iran, as if it tells the story of its context and *regional ties*, is the Qābus Tower[47].

Others affirm its signification of Tehran and its role as a gateway to the city, but at the same time, there is an ambiguous relationship between it, Tehran, and the country:

> It is a modern building ... it definitely reminds me of the [1979] Revolution ... it is more a symbol of Tehran than Iran ... [but then] it is also a symbol of Iran.[48]

> This was the symbol of greatness of Tehran ... in fact of the whole of Iran. It was the symbol of Iran's development. I swear to God ... on the life of my children ... how do I say it ... this Shahyad, it showed civilization. When this structure was built in the Middle East, in these Arab countries, in Dubai there was nothing ... it was desert ... this structure showed that we had development. When that Shah said that we have reached 'the gates of the Great Civilization', this is what he meant. Had it continued we would have been way ahead of Dubai now.[49]

In the second statement, by an army retiree, there is a much more reflective reading of the monument, one which is perhaps close to what the Pahlavis intended, but which also reflects nostalgia for a now-distant past, after forty years of the Islamic Republic. The statement also expresses a sense of loss for the past regime but, more significantly, evokes what a growing number of people in Iran seem to think that the regime represented. It is perhaps a function of the generational gap between the last two individuals quoted above, that for the latter, the Pahlavis stood for development and progress.[50]

As a symbol, the Shahyad also speaks to the unevenness of development processes in Iran, which in conjunction with unfortunate historical events after the Revolution, and the maladministration of development thereafter, have exacerbated the concentration of capacities in, and a population shift to, Tehran and other major cities. Statements implicitly or explicitly identify the unevenness of development and centre–periphery tensions in the country, as indicated in the following statements by people interviewed on-site (four individuals) and off-site (nineteen individuals through photo elicitation):

> But I guess if this [Shahyad] wasn't here, then Tehran would have been like Tabriz or Ardabil, an ordinary city. ... I don't know where they got it [the idea of its design] from, but when you arrive from the countryside and see this, you say: Tehran ... we arrived in Tehran ... when we see the image, it means we are in Tehran ... [it signifies Tehran].[51]

> Shahyad symbolizes Tehran ... because everything is concentrated in Tehran ... and this symbolizes Tehran, [then] we can say that this symbolizes Iran ... there is nothing here [in Tabriz]. When you get to Tehran, there is a mixed feeling of [appreciation for] its scale and amenities and a sense of envy because everything is concentrated here.[52]

The above statements also contain various levels of politics that intersect with both the Islamic Republic and Pahlavi state narratives across various administrations in Iran. Some refer to a transhistorical and inclusive sense of national unity:

> This is like [other] historic monuments ... when you see [visit] this, it is as if you've seen Iran. ... [the interviewee points at the motifs and decorations underneath the structure] the architecture of this place is more Islamic ... some say it is like a mosque [but he is not so sure about the base of the monument].[53]

> It is the symbol of national unity, meaning everyone gathers there and things culminate there [as he says these words, he moves his hands on the picture and up along the tower clasping them together]. If there is unity, we will [reach our] peak. See this building ... one wants to lift off [culminate] ... it is symmetrical ... it is like Persepolis ... that too is symmetrical [he shows a gesture of emphasis and strength with his hands] ... [this symbolizes] national unity.[54]

To others, the building suggests meaning in accordance with their own visual experiences, some subtly influenced by official discourses:

> The Shahyad building reminds me of a mosque because it is big and seen from everywhere ... if someone hasn't been here themselves, they would have seen it on television ... if this is destroyed, it is as if Tehran is destroyed.[55]

> The building somehow symbolizes Islam, it is something like unity ... all the lines that converge at the top.[56]

From the above examples, it becomes clear that, in the space of the monument, various scales of temporal and spatial experience converge and collide. Tensions of persistent ideologies thus begin to reveal themselves such that the mosque, for example, insinuated within the visual zone of the monument (below), serves functions beyond devotion for travellers and commuters. It is here that the convoluted space of the museum makes sense.

Contesting the monument: The 72 Tan Mosque

In recent years, a new edifice has been added to the visual field of the Shahyad – the *Haftād-o-do Tan* Mosque (the Mosque of 72 Martyrs). Referring to a symbolic number of martyrs who stood by Imam Hossein and were slain by Yazid, the caliph of the time, the title's association with martyrdom is further emphasized by its housing the graves of six unknown martyrs of the Iran–Iraq War (Figure 5.14). The mosque accommodates 650 people.[57] According to the authorities, it is intended to mark the entry to Tehran, and to perform a trans-regional function as well as serving the various bus and shuttle taxi interchanges around the square, especially for 'prayers in national and religious ceremonies'.[58] The new edifice therefore constitutes a clear ideological statement at an urban scale, and, according to Mr Jafari, the Operational Director of Tehran Municipality's Cultural Spaces Corporation, promotes 'Islamic prayers and our Islamic culture'.[59] In particular, the burial of 'martyrs' on the site points to an overt political agenda of silencing dissent and dominating otherwise mundane and secular spaces with sanctioned versions of sacrality held by at least a sector within the governing elite of the Islamic Republic. The imposition of the mosque, and its housing of the martyrs' remains, is a clear indication that to many ideologues in the Islamic Republic the Shahyad is still 'contaminated' with unwanted ideologies, or that it falls short of the kind of expression they

5.14 One of two main entries of the 72 Tan Mosque (2017).

Forming a national image through public projects 167

5.15 Views of the 72 Tan Mosque showing formal 'innovations' made possible by CAD design (2017).

understand and prefer. Jafari is explicit in noting that 'this mosque in fact stands for our national and religious realm in contradistinction to Azadi Square as the national symbol [in] Tehran.'[60] Contrary to the official claims that it works with the material and structure of Shahyad, and that the two are thus 'integrated', the newer edifice clearly registers the authorities' disregard for the presence of a heritage-registered monument, a disregard that accords with its general neglect – there have been clear warnings of its erosion and even possible risk of collapse due to structural fatigue and water damage.[61]

Here, the contrast in understanding and operation of traditional motifs and heritage is explicit. The mosque, in its proportion and finishes, resembles not the rich masterpieces of Iranian architecture, but rather the kind of grand mosques filled with flamboyant discord seen in places such as Dubai or Abu Dhabi (Figure 5.15). Furthermore, in its literal approach and overt use of symbolism, the design attests to a cultural perception that has lost all sense of creative adaptation of tradition. Indeed, it exemplifies a retrograde nostalgia which Boym refers to as 'restorative'.[62] Even at a technological level, the two are worthy of comparison. The Shahyad was designed and constructed through the utilization of the latest engineering, fabrication, and display technologies of its time. It could thus be interpreted as a cultural response to development and as productive of a cultural heritage, constituting modern heritage in its own right. By contrast, the mosque possesses little critical engagement with tradition, but is, instead, a set of dead symbols clashing with, and melding into, one another with the aid of computer programs, and yet exhibiting little more than shallow propaganda. The reduction of imaginative possibilities to an impoverished aesthetics of computer-aided design (CAD) is itself perhaps a tacit act of heritage destruction, reflecting the regression into an insecure dreamworld, in which the notion of an Iranian nation-state is still officially irreconcilable with pan-Shiism. The

168 *Development, architecture, and the formation of heritage*

result is failure all round and, in this respect, it resembles the Mosallā project (see Chapter 6). It is at this point that official stances towards heritage exhibit a clear dissonance with popular perceptions of the monument. But this sense of purposive neglect is also replicated in the museum underneath the Shahyad.

The museum underneath: A dissonant space

Foregoing the history of the museum, which is available elsewhere,[63] we will engage briefly with the current experience of the interior, in order to elicit the afterlife of the edifice and its complicated meanings. Upon entering the museum in 2017, one encountered a sense of general chaos. There was a bust of the builder, engineer Mohammad Pourfathi, but little mention of Amanat, perhaps because he is a 'heretical' Baha'i (Figure 5.16). On one side of the hall there were distorting mirrors meant for entertainment, on the other a desk with a group of people aimlessly chatting away, upon which there was a load of material that made the place look like the back of a handicraft shop (Figure 5.17). Cases opposite the entry housed various artefacts representing a mishmash of different ages. The galleries were divided into rough themes. Where there used to be exhibits depicting White Revolution development projects that were anticipated to come, many were now empty, while some were instead filled with Quranic verses. Some models were dusty and in disrepair. While recording the exhibits,

5.16 Bust of Pourfathi in the Shahyad Museum (2017).

5.17 View upon entry in the main exhibition hall underneath the tower (2017).

5.18 General layout of a gallery with exhibits about development (2017).

170 Development, architecture, and the formation of heritage

5.19 Detail of exhibits showcasing (clockwise from top-left) education, the Persian Gulf, the environment, and culture and the arts. The exhibits pertain to aspects of the White Revolution and projects envisioned therein. Thus, the cases for education and culture and the arts have been emptied after the Revolution of 1979, presumably due to ideological incompatibilities (2017).

Mozaffari was told not to take 'too many photos of all the cases' (Figures 5.18 and 5.19).

The walls were lined with, mostly unimpressive, calligraphic works and occasional casts of pre-Islamic Persepolitan bas-reliefs. Spaces were rented out, in order to make the gallery 'self-sufficient', a practice which contrasted with the evidently abundant money spent on mosques and religious spaces (Figure 5.20). The library, dating back to the museum's creation, was now closed. Instead, an automaton, sitting before a piano, was programmed to play the nationalistic march of *ey-Iran* for school students. A staff member who learnt of our interest started talking about the history of this building – her eyes filled with tears as she noted how the place was in disrepair. Simply put, there was a sense of nostalgia and loss. As we moved on to the Iranology gallery, there were still remnants of the original exhibits on display: the industrial highlights of each province of Iran were emphasized in a dark room, originally intended to be seen as the viewer was moved along on a conveyor belt; now, the conveyor belt no longer worked, a vision of the future that had succumbed to history (Figure

Forming a national image through public projects 171

5.20 Under the watchful eyes of Khomeini and Khamenei, the amphithcatre was being prepared for an 'endorsed' weekend rock concert (2017).

5.21 Remains from a different time: exhibits in the Iranology gallery depicting the development and industrial projects that were meant to happen in each province (2017).

5.21). At the end of the static conveyor belt, where the viewer was supposed to encounter the crescendo of the museum, there were now two empty fish tanks and a cursorily placed picture of Persepolis, and then another of the tomb of Cyrus the Great. Turning into that space, there were pictures of Khomeini, Khamenei, and other members of the Islamic Republic's top leadership, together

5.22 Fish tanks at the end of a travelator, leading to history of revolution in the back room (2017).

with images of protests at the time of revolution, badly presented caricatures of the Shah and his clique, and opposite them, a convoluted 'artwork'. The state of the museum was a reminder of Marx's oft-quoted idiom, 'history repeats itself, the first as tragedy, then as farce' (Figures 5.22–5.25).

Conclusion

As our examination of the Shahyad suggests, the monument is entangled in issues of heritage and development at various scales. Not only was it meant to symbolize a developing country (and to celebrate the Shah), it was also the product of the effects of development within the capital in terms of local, national, and international networks of transport and circulation of people and materials, as well as ideas of new lifestyles for the rapidly growing, educated urban class who, it was hoped, would quickly adapt to modern lifestyles. It is within this context that the edifice, through its design, begins to reconstruct history and project heritage (as we note below). Thus, critiquing the Shahyad from the perspective of power does not fully explain the making of heritage, nor the complex way in which consciously conceived works of architecture interact both materially and spatially with their public, and risks essentializing both the architecture and the state apparatuses.[64] Clearly, in this case, one must

Forming a national image through public projects 173

5.23 Tourism posters poorly mounted and lit at the end of the travelator at the Iranology gallery (2017).

5.24 Artwork about history of the Islamic Revolution (2017).

174 Development, architecture, and the formation of heritage

5.25 History of the Islamic Revolution depicted through prints (2017).

separate the function of the complex from its popular reception. The Shahyad's programme has, over its existence, changed from a glorification of the monarchy to neutral, perhaps even convoluted, displays of arts and crafts. Its physical presence, on the other hand, forms a monumental backdrop to successive, and opposing, ideological demonstrations, both official and unofficial, as Grigor and Lotfi have both noted, through which it is subsequently reproduced as photographic or cinematic image.[65]

The vaguely familiar forms, reminiscent of Islamic and pre-Islamic motifs, connect the structure to the past, however indirectly, as conveyed by the respondents' comments above. While the ascription of meanings, through the Pahlavi regime's ideologically informed programme, might have entailed a certain symbolism, this could in no way be considered immutable; the cultural memory of the site was dependent on the survival of the regime, and therefore the issue of reception needs to be addressed – the forms might be received in a different manner than that intended, misinterpreted knowingly or unknowingly. In the Pahlavi regime's absence, the forms now persist as an accreted image of national identity, beyond specific ideological associations. Here, 'meaning' and 'truth' are constituted, and reconstituted, through the network of interactions between the site and monument as material agent, and the multiple social agents who appropriate it; meaning does not transcend historical time and social practices. Thus, a thoroughly critical examination of monuments like the Shahyad needs to pay attention to three aspects: the object itself, through formal analysis; the site of its production – the commissioning, design, and construction processes; and finally, its reception by the public. The production of the monument comprises multiple, and sometimes conflictual, agencies and cultural frictions.[66] Indeed, while it is certainly true that the meanings ascribed to the monument have changed over its history, from our pilot study one might question the veracity of the assumption that hegemonic power dictates which new cultural memories are acquired, given the potential for historically imbricated, and dissonant, cultural memories, and thus for contestation. For the respondents, the monument was variously a symbol of Tehran, a symbol of Iran, an embodiment of Iran like Persepolis, a monument that stands for civilization and Iranian greatness, but for others it was like a mosque, and symbolized Islam.

The Shahyad monument is a liminal, transitional site, both in a physical sense, experienced through movement, and in a metaphorical one. In its conception, it was intended to demarcate the boundary of the city, construct an urban threshold and navigate between, and connect, the past, present, and future. While the monument is the tangible manifestation and concentration of power, it would, as well, be the expected place for contestation of that power. It was precisely this site that formed the main tableau for expressions of revolt, just as, Vidler documented, the royal places in Paris had done during the French Revolution.[67] There were both representational reasons for this, as well as practical ones – the site is a transport hub, and as the largest open space in the city could accommodate large crowds. However, other questions remain – why are members of the public drawn to this monument? How do they interact with, transform the meaning of, and are transformed by the monument? If the identity and constitution is dynamic because of its multifarious interactions with people in the course of time, then existing arguments around its association with power seem undifferentiated, and in need of nuance. To use Aldo Rossi's term,[68] the monument can be said to be *indifferent* both to its functions and to the inscriptions placed upon it by ideological discourses, yet at the same time it might be experienced as something familiar.

In considering the issue of affectivity and association in the Shahyad monument, it becomes necessary to subsume architectural discourse into heritage discourse, whereby landscapes, places, and sites of memory may be said to engage with their public in a reciprocal manner.[69] Memory, in this sense, is not simply a product of ascriptions applied to the passive vessel of architecture, but rather a two-way process. It is precisely the heritage emerging from this process, a construction that derives from what is *received* from these sites and monuments, and then put into practice in interactions with the environment, forming bodily habits and embodied memories, that will determine whether the site remains a dead trace, or evolves into a culturally productive agent. In the case of edifices such as the Shahyad-Azadi monument, its perception and meaning are formed through the human–edifice interaction and is constantly evolving. For any new association to take root, however, more than rhetoric or some vague notion of ideology and propaganda is required – new meanings demand embodied practice, which through time results in the formation of specific habits and anticipations, be they official,[70] or unofficial. The latter, quotidian meaning is reinforced through the building's and site's function as an urban transport hub and urban gateway, much more so than as monument or even museum site. The place is created through levels of sedimentation and habituation, by means of which, to cite Malpas, '[the] stuff of our "inner" lives is [...] to be found in the exterior spaces or places in which we dwell, while those same spaces and places are themselves incorporated "within" us'.[71]

The Shahyad monument has become Iran's quintessential national monument, inscribed with successive, and contested, meanings over time. It forms a kind of twinning with a second intended legacy project of Mohammad Reza Pahlavi, the Shahestan Pahlavi, a projected new governmental and cultural centre for both Tehran and the nation as a whole. Both projects partake in, and are products of, the attempt by a newly ambitious developing nation to project itself onto the world stage through elaborate representations, through tourism and the media, and to its own population, through both internal tourism and local media. And both sites share a similar monumental language, of vast squares, gateways to an imagined future, interpretational museums, and grand urban ensembles of avenues, landscaping, and spatial sequences, through which the nation could be represented as a modern, progressive entity, occupying the global stage while retaining its own cultural character. Both the Shahyad, in its transformation into the Azadi monument tower, and the evolution of Shahestan Pahlavi into the Abbās Ābād cultural gardens and Mosallā, also witnessed a surprising degree of continuity in the ambition to use architecture as a vehicle for the projection of national identities. The role of the Shahyad, as a symbolic gateway for both the capital city and for the nation, was paralleled by the projected Pahlavi Gateway in the Shah and Nation Square in the centre of Shahestan, then reappeared in Mirmiran's competition-winning symbolic gateway for the second National Library competition after the Revolution. If such ambitions were continually thwarted and compromised by the discord and confusion of competing interests, there is nonetheless evidence of the perceived role of architecture in the projection of national agendas.

Notes

1. P. Ayres, 'The Geometry of Shahyad Ariamehr', *The Arup Journal*, 5:1 (March, 1970), p. 29.
2. H. Amanat cited in P. Akbarzadeh (dir.), *Taq Kasra: Wonder of Architecture* [documentary film] (Amsterdam: Persian Dutch Network, 2018).
3. K. Hemmati, 'A Monument of Destiny: Envisioning A Nation's Past, Present, and Future through Shahyad/Azadi' (master's thesis, Simon Fraser University, 2015).
4. N. Kakhi, 'The Monument, Its Images and Histories', in R. A. Alcolea and J. Tárrago-Mingo (eds), *Congreso Internacional: Inter Photo Arch 'Interferencias'* (Navarra: Servicio de Publicaciones Universidad de Navarra, 2016), pp. 132–41, http://dadun.unav.edu/handle/10171/42419 (accessed 25 January, 2019).
5. Grigor, 'Of Metamorphosis'.
6. B. Lotfi, 'Spatial Agency: The Role of Tehran's Freedom Square in Protests of 1979 and 2009' (master's thesis, Central European University, 2010); T. Schneider and J. Till, 'Beyond Discourse: Notes on Spatial Agency', *Footprint*, 4 (2009), pp. 97–111.
7. Benjamin, 'Theses on the Philosophy of History', p. 18.
8. Grigor, 'Of Metamorphosis', p. 39.
9. Assmann and Czaplicka, 'Collective Memory', pp. 127–30, cited in Grigor, 'Of Metamorphosis', pp. 208–9.
10. Grigor, 'Of Metamorphosis', pp. 209, 212.
11. Grigor, 'Of Metamorphosis', p. 209.
12. Grigor, 'Of Metamorphosis', p. 224.
13. The term 'Green Movement' refers to the protest movement that emerged after the disputed election results in 2009 in which so-called reformist candidates were unsuccessful and Ahmadinejad was returned to office. Many, including state factions, claimed that there was widespread election fraud. As it had been for the 1979 Revolution, the Azadi monument and square formed a focus for rallies and demonstrations.
14. Tunbridge and Ashworth, *Dissonant Heritage*.
15. Kakhi, 'The Monument'; Hemmati, 'A Monument of Destiny'; Lotfi, 'Spatial Agency'; Grigor, 'Of Metamorphosis'.
16. Hossein Amanat (b. 1942) studied architecture at the Faculty of Fine Arts, University of Tehran, in the 1960s under Houshang Seyhoun. Ove Arup were probably commissioned on the basis of their achievement in the ground-breaking structure of the Sydney Opera House (completed 1973).
17. Grigor, 'Of Metamorphosis', p. 212.
18. Grigor, 'Of Metamorphosis', pp. 92–3, 96–8.
19. Herzfeld, *A Place in History*.
20. Hemmati, 'A Monument of Destiny', pp. 42, 70.

21 Hemmati, 'A Monument of Destiny', p. 67.
22 R. Habibi, 'Modern Mass Housing in Tehran: Episodes of Urbanism 1945–1979' (PhD diss., Katholieke Universiteit Leuven, 2015), p. 30, https://lirias.kuleuven.be/handle/123456789/497502 (accessed 25 January 2019).
23 Hemmati, 'A Monument of Destiny', pp. 32–3.
24 Grigor, 'Of Metamorphosis', pp. 215–16.
25 B. Tiven, 'Interview with Hossein Amanat', *Bidoun*, 28, (Spring, 2013), https://archive.bidoun.org/magazine/28-interviews/hossein-amanat-with-benjamin-tiven/.
26 Mozaffari, *Forming National Identity*.
27 Tiven, 'Interview with Hossein Amanat'.
28 J. R. Cole, *Modernity and the Millennium: The Genesis of the Baha'i Faith in the Nineteenth-Century Middle East, Volume 9* (New York: Columbia University Press, 1998), pp. 1–20.
29 Tiven, 'Interview with Hossein Amanat'.
30 Grigor, 'Of Metamorphosis', p. 215.
31 The monumental structures of Reza Shah and Mohammad Reza Shah reflect national modernization efforts and are also products of Iran's exposure to and engagement with global currents, which in turn prompted various forms of engagements with multiple pasts.
32 Army retiree in his late fifties from Tabriz, with a high school diploma, 2017 interview.
33 Twenty-six-year-old university student, Tehran.
34 Herzfeld, *A Place in History*.
35 The following description is elicited from Ali Mozaffari's fieldwork, 3 September 2017.
36 ملکی، ف.، پیرمردی که ۳۷سال است در میدان آزادی عکس یادگاری می‌گیرد، خبرگزاری مشرق، ۱۳۹۵/۵/۱۷، http://bit.ly/2WUd0tY دریافت (accessed 29 September 2018). در
37 Lynch, *Image of the City*.
38 Woman with a university degree from Tabriz, in her late thirties, 2017 interview.
39 Thompson, 'Tradition and Self'.
40 D. C. Harvey, 'Heritage and Scale: Settings, Boundaries and Relations', *International Journal of Heritage Studies*, 21:6 (2015), pp. 577–93.
41 Woman with a university degree from Tabriz, in her late thirties, 2017 interview.
42 Former political activist, male in his fifties from Tabriz, high school diploma, 2017 interview.
43 Harrison, *Heritage*, pp. 15–23.
44 Harvey, 'Heritage and Scale', p. 579.
45 A young businessman from Tabriz in his late twenties with an undergraduate degree, 2017 interview.
46 Former political activist, male in his fifties from Tabriz, with a high school diploma, 2017 interview.
47 The tower of Gonbad-e Gabus, dating back to 1006 CE, near the city of Gorgan in Northern Iran, was listed as a World Heritage site by UNESCO in 2012.
48 Thirty-year-old student of dentistry, Tehran, 2017 interview.
49 Army retiree, 2017 interview.
50 Army retiree, 2017 interview. He also states: 'It was good ... beautiful ... we hung out

there. We went up top. It had [a] cinema, restaurant ... we went to the Shahyad a lot [as cadets].'
51 Fifty-three-year-old tea vendor working at the Shahyad, with a high school diploma, 2017 interview.
52 Woman with a university degree from Tabriz, 2017 interview.
53 Azerbaijani photographer working at the Shahyad-Azadi monument, in his early fifties, with a high school diploma, 2017 interview.
54 Thirty-nine-year old man from Tabriz, with an undergraduate degree and from the 'average' class, 2017 interview.
55 Two uneducated labourers from Zahedan in their early twenties looking for day work around Shahyad, 2017 interview.
56 Twenty-six-year-old tax driver from Azerbaijan, working in Tehran, with a high school diploma, 2017 interview.
57 The 72 Tan Mosque occupies a footprint of 1,200 m² on a plot of 5,000 m², and is distributed over four levels (two underground, one ground level, and one at first floor level).
58 آغاز ساخت مسجد هفتاد و تن در تهران، *عصر ایران*، 29 مرداد 1396.
59 مدیر عامل شرکت توسعه فضاهای فرهنگی شهرداری تهران:مسجد 72 تن در نزدیکترین حریم مجاز میدان آزادی قرار دارد، *ایسنا*، دوشنبه / 14 تیر 1395 ، قابل دسترس در http://bit.ly/32tlw4u (accessed 16 January 2019).
60 ایسنا، مسجد 72 تن در نزدیکترین حریم مجاز میدان آزادی قرار دارد.
61 هوشیار یوسفی، ب.، معماری: فضای فرهنگی پانزده متر زیرزمین، مهر (فرهنگی، هنری، اجتماعی)، (1:21)،3 آبان 1382، ص. 16.
62 Boym, 'Nostalgia'.
63 Grigor, 'Of Metamorphosis', pp. 207–25; Hemmati, 'A Monument of Destiny', pp. 89–97.
64 M. Herzfeld, 'Spatial Cleansing: Monumental Vacuity and the Idea of the West', *Journal of Material Culture*, 11:1–2 (2006), pp. 127–49.
65 Lotfi, 'Spatial Agency'.
66 Tsing, *Friction*, pp. 4–6.
67 A. Vidler, 'The Scenes of the Street: Transformations in Ideal and Reality, 1750–1871', in S. Anderson (ed.), *On Streets: Streets as Elements of Urban Structure* (Cambridge, MA: MIT Press, 1978), pp. 29–112.
68 A. Rossi, *The Architecture of the City* (Cambridge, MA: MIT Press, 1982), p. 174.
69 Nora, 'Between Memory and History'.
70 An example of using the site for official purposes includes commemorations of the anniversary of the Revolution's victory (11 February 1979).
71 Malpas, *Place and Experience*, p. 6.

Plate 1 Kamran Diba, Shushtar Now (2015). User interventions in apartments and houses show the original ideas were undermined by the need to adapt the design to cars and to expanding spatial requirements of residents.

Plate 2 Kamran Diba, Jondishapur Academic staff residences (2017). Similar user adaptations are apparent in closing off balconies, blocking windows, and other spaces. Photos courtesy of Bakhtyar Lotfi.

Plate 3 Hossein Amanat, the Shahyad monument (2017), view from the platform looking west and general view of the entrance gallery with the bust of Mohammad Pourfathi at the centre-right of the picture.

Plate 4 Hossein Amanat, the Shahyad monument (2007), view of the minor arch from the platform looking south.

Plate 5 General landscape of the Abbās Ābād development (2017). Aerial view of the development showing the Book Garden in the foreground, the Holy Defence Museum in the far left, and parts of the National Library and the Academies on the right (courtesy of Mohammad Shahhosseini, © Mohammad Shahhosseini 2017).

Plate 6 Kambiz Navaei an Kambiz Haji-Ghassemi, the main central courtyard of the Iranian Academies complex in Tehran (above) (2013); Jila Norouzi and Naqsh-e Jahan Pars architects, Sacred Defence Museum and Art Lake (2013), partial view of the Art Lake and its stepped garden adjacent and parallel to the museum structure (below).

Plate 7 Entry to the Sacred Defence Museum marking the graves of seven unknown martyrs (top-left) (view from the Tāleqāni Park, 2017); Parviz Moayyed-Ahd and others, the Grand Mosallā (2017), a colonnade adjacent to the main courtyard (top-right) (note how both edifices utilize the same symbolic arches also used in the Shahyad); interior of the main prayer hall of the Grand Mosallā during a sports exhibition (bottom).

Plate 8 General view of Bam citadel, a medieval fortified town in south-eastern Iran, prior to its devastation by an earthquake in 2003. This was a source of inspiration for Kalantari's competition entry for the Iranian Academies.

6

Tehran's reluctant urban centre: Representing the national capital

Introduction

The design of a capital and its administrative centre are important expressions of national sovereign power and the country's international standing in the global community of nations. In modern Iran, this was realized initially under Reza Shah with his rebuilding of central Tehran, and then attempted in the unrealized design for a new civic centre under his son, Mohammad Reza Shah. In this chapter we examine the evolution of this urban design proposal conceived for Abbās Ābād, north of the existing city centre. Upon conception, this new administrative heart of Iran included museums and the National Library, projects that would contribute to the development of both literacy and scholarship. As such, the project clearly reflected the Pahlavi state's aims of modernization and development.

Initially conceived as Shahestān Pahlavi, through designs made by Louis Kahn and Kenzo Tange (1973), and then by Llewelyn-Davies International (LDI) (1975–76), the project, with major transformations, has straddled the pre- and post-Revolution eras. The site, as built, contains major civic and religious monuments – the National Library, the Iranian Academies, the Museum of Holy Defence (War Museum), and the Mosallā mosque and prayer grounds. It also reflects the changing attitude towards national expression and heritage-making under the revolutionary ideology. In Chapter 1, we noted that a nostalgia for authenticity contributed to late Pahlavi architecture. Some of the realized Abbās Ābād projects embody expressions of nostalgia while others do not. The Mosallā represents a utopian Shi'ite community of religion; a primary ideological concern of the Islamic Republic. Here planning and design play crucial functions: while today international trends are superficially embraced, and the technical, programmatic, and logistical requirements of the site are addressed, the civic and urban aspects of the site are muted. The exception to this is the central element of the gigantic Mosallā, a later addition to the site which, in its *qibla* orientation, extinguishes any formal relationship with the rest of the city. In fact, the post-Revolution Abbās Ābād project exemplifies an erosion of civic order in public projects of this period. In this chapter, we argue that the vicissitudes of urban plans for the site reflect successive imperial and Islamic utopias, borne of different imaginations of the nation. This transformation evidences a gradual decline in the relevance of tradition and its symbolic forms in the shaping of the city, and a return of generic and universalizing architectural forms and spaces.

Shahestān Pahlavi: Kahn and Tange

The site selected for Shahestān consisted of a bare, rocky hillside with a central declivity that afforded a panoramic view of the city below. It formed a key commercial and residential node,[1] but not a centre, in the 1968 Tehran Comprehensive Plan by Victor Gruen in collaboration with the Farmanfarmaian office.[2] Gruen's plan, which was commissioned under the aegis of the Plan Organization, and was funded by oil revenues, World Bank loans, and US aid, divided the city into ten large districts (*mantaghe*) of about half a million, subdivided into subdistricts (*nāhyeh*) of 15–30,000 people, and neighbourhoods (*mahalleh*) of about 5,000,[3] alleviating demographic pressures on the historic urban core of Tehran.[4] It was in Konstantinos Doxiadis's Tehran Action Plan of 1972 that Abbās Ābād was designated as an administrative and cultural centre, while providing housing for 250,000 new middle-class residents.[5] In 1971, on the recommendation of the then-mayor of Tehran, Gholam-Reza Nikpay, and Prime Minister Amir Abbas Hoveida, the Shah issued a directive to develop it as a new governmental centre.[6] While the council's formally diffuse proposal was subsequently rejected by the Shah,[7] the site's status was upgraded in later plans for a new national administrative and cultural centre; it was renamed 'Shahestān Pahlavi'.

The projects for Shahestān have been described in some detail by others.[8] Notably, in 1973 the Queen's Special Office commissioned the eminent international architects Louis Kahn (USA) and Kenzo Tange (Japan) to prepare master plans. Kahn had been a key participant in the 1970 Isfahan congress, while Tange was a presenter at the 1974 Persepolis congress. Kahn had been contacted in October 1973 by the American developer John L. Rayward, representing a consortium of international banking, engineering, and construction companies. He subsequently chose Ardalan's Mandala Collaborative as his local partner, in accordance to the government's desire for international collaborative projects.[9] Kahn's initial scheme featured a triangular grid of square ministry buildings with central courtyards, diagonally bisected by water channels feeding into a lake (Figure 6.1). He had previously used similar elements for the governmental centre at Dhaka (Bangladesh), and the diagonal configuration of student apartments at the Indian School of Management in Ahmedabad (1962–74). The proposed lake and oval plaza formed a bridge between the ministry offices to the north, and commercial district to the south (Figure 6.2).

182 Development, architecture, and the formation of heritage

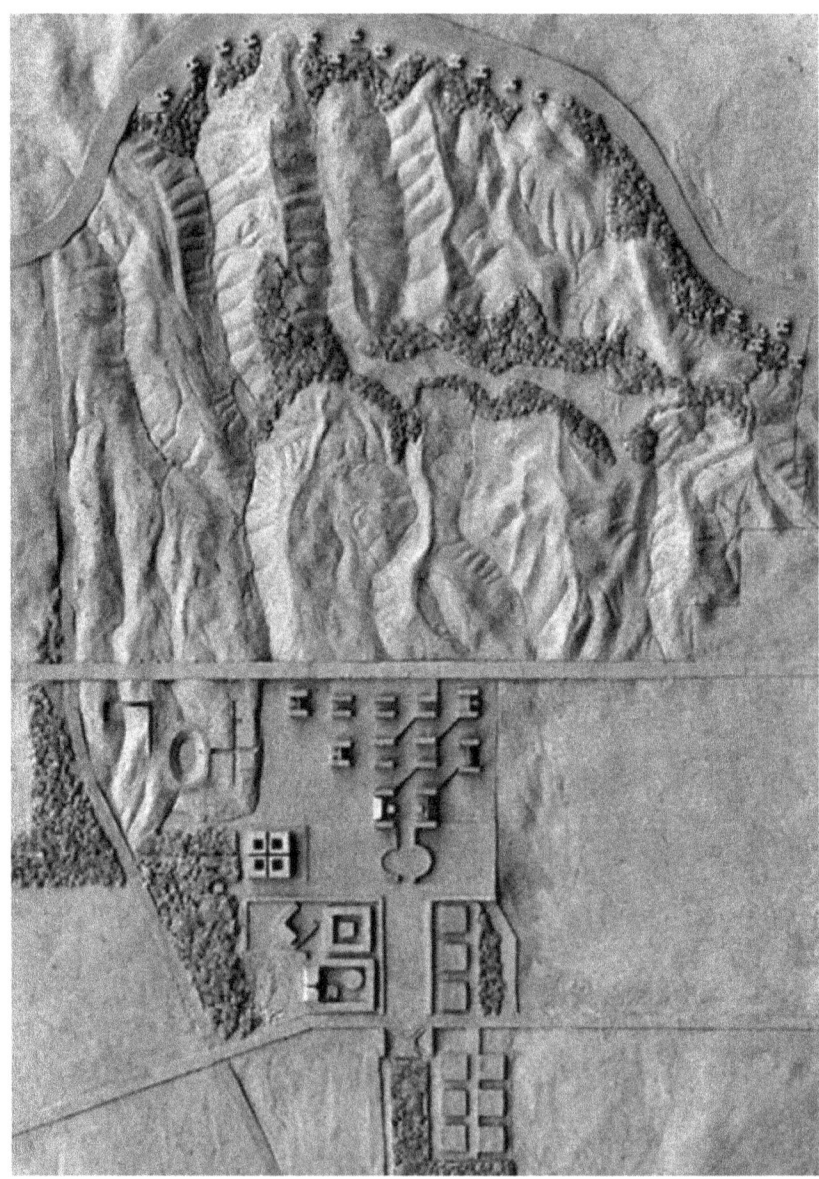

6.1 Louis Kahn project for Shahestān.

The Japanese 'Metabolist' architect Kenzo Tange took a very different approach, effectively creating a north–south linear megastructure that connected two lines of cylindrical office towers at the southern end, to the governmental buildings in the north, at the foothills of the Alborz mountains. Given the size of the programme, it is surprising that neither scheme's author seems

6.2 Kenzo Tange project for Shahestān.

to have considered how the project might have been staged incrementally, an issue of critical importance for a partially commercial project at an urban scale. This issue was, however, examined in detail in the succeeding LDI master plan.

Having been requested by the Queen's Special Office to collaborate on a second, joint submission, Kahn and Tange in 1974 designed a new project combining elements of their initial schemes.[10] In this project, the plaza is moved to the north, forming an acropolis of sorts, surrounded by a clustering of institutions: museum, library, national archive, theatre or opera, and mosque, stepping down to a vast lower terrace, or 'piazza' opposite the new City Hall, then descending to a diamond-shaped platform containing a grid of ministry offices, under which the east–west freeway would pass. To the south of the ministries was an ornamental lake and hotel (Figure 6.3).[11]

Following Kahn's untimely death, this collaborative scheme was abandoned, and with Nikpay's support,[12] the commission for Shahestān was awarded to the British architecture and planning firm of LDI, with Jaquelin Robertson as project architect. Surprisingly, the LDI master plan eliminated from its programme the mosque envisaged in previous plans, unless the diamond-shaped square defined by roads on the Shah and Nation Square, and approximately aligned with the current Mosallā (discussed later), was intended to also serve as a potential prayer space (Figure 6.4).[13] In place of a central mosque, the 'Isfahan aesthetic' of museums and spaces positioned oblique to the north–south grid appears to nostalgically reference the former significance of the mosque within the city, now reduced to a formalistic game. In the successive transformations of the master plans, an 'Islamic' character seems to have largely disappeared, replaced instead by a historicist urban picturesque. This last project for Shahestān has been characterized as the regime's attempts at self-aggrandizement,[14] but avoiding such arid and questionable assumptions, it is more fruitful to focus on the heritage aspects of this gigantic project – on its mode of engagement with a collective past.

Here it is necessary to dispel two myths advanced regarding these projects. Firstly, Kahn's initial scheme is erroneously interpreted as projecting a democratic counter-force to the authoritarian Pahlavi court.[15] Secondly, there is the claim that Ardalan's Traditionalism, underpinned by Illuminationist philosophy,[16] transformed Kahn's conceptions of silence and light and thus his Shahestān project.[17] Regarding the first myth, to posit Kahn's project as some kind of critique of Pahlavi self-aggrandizement[18] disregards the reality that Kahn must have seen this project as a great professional opportunity, given the dearth of commissions at the time. Indeed, the prospect of one of the major international projects of the period would have been intoxicating, enabling him to explore his ideas of urban institutions and what he termed 'commonness', perhaps first undertaken in his Philadelphia urban centre plan, with Anne Tyng.[19] Regarding the second myth, the influence of Ardalan should not be overstated. Kahn had, at Dhaka and Ahmedabad, already elaborated his concepts of the hollow column, the inhabited wall, and the space of community. For

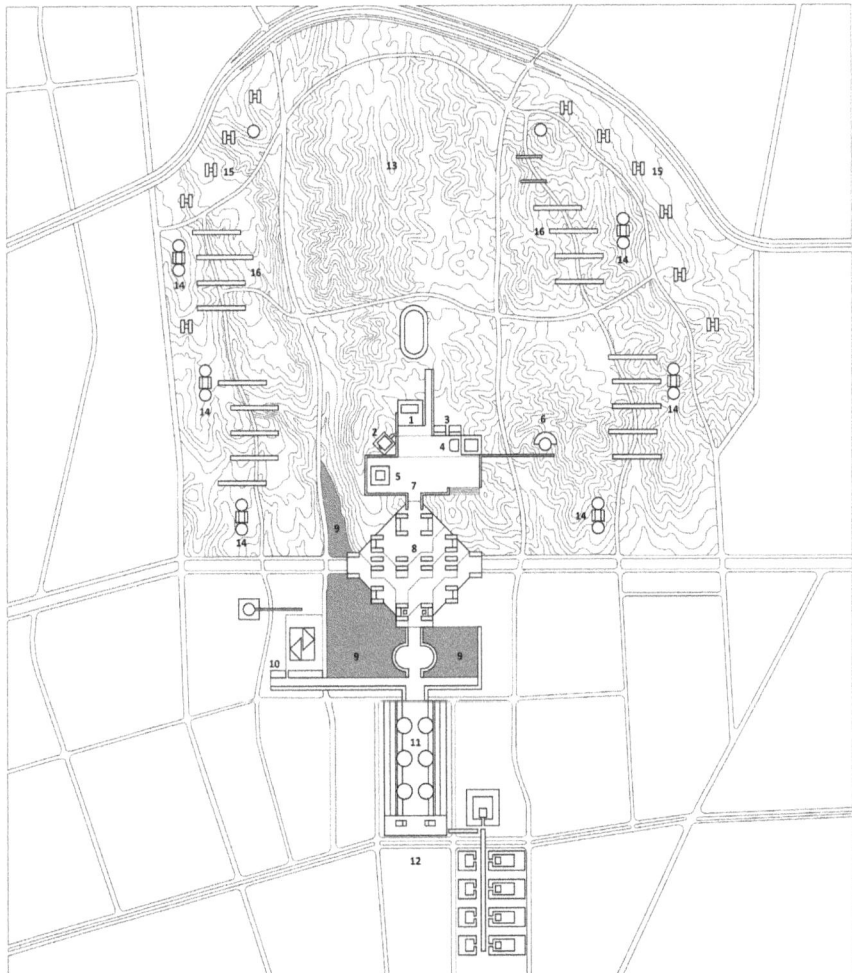

6.3 The joint Kahn-Tange Shahestan Pahlavi Master Plan 1974. Legend: 1. National Historical Archive; 2. Mosque; 3. Museum; 4. Theatre; 5. Cultural Centre; 6. Outdoor Theatre; 7. "Piazza"; 8. Ministries and City Hall; 9. Artificial Lake; 10. Hotel and International Conference Centre; 11. Business and Financial Centre; 12. Gateway; 13. Parkland; 14. High-rise apartments; 15. Medium-rise apartments; 16. Horizontally bridging apartments (derived from first Tange scheme).

there to have been a resonance between his intuitive responses and Ardalan's Traditionalism is not in itself surprising. Certainly Kahn, the historicist, adopted and adapted historic typologies, including Iranian ones. His approach was, however, always syncretic and synthesized through personal poetics – his concepts remain suspended above the forms, and at most intuited through them, unlike Ardalan's overt citation of canonical historical forms.[20]

186 *Development, architecture, and the formation of heritage*

6.4 The LDI scheme.

Kahn was essentially a modernist, with all the optimism that this implied.[21] He had been embraced in the 1960s by critics like Sibyl Moholy Nagy as bringing back a cultural dimension to architecture,[22] but in 1973, the same year that Kahn was working on Shahestān, the eminent Italian critic Manfredo Tafuri criticized Kahn's search for symbolic meaning through semiology and formalism as futile.[23] Indeed, he saw no essential difference between Kahn's historicism and the formalism of the modernist avant-garde – both were, he argued, alienated from the evolving processes of history.[24] While historical architecture was immersed in its evolving social context, historicism flattens this process into a surface, like so many signs detached from context, transforming history into material to be manipulated, refashioned, and recombined.[25] This is, of course, rather similar to a heritage process that inevitably addresses the present. Tafuri saw Kahn's historicism to be displaced from any deep engagement with history. Its order was 'institutional' rather than emerging from social and political praxis; it was an abstraction, made of values and forms 'at the mercy of any and all possible exploitation [that] can serve any and every end.'[26] At Abbās Ābād, Kahn deployed such an ahistorical formal rigour in his visualization, through image, of a social order that did not exist. In this sense, one can draw similarities between Kahn's project and the formalist abstraction of the subsequent LDI plan.

The Llewelyn-Davies International (LDI) plan

The final (1975)[27] project for Shahestān was the product of a large, multidisciplinary team – Jaquelin Robertson had previous experience as development architect for the New York Planning Commission, and both he and LDI had substantial experience in large-scale urban transformations, thus they were 'safe' from a developer's point of view. The design was also eminently implementable, following the economic logic of a grid layout that prepared it for a modular and staged execution as funds became available. The blocks could also be readily adapted to the construction of public offices and ministries, as well as private institutional buildings like banks and insurance companies.

While obviously Western in its general approach, the LDI plan differs from an American open-grid city,[28] rather resembling more the classical planning of Washington Mall. The north–south axis starts at the southern end with an existing park square, which in turn becomes a tree-lined avenue, 'Shah Boulevard', which gradually ascends to the north, passing through a 'wall' formed by the foreign ministry, a block labelled 'INTO Building' (Iranian National Tourism Organization?) and a theatre centre. This opens onto a vast public plaza, the Shah and Nation Square, 200 m x 400 m in size, where its axis meets the Shah monument, a 30 m high symbolic gate. The square, enclosed by a continuous loggia, decks over the east–west highway and a new metro line. On its western flank are the Prime Minister's offices, and to the north–west, a museum of modern art, textile museum, and national museum (Figure 6.5).

6.5 Reconstruction of area of Shah and Nation Square with City Hall scheme by Kenzo Tange and winning national library scheme by von Gerkan and Partners.

Directly fronting the square on the north is the Tehran City Hall, the commission of which would be awarded to Kenzo Tange, and a National Library, the subject of a later competition (see below). Within the square, as noted above, the *qibla*-oriented street layout reorients the plan to the east to a northerly directed parkway, the 'Shahbānou Boulevard and Park', lined by ministry buildings. To east and west, the proposed capitol is buffered from neighbouring districts by parkland. In other words, the plan is delimited, and vaguely reminiscent of the *chāhār-bāgh* of Isfahan; it exploits the hilly site to create a series of belvedere platforms overlooking the square and the city below.

Sharon Lee Ryder, in a 1976 survey on architectural developments in Iran, was hostile to the intent of the project, describing it as a 'misspent effort' in size, conception, and 'image value [...], as someone [Ardalan?] put it, an effort to create an image of civic dignity'. She dismissed the design as 'the ultimate in a sophisticated Western façade [...] rapidly obliterating all that might have been uniquely Persian in Tehran'.[29] Ironically, it seems that the LDI plan, rapidly produced for such a large project, was instead dependent on Ardalan and Bakhtiar's book on traditional Iranian architecture, *The Sense of Unity*; its citations of historical building and landscape forms reflect the desire for monumentality within late modernism that Sybil Moholy Nagy noted in the early 1960s,[30] a tendency which also characterizes the design by Kahn and Tange, as well as Ardalan's Iran Centre for Management Studies (see Chapter 1). Ardalan's Traditionalism, Kahn's citations of the past in his Abbās Ābād scheme and in his American and subcontinental projects of the time, and LDI's grand urban set pieces all evince forms of nostalgia.[31]

Like Ardalan's ICMS, Kahn's historicism could seamlessly mesh into Traditionalist perspectives. The nostalgia in his work was also productive of the affective aspects of memory and heritage through its allusions of spatial atmospheres and materials. Projects like Kahn's Dhaka capitol, referencing the past, were also imaginations, projections of a different future. This displacement of historical symbols within the universalizing matrix of the modern was a precursor of the postmodernist mining of history, whether the philosophical form of relativism, or the aesthetic form of bricolage, what Jameson has characterized as a 'new depthlessness'.[32] It is precisely this lack of depth, and its replacement by signification, that we argue would characterize the 'official' architecture after the Revolution, defined by the nostalgic desire for a return to authenticity. But before we move on, it is noteworthy that all the competing renditions of the Shahestān master plan included spaces that may be described as civic, or 'public realm', a quality that the post-1979 plans conspicuously lost.

The afterlife of Shahestān

After the Revolution, Gruen's plan was not replaced until 1992, with a master plan by Atek Architecture, Planning, and Engineering Consultants, approved by the Majlis (Consultative Assembly) in 1993,[33] in which the ten districts of the original plan were enlarged in number to twenty-two. This plan, however, was rejected as outdated by the Tehran Mayor Karbaschi, who commissioned the Tehran 80 Plan (Iranian calendar 1380 = 2000–1), which allowed for relatively uncontrolled development, but was either not approved by the government or not officially implemented.[34] Following the instabilities of revolution and war, elements of the Shahestān plan were incorporated in a plan for the district approved in 1984.[35] In this plan, a north–south axis, the main feature of the Shahestān projects, is retained, and the plan proposes an even larger central plaza, at the same location as the Shah and Nation Square. The largest complex in Abbās Ābād – the Grand Mosallā, an enormous mosque with related cultural, educational, and social facilities that is still under construction – is sited south of this plaza. The plan displaces the National Library together with a new Academies project to the north–east. In the site as constructed, the major change is the destruction of the north–south axis, the central structuring element of the LDI Shahestān plan, and the watered-down 1984 plan. North of the east–west Shahid Hemmat Expressway, the buildings and landscaping, designed in a Western-influenced 'deconstructive' style, weaken the original northern axis, which dissolves into as yet unfinished office buildings (Figures 6.6 and 6.7).

West of the axis is the Sacred Defence Museum, winner in a 2005 competition by the Barsiān Shaar office (Jila Norouzi), supervised by Hadi Mirmiran's Naqsh-e Jahan Pars Consulting Engineers, and completed in 2010. It is again dressed in fashionably folded and Western deconstructive style, further blurring the original urban configuration. To the east of the axis, is the Tehran Book Garden, by the Design Core 4S office, a scimitar-shaped building completed in

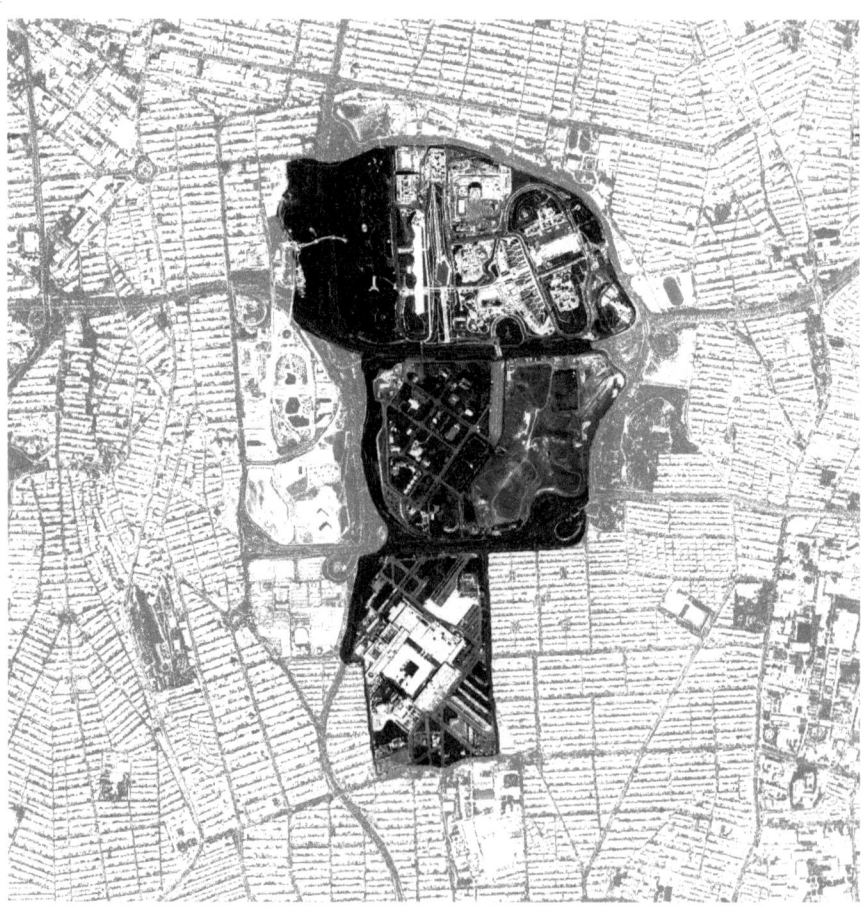

6.6 Aerial view of Abbās Ābād and Mosallā (2017).

6.7 Aerial view of the realized Abbās Ābād plan superimposed on the LDI model (2017).

2017, the roof of which is a folded landscape, and links to the Academies and National Library further to its east (Figure 6.8). Significantly, to the south, the land bridge over the freeway, the location of Kahn's governmental complex and later the 1984 plaza, was never constructed, thus isolating the north of Abbās Ābād from its southern development. South of the freeway, land that was reserved for ministries and the National Oil Company in the Shahestān plan, and for parks and gardens in the 1984 plan, has been taken over by the Islamic Culture and Communication Organization, which follows the *qibla* orientation

6.8 The Tehran Book Garden (2017).

of the Mosallā. In this reorientation, both geometric and cultural, the public realm of the 'urban' spaces of the LDI plan, and the buffering public parkland, have almost entirely disappeared. Specifically, either the public spaces are privatized, or they now function as forecourts for official buildings or as glorified pedestrian transit spaces linking to them (Plate 5). In this once-intended cultural and political heart of Tehran and Iran, the goal of representing a national identity has been abandoned. Where LDI had planned its 'acropolis' of civic monuments surrounding the Shah and Nation Square, there is now a complete void, but also a strange ghost of the Pahlavi project. Thus, the Defence Museum garden by Norouzi and Mirmiran overlays the site of the Shahbānou Boulevard and Park. But the representational capacity of the landscape and buildings has disappeared. Instead, a kind of formal play has been adopted, which could have taken place anywhere in the world, and which resembles the image-based architecture of Dubai and Singapore (Plate 6, below). The transformation of the master plan amounts to an attempted reimagination of the country's official image. While in the 1984 master plan there had been an emphasis upon landscaped open space, the realized plan is an over-scaled district of mega-blocks lacking both human scale and the promised green heart (Figure 6.9).

In its totality, the area appears to be the outcome of conflicting decision-making processes with competing interests, resulting in the loss of what Kevin Lynch termed 'imageability'.[36] This is symptomatic of a larger problem, which Mashayekhi has identified as the inability of either the city or the national planning ministry to develop a coherent replacement for the 1968 Tehran master plan, resulting from contestations and conflicting interests between civic authorities and para-state religious organizations. These have gained control over large tracts of previously private and public land, which they develop through a network of subsidiary companies.[37] This may go some way in explaining the impression of a disappearance of civic space in Abbās Ābād. Most

6.9 General view (above and below) of the bridge over the Art Lake connecting the Book Garden to the Sacred Defence Museum structure in the background (2017), and view along the main landscape axis (north–south) of the Art Garden in the form of a stepped promenade leading to the Art Lake (2010). The landscape and the museum were designed as part of the same project.

6.10 The promenade adjacent to the museum structure (2017).

of the institutions within the Mosallā grid appear to be aligned with the religious conservatives.³⁸ In the area given over to museums, cultural institutions, and gardens, which Mashayekhi does not discuss, the revised plans (or lack thereof) eradicate any impression of a civic realm.

Aside from the Mosallā complex, the two most visually significant building complexes are the isolated National Library and Iranian Academies, facing each other across a yet to be constructed public square. From here, an awkward western-directed stairway leads over the Tehran Book Garden, and the unfinished Art Garden (باغ هنر) and Lake, to the Sacred Defence Museum and Tāleqāni Park (Figure 6.10 and Plate 7, top-left). The space is disorienting, contingent, and fragmentary with circumstantial connections. Unconvincing modern architecture meets arbitrary landscaping and the sci-fi silver dome of the Panorama building of the Sacred Defence Museum. Despite the official rhetoric concerning expressions of Islamic identity, neither the landscape, nor the architectural elements within it, are particularly Islamic. While pre-Revolution critics, like Ardalan, and their Western supporters, had decried what they saw as the mimicry of Western cultural forms during the Pahlavi period, one sees in the post-Revolution 'public' projects in Abbās Ābād a profligate postmodernist licence for novel forms. Since these were sanctioned by an Islamist regime, one must question the perspective of critics, invoking Foucault, who have associated such mimicry with the Pahlavi regime.³⁹

We will limit our probing of the post-Revolution architecture of Abbās Ābād to three iconic buildings designed in the 1980s and 1990s, namely, the National

Library, the Iranian Academies, and the mountainous, but strangely alienated form of the Mosallā. These were all the subject of national competitions that formed the vehicle for public discourse on architecture and cultural identity in this period.

The National Library

The Pahlavi National Library was an imperial project planned for Abbās Ābād.[40] Decreed in 1973, it was intended to be a world-class project, embodying Iran's emergence as a modern nation.[41] The project was driven by the Deputy Minister of the Imperial Court for Cultural Affairs, Shojā`eddin Shafā, and the Imperial Cultural Council,[42] as integral to the promotion of both literacy and cultural knowledge, in concert with international bodies such as UNESCO, and thus aligned to the developmental objectives of the White Revolution.[43]

A board of consultants led by Chairman Dr Nasser Sharify[44] produced a six-volume document, 'The Pahlavi National Library of the Future: Its Resources, Services, Programmes, and Building Requirements', which was presented to Deputy Minister Shafā, in March 1976. This formed the basis for an international architectural competition (1977) with an international panel of judges including Ardalan,[45] to select an architect, and to serve as the basis for further functional planning.[46] The brief stipulated that designers should interpret traditional Iranian architecture, including a summary of principles based upon Ardalan's co-authored book, *The Sense of Unity*.[47] Thus, the competition sought modernization with Iranian characteristics.

From a large field, the competition was won by Meinhard von Gerkan and Partners.[48] Their project, while overtly modern, did reference traditional Islamic-era architecture with its octagonal court, and central space conceived as a gigantic *eyvān*, roofed by giant shade louvres and skylights that recall, and perhaps derive from, Jørn Utzon's 1959 design for the Bank Melli branch near the University of Tehran (1962).[49] Fountains and water channels descended from the courtyard by the central staircase to a square pool on the lower level. Overall, the design was mildly referential of bazaar and Persian garden spaces. Above the central staircase hall, a series of public patios would have overlooked the square and the city beyond. Nonetheless, the design language was also undeniably reminiscent of 1960s and 1970s Western institutional architecture (Figure 6.11).[50]

The winning design received a mixed reception in the professional press. One review, by an Iranian architect, Mansour Vakili, who had submitted an unsuccessful entry, decried the foreign and non-traditional character of the project: 'The result of an international competition is an international architecture.' He was particularly critical of the discord created by two adjacent buildings, Tange's Tehran City Hall and the Pahlavi National Library, arguing that this 'will cast a shadow of doubt over the future of the surrounding buildings and threaten the future square with disorder and chaos and [a] certain

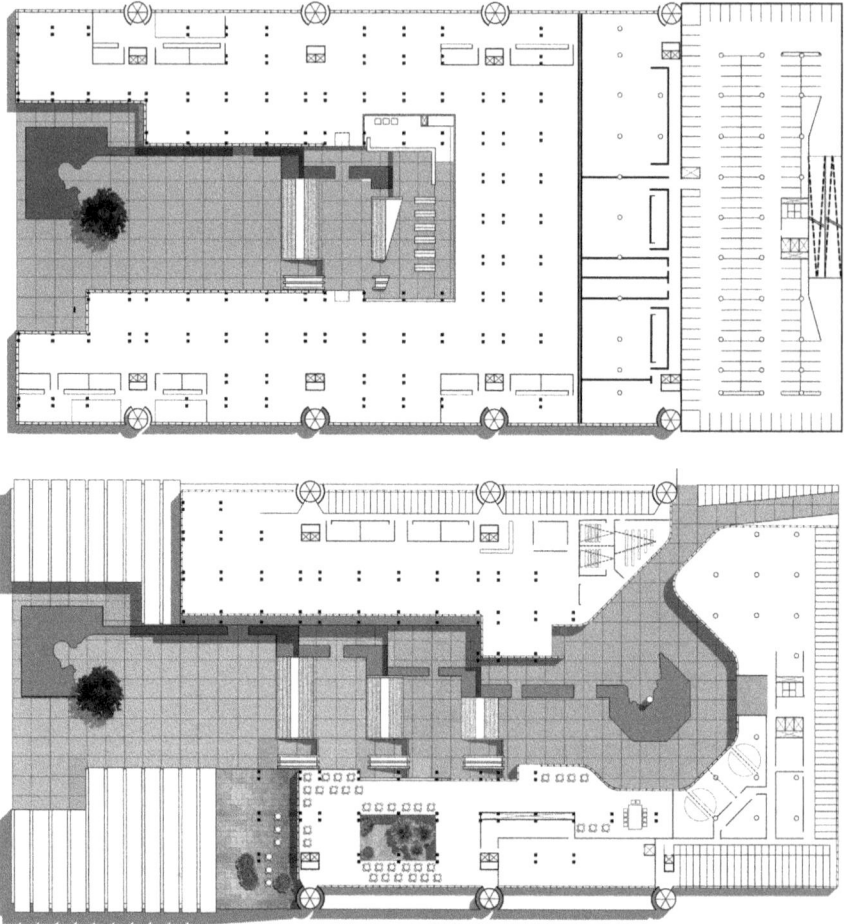

6.11 Meinhard von Gerkan and partners, National Library competition entry, site plan (1977).

destruction [of] architectural quality'.[51] These criticisms resonate with both the anti-Western sentiments of critics of the Shah's regime, and the rabidly anti-international reactions of the later revolutionary period.

After the Revolution, in 1995 the Rafsanjani government (1989–97) commissioned a second competition on a new site, based on a modified, reduced version of the 1976 brief. The winning scheme for the new National Library of Iran was subsequently revised by the architect Yousef Shariatzadeh of Pirraz Consulting Engineers,[52] who had trained under Houshang Seyhoun.[53] This new design was even less representational in its architectural expression than the von Gerkan scheme (Figure 6.12), but shared its experiential aspects. It utilized a sequence of fountains, pools, and water channels flowing through

6.12 Yousef Shariatzadeh and Pirraz Consulting Engineers, National Library (2013).

6.13 The Chogha-Zanbil archaeological site, Khuzestan, southern Iran (2018).

the external passages and courtyards of sand-coloured brickwork to create comfortable external rooms, but here the reference to Iranian heritage is rather remote, despite the horizontal striated form perhaps alluding to the Elamite pyramid of Chogha-Zanbil (Figure 6.13). Nor is there any overt reference to a Shi'ite Islamic identity; instead, it possesses what Darab Diba has described as 'an appropriate functionalism'.[54] In fact, individual stylistic differences aside, there is little conceptual difference between the von Gerkan and Pirraz projects.

The National Library design eschews monumentality, despite its great size, or for that matter recognizable iconography, in place of which there is an undemonstrative muteness. Shariatzadeh's design, which resonates with certain principles articulated by foreign delegates to the 1974 congress,[55] resides somewhere between brutalism and postmodernism – nonetheless, it creates a vaguely familiar spatial network, with overhead light admitted through linear and octagonal skylights, creating an ambience which could be familiar to a local population of users.[56]

Shariatzadeh was a committed modernist who based his architecture upon the demands of function, available technology, economy, and climate, rather than upon some Iranian cultural essence.[57] He abhorred overt figurative imitations of tradition. In his earlier projects, such as the Cinema Rivoli (1962), there is an exuberant exploration of abstract composition, but in the National Library, and his Shahid Bahonar University of Kerman (Pirraz, 1984 onwards), this has been reduced to simple massing, climatically sound spaces, and at most, subtle allusions to traditional motifs in abstracted traditional brickwork (Figure 6.14).[58] Rather than possessing the ideological Traditionalism that characterizes the Mosallā,[59] in Shariatzadeh's library one finds a muteness in which international trends are vaguely recalled, but which does not seem to echo the regime's ideology in any way. Its undemonstrative architecture contrasts sharply with the subsequent competition projects for the Iranian Academies.

The Iranian Academies: A contextual architecture?

The second major state institution proposed for Abbās Ābād, and the first significant post-Revolution architectural competition (1993), was the Iranian Academies, or *Farhangestān*. The Academies had been reformed in the second Pahlavi period under the supervision of Mehrdad Pahlbod, as a vehicle to enact cultural reform policies, such as the project to modernize and purify the Persian language that had begun under Reza Shah.[60] The project for a new complex, with three Academies (Science, Medicine, and Persian Literature), was commissioned during Rafsanjani's presidency at the beginning of his second term in office, and reflected his monumental and developmental ambitions. The competition was supported by the Ministry for Housing and Urban Development and promoted through *Abadi* journal, the first officially supported journal of architecture after the Revolution.[61] The submissions, and more importantly the selected projects, reflect the dominant tendencies of official Iranian architecture at the time.[62] Forty-four design teams registered for the competition, but only fifteen schemes were submitted, yet this was to be considered a significant participation rate, given the social and economic context and the shortage of technological expertise and competence.[63] The Revolution and then the war and international sanctions had impeded global circulation of design knowledge into Iran; at the time of the competition, the country was still relatively isolated from access to up-to-date developments, and information and university library collections were only starting to replenish. Given the lag in innovations, architects often had recourse to postmodernist symbolic representation predating the Revolution, seen as being well-suited to the country's 'cultural requirements'

6.14 Kerman, Shahid Bahonar University, by Yousef Shariatzadeh, Pirraz Architects: (above) the mosque with brickwork relief and (below) a general view into the courtyards with the amphitheatre at the right of the image (2004).

which were reinforced by the Aga Khan Award for Islamic Architecture.[64] Amid the flurry of post-war reconstructive architecture and master-planning projects, there is evidence of the strong influence of both Traditionalism and postmodernism.[65]

The competition had a noticeable effect in reinvigorating architectural debates in Iran. In his editorial in *Abadi* 12, editor Hashemi pointed out that since the Islamic Revolution, and the subsequent reopening of universities after the Cultural Revolution, there had been little serious architectural discourse in the profession or schools, but instead mostly jargonistic translations of non-Iranian architects and critics. In discussing the competition entries for the Academies, he noted this was the first time that such a complicated and significant project would be entrusted to Iranian designers – it was a step forward in self-reliance and independence in this field, and thus in line with revolutionary rhetoric.[66] Discourse within *Abadi* revolved around questions of authenticity, recalling the 1970s congresses, indicating that the hiatus in cultural contacts between Iran and the outside world had trapped Iranian architecture in a time capsule. This same outlook informed selection of the Academies' jury, and the brief which emphasized 'cultural aspects'. Other principles, such as the preference for 'simplicity' in design were, however, inherently consistent with the modernist principles of structural clarity, truth to the nature of materials, and honesty of expression.

In their report, the judges praised the first prize-winning entry by Naqsh-e Jahan Pars group (Mirmiran) for its 'simplicity in expression, clarity in design, and spatial organization' and monumental qualities (Figures 6.15 and 6.16). In fact, this design would have fitted in perfectly with the pre-Revolution cultural projects, consisting of a vast horizontal mastaba-like platform accessed by a monumental ramp, recalling in its archetypal forms the projects of Amanat and Ardalan. Surmounting the plinth was a monumental flattened dome, both modern and ancient. Mirmiran's double-bayed arch form resembles the battered pylons of ancient Egyptian temples, but also the symbolic arch of LDI's design for Shah and Nation Square. The project arranges and juxtaposes historical motifs in novel combinations. Ludovico Micara noted the winning entry's eclectic references to ancient architecture, and its reflection of the 'importance, value and respect attributed to the ground in Persian architecture', citing the Apadana at Persepolis.[67] The implied premise of this project was that 'archetypal' elements might be recreated, perpetually, in new contexts without losing their meanings. However, in the process, such motifs and elements were decontextualized, thus blurring the boundaries between traditional and modern iconography, indeed much as occurred in Western postmodernism. There was also thus a sense of nostalgia, a vaguely recalled past in this project that distinguished it.

The second prize went to Tajeer Architects (Ali Akbar Saremi and Taghi Radmard) for its 'new expression and the creation of consistent and flowing spaces'. Here, Kahn's influence can be detected in the project's bricolage-like composition.[68] Tajeer's approach, which rejected replication of the past, follows

6.15 Cover of *Abadi* 12 depicting the winning scheme for the Islamic Republic Academies showing the competition winning entry by Mirmiran's office, Naqsh-e Jahan-Pars.

6.16 Another view of the winning competition entry by Mirmiran.

what Saremi called 'loose order' (in contrast to Ardalan's faithful following of traditional forms and patterns), a quality which he detected in projects of James Stirling and Louis Kahn (Figure 6.17).[69]

The third prize was awarded to Ivan Hasht-Behesht (Darab Diba) for their project's 'rational distribution of spaces and simplicity of relationships'. This project demonstrated Diba's concern to establish architectural identity through a formal consistency with its cultural, historical, and environmental context, but also strongly recalls Kahn's historicism. Indeed, the architects made reference to both Islamic and non-Islamic precedents and typologies.[70] Certainly, this eclectic bricolage of Islamic and Western elements and motifs suggests an identity crisis, one that had persisted since before the 1970 Isfahan congress, when it was extensively debated, and reveals an ongoing infatuation with Kahn's abstracted monumental architecture (Figure 6.18).

The fourth place went to Bavand Consulting Engineers (Iradj Kalantari and Hossein Sheikh Zeineddin) for their project's 'balanced combination of vernacular and modern architectural elements'. This project followed an organizational hierarchy reminiscent of fortified traditional cities such as Bam (Figure 6.19), with the centre defined by a tower housing the libraries, and other functions housed at a domestic scale outside the wall (Plate 8).[71] The project's reference to the medieval Islamic city and playful use of historic architectural motifs, while essentially postmodernist, accords with one of the possibilities for contemporary Islamic architecture discussed in the 1970 congress by Kuran, who emphasized the need for tradition to be dynamic and responsive.[72]

The fifth place went to the Memar-Naqsh group, and its director Kambiz Haji-Ghassemi, a historian of Iranian Islamic-era architecture, for 'their

Tehran's reluctant urban centre 203

6.17 Tajeer Architects (Ali Akbar Saremi and Taghi Radmard), entry for the Academies competition.

6.18 Ivan Hasht-Behesht (Darab Diba), entry for the Academies competition.

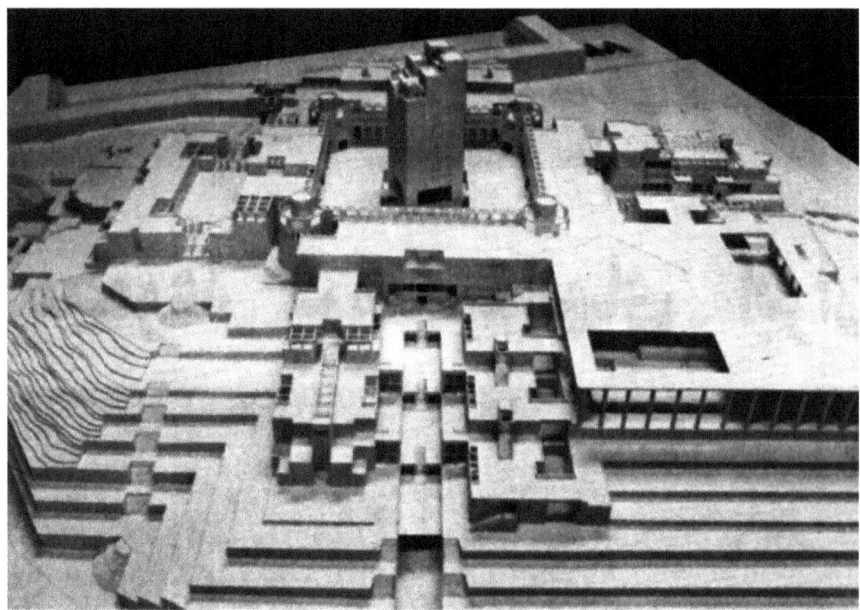

6.19 Competition entry by Bavand.

attention to cultural and functional aspects'.[73] In their entry, subsequently chosen for construction (Figure 6.20), Haji-Ghassemi seeks to authenticate the design through the deployment of axiality and centralized courtyards found in the traditional desert architecture of Iran.[74] On paper, the design faithfully reproduced traditional patterns, and formal relations, reflecting official projections of architectural identity. However, as evidenced in the constructed complex, the outcome again resembles postmodernism, with traditional motifs transformed into two-dimensional 'signs' applied to utilitarian concrete frame construction (Figure 6.21 and Plate 6, above). In theorizing their work, the designers claimed that they sought to attain order, clarity, and simplicity, normative principles that recall more the modernist architectural canon than traditional Iranian Islamic architectural heritage. In a recent interview, Haji-Ghassemi argued that the design was based upon the study of historic Iranian typologies, but also reflects the influence of the work and writing of Nader Ardalan:

> It is an architecture of directionless space. It is the architecture of 'abstinent simplicity' [*sahl va momtane* = سهل و ممتنع]. It seems simple on the surface but has many deep mysteries that will not be discovered without close connection. It does not speak to strangers, but those who become *mahram* [close] and familiar with it will feel an increasingly deeper connection to it.[75]

6.20 Competition entry by Memar-Naqsh.

6.21 Memar-Naqsh design for the Academies as constructed. Top row showing peripheral internal courtyards (2010) and bottom row showing the general massing of the project (2017).

In analysing the published projects in *Abadi* and through conversations with some of the authors,[76] one can identify several main tendencies: emphasis upon regional specificity, employment of vernacular elements, abstraction of archetypal forms and their recombination in novel compositions, and finally, the use of geometry and symmetry. All these characteristics had also been pursued in pre-Revolution architecture. These projects also reflect a regionalist discourse that was shaping up by this period as the preferred establishment style of the Islamic Republic. This mythologization of 'true' Iranian architecture as the embodiment of honesty, directness, and simplicity is clearly a modern projection onto the past, one which also resonates with Ardalan's and Diba's similar recourse to the forms of the past to valorize present-day projects.[77] This is an attempt to 'invent traditions' in precisely the sense that Hobsbawm and Ranger meant, an invention that is at once nostalgic and reactive to the outside world in its quest for identity and authenticity. The nostalgic references to tradition in these projects also recalls Quaroni and Candilis's critique of 'false tradition', the appearance of traditional forms, motifs, and patterns of geometrical relations as an ideological veil concealing modern programmes inconsistent with them.[78] Abstracted from their context, such forms could become fetishized, and serve an ideological purpose, reproducing the political relations that dominated the society. These Academies projects were highly aestheticized works of architecture, which owed much to the legacy of the Iran congresses, as well as to the later Western discourse of Critical Regionalism. Rather than grounding their projects in lived experience, architects reproduced a sanctioned rhetoric, while in the potential and actual effects of their projects – material impacts on the ground and emotional reception – they may have been doing something else.[79]

Within this identity rhetoric, these post-Revolution architects were arguably adapting familiar Western postmodernist critiques of functionalist rationality.[80] As discussed in previous chapters, this situation was not new and was apparent in the counter-Enlightenment responses of pre-Revolution Iranian intellectuals. Nevertheless, in striving for authenticity, and following other intellectuals, even well into the 1990s, architects obscured their global connections by clinging to a form of Critical Regionalism. While such an approach was consistent with the creeds of the Cultural Revolution, which advocated a return to Islamic principles[81] and viewed the indigenous and the Islamic as coterminous, this discourse was hardly a disruption of the old relations in the field. It was, rather, a continuation of the congress discourses, indicating that cultural transformations have a life of their own, which does not necessarily accord with political ruptures.

The 'Grand' or Imam Khomeini Mosallā: An inchoate Islamic centre for Tehran

The last of these 'national' projects envisaged in the Abbās Ābād site was a religious complex. The earliest master plans for Abbās Ābād had included a mosque, as did Kahn's scheme for Shahestān.[82] However, in relation to the subsequent master plan by LDI, Robertson noted that including a mosque was rejected by the Shah.[83] This raises the question of what the presence or absence of a mosque could mean.

Whereas the complete absence of a mosque in the LDI project may suggest a kind of secularism, its eventual dominant position in the post-Revolution Abbās Ābād layout signals a transformation of the mosque into the realm of symbols at both local and national scales. In the realized Abbās Ābād development, any formal continuity with the surrounding districts has been annulled. In its place the Imam Khomeini Grand Mosallā complex to the south of the Resālat Highway, and the Islamic Culture and Communication Organization and nearby cultural centre, share a *qibla* orientation; together they declare their otherness with respect to the surrounding districts. The Mosallā complex and its central prayer court are proposed to form the new social centre for Tehran, one that is controlled in every respect by the Islamic authorities (the contrast to previous civic schemes is notable). This intent is evident in the architect Parviz Moayyed-Ahd's aerial perspective drawing, in which the city has almost entirely disappeared. Instead, a closed complex of domes, shrines, fountain courts and 'Persian' gardens lined by arcaded porticoes, and minarets has the exotic unreality of Frank Lloyd Wright's Broadacre City project – ironically resembling the pleasure palace of some Eastern potentate rather than the spiritual heart of the Islamic Republic (Figure 6.22).

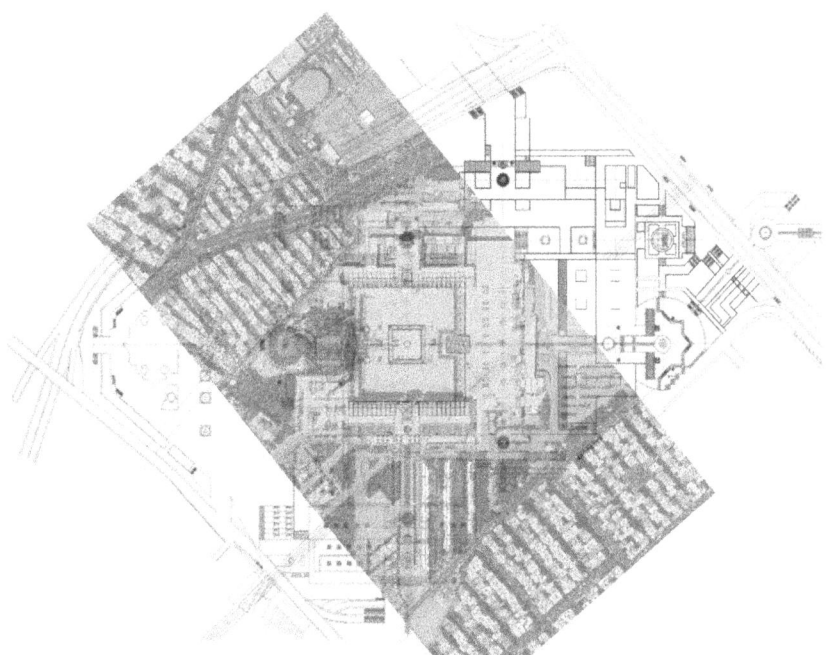

6.22 Plan of Imam Khomeini Grand Mosallā in its urban context.

The origin of the Mosallā project

Traditionally, mosallās were open-air enclosures outside Iranian cities. Their modern incarnations as great prayer halls is an innovation of the Islamic regime that wanted spaces for the performance of pan-Islamic ceremonies, serving as ideological representational spaces at both national (Shiite-Iranian) and transnational (the Muslim *Umma* at large) scales.[84] They were intended to promulgate the government's agenda through Friday sermons, a tradition which was reinstated by the new regime. In the capital, for over two decades this function was served by the University of Tehran's prayer ground, which, in the push to Islamize universities, was itself converted from a former university football pitch.[85] However, the Tehran Mosallā's architectural expression, through its form, scale, and decorative programme, under the current Supreme Leader Ali Khamanei departed from the preference for simplicity advocated by Ruhollah Khomeini.[86] Indeed, the Tehran Mosallā takes on an overtly ideological message in its siting, location, and scale.

The 1986 Mosallā competition located the project on a 65-hectare site in Abbās Ābād district, between Shahid Hemmat Expressway to the north, and Shahid Beheshti Street to the south. Befittingly, this was announced at Friday prayers in front of the University of Tehran in 1985.[87] The history of the Mosallā's planning, beginning as an idea for a grand mosque for which land had to be acquired, explains the disconnection between its layout and that of the rest of the Abbās Ābād area.[88] The location was a pragmatic choice as the most feasible and cheapest in terms of availability of land and the minimization of housing relocations. The planning went through three consultative stages, which included a large survey group (possibly religious officials), clerical input, and finally, input by architectural academics. One of the consistent emphases was that the complex had to reflect Islamic values and avoid alien styles. The outcome of this process was a booklet entitled *The Programme for the Grand Mosallā of Tehran*, ratified by Khamenei.[89] A panel of senior architects and heritage and conservation experts with links to the then-Iranian Cultural Heritage Organization (ICHO, now ICHHTO),[90] for the most part of a traditionalist orientation, judged the competition.[91] It is therefore not surprising that the judging panel failed to award a first prize from the short-listed entries, among which the Moayyed-Ahd project, while exploiting traditional motifs, recombined them in novel and unconventional ways. In the second round of the competition, Iranian academic architects were invited to produce schematics; however, only two responded – Latif Abolghasemi and Parviz Moayyed-Ahd. The latter architect's design was implicitly accepted in 1987. Subsequently, a second booklet of all the designs was compiled and sent to the Supreme Leader in 1991. Once again, Moayyed-Ahd was confirmed, upon which he was commissioned to undertake the design development.

The selected scheme proposed not just a mosque, but a new master plan for southern Abbās Ābād, extending north to Shahid Hemmat Expressway (Figure 6.23). Huge formal gardens, recalling the traditional Iranian *chāhār-bāgh*, were

Tehran's reluctant urban centre 209

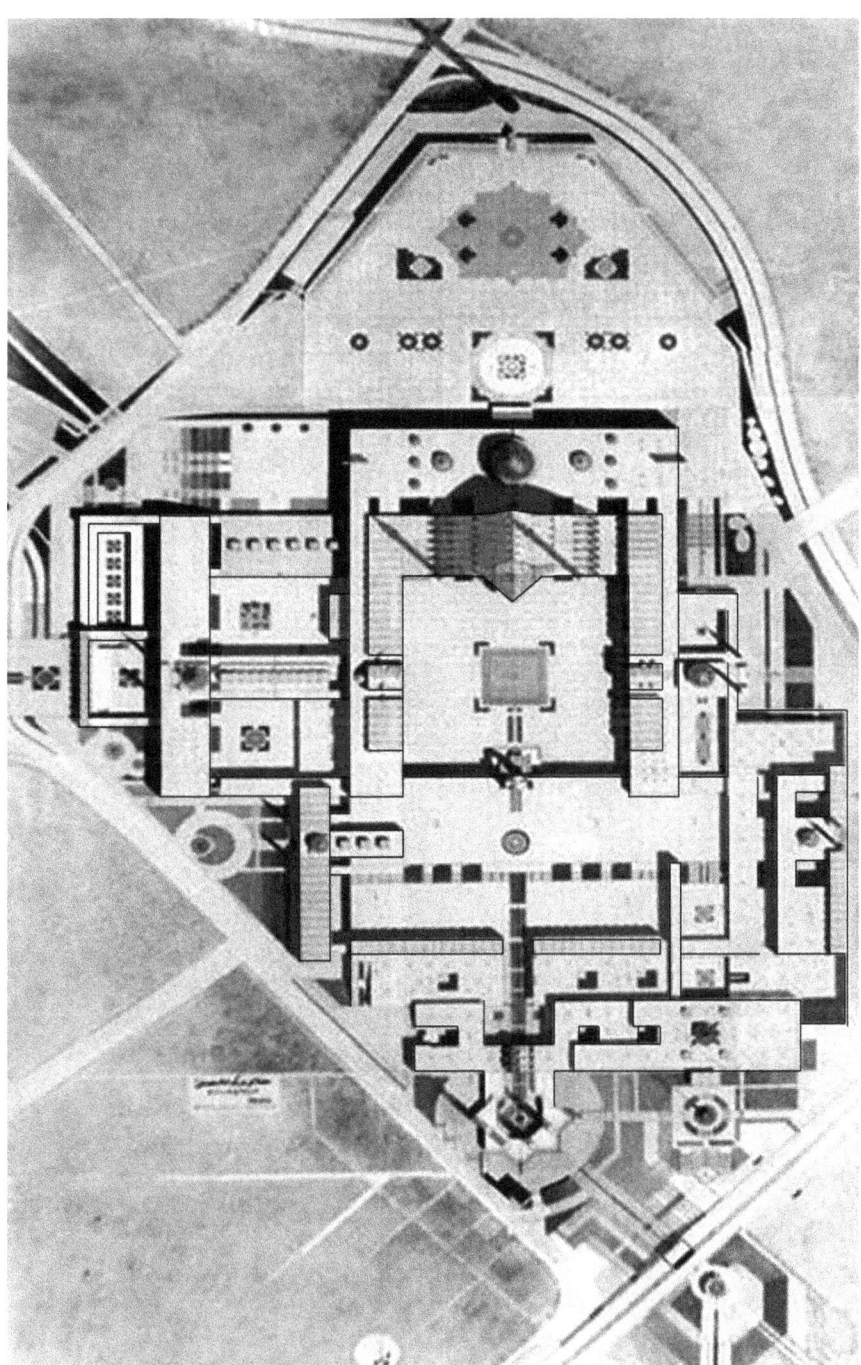

6.23 Moayyed-Ahd's winning scheme.

proposed to the north-east and north-west of the Mosallā, spanning across the north–south Modarres Highway and the east–west Resālat Highway. To the south-east, an enormous roundabout, centred upon a circular water basin and fountain, formed a gateway to the district from downtown Tehran. The original location of the mosque was in the bend of Modarres Highway north of Beheshti Street, which would have necessitated the demolition of an entire block of existing houses. In a later version of the design, Moayyed-Ahd relocated the mosque to the north-east of this block but replaced the housing with a large park and fountain basin. However, this was never implemented – in a more developed plan, the park is not shown – and presumably the housing was to be retained. As built, the rear of the mosque is now hemmed in by dense low-rise housing. Finally, neither of the decks bridging over the highways has been implemented, nor have the Persian-style gardens – in their place are car parks and depots. The reason for these changes is unclear, although the residents' resistance to displacement and sale of properties, and cost constraints, may have been influencing factors. Consequently, we can see in the development of the Mosallā, despite its vast size, a gradual diminution in ambition. What the architect envisaged as a spiritual utopia and focal point of the new 'Islamic city' became a petrified urban object, disconnected from its context and visually encountered from motorways.

The architecture of the Mosallā

In its unfinished state, the huge dome of the mosque, supported by reinforced concrete ribs and extensive steel framing, more resembles an exposition hall than a mosque. Meanwhile, the vaulted canopy facing the central courtyard, still incomplete, is loosely derived from the *eyvān* of the Sasanian palace at Ctesiphon in Iraq, as Rizvi has noted (Figure 6.24).[92] The motif, which is also reminiscent of Shahyad, is also repeated in the porticos around the main courtyard. In its exaggerated scale, the project reveals its ideological objectives as a national/transnational space interpreted in relation to the religious and political contestation between Shi'ite Iran and the Sunni states of the Persian Gulf.[93] As such, it is devoid of the usual 'spatial intimacy' found in a typical mosque, but is, instead, a space that potentially transforms individuals into masses (the *Umma*).[94] This dissolving of the individual into the collective is an old, familiar, and unavoidably sinister device, most blatantly exploited at the Nazi Zeppelinfeld rally ground, and analyzed in depth by Elias Canetti in his study of crowds and mass behaviour. Canetti notes the way in which a communal identity is created during the Shi'ite Moharram rituals: 'The whole crowd in a single movement lift their arms high and give a long reverberating shout "Ya Allah! O God!".'[95]

The Mosallā provides a multi-purpose space whose character can change at ritual times, thus becoming a hybrid of the secular and the religious. Outside ritual times, the space serves quotidian functions which are nonetheless subsumed and coloured by the sacred aspect of the space.[96] For example, during

6.24 Two views of the central courtyard of the Mosallā under construction (2017).

one author's visit to the site, there was a health and sports fair located in the courtyard of the Mosallā, full of sports and body-building equipment, both everyday and masculinist, supportive of a seductive cult of male physicality (Figure 6.25).[97] Another significant example, the transference of the Tehran Book Fair

6.25 Sports exhibition at the Mosallā (2017).

to the Mosallā in 2005 under then-mayor Amadinejad, should not necessarily be seen as a denial of the complex's intended religious and national identity-forming role, but instead perhaps as a cunning ploy to both muzzle the fair's previous function as a forum for public debate, as well as to harness the public's enthusiasm for it in the attempt to construct a submissive, massed crowd.[98]

Within the invented public space of the Mosallā, the architectural language suggests an image of the past validated by, and in turn authenticating, the Islamic Republic. This image of the past is activated through choreographed public spectacles and symbols that perform and represent collective identities. As the original judges had perceived, the architecture is not traditional, but instead uses familiar motifs – dome, arcade, fountain – as signs which could be deployed in the creation of a new assemblage. This kind of distinctly modern syncresis draws upon Islamic elements, such as Timurid domes, and pre-Islamic ones – the Ctesiphon vaulted *eyvān*, Tāq-e Kasrā (Plate 7, top-right). These elements are montaged together in a manner analogous to that deployed by Godard in his 1937 design for the Ancient Iran Museum.[99] Rather than following traditional techniques, in the Mosallā traditional forms – domes, arches, and minarets – are constructed out of modern industrial materials such as steel and concrete, and prefabricated ceilings, and the design is the product of international collaboration.[100] The resultant project is, as Rizvi noted in relation to the Khomeini shrine, a pastiche,[101] in the sense in which Jameson elegantly defined the term, as a parody that has lost its sense of humour, a stylistic mask. Here, the ideology of the Islamic Republic reveals itself to have commonalities with European postmodernist thought – borne of modernity, it adopts the signs of anti-modernity while employing modern processes, notably the control and manipulation of information.[102] The public realm – the space of political and cultural exchange and dissemination – is replaced by a space of mass mobilization. Personal architectural expression, the poetics of Amanat, or Diba, for example, is replaced by mass communicable signification: 'In a world in which stylistic innovation is no longer possible, all that is left is to imitate dead styles, to speak through the masks and with the voices of the styles in the imaginary museum.'[103]

This modern architecture is masked with the populist expressions of nostalgia for a past culture, home, and nation which cannot, however, be sated by a return. Furthermore, the gigantic scale of images and symbols creates a strange, defamiliarizing effect. In this regard, the commissioners and architect of the Mosallā were ultimately shrewd in eschewing a pure Traditionalist embrace of the architecture of an idealized past, such as Safavid Isfahan or Yazd, unlike the pre-Revolution culturalists, but have instead turned to the popular culture of the contemporary street. The motifs of this culture can mean anything or nothing, an image that has been severed from its originating context.[104] In this sense, the project, still at the time of writing incomplete, may never be completed – beneath its signs, it remains a kind of void, an emptiness at the heart of Tehran, one that is socially produced. Both the 'muscle fair', and the annual book fair held at the Mosallā, are carefully choreographed. While genuine public spaces retain a tension between their role as sites for the fabrication of a sense of 'community' and the threat that genuine openness poses to authority, through the contestation of power,[105] at the Mosallā activities must be authorized and approved (Plate 7, bottom). Certainly, expressions of political contestation must, like the rallies held there in 2009 in support of the presidential candidacy of Ahmedinejad, be approved of and in the interest of the ruling authorities. Even access to the site is heavily regulated. In this regard, the transferral of the function of main prayer space from the gates of the University of Tehran at *Enqelāb-e Islami* (Islamic Revolution Street) to the Mosallā might be seen as an assertion of the self-confidence of the regime, that there is no longer any substantive public opposition to contest. But it also suggests the opposite, that there is no public space at the Mosallā.

If the Shahyad and the Shahestān complexes were intended to represent the monarchic state, then the equivalent monuments that are representative of the ideology and aspirations of the Islamic Republic of Iran – the 72 Tan Mosque near the Shahyad and the Mosallā – connect politics and religion. The Pahlavi establishment identified with the tradition of kingship rooted in antiquity, but its White Revolution rhetoric was also reflected in these monuments' syncretic melding of pre-Islamic, Islamic, and futuristic motifs and forms. In the aftermath of the Revolution and ensuing war, the Tehran Mosallā, the visibly dominant and vast religious complex for state-promoted religious rallies and Friday prayers, but also mass secular events, joined the tomb of Ayatollah Ruhollah Khomeini in Tehran's southern necropolis of Behesht-e Zahrā, as an example of ambiguous structures that are simultaneously national monuments, quasi-shrines of statesmen and their families, but also populist destinations for tourist entertainment.

Conclusion

In summarizing the long gestation and vicissitudes of the Abbās Ābād site, and the institutional projects that were projected for it, both realized and unrealized, one can retrospectively draw parallels with the national modernist utopias that were planned for Western capital cities – Chandigarh, Brasilia, and Canberra. Arguably, in all these projects, the designers have addressed an ideal, rather than a lived reality. The centres are monumental but strangely empty. At Abbās Ābād, three characteristics are apparent in the current state of the development: the diminution of the public realm, the abandonment of citations of traditional Iranian architecture, and a decline in the assertion, through built form, of a national identity.

Conceived in the Pahlavi period as a capitol, centred upon a ceremonial plaza and cultural and governmental buildings, the area now operates as an island surrounded by freeways and disconnected from the city from all directions. Instead of integrating the administrative functions within the life of the city, the realized plan appears as a spatial metaphor for the gap between the state and the majority of the people – here, there is no genuinely civic realm. The major plaza that was still shown in the 1984 master plan, a carry-over of the urban heart concept at the core of the Kahn/Tange and LDI schemes, has been deleted, and instead replaced by privatized institutional spaces. Indeed, there is now no spatial centre at all, barring the inchoate plaza between the National Library and the Academies. The fragmentation and discontinuity of the urban spaces is the result of an abrupt disconnection in planning ideas about the area before and after the Revolution. Once the Mosallā was located adjacent to the Abbās Ābād area, its *qibla* orientation took over the vast site and became its dominant organizing device. A temporal regulation also governs the site; many of its functions (excluding the Book Garden building) operate within regulated hours, while even the National Library is not a public space – ordinary citizens with anything less than a master's degree are barred from entry!

The second apparent change is that the nostalgia that characterized the Pahlavi period projects, but also the Academies project, appears to have abated. Architectural languages no longer cite pre-Islamic or Islamic period architectural typologies. Fragmentation can be seen in the design of the Sacred Defence Museum, the adjacent Tāleqāni Park, the Art (*Honar*) Garden and Lake, and the adjacent Tehran Book Garden. The urban design is equally fragmented, with buildings standing marooned like islands. While the competitions for the National Library and Academies had sought overt expressions of authenticity and identity, thus encouraging projects that were romantic and nostalgic, the later competitions were not so prescriptive. Perhaps this relates to both the function of the elements (a Mosallā would demand Islamic symbolism) and the timing of the competitions, as well as their relationship to the internal evolution of ideology within the Islamic Republic. In the early days, the Republic was still in the process of asserting its ideology, self-representing, as it were. But four decades on, things have changed.

Finally, while Shahestān reflected the attempt by a developmentalist state to syncretically formulate an Iranian identity projected to the world, in the post-1979 constructions this goal has shifted. Firstly, the symbolic communication of identity in the architecture, reinforced by the official propaganda, addresses the transnational 'Muslim world' rather than the nation-state, and is ambivalent about Iranian culture. Secondly, on a national level, the emphasis on representation has gradually waned along with the vicissitudes of Iran's international relations with the region and beyond. While the previous regime attempted to forge an identity that was representative of a national imagination, and conceived of development in cultural terms, the Islamic Republic's pursuit of a transnational pan-Islamic agenda has caused a rift between its propaganda spaces and the everyday space of the city. Rather than any genuine engagement with the past, in this new era, the past – like politics – is reduced to the aesthetic play of depthless signs. There is no systematic push for engaging with the past, and thus little by way of a heritage imperative in these designs, or in the general space of the Abbās Ābād area.

Examining the evolution of Abbās Ābād, it is apparent that, on a programmatic and instrumental level, the change in plans – from the first collaborative plan by Kahn and Tange, through the LDI plan, the 1984 and 1998 revised plans, and finally the 2005 Mirmiran plan and subsequent additions – is negligible. However, what has evidently been abandoned is the attempt to reference Iranian heritage in a civic place. If Amanat's Shahyad monument managed, through its history, both to reference and in time embody such a heritage, then the Abbās Ābād project has evidently failed. Regardless of the respective merits of the Pahlavi project, inherent to these projects was the attempt to construct meaning – in this sense they are all similar. In the aftermath of the Islamic Revolution and ensuing decades, these ambitions have been substituted with placelessness. The Google Earth view of Abbās Ābād today reveals a more perplexing situation. The new additions to the district could have been designed for any city. Despite Iran's ideological assertion of an exceptionalism, in the face of the West and the Sunni world, the architecture and urban design weakly reflects global trends. We have noted how the master planning for the sites of the first two competition projects, for the Academies and for the National Library, relocated them away from the original planned centre. Then the square, the heart of the project, itself disappeared. In the resulting conceptual void, a series of 'gardens' and pavilions were created – the Sacred Defence Museum, Book Garden, and Art Garden, which collectively resemble a kind of spatial embroidery, a civic picturesque devoid of any perceptible meaning.

In analysing the projects for Abbās Ābād, which in their origin derived from the ambition to create a capital that accorded with Iran's intended status as a developed nation, we have also charted the function of their citation of the past, how elements of the past were used to forge an image of what Mohammad Reza appears to have regarded as his second architectural testament. Regardless of their respective merits, all the schemes for Shahestān had constituted attempts to construct meaning in a place, as representational civic projects. In the aftermath of the Islamic Revolution and ensuing decades, these ambitions have been substituted with a strange appearance of genericity. The new additions to the Abbās Ābād district could have been designed for any city, and do not represent the cultural ambitions of the state. There is no socio-spatial context at all, and yet the underlying reality is a theocratic state in which Iran has asserted an exceptionalist position. Only the Mosallā stands apart as the product of a failed attempt to create a utopia, nostalgically amplifying traditional Shi'ite forms, but in a fantastical and distended manner. In Abbās Ābād there is no concrete sense of the past, but equally no sense of the civic, of a space of the public in the present. All of this suggests that the reconciliation of development and culture is no longer a major concern in current state projects, and that nostalgia has been replaced by distraction.

Notes

1. Emami, '"Civic Visions"', p. 41.
2. A. Madanipour, 'Urban Planning and Development in Tehran', *Cities*, 23:6 (2006), p. 435.
3. A. Madanipour, 'The Limits of Scientific Planning: Doxiadis and the Tehran Action Plan', *Planning Perspectives*, 25:4 (2010), p. 488.
4. Madanipour, 'Urban Planning and Development', pp. 434–5.
5. Costello, 'Planning Problems', p. 152; J. T. Robertson, *Shahestan Pahlavi: A New City Centre for Tehran, Book 1: The Master Plan* (London: Llewelyn-Davies International, Planning Consultants, 1976); H. Amirahmadi and A. Kiafar, 'The Transformation of Tehran from Garrison Town to a Primate City: A Tale of Rapid Growth and Uneven Development', in Amirahmadi and El-Shakhs (eds), *Urban Development*, p. 124.
6. Mohajeri, 'Shahestan Blueprint', p. 257.
7. Emami, 'Urbanism of Grandiosity', p. 75.
8. Mohajeri, 'Shahestan Blueprint', pp. 147–72; Mohajeri, 'Louis Kahn's Space'; Emami, '"Civic Visions"'; Emami, 'Urbanism of Grandiosity', pp. 69–102.
9. Emami, '"Civic Visions"', pp. 54–6.
10. Emami, 'Urbanism of Grandiosity', p. 46.
11. Mohajeri, 'Louis Kahn's Space', p. 486.
12. Emami, '"Civic Visions"', p. 65; Mohajeri, 'Shahestan Blueprint', p. 257 and endnote 37.
13. Mohajeri, *Architectures of Transversality: Paul Klee, Louis Kahn and the Persian Imagination* (Abingdon: Routledge, 2019), p. xvi; Mohajeri, 'Louis Kahn's Space', p. 265.
14. Mohajeri, 'Louis Kahn's Space'; Emami, 'Urbanism of Grandiosity'.
15. Mohajeri, 'Louis Kahn's Space', p. 486.
16. H. Ziai, 'The Illuminationist Tradition', in S. H. Nasr and O. Leaman (eds), *History of Islamic Philosophy* (London: Routledge, 1995), p. 465.
17. Mohajeri, 'Louis Kahn's Space', p. 492.
18. Mohajeri, 'Louis Kahn's Space', p. 501.
19. Kahn, 'Spaces, Order and Architecture', in A. Latour (ed.), *Louis I. Kahn: Writings, Lectures and Interviews* (New York: Rizzoli, 1991 [1957]), cited in A. Pedret, 'Within the Text of Kahn' (master's thesis, Massachusetts Institute of Technology, 1993), pp. 68, 76.
20. Mohajeri, 'Louis Kahn's Space', p. 496.
21. Unlike Robert Venturi, Kahn was unable to fully embrace the semiotics of historical form or the direct referencing of traditional form that certain regionalists would advocate.
22. S. Moholy Nagy, 'The Future of the Past', *Perspecta*, 7 (1961), pp. 65–76.
23. Tafuri was formerly an enthusiast of Kahn, whose projects in his brief professional career resembled the latter's work. Frajndlich, 'Two Projects: The Formative Years of Manfredi Tafuri', *PÓS*, 23:29 (2016), pp. 72–89; Tafuri, *Architecture and Utopia*, 161; Tafuri, *Theories and History*, p. 130.
24. Tafuri, *Theories and History*, pp. 6–7.
25. M. Biraghi, *Project of Crisis: Manfredo Tafuri and Contemporary Architecture*, trans. A. L. Price (Cambridge, MA: MIT Press, 2013 [2005]), pp. 51–67.

26 Tafuri and F. D. Co, *Modern Architecture*, trans. R. E. Wolf (New York: Harry N. Abrams, 1979), p. 376.
27 The Shahestan project was commenced on-site on 19 August 1975, after compulsory acquisition of the required land, with the planting of fifty trees in concentric rings, to commemorate the fiftieth anniversary of the Pahlavi dynasty. J. M. Dixon, 'A Place in Progress', *Progressive Architecture*, 10 (October, 1976), p. 53.
28 Sudjic has pejoratively characterized this plan as a slice of Manhattan. D. Sudjic, *The Edifice Complex: How the Rich and Powerful Shape the World* (New York: Penguin Press, 2005), p. 93.
29 Dixon, 'A Place in Progress', p. 53.
30 Moholy Nagy, cited in Tafuri, *Theories and History*, p. 12 and note 4; Moholy Nagy, 'The Future of the Past'.
31 Tafuri's ideas on the relationship between memory and concrete forms accords with Boym's 'restorative nostalgia'. M. Tafuri, 'storicità di Louis Kahn', *Communità*, 117 (1964), p. 41, cited in Biraghi, *Project of Crisis*, p. 54.
32 Jameson, *Postmodernism*, pp. 1–6.
33 Mohajeri, *Architectures of Transversality*, p. 150, note 2, no sources given.
34 Madanipour, 'Urban Planning and Development', p. 436; A. Mashayekhi, 'The Politics of Building in Post-Revolution Tehran', in H. Jacobi and M. Nasasra (eds), *Routledge Handbook on Middle East Cities* (London and New York: Routledge, 2019 [2020]), p. 208.
35 See the history of this development in Abbās Ābād Development Corporation's site, Abbasabad Cultural Complex: http://abasabad.tehran.ir/Default.aspx?tabid=767.
36 Lynch, *Image of the City*.
37 Mashayekhi, 'The Politics of Building', pp. 211–13.
38 The institutions in this area include the Supreme Council of the Quran, the Sadra Islamic Philosophy Foundation, the Al-Zahra Hossainia, the Islamic Culture and Communication Organization, and a number of other large buildings, all of which appear to belong to the same development.
39 Mohajeri, 'Shahestan Blueprint', p. 154.
40 On the original National Library building by Maxime Siroux (1936), see Grigor, *Building Iran*, p. 262.
41 N. Sharify, *The Pahlavi National Library of the Future: Its Resources, Services, Programs, and Building Requirement: Final Report* (East Norwich, NY: Board of Consultants, Pahlavi National Library, 1976), p. 1; R. Steele, 'The Pahlavi National Library Project: Education and Modernization in Late Pahlavi Iran', *Iranian Studies*, 52:1–2 (2019), pp. 85–110, https://doi.org/10.1080/00210862.2018.1557512.
42 Ketābkhāneh-ye Pahlavi cited in Steele, 'The Pahlavi National Library', p. 90 and note 25.
43 Steele, 'The Pahlavi National Library', p. 95.
44 Sharify was the Iranian-born Dean of the Graduate School of Library and Information Science at the Pratt Institute in New York.
45 Although the author was not stated, the competition brief document may have been the work of Ardalan, who was also member of the jury. International judges included Team Ten member Giancarlo de Carlo, Mexican Pedro Ramirez, British Trevor Dannatt, Chinese American Leoh Ming Pei, Fumihiko Maki, and Charles Correa.

46 Sharify, *The Pahlavi National Library*, p. 12.
47 Steele, 'The Pahlavi National Library Project', p. 99.
48 There were 3,056 architects registered from 87 countries, of which 618 submitted, only 13 of whom were Iranian. Mansour Vakili, writing in the Iranian journal *Art and Architecture*, complained about the low number of Iranian entrants in the competition. M. Vakili, 'International Competition, International Archiecture', *Art and Architecture*, no. 45–6 (April–July, 1978), pp. 34–5.
49 Utzon's stepped skylights were apparently influenced by his visit to the Isfahan bazaar in 1959. See R. Weston, *Utzon: Inspiration, Vision, Architecture* (Copenhagen: Bløndal, 2002), pp. 225–9.
50 Comparable examples in concrete Brutalist idiom include Giurgola's design for Australia's Federal Parliament House (1979), John Andrews' Cameron Offices in Belconnen, Canberra (1976), Andrews' University of Toronto Scarborough College, Ontario, Canada (1963, first stage), and his Gund Hall, Harvard University (1972).
51 Vakili, 'International Competition'.
52 The first prize was awarded to Pirraz, by judges Seyed Reza Hashemi, Mohamad Beheshti (head, ICHTO), Hadi Nadimi, Mahdi Chamran, Serajadin Kazerooni, Bagher Shirazi, and Mohamad Hasan Mo'meni. The client was the Ministry of Housing and Urbanization.
53 Farahani et al., 'Impact of Architectural Competitions', p. 40.
54 D. Diba and M. Dehbashi, 'Trends in Modern Iranian Architecture', in P. Jodido (ed.), *Iran, Architecture for Changing Societies* (Turin: The Aga Khan Award for Architecture, 2004), p. 36.
55 One might see here the anti-formalist influence of Bruno Zevi, who was an invited delegate at the 1974 Persepolis congress.
56 E. Afshar, 'The National Library of Iran: A New Building and a New Future', *Australian Academic and Research Libraries*, 37:3 (2006), p. 230.
57 Shariatzadeh had little time for ideologies of tradition and authenticity in his work; decades ago he had a spat with Jalal Al-Ahmad over the appropriateness of including a dome over a contemporary extension to a religious shrine, Shariatzadeh vehemently dismissing the idea. See:

آ.ا. [جلال آل احمد]، مسجد جدید قم: آبرویمعماری قرن تخیر، علم و زندگی، 1338 ش. 3، صص. 61–55؛ در باره مقاله مسجد جدید قم [بینا، ولی به قلم یوسف شریعت‌زاده]، علم و زندگی، 1338 ش. 4، صص. 60–62.

58 D. Diba, 'The University of Kerman', *Mimar: Architecture in Development*, 42 (1992), pp. 62–4.
59 Mohajeri (*Architectures of Transversality*, p. 116, note 64) erroneously ascribes this characteristic to Shariatzadeh's work.
60 Afkhami, 'Pahlbod'.
61 مسابقه معماری فرهنگستانها: معرفی طرح های برنده، آبادی (4 :13)، تابستان 1373، صص. 4–17؛ مسابقه معماری فرهنگستانها، آبادی، (3 :12) ، صص. 49–50. On the *Abadi* journal, see Roudbari, 'Instituting Architecture'.
62 The brief accommodated three Academies – Science, Medicine, and Persian Literature – and their support spaces, totalling 58,400 m^2 on an 82,350 m^2 plot of land in what would become the new official cultural centre of Tehran:

مسابقه معماری فرهنگستانها: معرفی طرح های برنده، صص. 49.

63 مسابقه معماری فرهنگستانها: معرفی طرح های برنده، صص. ۲–۳، ۵۰.
64 This postmodernist semiotic-based approach was also influenced by the Traditionalist principles of symbolic geometry articulated in Ardalan and Bakhtiar's *The Sense of Unity*.
65 L. Micara, 'Contemporary Iranian Architecture in Search for a New Identity', *Environmental Design: Journal of the Islamic Environmental Design Research Centre*, 1 (1996), p. 62; Diba and Dehbashi, 'Trends in Modern Iranian Architecture', p. 33; N. Rabbat, 'What Is Islamic Architecture Anyway', *Journal of Art Historiography*, 6 (2012), p. 9.
66 R. S. Hashemi, 'Editorial', *Abadi*, 3:12 (1994), pp. 2–3.
67 Micara, 'Contemporary Iranian Architecture', p. 67.
68 Saremi had studied initially under Louis Kahn (see Chapter 4).
69 Saremi believed that architects had to desist from blindly following tradition and establish a distance from the formulas of revolutionary ideology. See Javaherian-Mehrjui, 'Ali-Akbar Saremi', pp. 94–5.
70 مسابقه معماری فرهنگستانها ، آبادی، (۳ :۱۲) ، صص. ۱۲–۱۳.
71 مسابقه معماری فرهنگستانها ، آبادی، (۳ :۱۲) ، صص. ۴۹–۵۰.
72 Kuran cited in L. Farhad and L. Bakhtiar (eds), *Investigating the Possibility of Linking Traditional Architecture with Modern Building Methods: Report of the Proceedings of the First International Congress of Architects* (Isfahan: Ministry for Development and Housing, 1970), p. 85.
73 مسابقه معماری فرهنگستانها: معرفی طرح های برنده، ص. ۱۴.
74 مسابقه معماری فرهنگستانها ، آبادی، (۳ :۱۲) ، صص. ۱۶–۱۷.
75 K. Haji-Ghassemi, interview with A. Mozaffari, Tehran, September 2013. Haji-Ghassemi was critical of the interference of the authorities in the execution of the scheme, which led to a number of deleterious changes.
76 Hashemi, 'Editorial', pp. 2–3.
77 For examples of surveys of regionalist tendencies in Iran, see ا.بانی مسعود، معماری معاصر ایران (تهران: انتشارات هنر معماری قرن، ۱۳۹۴)؛ S. M. Habibi, *Intellectual Trends in the Contemporary Iranian Architecture and Urbanism (1979–2003)* (Tehran: Cultural Research Bureau, 2007). These have not explored the political imperatives shaping and supporting this movement, in which the construction of traditional images of national folk culture is used in support of state ideological imperatives.
78 Bakhtiar and Farhad (eds), *Investigating the Possibility*, pp. 54–6, 70–2.
79 Sheikh Zeineddin, interview with Mozaffari, 2013.
80 A. Mirsepassi, *Political Islam, Iran, and the Enlightenment: Philosophies of Hope and Despair* (Cambridge and New York: Cambridge University Press, 2011), pp. 67–84.
81 The Secretariat for the High Council for Cultural Revolution (HCCR), pp. 13–14.
82 Kahn and Tange's proposed mosque site was aligned with an east–west garden rather than the *qibla*.
83 K. Rizvi, *The Transnational Mosque: Architecture and Historical Memory in the Contemporary Middle East* (Chapel Hill, NC: University of North Carolina Press, 2015), p. 120.
84 See Rizvi, *The Transnational Mosque*, pp. 24–5.
85 Ehsani, 'Cultural Politics', pp. 225–6; Rizvi, *The Transnational Mosque*, pp. 119–20.
86 Rizvi, *The Transnational Mosque*, p. 121.

87 Rizvi, *The Transnational Mosque*, pp. 120–1; Farahani et al., 'Impact of Architectural Competitions', pp. 35–44.
88 The decision to make a mosque was taken before acquiring the site upon which the design was imposed. The chief proponents for the Mosallā were Ali Khamenei (the current Supreme Leader and then-president, 1981–89) and Akbar Hashemi Rafsanjani (president for two terms, 1989–97). Khamenei was concurrently the president and Friday prayers leader (University of Tehran). These leaders went directly to Khomeini, who issued the decree to acquire the land.
89 The history of the site's transformation is described in an archived web version from 2009: https://web.archive.org/web/20080208075234/http://www.musalla.ir/tabid/58/Default.aspx.
90 The current title is Iranian Cultural Heritage, Handicrafts, and Tourism Organization (ICHHTO).
91 Farahani et al., 'Impact of Architectural Competitions', pp. 36–7. Bagher Ayatollah-zadeh Shirazi (1936–2007) was a conservation and heritage restoration architect and deputy director of the ICHO. Mohammad Karim Pirnia (1920–97) was a prominent architect, historian of traditional Iranian architecture, and professor at the University of Tehran, teaching a course on Islamic architecture. Ironically, given the project outcome, he emphasized the need for Iranian architecture to be 'human scaled'. He worked with Shirazi and others on the 1979 book *Masjid-i Jāmi'-i Isfahān* (Isfahan's Friday Mosque). Mehdi Chamran was at the time an Islamist member of Tehran City Council. He would later be a supporter of Ahmadinejad and the chairman of the council. Mehdi Hodjat was a conservation architect at ICHO and was at the time the Deputy Minister of Culture and later president of the Iranian ICOMOS committee. The last member, Ali Ghaffari, is Professor of Urban Design at Shahid Beheshti University, and a former head of school there. His field, like most of the panel, is traditional architecture. With his partner Hadi Nadimi, he was responsible for the restoration of the shrine of Imam Ali in Najaf, Iraq. Other than Pirnia, who was essentially an 'ethical modernist' in his design approach, and councilor Chamran, the rest of the panel members could be classified as traditionalist architects aligned with ICHO and its interpretation of Iranian heritage.
92 Rizvi, *The Transnational Mosque*, p. 122.
93 The Mosallā derives its effect of overwhelming power through the combination of massed crowds and vast size – a central courtyard about 200 m x 225 m, an outer courtyard about 125 m x 375 m, two minarets about 140 m in height flanking the mosque and 140 m wide *eyvān*, and the mosque's dome itself spans 57 m (compared to that of Hagia Sophia at 31 m and St. Peters basilica in Rome, of 41.5 m).
94 Ehsani, 'Cultural Politics', p. 225.
95 E. Canetti, *Crowds and Power* (London: Gollancz, 1962), p. 152.
96 Mozaffari, *Forming National Identity*, p. 88.
97 On hypermasculinity in Iran, see S. Gerami, 'Mullahs, Martyrs, and Men: Conceptualizing Masculinity in the Islamic Republic of Iran', *Men and Masculinities*, 5:3 (2003), pp. 257–274.
98 Ehsani, 'Cultural Politics', pp. 226–8.
99 Mozaffari, *Forming National Identity*, pp. 117–53.
100 Rizvi, *The Transnational Mosque*, p. 121.

101 K. Rizvi, 'Religious Icon and National Symbol: The Tomb of Ayatollah Khomeini in Iran', *Muqarnas*, 20 (2003), pp. 209, 222; Grigor, *Contemporary Iranian Art*, pp. 77–8.
102 On the manipulation of information in the Islamic Republic, see H. Mowlana, *Global Communication in Transition: The End of Diversity? Volume 19* (Newbury Park, CA: SAGE, 1996); G. Khiabany, 'De-Westernizing Media Theory, or Reverse Orientalism: Islamic Communication as Theorized by Hamid Mowlana', *Media, Culture & Society*, 25:3 (2003), pp. 415–22.
103 F. Jameson, 'Postmodernism and the Consumer Society', in Foster (ed.), *The Antiaesthetic*, p. 115.
104 Jameson, 'Postmodernism and the Consumer Society', p. 120.
105 Ehsani, 'Cultural Politics', p. 213.

Conclusion: Design as the mediator of development and heritage

Introduction

This book has explored some of the effects of development, which we have identified as a fundamental driver of historical change in late twentieth-century Iran. Throughout the twentieth century, but particularly during the second Pahlavi period, development constituted a raft of modernizing projects, displacements, and shifts in population composition, and changes in modes of production, all on a multitude of scales. Our point of departure has been that development unmoors traditions and gives rise to shifting historical perspectives, and is, therefore, closely associated with the production of heritage. Furthermore, conceptualizing development as a process of historical change, there are few areas where the relationship between heritage and development is more concrete and immediate, in the sense of being an object of daily and corporeal experience, than in architectural design.

As we noted in the earlier chapters and shall elaborate below, the term heritage is here construed critically as a cultural process[1] cutting across the divisions of tangible and intangible, material and social, human and non-human, rather than an objectified thing. In referring to multiple case studies at various scales, we have attempted to show how complex and at times elusive concepts such as tradition, heritage, identity, development, and design intersect and propel one another through time, and how their meanings and dynamics are affected by historical change. Here, we emphasized the central affective role played by nostalgia – the complex structure of feelings invoked via historical change – in propelling and perpetuating the above dynamics. Our explorations were underpinned by three intersecting areas – development, architecture, and heritage – each of which has tacit and explicit global and local dimensions. Through the period we have examined, each of these areas was engaged with questions of authenticity, traditions, and civilization, all of which pertain to identity and can give rise to or sustain various forms of nostalgic formulations and experiences across multiple scales. In this process, architectural design plays a central, mediating role.

Development: An 'engaged universal' displacing a past

As noted, from among the various conceptions of development, we have chosen to approach it broadly, in terms of historical change, a process that we have specifically interpreted in relation to the built environment and architecture.[2] Like other projects borne of the Enlightenment, development's intellectual origins have universalist underpinnings and Eurocentric undertones. In the twentieth century, development also incorporated notions of social, and thus historical, change brought about by both Marxist regimes and progressively minded administrators in their responses to crises in colonial territorial possessions.[3]

Far from traversing a smooth and linear trajectory, development has been a fragmented and messy process, the outcomes of which have been determined by the particularities of given localities at specific historical moments. As we noted in Chapter 1, this is an instance of what Tsing has explained in terms of friction and as such, development is an example of an 'engaged universal', a 'practical project accomplished in a heterogenous world'.[4] Heritage, as others have argued elsewhere,[5] is another instance of such engaged universals. In the first half of the twentieth century, as conceived by modernization theorists, development was bureaucratic, technocratic, and state centred. Critiques of development were evident from the inception of modernization projects in the 1950s and became increasingly vocal in the 1970s until the rise of post-development in the 1980s and 1990s, charging that the dominant American doctrines of development were directed towards reshaping the world (or at least the non-Eastern Bloc) in its image. Given America's primacy in world politics in the post-war era and its extensive aid programmes, this critique implied that development was a neo-colonialist (or imperialist) endeavour. Throughout the decades, the main critiques have been inspired by Marxist, neo-Marxist, dependency, and postcolonial theories.[6] They have charged that besides their links to imperialism and neo-colonialism and as part of a universalizing and globalizing project, development and its concomitant modernization processes have been oppressive and state imposed (that is to say, top-down), have eroded local specificities, diminished cultural assets and capabilities, and benefitted sectors of the ruling elite and their foreign collaborators to the detriment of the broader populace. In short, from this perspective, development was doomed from the start. However, as our examples implied, this perspective has painted an inaccurate, ideological picture and lacks nuance.

In examples given throughout the previous chapters, we have demonstrated that within Iran there was from the outset a genuine interest in responding to development, one that cannot be reduced to the reactionism implied in the term resistance, although reactionary trends also existed. Here, the position of the state comes to the fore, as it plays a pivotal role in governance and in implementing development. The government, architects, and other sectors exercised various degrees of agency in implementing development in Iran. It is true that Iran's economic planning privileged capitalism, a point of critique for many leftist and Marxian theories, such as dependency theory, at the time. But by the late 1970s, these theories and their approaches too were being revised and critiqued and the value of capitalism to development was noted.[7]

As was evidenced in the White Revolution, the quintessential Pahlavi development project, national development programmes were primarily domestic Iranian initiatives, constituting attempts to incorporate and moderate social, economic, and cultural change. Such measures included action on land redistribution and ownership, women's emancipatory rights, and in education, where new forms, ideas, and fields, responding to foreign innovations, were introduced into the Iranian system. These were not purely following a capitalist model, either. Rather, it appears that the attention to land redistribution, culture, and women's rights, to name a few, was also informed by the slogans and some policies of the Soviet Union during the Cold War – especially at the time of their occupation of Azerbaijan and the establishment of the Pishevari government that promoted land reform and a strong degree of culturalism.[8] The Pahlavi establishment was cognizant of the profound social change that development induced, and it endeavoured to respond to and manage that change in its social policies, albeit at times unsuccessfully.

The congresses, discussed in Chapter 2, provide ample evidence of the development–culture relationship in Iran. For example, the Ramsar congress demonstrates how the questions of women's education and emancipation, and architectural identity, were folded into one another in an innovative manner. Thus, responses in Iran foreshadowed some of the post-development arguments concerned with cultural effects of development, and its potential role in the loss of diversity and distinctive identities. This concern for the loss of cultural identity was an overarching theme debated in all the architectural congresses, and a leitmotif of cultural production in that period. Another example of responding to development is the variation and stratification in the design of housing stock. In theory, it was recognized that housing played the dual role of both modernizing populations and mitigating the effects of change. In practice, there were only a handful of attempts to consider culture in design, and here Shushtar Now stands out. The design thinking embodied in the Shushtar Now project contrasts with the Western-inspired models driving other large-scale housing projects such as the Ekbatan complex, which addressed a different, middle-class social group and today, evidence suggests,[9] provides the setting for a vibrant and desirable urban life.

Arguments that were partially or largely similar to post-development and postcolonial critiques, conflated with anti-Westernism, had currency in Iran long before the Islamic Revolution. However, unlike post-development theorists, the Iranian actors, by and large, did not dismiss developmentalist ideas and plans as inherently colonialist and bankrupt. Instead, there was a process of productive negotiation and change – 'friction', as this 'engaged universal' development, entered the Iranian scene. There was a genuine desire for development and the state's role in it was also recognized.[10] Here, the architectural projects were leading by example in a process in which Iranian agency was abundantly clear. More importantly, these Iranian efforts were not intended to simply and solely benefit a ruling elite, or the international hegemons. This blurs the assumed dichotomies between state and society, tradition and modernity, and the like. As fresh scholarship on developmentalism in Iran also corroborates, this stands in contrast with some of the ideological assumptions in post-development studies that ascribe Manichean characteristics to development.[11]

There are other inconsistencies too. Much of the neo-liberal debate, which took centre stage in the 1980s but had started almost four decades earlier,[12] concerned the goal of limiting the role of the state, which the proponents of this debate thought of as the oppressor of individual freedom.[13] Iran clearly took a different direction during the Shah period by increasing the role of the government in development and employment, and imposing protectionist measures borrowed from Latin American, leftist economic plans, in clear contrast to liberal economic planning.[14] In other developing countries, the pivotal role of the state continued well into the 1980s, and in Iran well into the 1990s.

At the time, within architecture and urbanism this state agency also translated into, for example, the provision of representational spaces. Shahestān Pahlavi was an example of the nation-state being represented, and materially embodied, at a grand scale. Like the Shahyad monument, it also contained urban spaces that could represent the nation to itself, recognizing the role of a public, however tokenistically, in the body politic of the country. In making gestures towards the past, these spaces utilized nostalgia as a positive collective experience, one that brought people together and forged collective identities and moral communities. It is precisely this aspect that was consistently transformed, even diminished, after the Revolution, as authorities imposed draconian controls on public behaviour through widespread surveillance. This has contributed to the contraction of the public sphere. Here, Ehsani argues that 'while public spaces are not inherently emancipatory, nevertheless the enactment of citizenship takes shape in the public sphere of discourse and in the public spaces of collective urban life'.[15] We noted in Chapter 6 that all the projects for Shahestān constituted attempts to construct a nascent public sphere. In contrast, in the realized constructions at Abbās Ābād since the Revolution, in response to the disputed question of what should constitute the representational urban centre, the authorities replaced the idea of a symbolic heart of the national capital with a transnational mosque, the Mosallā – as a symbol of both the Islamic (and Shi'ite) nation, but also of global Islam. The product of this displacement is the shrinking of the public sphere, beyond activities coordinated and sanctioned by the authorities. This disappearance is compounded by the reduced responsibility of state and civic authorities in national development. In both the development of institutions, and in the construction of housing, as discussed in Chapter 4, the state has also devolved responsibilities and resources to quasi-governmental or non-governmental 'foundations', ostensibly charitable institutions and individuals with connections to power.

As the above examples and those discussed throughout the book have suggested, development studies as a field is concerned with processes of social change that are registered in the design of architecture and urban spaces. In this respect, this book has opened up new avenues in discussing architecture and policies towards the past framed and actualized as heritage and articulated in the process of development.

From development to heritage: The mediating role of architecture

> The [Iranian] architecture of today has to belong to the present and use all facilities presently on offer and speak the language of the present but be in such a way ... that when you enter the space or when you encounter it from a distance, you get the sense that this is Iranian, not that it comes from the other side of the world. Its atmosphere and the qualities it offers have to relate to the history of our architecture. [...]
>
> I used to discuss this with various people [in different fields], that for our future architecture we should be looking into our architectural past. Not to produce arches and domes, no, but to induce the spatial qualities that exist in that architecture so that when we encounter an old house even now it leaves an influence and we feel calm, we [wish] to create that with new material, facilities, and technologies. The people to whom I spoke see this as self-evident. The only group that resists this [is that of] the architects themselves.[16]

As we have argued, development intersects inevitably with heritage. This intersection is usually discussed in relation to the areas of conservation and tourism.[17] However, cognizant of the role the past plays in daily life and in arenas outside economic planning, we have approached heritage from a critical angle, focusing on how it is constructed, and on what function it performs. In this approach, heritage is underpinned by changing notions of temporality, scale, and practice. Although critical heritage began with a focus on the appraisal of power relations, its scope and definition are slowly evolving away from essentialized dichotomies that pit, for example, the state against the people.[18] Still, the lure of abstractions that present a 'neat' picture conceived to fit pre-existing theoretical constructs, those that are often deployed uncritically, remains strong. Such abstractions, in the Iranian context, include notions of a bourgeoisie that universalizes Eurocentric social stratifications, resistance, which presumes the categorical separation between state apparatuses and the people in an out-of-context application of postcolonial theories, and the dominance of a Persian (فارس) ethnicity, which oversimplifies a complex historical dynamic and invents an ethnicity, the boundaries of which are barely clarified.[19]

The difficulty with such 'neat' interpretations lies in their inherent essentialism and in their empirical weakness. These qualities are bound to provide a limited and distorted reading of the dynamics of culture in a developing context. Avoiding this pitfall and driven by our specific focus on the built environment, we have also considered heritage in the context of more-than-human ontologies. As Harrison has aptly articulated it, this focuses on how heritage is constructed, that is to say, made through the assembly of the tangible and the intangible. He asserts that 'things, places and practices'[20] are deployed in relation to specific material, historical, and social contexts. Here, heritage is relationally conceived, connoting an inextricable link between objects, concepts, and practices. And it is through this link that heritage pertains to both memory and identity, but also to emotions – hence its clear and well-established relationship with nostalgia.[21] In many instances, nostalgia is a necessary component of the collective experience of heritage.

But perhaps most importantly for this book, we have worked with the premise that heritage and place are coextensive and co-constituted.[22] This has direct implications for the reading of the heritage–design relationship by highlighting the role of architecture in the process of heritage production. Among others, Harrison has noted that heritage is mutable and transformable, as 'a set of attitudes to, and relationships with, the past'.[23] One of the vehicles through which these attitudes materialize is architecture – heritage, we have argued, is concretely fashioned through design processes that are intentional, and pertains to cultural specificity and tradition. This intentionality distinguishes heritage from mere repetitions of traditions and the past. Design, which forms the basis of architectural creativity, is a highly transferable practice resting on concepts and theories (not to mention ideologies) that circulate across contexts and cultures. Technology, too, is transferable – albeit perhaps with a different inertia. The transposition of design techniques and ideas and construction materials heightens the attention to localities, with paradoxical effects characteristic of Tsing's idea of friction.[24]

One such effect, attained in light of development, has been that between the 1970s and the 1980s and with an increasing pace, Iran re-examined and recast its relationship to history and tradition in architecture and many other areas. Regardless of design prowess, the past was used and deployed concretely in the service of the present, and the imagination of a future. Heritage was composed, visualized, and experienced bodily through the fabric of buildings, producing feelings of nostalgia. In practice, there have been multiple interweavings of the past into the fabric of the present through architecture. Here, tradition and the past, usually parallel yet distinct concepts, transmute into one another. In the period covered by this book, certain aspects of tradition were beginning to be experienced as something of the past, historicized, rather than as an intrinsic part of the everyday world. The examples discussed in our chapters reveal modes of interpreting and engaging with this past, and its traditions, through material engagements, the choice of material and techniques of construction, and the tacit knowledge of the sociocultural patterns of use shared by adherents to a specific cultural tradition. The various interpretations of tradition and culture within architectural design reveal ideological traces. Within Iran, arguably the most explicit example, one that came to fully realize its nostalgic spatial function after the Islamic Revolution, was Ardalan's Iran Centre for Management Studies in Tehran, now Imam Sādiq University (Chapter 1). But this project, and other forms of engaging the past, constituted reactive responses to a strand of universal ideas pertaining to developmental, modernizing projects. Such responses, manifested in a quest for identity, belonging, and community, and driven by nostalgia, were instigated by the sense of displacement and loss invoked by historical change and by global encounters. In place of the everyday world of the traditional was inserted its image.

Global exchanges tend to universalize approaches to design and its techniques, instilling a tension in the process. On the one hand, approaches to design take on other universalist values, such as human rights – perhaps this is why housing is reconceived as habitat and seen as deserving of a Bill of Rights? On the other, the values that go with design are engaged in specific contexts and thus take interesting turns. This underscores the significance of localities, and their specific domestic ideologies and concomitant politics, in the production of particular design outcomes, and through them, particular forms of heritage. For example, the theoretical and practical origins of a return to tradition existed before the Revolution; however, the oppressive and nostalgic trends that underpinned the ideology of the Islamic Revolution forced architects to design in constricted ways. The ideological push of Islamism prioritized the rhetoric of authenticity and anti-Westernism, by reducing lived experience to image and cliché. Here, the intent behind this push was recognized by some scholars and practising architects alike:

> Since the Revolution, there has been a contest over the fact the they [the establishment] insist in attaching basic elements and ingredients of identity to Islamic culture and civilization. They only follow this discourse. The other problem is that some of our colleagues, even though they may be knowledgeable, spend all their energy to go into the rucksack of tradition and whatever [patrimony] that is left and constantly talk about and analyse the characteristics of that heritage. And there is [yet] another group in the professional and academic societies, who because of demographic situation of the society are necessarily young and are intensely inclined towards being contemporary and attempt to find their identity in that and have strong modern tendencies. [...] there is a kind of resistance and deviation from the elements of identity-making that the former group have designated from their studies of tradition. [...]
>
> We had identity in the past without the need to use any clichés as to how one should work [design] in order to attain identity. ... in the 1960s, this existed in 3D [corporeally] in our cultural and artistic society.[25]

Iran, and arguably other Muslim developing nations, followed three responses to mitigating developmental instabilities: the embrace of change, through which traditions transmute and evolve; the radical rejection of tradition, in which modernity was fully embraced; and the attempted return to a traditional life, or the discourse of Traditionalism. Our examples have clearly illustrated how each one of these responses was manifested in spatial and design terms and how the boundaries between these responses is at times ambiguous.

From a different perspective, we have used Iran to shed further light on the intersection of multiple global (or globalizing) discourses operating at different scales. This scalarity has been mentioned above but is less explicitly examined in relation to development or architecture and only recently in heritage. Like identity and place, heritage has a scalar characteristic,[26] which yields new insights into the heritage–design relationship. We pointed out one aspect of this scalarity in Chapter 5, in our study of the Shahyad monument, demonstrating that the same heritage can invoke different meanings and emotions and therefore perform different functions depending on the scale on which it is deployed and operationalized (as Graham and colleaugues have observed).[27] This was only one manifestation of scale, as nested, hierarchical relations, and it is at these levels that there is, in Harvey's words, a 'politics of scale'.[28] As Lähdesmäki and colleagues correctly observe, '[h]eritage functions as a tool to create and rethink national consciousness and unity, and to promote economic and social development'.[29] We shall elaborate on the discussion of scale further below, but here we note that when posited at a larger, international scale, the question of heritage pertains to conceptions of civilization. As such, at a global scale, heritage is taken as evidence of distinction and specificity of one civilization (Persian, Arab, Muslim, etc.) in comparison to others, and especially the West. In the Shah's words, 'we Iranians are not only of possessing the rich relics of a valuable culture and civilization, but also of the fact that we have played an effective role in the production of other countries' civilisations and cultures'.[30]

The scalar dynamics between design, heritage, and development

In a broader perspective, our findings pertain to three interrelated scales in which historical change and heritage must be considered: local, regional, and global. From the discussions in the book, it is possible to draw several observations on these scales, in relation to which identities, heritages, and places are constructed and disseminated. The relationship between identity-making, nostalgia, and development survived the Islamic Revolution, although the other concepts and discourses that supported the assertion of identities, namely, tradition, authenticity, and civilization, have shifted in their connotations. Also shifting has been the relationship between the global forces and domestic dynamics in development, and the position of heritage and its production through design. It is therefore worth commenting on how these concepts and their use have evolved through time and across various scales, from global exchanges, to the experience of heritage in the intimate scale of the everyday through housing, and then back to the national and global expressions of belonging and heritage through monumental expressions. But before proceeding to the discussion, it is useful to recognize the characteristics of scale.

Architects work intimately with scale, pertaining (instrumentally) to size but also to relative dimensions among comparable objects within a design area – hence their use of terms such as 'appropriate scale'. This relationality closely approximates the geographical understanding of the term as a 'hierarchy'. Here, the idea of scale is itself fixed onto spatial entities, in so doing projecting socio-political implications of hierarchies of power, and therefore implying a certain type of governance which is familiar in developmental programming. But this fixation of scale to bounded territories and space can result in conceptions of permanence in identity and place. As such, for example, a globalizing programme is, perhaps necessarily, a potential threat to national sovereignty, hence giving rise to the autochthonous rhetoric of anti-globalization, Traditionalism, and self-reliance, which began long before the 1979 Revolution and continues to the present. Here, as evidenced in the discussion in Chapter 4 of the post-Revolution housing competitions, agency and negotiation are reduced to 'resistance'. Such instances also indicate that scale is socially contestable and processually negotiable. And yet, in contrast to this identity-bound scale, the global circulation of ideas, expertise, materials, and concepts disrupts fixed scales, simultaneously challenging and propagating identities, as we witnessed in the architectural congresses, and as has been the case in development projects. We have also noted how local actors, such as Ardalan, sought legitimation of their ideas through scalar contacts with international institutions, and individuals like Louis Kahn.[31]

National scale

At a national scale, the dynamics of developmentalism in Iran have been registered in the built environment. Even so, both the architecture, and the uses of the past within it, have shifting and dissonant temporal interpretations. While we have noted the ideological traces revealed by various ways of engaging past traditions in design, it would be simplistic and erroneous to assume that all symbolic and public architecture, then and now, is 'designed to order'. Rather, the search for an idea of historical connection, the attempt to trace the contours of a moral community, tantamount to the quest for constructing and propagating a common ground for the nation, was seen as a valid endeavour both before and after the 1979 Revolution and, in both cases, was effected through nostalgia. However, whereas the Pahlavi state asserted a national identity that drew upon its pre-Islamic and Islamic heritage, the Islamic Republic, as illustrated by the example of the Mosallā, and discussed in heritage scholarship,[32] tends to prefer the conception of a Shi'ite community of religion as the main identifier of the nation. Either way, in such attempts, nostalgia plays a functional role. In the case of the Islamic Republic, as others have previously discussed,[33] the practicalities of governing have instilled a tension between the demands of a modern nation-state and those of an ideologically driven, revolutionary entity, a tension that has lasted for four decades so far. As noted above and elsewhere by others, development activities that pertained to poverty alleviation were undertaken by quasi-state organizations.[34] Similarly, the issue of spatial and cultural development was 'outsourced' from various arms of government to a raft of parallel 'charitable' and revolutionary organizations. In the successive urban plans, Iranians have witnessed a progressive disappearance of public spaces, as exemplified by the transformations of Abbās Ābād. Instead, representational spaces are increasingly and exclusively religiously based, even in contesting the urban presence of pre-Revolution edifices, as we have seen in relation to the Shahyad and the 72 Tan Mosque. Urban spaces and activities are further curbed by quasi-privatization processes that tend to remove the public. This has proven problematic, as there is an increasing nostalgia for non-Islamic spaces and identity, especially among the younger generation when they publicly challenge or flout the morality codes imposed the government.[35]

From the regional to the global scale

Development and the making of heritage through design had regional repercussions. We have demonstrated, after Tsing, that local transformations are embedded in global exchanges and, in encountering specific localities, universalizing projects take new surprising directions, and that culture and heritage are borne of such encounters between the two. In developmental contexts that are characterized by palpable historical change, the emotional, embodied, and affective aspect of such exchanges are experienced as nostalgia. While nostalgia is the by-product of change, it can also propel action in design, as in politics.[36] Heritage is the medium through which nostalgia is operationalized, used for different motivations, assembled through various materials, and engaged in various social, political, and economic processes. The characteristic of nostalgia in this context is its ambiguous connotations; while there may be an apparent consensus over those connotations – the past, a sense of moral and communal belonging – that consensus may be as much a product of projected assumptions, amnesia, and misunderstanding as the result of reflective and rational thought processes.[37]

Throughout the book and its examples, we have emphasized relationality and historical specificity in discussing nostalgia in architecture, concurring with recent perspectives that note nostalgia's ethical, social, even emancipatory potentials. However, as noted in relation to Ardalan's ICMS design, as well as observed by a few interviewees in the course of the field research for the book, what may have seemed as nostalgic and appropriate in the 1970s, may in hindsight appear as reactionary and oppressive. Changing socio-historical and spatial contexts influences the meaning of the nostalgic phenomena, which may appear otherwise in a new context.

In the 1970s, Iran played the role of a leading exemplar in the predominantly Muslim societies and cultures of the region. Bolstered by strong economic growth, the country was active in the regional and international machinations of UNESCO.[38] But more importantly, the questions it posited, for example through the congresses, conveyed regional concerns, some of which have retained their currency to the present. Rather than just being initiated by global trends, transformations in Iran also provoked and prompted regional responses, some of which were driven by Iran itself.

In Iran, the past was invoked, not simply in terms of romantic imperialism, but also in support of Islamic causes and identities within the broader strategic machinations of the Cold War. This served to assert implicit and explicit civilizational claims against those of rivals in the region and beyond, and in the process also legitimating Iran's, and by extension the monarchy's, historical place. One consequence of this assertiveness was the ambivalent relationship with the so-called Muslim or Arab world.[39] Iran intervened in the Middle East and North African (MENA) region as part of a larger strategic policy pursuit within the context of the Cold War, and in the Middle East and the Islamic world in general after the Revolution. In its rivalry over cultural supremacy among Muslim societies, Iran advanced its civilizational claims, evidenced through material culture. Architecture and design were arenas substantiating its contemporaneity and thus the mirror image of a glorious past. After the Revolution, given the shift in official positions relating to identity and history, Iran's civilizational and cultural repository was construed primarily in Shi'ite Islamic terms interpreted with a nostalgic and reactionary slant. Within architecture, the cultural manifestations of this tendency have been the programmes and designs for the Mosallā and Khomeini's tomb, monuments which are both national and transnational, and which also evidence a strong sense of oblivion and cultural forgetting, despite the presence of images of multiple pasts.

Another regional outcome arising from the cultural identity debates of the 1970s is the Aga Khan Network for Development, which paid specific attention to architecture through its ongoing awards programme and its journal, *Mimar*, dedicated to architecture in Muslim societies. It is possible to relate the creation of this thriving network to developments in the Iranian context. Such networks cut across hierarchies of scale and link geographies, and end up defining new communities of identity – civilizational blocs, with regional affiliations and a global footprint. As academic architects who believed in the ideals of the Islamic Revolution recalled,

> [Compared to the usual Western journals,] there was one exceptional journal, *Mimar*, published by the Aga Khan Institute ... it focused on the architecture of Islamic countries and their identitarian aspects and I remember that it was as if this was what we longed for and expected. And I recall that the thing it articulated through its projects was the ultimate goal of all our efforts (the paths we had in mind) and it was bringing an identity for Islamic countries. ... we were considerably influenced by it ... and I think now this journal cannot be disregarded.[40]

234 *Development, architecture, and the formation of heritage*

This disruption of hierarchical scales is cause for concern for some state actors, including hard-line Islamists at the dawn of the Revolution, who were concerned with the Aga Khan's role as the leader of the Shi'ite Ismailis. In Iran in particular, the Islamist rhetoric, propagated by the revolutionary state, resulted in a dampening of creative explorations around heritage and design, through which there was a weakening of the geopolitical and transnational role that heritage and architecture could play.

Concluding remarks

This book has examined much of the current scholarship on Iranian architecture, heritage, and the built environment in a critical light. It is immediately apparent that even in the official architecture, there has been a multiplicity of intentions at any given time, in which there is a clear distinction between the rhetoric and practice of architecture, and the making of heritage. It is also apparent that various modes of cultural and political production contain different durations. We have emphasized that in discussing the 1970s, the complexity of architectural and cultural production cannot be oversimplified as monarchic hubris, nor can there be a recourse to a dismissive ascription of the production of that period as 'Aryanist'. Furthermore, it is evident that there were certain continuities in design practices before and after the Revolution. In relation to the nature of modernization and modernity in Iran, it has become something of an orthodoxy to refer to these processes as 'top-down'. Perhaps this is a description of the monopoly that the state held in development, one that was also held by other states in other developmental contexts.[41] But beyond this description, the term carries very little analytical purchase, and thus analyses built upon it in areas of heritage and architecture must also be re-examined. Similarly, the 'Islamic' turn in cultural production in the late Pahlavi period reflected a genuine desire to arrive at an authentic cultural identity, perhaps less ideologically driven than it did in the wake of the Revolution. More importantly, this search for authenticity was a common, albeit misplaced, tendency among the establishment and its critics alike. The turn to tradition and to religion cannot be dismissed as simply an administration 'ploy' to suppress and absorb opposition forces – despite the fact that invoking Shi'ite Imams was in vogue even among the Marxist opposition.[42]

We have further noted that some official architecture sought to represent authenticity in its public expression through an Islamic (and at times pre-Islamic) nostalgia. Although Traditionalism is emphasized in the published congress proceedings and was favoured in the wake of the Revolution, it would be erroneous to assume that it was the only discourse in cultural and architectural production. To do so amounts to reducing the polyphony of voices to a singular note. While significant works of public architecture possessed some of these traditionalist tendencies, there were many other modes of production. Thus, even after the Revolution, the discourse of architectural production could not be reduced to Islamic architecture, no matter how hard the officialdom tried. Here, we have recognized the critical potentials of nostalgia, through projections into both the past and future. Nostalgia is not itself value laden but acquires values through the uses to which it is put, and some observe this even in the machinations of prestigious institutions and awards:

> A small problem with the Aga Khan Institute is that they invite people such as Glenn Murcutt or Frank Gehry or Zaha Hadid, and MIT academics like Mostafavi, who are after promoting a kind of exoticism and … rank projects with a vernacularist formal approach [and this contains a kind of Orientalism in it] and for a few years there was a kind 'miserabilism' which [again glorified the vernacular and] the village but also award something to the work of Louis Kahn to say that we are neither populists nor elitist but seek excellence in architecture.[43]

Finally, we have demonstrated that, far from reflecting an inward-looking gaze, the developments in Iranian architecture have often been influenced by global projects and movements. Unlike some other readings that evaluate this globalizing streak in a negative light, perhaps as a continuation of imperial and class dominations, we consider this to have been an inevitable process, and one which has demonstrated significant potentials for genuine cultural expression, through which local actors possessed agency, and in turn exerted their influence on international developments. For the majority, as suggested by the late Abdolhamid Eshragh reflecting on the 1970s congresses, the point of departure was the desire 'to emerge out of tradition [a desire shared by many others] and exactly the same [desire] existed in music [to construct] a different world [out of tradition]'.[44] Today, that 'different world' remains an ongoing project.

Notes

1 Smith, *Uses of Heritage*.
2 On development and historical change, see Kitching, *Development and Underdevelopment*, ch. 4; Kothari, 'Introduction'; Craggs, 'Development in a Global-Historical Context'.
3 J. Harris, 'Great Promise, Hubris and Recovery: A Participant's History of Development Studies', in Kothari (ed.), *A Radical History*, pp. 19–44.
4 Tsing (*Friction*, pp. 6–11, 23) describes how engaged universals 'travel across difference and are charged and changed by their travels', which is precisely what happened in development projects and in transpositions of design techniques and ideas.
5 T. Jones et al., 'Heritage Designation and Scale: A World Heritage Case Study of the Ningaloo Coast', *International Journal of Heritage Studies*, 22:3 (2016), pp. 242–60, https://doi.org/10.1080/13527258.2015.1120226.
6 Peet and Hartwick, *Theories of Development*, pp. 166–72; A. Escobar, 'Imagining a Post-development Era? Critical Thought, Development and Social Movements', *Social Text*, 31/32 (1992), pp. 20–56; A. Escobar, 'Imagining a Post-development Era', in J. Crush (ed.), *Power of Development* (London: Routledge, 2005), pp. 221–38.
7 Peet and Hartwick, *Theories of Development*, pp. 181–6.

8 See J. P. Hasanli, *At the Dawn of the Cold War: The Soviet-American Crisis over Iranian Azerbaijan, 1941–1946* (Oxford: Rowman and Littlefield, 2006). These were also policies promoted by the Tudeh Party.
9 See Haji Molana, 'Sense of Community'; Zabihi et al., 'Study of Relationship between Satisfaction Rate of the Residential Complexes and Their Impacts on Human Relations (Case Study of Some Residential Complexes in Tehran)', *American Journal of Scientific Research*, 67 (2012), pp. 36–49.
10 It is particularly important to note that since the mid-1960s, independence was emphasized and put into practice by the Pahlavi establishment. Culture, civilization, power (in the regional sense), and development were folded into one another in the (particularly official) Iranian imagination. See C. Schayegh, 'Iran's Global Long 1970s: An Empire Project, Civilizational Developmentalism, and the Crisis of the Global North', in Alvandi (ed.), *The Age of Aryamehr*, pp. 492–548.
11 See M. J. Willcocks, 'Agent or Client: Who Instigated the White Revolution of the Shah and the People of Iran, 1963?' (PhD diss., University of Manchester, 2015). Also, on developmentalist approaches in Iran, see Nassehi, 'Domesticating Cold War'.
12 Peet and Hartwick, *Theories of Development*, pp. 78–84.
13 This shift was about the displacement of the role of the state apparatuses and the creation of 'civil society', as philosophers such as Karl Popper – later, the hero of Islamic reformism in Iran – saw the state as the oppressor of the individual and obstacle to development.
14 See also Nassehi, 'Domesticating Cold War'.
15 Ehsani, 'Cultural Politics', p. 223.
16 Sheikh Zeineddin, interview with Mozaffari, 2013.
17 For example, see D. G. Reid, *Tourism, Globalization and Development: Responsible Tourism Planning* (London and Sterling, VA: Pluto Press, 2003); D. E. Hawkins and S. Mann, 'The World Bank's Role in Tourism Development', *Annals of Tourism Research*, 34:2 (2007), pp. 348–63; D. J. Telfer and R. Sharpley, Tourism and Development in the Developing World (London and New York: Routledge, 2007); J. Brohman, 'New Directions in Tourism for Third World Development', *Annals of Tourism Research*, 23:1 (1996), pp. 48–70; P. Kareiva et al., 'Development and Conservation Goals in World Bank Projects', *Science*, 321:5896 (2008), pp. 1638–39, https://doi.org/10.1126/science.1162756; N. Nasser, 'Planning for Urban Heritage Places: Reconciling Conservation, Tourism, and Sustainable Development', *Journal of Planning Literature*, 17:4 (2003), pp. 467–79; A. Orbaşli, *Tourists in Historic Towns: Urban Conservation and Heritage Management* (London: Spon, 2000).
18 For examples of a critique of this position, see T. Rico, 'After Words: A Dedichotimization in Heritage Discourse', in K. L. Samuels and T. Rico (eds), *Heritage Keywords: Rhetoric and Redescription in Cultural Heritage* (Boulder, CO: University Press of Colorado, 2015), pp. 285–92.
19 On the essentialization of the concept of 'the state' in academic thinking, see M. Herzfeld, *Cultural intimacy: Social Poetics in the Nation-State* (London and New York: Routledge, 2014), pp. 1–44.
20 Harrison, *Heritage*, p. 4.
21 D. Crouch, 'Affect, Heritage, Feeling', in Waterton and Watson (eds), *Handbook of Contemporary Heritage Research*, pp. 177–90; Campbell et al., 'Nostalgia and

Heritage', pp. 609–11; L. Smith and G. Campbell, 'The Elephant in the Room: Heritage, Affect and Emotion', in Logan et al. (eds), *A Companion to Heritage Studies*, pp. 443–60; D. P. Tolia-Kelly et al. (eds), *Heritage, Affect and Emotion: Politics, Practices and Infrastructures* (London: Routledge, 2016).

22 On place and identity, see D. Massey, 'Power-Geometry and a Progressive Sense of Place', in J. Bird et al. (eds), *Mapping Futures: Local Cultures, Global Change* (London: Routledge, 1993), pp. 59–69. On relationality in place, see Massey, *For Space*. The heritage–place relationship within an Iranian context was developed for the first time by A. Mozaffari (ed.), *World Heritage in Iran: Perspectives on Pasargadae* (Surrey: Ashgate, 2014). On place and heritage, see A. Mozaffari, 'Conceptualising a World Heritage Site', in Mozaffari (ed.), *World Heritage in Iran*, pp. 17–44.

23 Harrison, *Heritage*, p. 14.

24 The evolution of Iranian architectural theory and practice remains directly related to international trends. Perhaps it is an indication of the connectedness of design that with the shutting down of contacts and exchanges in the 1980s, productive design and theory discourses in Iran showed clear signs of stagnation. These exchanges have more recently been revived, but largely outside the institutions of universities, ministries, or professional bodies.

25 I. Kalantari, interview with A. Mozaffari, Tehran, September 2013.

26 Harvey, 'Heritage and Scale'; T. Jones et al., 'Heritage Designation and Scale: A World Heritage Case Study of the Ningaloo Coast', *International Journal of Heritage Studies*, 22:3 (2016), pp. 242–60, https://doi.org/10.1080/13527258.2015.1120226; T. Lähdesmäki et al. (eds), *Politics of Scale: New Directions in Critical Heritage Studies, Volume 1* (New York and Oxford: Berghahn Books, 2019).

27 B. Graham et al., *A Geography of Heritage: Power, Culture and Economy* (London: Routledge, 2016), p. 4.

28 Harvey, 'Heritage and Scale', p. 590.

29 Lähdesmäki et al., *Politics of Scale*, p. 20.

30 M. R. Pahlavi, Selection from the Shahanshah Aryamehr's Speeches and Writings on Culture, Tehran 1975, p. 30; part of the speech for the occasion of inaugurating the Pahlavi building at the University of Chicago in 1968, cited in Schayegh, 'Iran's Global Long 1970s', p. 34.

31 N. Brenner, 'The Limits to Scale? Methodological Reflections on Scalar Structuration', *Progress in Human Geography*, 25:4 (2001), pp. 591–614.

32 Mozaffari, 'The Heritage "NGO"'; A. Mozaffari et al., 'Tourism and Political Change: The Return of the "Idea of Iran" (2005–2015)', in R. Butler and W. Suntikun (eds), *Tourism and Political Change* (Oxford: Goodfellow Publishers, 2017), pp. 186–99.

33 Mozaffari, *Forming National Identity*, pp. 85–9, 176–9.

34 Mashayekhi, 'The Politics of Building'.

35 This is apparent in, for example, the use of parks to stage water fights between boys and girls, an activity seen to be subversive by the Islamic Republic.

36 Mirsepassi, *Transnationalism*.

37 On the different meanings of heritage in Luang Prabang, see Berliner, 'Multiple Nostalgias', p. 782.

38 On heritage as an instrument of diplomacy, see T. Winter, 'Heritage Diplomacy: Entangled Materialities of International Relations', *Future Anterior*, 13:1 (2016), pp. 16–34.

39 احمدی، ح.، روابط ایران و عربستان در سده بیستم (دوره پهلوی)، مرکز اسناد و تاریخ دیپلماسی، تهران: مرکز چاپ و انتشارات وزارت امور خارجه، 1386.
40 H. Mazaherian, interview with A. Mozaffari, Tehran, November 2013.
41 Nassehi, 'Domesticating Cold War'.
42 H. Dabashi, *Shi'ism* (Cambridge, MA: Harvard University Press, 2011).
43 Academic architect in Iran (name withheld), interview with A. Mozaffari, Tehran, 2013.
44 A. Eshragh, interview with A. Mozaffari, Paris, 2011.

Bibliography

Interviews

Ardalan, A.-H., interview with A. Mozaffari, Tehran, 2017.
Diba, L., interview with T. Farmanfarmaian, 1984, vols 1 and 2, Foundation for Iranian Studies, https://fis-iran.org/en/content/diba-leyla (accessed 16 October 2018).
Eshragh, A., interwiew with A. Mozaffari, Paris, 2011.
Etemad, G., interview with A. Mozaffari, Tehran, 2017.
Haji-Ghassemi, K., interview with A. Mozaffari, Tehran, September 2013.
Kalantari, I., interview with A. Mozaffari, Tehran, September 2013.
Kashanijoo, M., interview with A. Mozaffari, Skype, November 2014.
Mazaherian, H., interview with A. Mozaffari, Tehran, November 2013.
Nourhkeihani, S. H., interview with A. Mozaffari, Tehran, 2017.
Nourkeihani, H., interview with A. Mozaffari, Skype, November 2014.
Shafe`i, B., interview with A. Mozaffari, Tehran, 2017.
Sheikh Zeineddin, H., interview with A. Mozaffari, Tehran, September 2013.
Various, interviews with B. Lotfi, Tabriz, September and October 2017.

Works cited (English)

Abrahamian, E., 'Ali Shariati: Ideologue of the Iranian Revolution', in E. Burke and I. Lapidus (eds), *Islam, Politics, and Social Movements* (Los Angeles, CA: University of California Press, 1993), pp. 56–63.
Abrahams, R. D., 'Phantoms of Romantic Nationalism in Folkloristics', *American Folklore*, 106:419 (Winter, 1993), pp. 3–37.
Adle, C. and B. Hourcade (eds), *Téhéran Capitale Bicentenaire* (Paris and Tehran: Institut Français de Recherche en Iran, 1992).
Adorno, T., *The Jargon of Authenticity*, trans. K. Tarnowski and F. Will (Evanston, IL: Northwestern University Press, 1973).
Adorno, T. W. and M. Horkheimer, *Dialectic of Enlightenment*, trans. E. Jephcott (Stanford, CA: Stanford University Press, 2002).
Afkhami, M., 'Pahlbod, Mehrdad', Oral History interview (Los Angeles, CA: Foundation for Iranian Studies, 25 and 30 May 1984), https://fis-iran.org/en/content/pahlbod-mehrdad (accessed 14 January 2018).
Afshar, E., 'The National Library of Iran: A New Building and a New Future', *Australian Academic and Research Libraries*, 37:3 (2006), pp. 221–32.
Aga Khan Award for Architecture (ed.), 'Shushtar New Town On-site Review Report', 1980, http://bit.ly/35sPGHX (accessed 23 October 2017).

Akbarzadeh, P. (dir.), *Taq Kasra: Wonder of Architecture* [documentary film] (Amsterdam: Persian Dutch Network, 2018).

Akhavi, S., 'Islam, Politics and Society in the Thought of Ayatullah Khomeini Taliqani and Ali Shariati', *Middle Eastern Studies*, 24:4 (1988), pp. 404–31.

Akhavi-Pour, H., 'The Economy', in G. E. Curtis and E. Hooglund (eds), *Iran: A Country Study* (Washington, DC: Federal Research Division, Library of Congress, 2008), pp. 143–205.

Alexander, C., *The Timeless Way of Building* (Oxford: Oxford University Press, 1979).

Alexander, C., S. Ishikawa, and M. Silverstein, *A Pattern Language: Towns, Buildings, Construction* (Oxford: Oxford University Press, 1977).

Alsayyad, N., 'Consuming Heritage or the End of Tradition: The New Challenges of Globalization', in Y. Kalay, T. Kvan, and J. Affleck (eds), *New Heritage: New Media and Cultural Heritage* (Abingdon: Routledge, 2007), pp. 155–69.

Altman, I. and C. M. Werner (eds), *Home Environments, Human Behavior and Environment: Advances in Theory and Research, Volume 8* (New York: Plenum Press, 1985).

Alvandi, R., 'Introduction: Iran in the Age of Aryamehr', in R. Alvandi (ed.), *The Age of Aryamehr: Late Pahlavi Iran and Its Global Entanglements* (London: Gingko Library, 2018), ebook.

Alvandi, R. (ed.), *The Age of Aryamehr: Late Pahlavi Iran and Its Global Entanglements* (London: Ginko Library, 2018).

Amini, N., 'Modern Architecture as an Agency of Political Competition: The Case of Iran and Pakistan', *Studies in History and Theory of Architecture*, 6 (2018), pp. 92–107.

Amirahmadi, H., 'Regional Planning in Iran: A Survey of Problems and Policies', *The Journal of Developing Areas*, 20:4 (1986), pp. 501–30.

Amirahmadi, H. and A. Kiafar, 'The Transformation of Tehran from Garrison Town to a Primate City: A Tale of Rapid Growth and Uneven Development', in H. Amirahmadi and S. S. El-Shakhs (eds), *Urban Development in the Muslim World* (New Brunswick, NJ: Rutgers University Press, 1993 [2012]), pp. 109–36.

Amirahmadi, H. and S. S. El-Shakhs (eds), *Urban Development in the Muslim World* (New Brunswick, NJ: Rutgers University Press, 1993 [2012]).

Amirjani, R., 'An Analogical Quotation', in J. Ting and G. Hartoonian (eds), *Quotation: What Does History Have in Store for Architecture Today?* Proceedings of the 34th Annual Conference of the Society of Architectural Historians of Australia and New Zealand, 5–8 July 2017 (Canberra, ACT: Society of Architectural Historians, Australia and New Zealand, 2017), pp. 13–23.

Amir-Moezzi, M. A. and C. Jambet, *What Is Shia Islam? An Introduction* (Abingdon: Routledge, 2018).

Amuzegar, J., 'The Iranian Economy before and after the Revolution', *Middle East Journal*, 46:3 (Summer, 1992), pp. 413–25.

Anderson, S. (ed.), *On Streets: Streets as Elements of Urban Structure* (Cambridge, MA: MIT Press, 1978).

Andritsky, M., L. Burkhardt, and O. Hoffman (eds), *Für Eine Andere Architektur* (Frankfurt am Main: Fisher 1981).

Angé, O., 'Social and Economic Performativity of Nostalgic Narratives in Andean Barter Fairs', in O. Angé and D. Berliner (eds), *Anthropology and Nostalgia* (New York and Oxford: Berghahn Books, 2015), pp. 178–97.

Angé, O. and D. Berliner, 'Introduction: Athropology of Nostalgia – Anthropology as Nostalgia', in O. Angé and D. Berliner (eds), *Anthropology and Nostalgia* (New York and Oxford: Berghahn Books, 2015), pp. 1–15.

Angé, O. and D. Berliner (eds), *Anthropology and Nostalgia* (New York and Oxford: Berghahn Books, 2015).

Ansari, A. M., 'The Myth of the White Revolution: Mohammad Reza Shah, "Modernization" and the Consolidation of Power', *Middle Eastern Studies*, 37:3 (2001), pp. 1–24, https://doi.org/10.1080/714004408.

Appadurai, A., *Modernity at Large: Cultural Dimensions of Globalization* (Minneapolis, MN: University of Minnesota Press, 1996).

Ardalan, N., 'Places of Public Gathering', in L. Safran (ed.), *Places of Public Gathering in Islam* (Philadelphia, PA: The Aga Khan Award for Architecture, 1980), pp. 5–16.

Ardalan, N., 'The Quest for a Spiritually Inspired, Holistically Sustainable Habitat: Nuran – The City of Illumination, Isfahan', in Utopia, Architecture, and Spirituality, Architecture, Culture, and Spirituality Symposium (ACS8), 23–26 June 2016, New Harmony, Indiana, www.acsforum.org/symposium2016/papers/ardalan.pdf (accessed 18 September 2018).

Ardalan, N. and L. Bakhtiar, *The Sense of Unity: The Sufi Tradition in Persian Architecture*, with a foreword by S. H. Nasr (Chicago, IL: The University of Chicago Press, 1973).

Ardalan, N., G. Candilis, B.V. Doshi, M. Safdie, and J. L. Sert, *Habitat Bill of Rights: Presented by Iran* (Tehran: Hamdami Foundation, 1976).

Arefian, F. F. and S. H. I. Moeini (eds), *Urban Change in Iran: Stories of Rooted Histories and Ever-accelerating Developments* (Basel: Springer, 2015).

Arendt, H., *Between Past and Future: Eight Exercises in Political Thought* (New York: Penguin Books, 1993 [1961]).

Arendt, H. and H. Zohn (eds), *Illuminations: Essays and Reflections* (New York: Schoken Books, 1969 [1968]).

Arnell, P., T. Bickford, and C. Rowe (eds), *James Stirling: Buildings and Projects, James Stirling and Michael Wilford and Associates* (London: Architectural Press, 1984).

Ashuri, D., 'Fardid Was Not Very Religious', in A. Mirsepassi (ed.), *Iran's Troubled Modernity: Debating Ahmad Fardid's Legacy* (Cambridge: Cambridge University Press, 2019), pp. 73–97.

Ashworth, G. J., B. J. Graham, and J. E. Tunbridge, *Pluralising Pasts: Heritage, Identity and Place in Multicultural Societies* (London and Ann Arbor, MI: Pluto Press, 2007).

Assmann, J., 'Communicative and Cultural Memory', in A. Erll and A. Nünning (eds), *Cultural Memory Studies: An International and Interdisciplinary Handbook* (Berlin and New York: de Gruyter, 2008), pp. 109–18.

Assmann, J. and J. Czaplicka, 'Collective Memory and Cultural Identity', *New German Critique*, 65 (Spring–Summer, 1995), pp. 125–33.

Atia, N. and J. Davies, 'Nostalgia and the Shapes of History', Editorial, *Memory Studies*, 3:3 (2010), pp. 181–6.

Avermaete, T., 'Nomadic Experts and Travelling Perspectives: Colonial Modernity and the Epistemological Shift in Modern Architectural Culture', in T. Avermaete, S. Karakayali, and M. von Osten (eds), *Colonial Modern: Aesthetics of the Past, Rebellions for the Future* (London: Black Dog Publishing, 2010), pp. 131–51.

Avermaete, T., 'Coda: The Reflexivity of Cold War Architectural Modernism', *The Journal of Architecture*, 17:3 (2012), pp. 475–7.

Avermaete, T., S. Karakayali, and M. von Osten (eds), *Colonial Modern: Aesthetics of the Past, Rebellions for the Future* (London: Black Dog Publishing, 2010).

Aydin, C., *The Politics of Anti-Westernism in Asia: Visions of World Order in Pan-Islamic and Pan-Asian Thought* (New York: Columbia University Press, 2007).

Aydin, C., 'Japan's Pan-Asianism and the Legitimacy of Imperial World Order, 1931–1945', *The Asia-Pacific Journal*, 6:3 (2008), pp. 1–33.

Ayres, P., 'The Geometry of Shahyad Ariamehr', *The Arup Journal*, 5:1 (March, 1970), pp. 29–36.

Azizi, M. M., 'Evaluation of Urban Land Supply Policy in Iran', *International Journal of Urban and Regional Research*, 22:1 (1998), pp. 94–105.

Azizi-Matr, N., 'Regeneration Process in Tehran: The Ineffectiveness of Regeneration of Deteriorated Parts of Tehran', master's thesis, Politecnico Di Milano, 2014.

Babadzan, A., 'Anthropology, Nationalism and "the Invention of Tradition"', *Anthropological Forum*, 10:2 (2000), pp. 131–55.

Bahrainy, H. and B. Aminzadeh, 'Autocratic Urban Design: The Case of the Navab Regeneration Project in Central Tehran', *International Development Planning Review*, 29:2 (2007), pp. 241–70.

Bahrainy, H. and B. Aminzadeh, 'Evaluation of Navab Regeneration Project in Central Tehran, Iran', *International Journal of Environmental Research*, 1:2 (2007), pp. 114–27.

Baker, G. H., *The Architecture of James Stirling and His Partners James Gowan and Michael Wilford* (Surrey and Burlington, CT: Ashgate, 2011).

Bakhtiar, L. (ed.), *Towards a Quality of Life: The Role of Industrialization in the Architecture and Urban Planning of Developing Countries: Report of the Proceedings of the Second International Congress of Architects, Persepolis, Iran, 1974* (Tehran: Ministry of Housing and Development, 1974).

Bakhtiar, L. (ed.), *The Crisis of Identity in Architecture: Report of the Proceedings of the International Congress of Women Architects, Ramsar Iran, 13–17 October 1976* (Tehran: Hamdami Foundation, 1976).

Barnes, T. and D. Gregory (eds), *Reading Human Geography: The Poetics and Politics of Inquiry* (London and New York: Arnold, 1997).

Bartoletti, R. 'Memory Tourism and Commodification of Nostalgia', in P. Burns, C. Palmer, and J.-A. Lester (eds), *Tourism and Visual Culture: Volume 1: Theories and Concepts* (Wallingford: CABI, 2010), pp. 23–42.

Bauman, Z., 'Morality in the Age of Contingency', in P. Heelas, S. Lash, and P. Morris (eds), *Detraditionalization: Critical Reflections on Authority and Identity* (Cambridge, MA: Blackwell, 1996).

Bayat, A., 'Squatters and the State: Back Street Politics in the Islamic Republic', *Middle East Report*, 191 (1994), pp. 10–14.

Bechtel, R. B., 'Behaviour in the House: A Cross-cultural Comparison using Behaviour-Setting Methodology', in S. M. Low and E. Chambers (eds), *Housing, Culture and Design: A Comparative Perspective* (Philadelphia, PA: University of Pennsylvania Press, 1989), pp. 165–81.

Beck, L., 'Revolutionary Iran and its Tribal Peoples', in T. Asad and R. Owen (eds), *The Middle East* (London: Palgrave, 1983), pp. 115–26.

Bendix, R., 'Tradition and Modernity Reconsidered', *Comparative Studies in Society and History*, 9:3 (1967), pp. 292–346.

Benjamin, W., 'Theses on the Philosophy of History', in H. Arendt and H. Zohn (eds), *Illuminations: Essays and Reflections* (New York: Schoken Books, 1969 [1968]), pp. 235–64.

Benjamin, W., *The Arcades Project*, trans. H. Eiland and K. McLaughlin (Cambridge, MA, and London: Belknapp Press, 1999).

Beny, R., *Persia: Bridge of Turquoise* (Toronto: McClelland and Stewart, 1975).

Beny, R., *Iran: Elements of Destiny* (Toronto: McClelland and Stewart, 1978).

Berliner, D., 'Multiple Nostalgias: The Fabric of Heritage in Luang Prabang (Lao PDR)', *The Journal of the Royal Anthropological Institute*, 18:4 (2012), pp. 769–86.

Biraghi, M., *Project of Crisis: Manfredo Tafuri and Contemporary Architecture*, trans. A. L. Price (Cambridge, MA: MIT Press, 2013 [2005]).

Bissel, W. C., 'Engaging Colonial Nostalgia', *Cultural Anthropology*, 20:2 (2005), pp. 215–48.

Blake, K., *The U.S.–Soviet Confrontation in Iran 1945–1962: A Case in the Annals of the Cold War* (Lanham, MD, and Plymouth: University Press of America, 2009).

Bonnett, A., *The Geography of Nostalgia: Global and Local Perspectives on Modernity and Loss* (London and New York: Routledge, 2016).

Bordeau, L., M. Gravari-Barbas, and M. Robinson (eds), *World Heritage, Tourism and Identity: Inscription and Co-production* (Abingdon: Ashgate, 2016).

Boroujerdi, M., *Iranian Intellectuals and the West: The Tormented Triumph of Nativism* (New York: Syracuse University Press, 1996).

Borsano, G. and P. Portoghesi (eds), *The Presence of the Past: First International Exhibition of Architecture – The Corderia of the Arsenale: la Bienale di Venezia* (London: Academy Editions, 1980).

Bostock, F. and G. Jones, *Planning and Power in Iran: Ebtehaj and Economic Development under the Shah* (London: Frank Cass, 1989).

Bourdieu, P., *Outline of a Theory of Practice* (Cambridge: Cambridge University Press, 1977).

Bourdieu, P., 'Habitus', in J. Hillier and E. Rooksby (eds), *Habitus: A Sense of Place* (Burlington, VT: Ashgate, 2002), pp. 27–34.

Boyer, D., 'From Algos to Autonomos: Nostalgic Eastern Europe as Postimperial Mania', in M. Todorova and Z. Gille (eds), *Postcommunist Nostalgia* (Oxford: Berghahn Books, 2012), pp. 17–28.

Boym, S., *The Future of Nostalgia* (New York: Basic Books, 2001).

Boym, S., 'Nostalgia and Its Discontents', *Hedgehog Review*, 9:2 (2007), pp. 7–18.

Bozdogan, S., *Sedad Eldem* (Istanbul: Literatür Yayınları, 2005).

Briggs, C. L., 'The Politics of Discursive Authority in Research on the "Invention of Tradition"', *Cultural Anthropology*, 11:4 (1996), pp. 435–69.

Brohman J., 'New Directions in Tourism for Third World Development', *Annals of Tourism Research*, 23:1 (1996), pp. 48–70.

Brenner, N., 'The Limits to Scale? Methodological Reflections on Scalar Structuration', *Progress in Human Geography*, 25:4 (2001), pp. 591–614.

Brownlee, D. and D. de Long, *Louis Kahn: In the Realm of Architecture* (Los Angeles, CA: Museum of Contemporary Art, and New York: Rizzoli, 1991).

Bryant, R., 'Nostalgia and the Discovery of Loss: Essentializing the Turkish Cypriot Past', in O. Angé and D. Berliner (eds), *Anthropology and Nostalgia* (New York and Oxford: Berghahn Books, 2015).

Burke, E. and I. Lapidus (eds), *Islam, Politics, and Social Movements* (Los Angeles, CA: University of California Press, 1993).
Burke, P., *Cultural Hybridity* (Cambridge: Polity Press, 2009).
Butler, R. and W. Suntikun (eds), *Tourism and Political Change* (Oxford: Goodfellow Publishers, 2017).
Buttimer, A., 'Grasping the Dynamism of Lifeworld', *Annals of the Association of American Geographers*, 66:2 (1976), pp. 277–92.
Buttimer, A. and D. Seamon (eds), *The Human Experience of Space and Place* (New York: St. Martin's Press, 1980).
Campbell, G., L. Smith, and M. Wetherell, 'Nostalgia and Heritage: Potentials, Mobilisations and Effects', *International Journal of Heritage Studies*, 23:7 (2017), pp. 609–11, https://doi.org/10.1080/13527258.2017.1324558.
Canetti, E., *Crowds and Power* (London: Gollancz, 1962).
Carey, J. P. C. and A. G. Carey, 'Industrial Growth and Development Planning in Iran', *Middle East Journal*, 29:1 (Winter, 1975), pp. 1–15.
Casakin, H. and F. Bernado (eds), *The Role of Place Identity in the Perception, Understanding, and Design of the Built Environment* (Sharjah, UAE: Bentham Science Publisher, 2012).
Casciato, M., 'Neorealism in Italian Architecture', in S. W. Goldhagen and R. Legault (eds), *Anxious Modernisms: Experimentation in Postwar Architectural Culture* (Cambridge, MA: MIT Press, 2000), pp. 25–53.
Casey, E., *The Fate of Place: A Philosophical Inquiry* (Berkley, CA: University of California Press, 1997).
Casey, E., *Remembering: A Phenomenological Study*, 2nd edn (Bloomington, IN: Indiana University Press, 2000 [1987]).
Cashman, R., 'Critical Nostalgia and Material Culture in Northern Ireland', *The Journal of American Folklore*, 119:472 (Spring, 2006), pp. 137–60.
Chehabi, H., P. Jafari, and M. Jefroudi (eds), *Iran in the Middle East: Transnational Encounters and Social History* (London: I.B. Tauris, 2015).
Chittick, W. C. (ed.), *The Essential Seyyed Hossein Nasr* (Bloomington, IN: World Wisdom Inc., 2007).
Clarke, A., 'World Heritage, Tourism and Identity: Inscription and Co-production', *Journal of Heritage Tourism*, 12:2 (2017), pp. 220–1.
Clifford, J., 'Traditional Futures', in M. S. Phillips and G. Schochet (eds), *Questions of Tradition* (Toronto: University of Toronto Press, 2004), pp. 152–68.
Cofano, P., D. Konstantinidis, and A. Konstantinidis, *Aris Konstantinidis, 1913–1993* (Milan: Electa Architettura, 2010).
Cohen, J.-L. and M. Eleb, *Casablanca: Colonial Myths and Architectural Ventures* (New York: Monacelli Press, 2002).
Cole, J. R., *Modernity and the Millennium: The Genesis of the Baha'i Faith in the Nineteenth-Century Middle East, Volume 9* (New York: Columbia University Press, 1998).
Congrès international d'architecture moderne (CIAM), *La Charte d'Athenes or The Athens Charter, 1933*, trans J. Tyrwhitt (Paris: Library of the Graduate School of Design, Harvard University, 1946).
Congrès international d'architecture moderne (CIAM), *Documents: 7 CIAM, Bergamo, 1949* (Nendeln: Kraus Reprint, 1979).
Connerton, P., *How Societies Remember* (Cambridge: Cambridge University Press, 1989).

Constitution of Islamic Republic of Iran, 'Preamble', Iran Chamber Society, 1980, www.iranchamber.com/government/laws/constitution.php (accessed 12 February 2019).

Constitution of the Islamic Republic of Iran 1979, 'The Form of Governance in Islam', World Intellectual Property Organization (WIPO), amended 28 July 1989, https://wipolex.wipo.int/en/text/332330 (accessed 21 January 2018).

Costello, V. F., 'Planning Problems and Politics in Tehran', in H. Amirahmadi and S. S. El-Shakhs (eds), *Urban Development in the Muslim World* (New Brunswick, NJ: Rutgers University Press, 1993 [2012]), pp. 137–63.

Cowan, J. K., M.-B. Dembour, and R. A. Wilson (eds), *Culture and Rights: Anthropological Perspectives* (Cambridge: Cambridge University Press, 2001).

Cowen, M. P. and R. W. Shenton, *Doctrines of Development* (London and New York: Routledge, 1996).

Craggs, R., 'Development in a Global-Historical Context', in V. Desai and R. B. Potter (eds), *The Companion to Development Studies*, 3rd edn (London and New York: Routledge, 2014), pp. 5–10.

Cresswell, T., *In Place/Out of Place: Geography, Ideology and Transgression* (Minneapolis, MN: University of Minnesota Press, 1996).

Crossley, N., 'The Phenomenological Habitus and Its Construction', *Theory and Society*, 30:1 (2001), pp. 81–120.

Crossley, N., *The Social Body: Habit, Identity and Desire* (London: SAGE Publications, 2001).

Crouch D., 'Affect, Heritage, Feeling', in E. Waterton and S. Watson (eds), *The Palgrave Handbook of Contemporary Heritage Research* (New York: Palgrave, 2015), pp. 177–90.

Curtis, G. E. and E. Hooglund (eds), *Iran: A Country Study* (Washington, DC: Federal Research Division, Library of Congress, 2008).

Curtis, W., 'Towards an Authentic Regionalism', in H.-U. Khan (ed.), *Mimar 19: Architecture in Development* (Singapore: Concept Media, 1986), pp. 24–31.

Dabashi, H., *Shi'ism* (Cambridge, MA: Harvard University Press, 2011).

Dados, N. and R. Connell, 'The Global South', *Contexts*, Taking on the Issues, 11:1 (Winter, 2012), pp. 12–13.

Daftary, F., 'Development Planning in Iran: A Historical Survey', *Iranian Studies*, 6:4 (1973): 176–228.

Dames, N., 'Nostalgia and Its Disciplines', *Memory Studies*, 3:3 (2010), pp. 269–75.

Dānishvar, R., *A Garden between Two Streets* (Persian) (Paris: Alborz, 2010).

Davis, F., *Yearning for Yesterday: A Sociology of Nostalgia* (New York: Free Press, 1979).

de Certeau, M., *The Practice of Everyday Life*, trans. S. Rendall (Berkeley, CA: University of California Press, 1984).

'Declaration Presented by Princess Ashraf Pahlavi to the Secretary General of the U.N' (Tehran: Women's Organization of Iran, 10 December 10, 1974), https://fis-iran.org/sites/fis/files/Princess%20Ashraf%20Declaration%20to%20UN%20P1.pdf (accessed 23 March 2018).

Delevoy, R. L., A. Vidler, and L. Krier (eds), *Architecture Rationelle: La Reconstruction de la Ville Europeenne* [Rational Architecture: The Reconstruction of the European City] (Brussels: AAM, 1978).

Department of Housing and Development (Islamic Republic of Iran), *Housing Complexes Design Competition* (Department of Housing, September 1989) [مسابقه طراحی مجتمع های مسکن].

Der-Grigorian, T., 'Construction of History: Mohammad-Reza Shah Revivalism, Nationalism, and Monumental Architecture of Tehran, 1951–1979', PhD diss., Massachusetts Institute of Technology, 1998.

Desai, V. and R. B. Potter (eds), *The Companion to Development Studies*, 3rd edn (London and New York: Routledge, 2014).

Devos, B. and C. Werner (eds), *Cultural Politics under Reza Shah: The Pahlavi State, New Bourgeois Culture and the Creation of a Modern Society in Iran*, Iranian Studies Series (London: Routledge, 2013).

Diba, D., 'Architect's Design Report: Aga Khan Technical Review Summary' (Philadelphia, PA: The Aga Khan Award for Architecture, 1986 [1980]).

Diba, D., 'The University of Kerman', *Mimar: Architecture in Development*, 42 (1992), pp. 62–4.

Diba, D. and M. Dehbashi, 'Trends in Modern Iranian Architecture', in P. Jodido (ed.), *Iran, Architecture for Changing Societies* (Turin: The Aga Khan Award for Architecture, 2004), pp. 31–7.

Diba, K. T. [D.A.Z. Architects and Planners, Kamran T. Diba principal], 'A Case Study: Design Concepts of Shushtar New Town', in L. Safran (ed.), *Housing Process and Physical Form*, Proceedings of Seminar Two in the series Architectural Transformations in the Islamic World, Istanbul, Turkey, 26–28 September 1978 (Philadelphia, PA: The Aga Khan Award for Architecture, 1980), pp. 41–4.

Diba, K. T. 'The Recent Housing Boom in Iran – Lessons to Remember', in L. Safran (ed.), *Housing: Process and Physical Form, Housing Process and Physical Form*, Proceedings of Seminar Three in the series Architectural Transformations in the Islamic World, Jakarta, Indonesia, 26–29 March 1979 (Philadelphia, PA: The Aga Khan Award for Architecture, 1980), pp. 41–4.

Diba, K. T., *Kamran Diba: Buildings and Projects* (Berlin: Verlag Gerd Hatje, 1981).

Diba, K. T., 'Shustar New Town, a Company Town in Persia', *Lotus International*, 36 (1982), pp. 118–24.

Diba, K. T., *Shustar New Town* (Aga Khan Award for Architecture –Technical Report, 0117.IRA, 1986).

Diba, K. T., 'Aspects of a University Project and a New Town in Iran', in W. Reilly (ed.), *Sustainable Landscape Design in Arid Climates* (Geneva: Aga Khan Trust for Culture, 1989), pp. 34–7.

Dixon, J. M., 'A Place in Progress', *Progressive Architecture*, 10 (October, 1976), pp. 49–55.

Eagleton, T., *Ideology: An Introduction* (London and New York: Verso, 1991).

Edgerton, J. D. and L. W. Roberts, 'Cultural Capital or Habitus? Bourdieu and Beyond in the Explanation of Enduring Educational Inequality', *Theory and Research in Education*, 12:2 (2014), pp. 193–220.

Eggener, K. L., 'Placing Resistance: A Critique of Critical Regionalism', *Journal of Architectural Education*, 55:4 (May, 2002), pp. 228–37.

Ehsani, K., 'The Cultural Politics of Public Space in Tehran's Book Fair', in H. Chehabi, P. Jafari, and M. Jefroudi (eds), *Iran in the Middle East: Transnational Encounters and Social History* (London: I.B. Tauris, 2015), pp. 213–31.

Eisenstadt, S. N., 'Intellectuals and Tradition', *Daedalus*, 101:2 (Spring, 1972), pp. 1–19.

Eleb, M., 'An Alternative to Functionalist Universalism: Écochard, Candilis, and ATBAT-Afrique', in S. W. Goldhagen and R. Legault (eds), *Anxious Modernisms:*

Experimentation in Postwar Architectural Culture (Cambridge, MA: MIT Press, 2001), pp. 55–73.

Eliade, M., *Cosmos and History: The Myth of the Eternal Return* (New York: Harper Torchbooks, 1959).

El-shorbagy, A.-A. M., 'The Architecture of Hassan Fathy: Between Western and Non-Western Perspectives', PhD diss., University of Canterbury, 2001.

Emami, F., '"Civic Visions", National Politics, and International Designs: Three Proposals for a New Urban Centre in Tehran (1966–1976)', master's thesis, Massachusetts Institute of Technology, 2011.

Emami, F., 'Urbanism of Grandiosity: Planning a New Urban Centre for Tehran', *International Journal of Islamic Architecture*, 3:1 (2014), pp. 69–102.

English, P. W. and R. C. Mayfield (eds), *Man, Space and Environment: Concepts in Contemporary Human Geography* (Oxford: Oxford University Press, 1972).

Erikson, T. H., 'Between Universalism and Relativism: A Critique of the UNESCO Concept of Culture', in J. K. Cowan, M.-B. Dembour, and R. A. Wilson (eds), *Culture and Rights: Anthropological Perspectives* (Cambridge: Cambridge University Press, 2001), pp. 127–48.

Erll, A. and A. Nünning (eds), *Cultural Memory Studies: An International and Interdisciplinary Handbook* (Berlin and New York: de Gruyter, 2008).

Escobar, A., 'Imagining a Post-development Era? Critical Thought, Development and Social Movements', *Social Text*, 31/32 (1992), pp. 20–56.

Escobar, A., 'Imagining a Post-development Era', in J. Crush (ed.), *Power of Development* (London: Routledge, 2005), pp. 221–38.

Escobar, A., *Territories of Difference: Place, Movements, Life, Redes* (Durham, NC, and London: Duke University Press, 2008).

Esfahani, H. S. and M. H. Pesaran, 'The Iranian Economy in the Twentieth Century: A Global Perspective', *Iranian Studies*, 42:2 (2009), pp. 177–211, https://doi.org/10.1080/00210860902764896.

Fanni, Z., 'Cities and Urbanization in Iran after the Islamic Revolution', *Cities*, 23:6 (2006), pp. 407–11.

Farahani, R. F., I. Etesam, and S. R. Eghbali, 'The Impact of Architectural Competitions on the Improvement of the Post-Revolution Architecture in Iran', *International Journal of Architecture and Urban Development*, 2:2 (Spring, 2012), pp. 35–44.

Farhad, L. and L. Bakhtiar (eds), *Investigating the Possibility of Linking Traditional Architecture with Modern Building Methods: Report of the Proceedings of the First International Congress of Architects* (Isfahan: Ministry for Development and Housing, 1970).

Farhad, L. and L. Bakhtiar, *The Interaction of Tradition and Technology: Report of the Proceedings of the First International Congress of Architects, Isfahan, 1970* (Tehran: Ministry for Development and Housing, 1970).

Fathy, H., *Architecture for the Poor: An Experiment in Rural Egypt* (Chicago, IL: The University of Chicago Press, 1976 [1973]).

Feniger, N. and R. Kallus, 'Building a "New Middle East": Israeli Architects in Iran in the 1970s', *The Journal of Architecture*, 22:4 (May, 2017), pp. 765–85, https://doi.org/10.1080/13602365.2016.1204073.

Ferraro, V., 'Dependency Theory: An Introduction,' in G. Secondi (ed.), *The Development Economics Reader* (London: Routledge, 2008), pp. 58–64.

Foltz, R. C., F. M. Denny, and A. Baharuddin (eds), *Islam and Ecology: A Bestowed Trust* (Cambridge, MA: Harvard University Press, 2003).

Forouzandeh, N. and S. Motallebi, 'The Role of Open Spaces in Neighborhood Attachment (Case Study: Ekbatan Town in Tehran Metropolis)', *International Journal of Architecture and Urban Development*, 2:1 (2012), pp. 11–20.

Foster, H. (ed.), *The Anti-aesthetic: Essays on Postmodern Culture* (Seattle, WA: Bay Press, 1983).

Foucault, M., *The Foucault Effect: Studies in Governmentality* (Chicago, IL: The University of Chicago Press, 1991).

Frajndlich, R. U., 'Two Projects: The Formative Years of Manfredi Tafuri', *PÓS*, 23:29 (2016), pp. 72–89.

Frampton, K., 'Prospects for a Critical Regionalism', *Perspecta*, 20 (1983), pp. 147–62.

Frampton, K., 'Towards a Critical Regionalism: Six Points for an Architecture of Resistance', in H. Foster (ed.), *The Anti-aesthetic: Essays on Postmodern Culture* (Seattle, WA: Bay Press, 1983), pp. 16–30.

Friedman, J., 'The Past in the Future: History and the Politics of Identity', *American Anthropologist*, 94:4 (1992), pp. 837–59.

Frye, R. N. (ed.), *The Cambridge History of Iran, Volume 4: From the Arab Invasion to the Saljuqs* (Cambridge: Cambridge University Press, 1975).

Fuller, M., 'Mediterraneanism: French and Italian Architects' Designs in 1930s North African Cities', in S. K. Jayyusi, R. Holod, A. Petruccioli, and A. Raymond (eds), *The City in the Islamic World, Volume 2* (Leiden and Boston, MA: Brill, 2008).

Fuller, R. B., *Utopia or Oblivion: The Prospects for Humanity* (Toronto and New York: Bantam Books, 1969).

Gandelsonas, M. and D. Morton, 'On Reading Architecture', *Progressive Architecture* (March, 1972), pp. 29–59.

García-Huidobro, F., D. T. Torriti, and N. Tugas (eds), *¡El Tiempo Construye! Time Builds!* (Barcelona: Gustavo Gili, 2008).

Garlitz, R., 'Academic Ambassadors in the Middle East: The University Contract Program in Turkey and Iran, 1950–1970', PhD diss., Ohio University, 2008.

Garlitz, R., 'U.S. University Advisors and Education Modernization in Iran, 1951–1967', in R. Garlitz and L. Jarvinen (eds), *Teaching America to the World and the World to America* (New York: Palgrave Macmillan, 2012), pp. 195–215.

Garofalo, F. and L. Veresani, *Adalberto Libera* (New York: Princeton Architectural Press, 1992).

Gerami, S., 'Mullahs, Martyrs, and Men: Conceptualizing Masculinity in the Islamic Republic of Iran', *Men and Masculinities*, 5:3 (2003), pp. 257–74.

Ghairpour, M. (ed.), *The Historiography of Persian Architecture* (London and New York: Routledge, 2015).

Gharipour, M. (ed.), *Contemporary Urban Landscapes of the Middle East* (Londona and New York: Routledge, 2016).

Gheissari, A. and V. Nasr, 'Iran's Democracy Debate', *Middle East Policy*, 11:2 (Summer, 2004), pp. 94–106.

Gholipour, A., *Cultivation of Popular Taste in the Pahlavi Era: The Nation's aesthetic Training in the Government's Cultural Policies* (Tehran: Nazar Publications, 2019).

Giddens, A., *Consequences of Modernity* (Cambridge and Malden, MA: Polity Press, 2012).

Gilman, N., *Mandarins of the Future: Modernization Theory in Cold-War America*, New Studies in American Intellectual and Cultural History (Baltimore, MD, and London: Johns Hopkins University Press, 2003).

Glikson, A., 'L'Unité d'Habitation Intégrale', *Le Carré Bleu*, 1 (1962), pp. 1–6.

Gluck, R., 'The Shiraz Arts Festival: Western Avant-Garde Arts in 1970s Iran', *Leonardo*, 40:1 (2007), pp. 20–8.

Goldhagen, S. W., *Louis Kahn's Situated Modernism* (New Haven, CT: Yale University Press, 2001).

Goldhagen, S. W. and R. Legault (eds), *Anxious Modernisms: Experimentation in Postwar Architectural Culture* (Cambridge, MA: MIT Press, 2000).

Golkar, S., 'Cultural Engineering under Authoritarian Regimes: Islamization of Universities in Postrevolutionary Iran', *DOMES: Digest of Middle East Studies*, 21:1 (2012), pp. 1–23.

Goonewardena, K., 'The Urban Sensorium: Space, Ideology and the Aestheticization of Politics', *Antipode*, 37:1 (2005), pp. 46–71.

Grabar, O., 'The Visual Arts', in R. N. Frye (ed.), *The Cambridge History of Iran, Volume 4: From the Arab Invasion to the Saljuqs* (Cambridge: Cambridge University Press, 1975), pp. 341–2.

Graham, B., G. Ashworth, and J. Tunbridge, *A Geography of Heritage: Power, Culture and Economy* (London: Routledge, 2016).

Grainge, P., *Monochrome Memories: Nostalgia and Style in Retro America* (Westport, CT: Praeger, 2002).

Gravari-Barbas, M., L. Bordeau, and M. Robinson, 'World Heritage and Tourism, from Opposition to Co-production', in L. Bordeau, M. Gravari-Barbas, and M. Robinson (eds), *World Heritage, Tourism and Identity: Inscription and Co-production* (Abingdon: Ashgate, 2016), pp. 1–24.

Grigor, T., 'Of Metamorphosis: Meaning on Iranian Terms', *Third Text*, 17:3 (2003), pp. 207–25.

Grigor, T., 'Recultivating "Good Taste": The Early Pahlavi Modernists and Their Society for National Heritage', *Iranian Studies*, 37:1 (March, 2004), pp. 17–45.

Grigor, T., *Building Iran: Modernism, Architecture, and National Heritage under the Pahlavi Monarchs* (New York: Periscope Publishing, 2009).

Grigor, T., 'King's White Walls: Modernism and Bourgeois Architecture', in B. Devos and C. Werner (eds), *Cultural Politics under Reza Shah: The Pahlavi State, New Bourgeois Culture and the Creation of a Modern Society in Iran*, Iranian Studies Series (London: Routledge, 2013), pp. 95–118.

Grigor, T., *Contemporary Iranian Art: From the Street to the Studio* (London: Reaktion, 2014).

Gross, J. J. (ed.), *Handbook of Emotion Regulation* (New York: The Guilford Press, 2015).

Gruen, V., *Shopping Town: Designing the City in Suburban America*, ed. A. Baldauf (Minneapolis, MN: University of Minnesota Press, 2017).

Habibi, R., 'Modern Mass Housing in Tehran: Episodes of Urbanism 1945–1979', PhD diss., Katholieke Universiteit Leuven, 2015, https://lirias.kuleuven.be/handle/123456789/497502 (accessed 25 January 2019).

Habibi, R., 'The Institutionalization of Modern Middle Class Neighborhoods in 1940s Tehran – Case of Chaharsad Dastgah', *Cities*, 60 (2017), pp. 37–49.

Habibi, R., 'Unveiled Middle-Class Housing in Tehran, 1945–1979', in A. Staub (ed.),

The Routledge Companion to Modernity, Space and Gender (Abingdon: Routledge, 2018), pp. 253–69.

Habibi, R. with B. de Meulder, 'Architects and "Architecture without Architects": Modernization of Iranian Housing and the Birth of a New Urban Form Narmak (Tehran, 1952)', *Cities*, 45 (2015), pp. 29–40.

Habibi, R., B. de Meulder, and S. M. Habibi, 'Re-visiting Three Neighbourhoods of Modern Tehran: Chaharsad-Dastgah, Narmak and Nazi-Abad', in F. F. Arefian and S. H. I. Moeini (eds), *Urban Change in Iran: Stories of Rooted Histories and Ever-accelerating Developments* (Basel: Springer, 2015), pp. 31–46.

Habibi, S. M., *Intellectual Trends in the Contemporary Iranian Architecture and Urbanism (1979–2003)* (Tehran: Cultural Research Bureau, 2007).

Haddad, E. G. and D. Rifkind (eds), *A Critical History of Contemporary Architecture, 1960–2010* (Abingdon: Ashgate, 2014).

Haddad, Y. and J. L. Esposito (eds), *Islam, Gender, and Social Change* (New York: Oxford University Press, 1998).

Haeri, S., 'Ardalan, Nader', Oral History interview (Boston, MA: Foundation for Iranian Studies, 21 July 1991), https://fis-iran.org/en/content/ardalan-nader (accessed 11 September 2017).

Haji Molana, H., 'Sense of Community and Residential Neighborhoods in Tehran, Iran', master's thesis, Kent State University, 2016.

Hanson, B., 'The "Westoxication" of Iran: Depictions and Reactions of Behrangi, Āl-e Ahmad, and Shariati', *International Journal of Middle East Studies*, 15:1 (1983), pp. 1–23.

Harris, J., 'Great Promise, Hubris and Recovery: A Participant's History of Development Studies', in U. Kothari (ed.), *A Radical History of Development Studies: Individuals, Instituions and Ideologies* (London: Zed Books, 2016), pp. 19–44.

Harrison, R. (ed.), *Understanding the Politics of Heritage* (Manchester: Manchester University Press, 2010).

Harrison, R., 'What Is Heritage?', in R. Harrison (ed.), *Understanding the Politics of Heritage* (Manchester: Manchester University Press, 2010), pp. 4–42.

Harrison, R., *Heritage: Critical Approaches* (London and New York: Routledge, 2013).

Harrison, R., 'Heritage and Globalization', in E. Waterton and S. Watson (eds), *The Palgrave Handbook of Contemporary Heritage Research* (New York: Palgrave, 2015), pp. 297–312.

Harvey, D., *The Condition of Postmodernity: An Enquiry into the Origins of Cultural Change* (New York: Wiley, 1992).

Harvey, D., 'Die Postmoderne und die Verdichtung von Raum und Zeit (The Postmodern and the Compression of Space and Time)', in A. Kuhlmann (ed.), *Philosophische Ansichten der Kultur der Moderne* (Frankfurt: Fischer Taschenbuch Verlag, 1994), pp. 48–78.

Harvey, D. C., 'Heritage Pasts and Heritage Presents: Temporality, Meaning and the Scope of Heritage Studies', *International Journal of Heritage Studies*, 7:4 (2001), pp. 319–38.

Harvey, D. C., 'Heritage and Scale: Settings, Boundaries and Relations', *International Journal of Heritage Studies*, 21:6 (2015), pp. 577–93.

Hasanli, J. P., *At the Dawn of the Cold War: The Soviet-American Crisis over Iranian Azerbaijan, 1941–1946* (Oxford: Rowman and Littlefield, 2006).

Hashemi, R. S., 'Editorial', *Abadi*, 3:12 (1994), pp. 2–3.
Hawkins, D. E. and S. Mann, 'The World Bank's Role in Tourism Development', *Annals of Tourism Research*, 34:2 (2007), pp. 348–63.
Hays, K. M. (ed.), *Architectural Theory Since 1968* (Cambridge, MA: MIT Press, 1998).
Hays, K. M., *Architecture's Desire: Reading the Late Avant-Garde* (Cambridge, MA: MIT Press), 2010.
Heelas, P., 'Introduction: Detraditionalization and Its Rivals', in P. Heelas, S. Lash, and P. Morris (eds), *Detraditionalization: Critical Reflections on Authority and Identity* (Cambridge, MA: Blackwell, 1996).
Heelas, P., S. Lash, and P. Morris (eds), *Detraditionalization: Critical Reflections on Authority and Identity* (Cambridge, MA: Blackwell, 1996).
Hemmati, K., 'A Monument of Destiny: Envisioning A Nation's Past, Present, and Future through Shahyad/Azadi', master's thesis, Simon Fraser University, 2013.
Herscher, A., 'In Ruins: Architecture, Memory, Countermemory', *Journal of the Society of Architectural Historians*, 73:4 (2014), pp. 464–77.
Herzfeld, M., *A Place in History: Social and Monumental Time in a Cretan Town* (Princeton, NJ: Princeton University Press, 1991).
Herzfeld, M., 'Spatial Cleansing: Monumental Vacuity and the Idea of the West', *Journal of Material Culture*, 11:1–2 (2006), pp. 127–49.
Herzfeld, M., *Cultural Intimacy: Social Poetics in the Nation-State* (London and New York: Routledge, 2014).
Hillier, J. and E. Rooksby (eds), *Habitus: A Sense of Place* (Burlington, VT: Ashgate, 2002).
Hobsbawm, E., 'Introduction: Inventing Traditions', in E. Hobsbawm and T. Ranger (eds), *The Invention of Tradition* (Cambridge: Cambridge University Press, 1983), pp. 1–14.
Hodge, J., 'Writing the History of Development (Part 1: The First Wave)', *Humanity: An International Journal of Human Rights, Humanitarianism and Development*, 6:3 (Winter, 2015), pp. 429–63.
Hodge, J., 'Writing the History of Development (Part 2: Longer, Deeper, Wider)', *Humanity: An International Journal of Human Rights, Humanitarianism and Development*, 7:1 (Spring, 2016), pp. 125–74.
Holod, R. (ed.), *Towards an Architecture in the Spirit of Islam* (Aiglemont: The Aga Khan Award for Architecture, 1978).
Hooglund, E., *Land and Revolution: 1960–1980* (Austin, TX: University of Texas Press, 2014).
Hunter, S. T., 'Islamic Reformist Discourse in Iran: Proponents and Prospects', in S. T. Hunter (ed.), *Reformist Voices of Islam: Mediating Islam and Modernity* (London and New York: Routledge, 2009), pp. 33–97.
Hunter, S. T. (ed.), *Reformist Voices of Islam: Mediating Islam and Modernity* (London and New York: Routledge, 2009).
Hutton, P. H., 'Ideas about Tradition in the Life and Work of Phillipe Ariès', in M. S. Phillips and G. Schochet (eds), *Questions of Tradition* (Toronto: University of Toronto Press, 2004), pp. 274–95.
Islamic Republic Constitution, reproduced in Malaee-Tavani, A., L. Maleki, and S. M. H. Mohammadi SMH, *Documents from the Iranian Centre for the Study of Cultures* (Tehran: Research Institute for Humanities and Cultural Studies, 2018).
Jackson, I. and J. Holland, *The Architecture of Edwin Maxwell Fry and Jane Drew: Twentieth*

Century Architecture, Pioneer Modernism and the Tropics, Ashgate Studies in Architecture (London and New York: Routledge, 2014).

Jameson, F., 'Postmodernism and the Consumer Society', in H. Foster (ed.), *The Anti-aesthetic* (Port Townsend, WA: Bay Press, 1983), pp. 111–25.

Jameson, F., *Postmodernism or, the Cultural Logic of Late Capitalism* (Durham, NC: Duke University Press, 1991).

Javaherian-Mehrjui, F. J., 'Ali-Akbar Saremi in Conversation with Faryar Javaherian Mehrjui', *Environmental Design: Journal of the Islamic Environmental Design Research Centre*, 1 (1996), pp. 94–7.

Jodidio, P. (ed.), *Iran, Architecture for Changing Societies* (Turin: The Aga Khan Award for Architecture, 2004).

John-Alder, K., 'Paradise Reconsidered: The Early History of Pardisan Park in Tehran', in M. Gharipour (ed.), *Contemporary Urban Landscapes of the Middle East* (London and New York: Routledge, 2016), pp. 120–48.

Jones, T., R. Jones, and M. Hughes, 'Heritage Designation and Scale: A World Heritage Case Study of the Ningaloo Coast', *International Journal of Heritage Studies*, 22:3 (2016), pp. 242–60, https://doi.org/10.1080/13527258.2015.1120226.

Jones, T., A. Mozaffari, and J. M. Jasper, 'Heritage Contests: What Can We Learn from Social Movements?', *Heritage & Society*, 10:1 (2018), pp. 1–25, https://doi.org/10.1080/2159032X.2018.1428445.

Kadoi, Y., 'Persia through the Lens: Poetics and Politics of Architectural Photographs in Pahlavi Iran', *Iranian Studies*, 50:6 (2017), pp. 873–93, https://doi.org/10.1080/00210862.2017.1293374.

Kahn, L., 'Spaces, Order and Architecture', in A. Latour (ed.), *Louis I. Kahn: Writings, Lectures and Interviews* (New York: Rizzoli, 1991 [1957]).

Kakhi, N., 'The Monument, Its Images and Histories', in R. A. Alcolea and J. Tárrago-Mingo (eds), *Congreso Internacional: Inter Photo Arch 'Interferencias'* (Navarra: Servicio de Publicaciones Universidad de Navarra, 2016), pp. 132–41, http://dadun.unav.edu/handle/10171/42419 (accessed 25 January 2019).

Kalay, Y., T. Kvan, and J. Affleck (eds), *New Heritage: New Media and Cultural Heritage* (Abingdon: Routledge, 2007).

Kallus, R., 'Nation-Building Modernism and European Post-War Debates: Glikson's "Integral Habitational Unit" and Team 10 Discourse', *Architectural Research Quarterly*, 18 (2014), pp. 123–33.

Kamiar, M., 'Changes in Spatial and Temporal Patterns of Development in Iran', *Political Geography Quarterly*, 7:4 (1988), pp. 323–37.

Kandiyoti, D. (ed.), *Women, Islam and the State* (London: MacMillan Press, 1991).

Kareiva, P., A. Chang, and M. Marvier, 'Development and Conservation Goals in World Bank Projects', *Science*, 321:5896 (2008), pp. 1638–9, https://doi.org/10.1126/science.1162756.

Karimi, P., 'Wes toxification', *Perspecta: The Yale Architectural Journal*, 43 (2010), pp. 191–9.

Karimi, P., 'Architecture, Matter, and Mediation in the Middle East', *Traditional Dwellings and Settlements Review*, 25:1 (Fall, 2013), pp. 45–53.

Karimi, P., *Domesticity and Consumer Culture in Iran: Interior Revolutions of the Modern Era* (London and New York: Routledge, 2013).

Karimi, P., 'Old Sites, New Frontiers: Modern and Contemporary Architecture in Iran', in E. G. Haddad and D. Rifkind (eds), *A Critical History of Contemporary Architecture, 1960–2010* (Abingdon: Ashgate, 2014), pp. 339–58.

Karimi, Z. P., 'Policymaking and Housekeeping: President Truman's Point IV Program and the Making of the Modern Iranian House', *Thresholds*, 30 (2005), pp. 28–37.

Kassarjian, J. B. and N. Ardalan, 'The Center for Management Studies, Tehran', in M. B. Sevçenko (ed.), *Higher-Education Facilities* (Cambridge, MA: Aga Khan Program for Islamic Architecture, 1982).

Katouzian, H., *Sadeq Hedayat: The Life and Legend of an Iranian Writer* (London and New York: I.B. Tauris, 2002).

Katouzian, H., *Iranian History and Politics: The Dialectic of State and Society* (London: Routledge, 2003).

Katouzian, H., 'Of the Sins of Khalil Maleki', *Iran Namag*, 2:1 (2017), pp. 50–65.

Kazemi, F., 'Urban Migrants and the Revolution', *Iranian Studies*, 13:1–4 (1980), pp. 257–77.

Kazerooni, M. T., A. Esteqlal, M. Fallah, and S. J. Derakhshan, 'Comparative Exploration of Social Housing in Iran', *MAGNT Research Report*, 2:7 (December, 2014), pp. 28–49.

Keddie, N. R., 'Iranian Revolutions in Comparative Perspective', *The American Historical Review*, 88:3 (1983), pp. 579–98.

Keddie, N. R., 'The Midas Touch: Black Gold, Economics and Politics in Iran Today', *Iranian Studies*, 10:4 (Autumn, 1977), pp. 243–66.

Kemp, C., 'Building Bridges between Structure and Agency: Exploring the Theoretical Potential for a Synthesis between Habitus and Reflexivity', *Essex Journal of Sociology*, 10 (2010), pp. 4–12.

Kester, G. H., 'Aesthetics after the End of Art: An Interview with Susan Buck-Morss', *Art Journal*, 56:1 (1997), pp. 38–45.

Khan, H.-U. (ed.), 'Shushtar New Town', *Mimar: Architecture in Development*, 17 (July–September, 1985), pp. 49–53.

Khan, H.-U. (ed.), *Mimar 19: Architecture in Development* (Singapore: Concept Media, 1986).

Khiabany, G., 'De-Westernizing Media Theory, or Reverse Orientalism: Islamic Communication as Theorized by Hamid Mowlana', *Media, Culture & Society*, 25:3 (2003), pp. 415–22.

Khosravi, H., 'Politics of DeMonst(e)ration', *San Rocco*, 6, Collaboration (Spring, 2013), pp. 28–37, www.tehranprojects.com/Politics-of-DeMonst-e-ration (accessed 4 March 2019).

Khosravi, H., 'Planning a Revolution: Labour Movements and Housing Projects in Tehran, 1943–1963', in C. Hein (ed.), *History – Urbanism – Resilience, Volume 2: 'The Urban Fabric, Housing and Neighbourhoods', Proceedings of the 17th IPHS Conference, Delft, 17–21 July 2016*, 17:2 (Delft: International Planning History Society, 2016), pp. 43–52.

Kian, A., 'Gendered Occupation and Women's Status in Post-revolutionary Iran', *Middle Eastern Studies*, 31:3 (1995), pp. 407–21.

Kiely, R., 'Dependency and World-Systems Perspectives on Development', *Oxford Research Encyclopedia of International Studies* (November, 2017), https://doi.org/10.1093/acrefore/9780190846626.013.142.

Kitching, G. N., *Development and Underdevelopment in Historical Perspective: Populism, Nationalism and Industrialisation* (Abingdon: Routledge, 2010).

Knudsen, B. T. and A. M. Waade, *Performative Authenticity in Tourism and Spatial Experience: Rethinking the Relation Between Travel, Place and Emotion in the Context of Cultural Economy and Emotional Geography* (Leeds: Channel View Publications, 2010).

Koselleck, R., *Futures Past: On the Semantic of Historical Time*, trans. K. Tribe (Cambridge, MA: MIT Press, 1985).

Kothari, U. (ed.), *A Radical History of Development Studies: Individuals, Institutions and Ideologies* (London: Zed Books, 2016).

Kothari, U., 'Introduction', in U. Kothari (ed.), *A Radical History of Development Studies: Individuals, Institutions and Ideologies* (London: Zed Books, 2016), pp. 7–8.

Kuhlmann, A. (ed.), *Philosophische Ansichten der Kultur der Moderne* (Frankfurt: Fischer Taschenbuch Verlag, 1994).

Kuutma, K., 'From Folklore to Intangible Heritage', in W. Logan, M. N. Craith, and U. Kockel (eds), *A Companion to Heritage Studies* (Chichester, UK, and Malden, MA: Wiley-Blackwell, 2015), pp. 41–54.

La Belle, T. J., 'Inter-institutional Cooperation: A Case Study of UCLA (U.S.) and UTE (Iran)', *UCLA Educator*, 22:1 (1981), pp. 60–7.

Lähdesmäki, T., S. Thomas, and Y. Zhu (eds), *Politics of Scale: New Directions in Critical Heritage Studies, Volume 1* (New York and Oxford: Berghahn Books, 2019).

Larice, M. and E. MacDonald (eds), *The Urban Design Reader* (Abingdon and New York: Routledge, 2013).

Lasch, C., 'Memory and Nostalgia, Gratitude and Pathos', *Salmagundi*, 85/86 (1990), pp. 18–26.

Leatherbarrow, D., *Uncommon Ground: Architecture, Technology and Topography* (Cambridge, MA: MIT Press, 2000).

Lejeune, J.-F., and M. Sabatino (eds), *Modern Architecture and the Mediterranean: Vernacular Dialogues and Contested Identities* (London: Routledge, 2010).

Lejeune, J.-F. and M. Sabatino, 'North versus South: Introduction', in J.-F. Lejeune and M. Sabatino (eds), *Modern Architecture and the Mediterranean: Vernacular Dialogues and Contested Identities* (London: Routledge, 2010), pp. 1–12.

Lerner, D., *The Passing of Traditional Society: Modernizing the Middle East* (New York: Free Press of Glencoe, 1958).

Li, T. M., *The Will to Improve: Governmentality, Development, and the Practice of Politics* (Durham, NC: Duke University Press, 2007).

Li, T. M., *Land's End: Capitalist Relations on an Indigenous Frontier* (Durham, NC: Duke University Press, 2014).

Litvak, M. (ed.), *Constructing Nationalism in Iran* (Abingdon: Routledge, 2017).

Logan, W., M. N. Craith, and U. Kockel (eds), *A Companion to Heritage Studies* (Chichester, UK, and Malden, MA: Wiley-Blackwell, 2015).

Lotfi, B., 'Spatial Agency: The Role of Tehran's Freedom Square in Protests of 1979 and 2009', master's thesis, Central European University, 2010.

Low, S. M. and E. Chambers (eds), *Housing, Culture and Design: A Comparative Perspective* (Philadelphia, PA: University of Pennsylvania Press, 1989).

Luke, T. W., 'Identity, Meaning and Globalization: Detraditionalization in Postmodern Space-Time Compression', in P. Heelas, S. Lash, and P. Morris (eds), *Detraditionalization: Critical Reflections on Authority and Identity* (Cambridge, MA: Blackwell, 1996), pp. 109–33.

Lynch, K., *The Image of the City* (Cambridge, MA: MIT Press, 1960).
Lynch, K., *What Time Is This Place?* (Cambridge, MA: MIT Press, 1972).
MacCannell, D., 'Staged Authenticity: Arrangements of Social Space in Tourist Settings', *American Journal of Sociology*, 79:3 (November, 1973), pp. 589–603.
MacDougall, E. B. and R. Ettinghausen (eds), *The Islamic Garden* (Washington, DC: Dumbarton Oaks, 1976).
Madanipour, A., 'Urban Planning and Development in Tehran', *Cities*, 23:6 (2006), pp. 433–8.
Madanipour, A., 'The Limits of Scientific Planning: Doxiadis and the Tehran Action Plan', *Planning Perspectives*, 25:4 (2010), pp. 485–504.
Mahdavy, H., 'The Coming Crisis in Iran', *Foreign Affairs* (October, 1966), www.foreignaffairs.com/articles/iran/1965-10-01/coming-crisis-iran (accessed 8 August 2018).
Mahmoudiyan, H., 'Internal Migration and Urbanization in Iran: Status Quo, Challenges and Policy Guidelines', *Policy Papers: Emerging Population Issues in IR of Iran*, 1:1 (2015), pp. 47–55.
Malaee-Tavani, A., L. Maleki, and S. M. H. Mohammadi SMH, *Documents from the Iranian Centre for the Study of Cultures* (Tehran: Research Institute for Humananities and Cultural Studies, 2018).
Malpas, J., *Place and Experience: A Philosophical Topography* (Cambridge: Cambridge University Press, 1999).
Malpas, J., 'Place, Space, and Modernity', lecture, 14 November 2016, International Studies Institute, University of New Mexico, www.youtube.com/watch?v=mFqX6AA19T4 (accessed 29 May 2018).
Mansouri-Zeyni, S. and S. Sami, 'The History of Ressentiment in Iran and the Emerging Ressentiment-less Mindset', *Iranian Studies*, 47:1 (2014), pp. 49–64.
Marans, R. W., 'Neighborhood Planning: The Contributions of Artur Glikson', *Journal of Architectural and Planning Research*, Theme Issue: Artur Glikson and the Making of Place: A Look at His Lasting Impact on Planning and Architecture, 21:2 (Summer, 2004), pp. 112–24.
Marefat, M., 'Building to Power: Architecture of Tehran 1921–1941', PhD diss., Massachusetts Institute of Technology, 1988.
Mashayekhi, A., 'The 1968 Tehran Master Plan and the Politics of Planning Development in Iran (1945–1979)', *Planning Perspectives*, 34:5 (2018), pp. 849–76, https://doi.org/10.1080/02665433.2018.1468805.
Mashayekhi, A., 'The Politics of Building in Post-Revolution Tehran', in H. Jacobi and M. Nasasra (eds), *Routledge Handbook on Middle East Cities* (London and New York: Routledge, 2019 [2020]), pp. 196–216.
Massey, D., 'Power-Geometry and a Progressive Sense of Place', in J. Bird, B. Curtin, T. Putnam, G. Robertson, and L. Tickner (eds), *Mapping Futures: Local Cultures, Global Change* (London: Routledge, 1993), pp. 59–69.
Massey, D., 'A Global Sense of Place', in T. Barnes and D. Gregory (eds), *Reading Human Geography: The Poetics and Politics of Inquiry* (London and New York: Arnold, 1997), pp. 315–23.
Massey, D., *For Space* (London: Sage, 2005).
Mateo, J. L., 'Overview: PREVI Eperience', TTANSF–ER: Global Architecture Platform, www.transfer-arch.com/reference/previ-lima-1969/.

Matin-Asgari, A., *Both Eastern and Western: An Intellectual History of Iranian Modernity* (Cambridge: Cambridge University Press, 2018).
Matin-Asgari, A., *Both Eastern and Western: An Intellectual History of Irananian Modernity* (Cambridge: Cambridge University Press, 2018).
Mazumdar, S. and Sh. Mazumdar, 'Societal Values and Architecture: A Socio-Physical Model of the Interrelationships', *Journal of Architectural and Planning Research*, 11:1 (Spring, 1994), pp. 66–90.
McCallum, D. and S. Benjamin, 'Low-Income Urban Housing in the Third World: Broadening the Economic Perspective', *Urban Studies*, 22:4 (1985), pp. 277–87, https://doi.org/10.1080/00420988520080521.
McCarter, R., *Louis Kahn* (New York: Phaedon, 2005).
McFarland, S. L., 'A Peripheral View of the Origins of the Cold War: The Crises in Iran, 1941–47', *Diplomatic History*, 4:4 (Fall, 1980), pp. 333–51.
McKeon, M., 'Tacit Knowledge: Tradition and Its Aftermath', in M. S. Phillips and G. Schochet (eds), *Questions of Tradition* (Toronto: University of Toronto Press, 2004), pp. 171–202.
McLeod, T. H., *National Planning in Iran: A Report Based upon the Experiences of the Harvard Advisory Group in Iran* (Regina, Saskatchewan: The Library and Archive of the Plan Organization of Iran, 23/07.1978 no. 2261, 31 December 1964).
Memarian, G. and F. E. Brown, 'Climate, Culture, and Religion: Aspects of the Traditional Courtyard House in Iran', *Journal of Architectural and Planning Research*, 20:3 (2003), pp. 181–98.
Merhavi, M., '"True Muslims Must Always Be Tidy and Clean": Exoticism of the Countryside in Late Pahlavi Iran', in M. Litvak (ed.), *Constructing Nationalism in Iran* (Abingdon: Routledge, 2017), pp. 158–72.
Meskell, L., 'The Practice and Politics of Archaeology in Egypt', *Annals of the New York Academy of Sciences*, 925:1 (2000), pp. 146–69.
Meskell, L. (ed.), *Global Heritage: A Reader* (Oxford: Wiley-Blackwell, 2015).
Mesquita, B., J. D. Leersnyder, and D. Albert, 'The Cultural Regulation of Emotions', in J. J. Gross (ed.), *Handbook of Emotion Regulation* (New York: The Guilford Press, 2015), pp. 284–301.
Micara, L., 'Contemporary Iranian Architecture in Search for a New Identity', *Environmental Design: Journal of the Islamic Environmental Design Research Centre*, 1 (1996), pp. 52–91.
Micara, L. and V. Salomone, 'Shushtar New Town: The Idea of a Community. Interview with Kamran Diba', *L'ADC L'architettura delle città, The Journal of the Scientific Society Ludovico Quaroni*, 8 (2016), pp. 121–55.
Milani, A., *The Men and Women Who Made Modern Iran, 1941–1979, Volume 1* (New York: Syracuse University Press and Persian World Press, 2008).
Millward, W., 'Traditional Values and Social Change in Iran', *Iranian Studies*, 4 (1971), pp. 29–30.
Mirsepassi, A., *Intellectual Discourse and the Politics of Modernization: Negotiating Modernity in Iran* (Cambridge: Cambridge University Press, 2000).
Mirsepassi, A., *Political Islam, Iran, and the Enlightenment: Philosophies of Hope and Despair* (Cambridge and New York: Cambridge University Press, 2011).
Mirsepassi, A., *Transnationalism in Iranian Political Thought: The Life and Times of Ahmad Fardid, Volume 1* (Cambridge: Cambridge University Press, 2017).

Mirsepassi, A. (ed.), *Iran's Troubled Modernity: Debating Ahmad Fardid's Legacy* (Cambridge: Cambridge University Press, 2019).

Mohajeri, S., 'Louis Kahn's Space of Critique in Tehran, 1973–74', *Journal of Society of Architectural Historians*, 74:4 (2015), pp. 485–504.

Mohajeri, S., 'The Shahestan Blueprint: The Vestigial Site of Modernity in Iran', in M. Ghairpour (ed.), *The Historiography of Persian Architecture* (Abingdon and New York: Routledge, 2016), pp. 147–72.

Mohajeri, S., *Architectures of Transversality: Paul Klee, Louis Kahn and the Persian Imagination* (Abingdon: Routledge, 2019).

Mohler, A. P. and P. Papademetriou, *Louis I. Kahn: Conversations with Students* (New York: Princeton Architectural Press, 1998).

Moholy Nagy, S., 'The Future of the Past', *Perspecta*, 7 (1961), pp. 65–76.

Mota, N., 'Between Populism and Dogma: Álvaro Siza's Third Way', *Footprint*, 5:1 (Spring, 2011), pp. 35–58.

Mowlana, H., *Global Communication in Transition: The End of Diversity? Volume 19* (Newbury Park, CA: SAGE, 1996).

Mozaffari, A., *Forming National Identity in Iran: The Idea of Homeland Derived from Ancient Persian and Islamic Imaginations of Place* (London: I.B. Tauris, 2014).

Mozaffari, A., 'Conceptualising a World Heritage Site', in A. Mozaffari (ed.), *World Heritage in Iran: Perspectives on Pasargadae* (Surrey: Ashgate, 2014), pp. 17–44.

Mozaffari, A. (ed.), *World Heritage in Iran: Perspectives on Pasargadae* (Surrey: Ashgate, 2014).

Mozaffari, A., 'The Heritage "NGO": A Case Study on the Role of Grass Roots Heritage Societies in Iran and Their Perception of Cultural Heritage', *International Journal of Heritage Studies*, 21:9 (2015), pp. 845–61, https://doi.org/10.1080/13527258.2015.1028961.

Mozaffari A. and N. Westbrook, 'The (Unfinished) Museum at Pasargadae', in A. Mozaffari (ed.), *World Heritage in Iran: Perspectives on Pasargadae* (Surrey: Ashgate, 2014), pp. 197–224.

Mozaffari, A. and N. Westbrook, 'Shushtar No'w: Urban Image and Fabrication of Place in an Iranian New Town, and Its Relation to the International Discourse on Regionalism', *Fusion Journal*, 6 (2015), pp. 1–15, www.fusion-journal.com/iissue/006-fusion-the-rise-and-fall-of-social-housing-future-directions/shushtar-now-urban-image-and-fabrication-of-place-in-an-iranian-new-town-and-its-relation-to-the-international-discourse-on-regionalism/ (accessed 14 September 2017).

Mozaffari, A., R. Karimian, and S. Mousavi, 'Tourism and Political Change: The Return of the "Idea of Iran" (2005–2015)', in R. Butler and W. Suntikun (eds), *Tourism and Political Change* (Oxford: Goodfellow Publishers, 2017), pp. 186–99.

Mozaffari, A. and N. Westbrook, 'Designing a Revolutionary Habitat: Tradition, Heritage and Housing in the Immediate Aftermath of the Iranian Revolution – Continuities and Disruptions', *Fabrications*, 28:2 (2018), pp. 185–211.

Müller, M., 'Avant-Garde, Aestheticization and the Economy', *Footprint*, 5:1 (Spring, 2011), pp. 7–22, https://journals.open.tudelft.nl/index.php/footprint/article/view/729/905.

Mumford, E. P., *The CIAM Discourse on Urbanism 1928–1960* (Cambridge, MA: MIT Press, 2000).

Mumford, L., *Sticks and Stones: A Study of American Architecture and Civilization* (New York: Bonui and Liveright, 1924).

Mumford, L., 'Regionalism and Irregionalism', *The Sociological Review*, 19 (October, 1927), pp. 277–8.

Mumford, L., *The Brown Decades: A Study of the Arts in America 1865–1895* (New York: Harcourt Brace and Co., 1931).

Mumford, L., *Technics and Civilization* (New York: Harcourt Brace and Co., 1934).

Mumford, L., 'l'Oeuvre d'Artur Glikson', *Le Carré Bleu*, 4 (1966), www.lecarrebleu.eu/PDF_INTERA%20COLLEZIONE%20LCB/FRAPNO2_CARR_1966_004.pdf (accessed 3 December 2017).

Nabavi, N., 'The Changing Concept of the "Intellectual" in Iran of the 1960s', *Iranian Studies*, 32:3 (Summer, 1999), pp. 333–50.

Nabavi, N., *Intellectuals and the State in Iran: Politics, Discourse, and the Dilemma of Authenticity* (Gainesville, FL: University Press of Florida, 2003).

Nabavi, N., 'The Discourse of "Authentic Culture" in Iran in the 1960s and 1970s', in N. Nabavi (ed.), *Intellectual Trends in Twentieth-Century Iran: A Critical Survey* (Gainesville, FL: University Press of Florida, 2003), pp. 91–108.

Nafisi, M., 'Khamenei's Fight against "Un-Islamic" Architecture in Iran', *Your Middle East*, 12 December 2014, https://yourmiddleeast.com/2014/12/12/khameneis-fight-against-un-islamic-architecture-in-iran/ (accessed 26 May 2015).

Nahad, N. R., *Cultural Revolution in Islamic Republic of Iran* [*Enghelabe Farhangi dar Jomhoorie Eslamie Iran*] (Tehran: Markaze Asnade Enghelabe Eslami [Centre for Islamic Revolution Documents], 2004).

Najmabadi, A., 'Hazards of Modernity and Morality: Women, State and Ideology in Contemporary Iran', in D. Kandiyoti (ed.), *Women, Islam and the State* (London: MacMillan Press, 1991), pp. 48–76.

Najmabadi, A., 'Feminism in an Islamic Republic: Years of Hardship, Years of Growth', in Y. Haddad and J. L. Esposito (eds), *Islam, Gender, and Social Change* (New York: Oxford University Press, 1998), pp. 59–84.

Naseriazar, A. and A. Badrian, 'Iran', in B. Vlaardingerbroek and N. Taylor (eds), *Getting into Varsity: Comparability, Convergence and Congruence* (Amherst, NY: Cambria Press, 2010), pp. 169–83.

Nasr, S. H., 'The Contemporary Muslim, and the Architectural Transformation of the Islamic Urban Environment', in R. Holod (ed.), *Towards an Architecture in the Spirit of Islam* (Aiglemont: The Aga Khan Award for Architecture, 1978), pp. 1–5.

Nasr, S. H., *Knowledge and the Sacred: Revisioning Academic Accountability* (New York: SUNY Press, 1989).

Nasr, S. H., 'Islam, the Contemporary Islamic world, and the Environmental Crisis', in R. C. Foltz, F. M. Denny, and A. Baharuddin (eds), *Islam and Ecology: A Bestowed Trust* (Cambridge, MA: Harvard University Press, 2003), pp. 85–105.

Nasr, S. H. and O. Leaman (eds), *History of Islamic Philosophy* (London: Routledge, 1995).

Nassehi, R., 'Domesticating Cold War Economic Ideas: The Rise of Iranian Developmentalism in the 1950s and 1960s', in R. Alvandi (ed.), *The Age of Aryamehr: Late Pahlavi Iran and Its Global Entanglements* (London: Ginko Library, 2018), pp. 77–139.

Nasser, N., 'Planning for Urban Heritage Places: Reconciling Conservation,

Tourism, and Sustainable Development', *Journal of planning literature*, 17:4 (2003), pp. 467–79.

Nederveen Pieterse, J., *Globalization and Culture: Global Melange*, 2nd edn (Blue Ridge Summit, PA: Rowman & Littlefield Publishing, 2009).

Nora, P., 'Between Memory and History: Les Lieux de Mémoire', *Representations*, 26 (Spring, 1989), pp. 7–24.

Norberg-Schulz, C., 'The Phenomenon of Place', in M. Larice and E. Macdonald (eds), *The Urban Design Reader* (Abingdon and New York: Routledge, 2013), pp. 125–37.

Oliver, P. (ed.), *Shelter and Society* (New York: Praeger, 1969).

Orbaşli, A., *Tourists in Historic Towns: Urban Conservation and Heritage Management* (London: Spon, 2000).

Otto, T. and P. Pedersen, 'Disentangling Traditions: Culture, Agency and Power', in T. Otto and P. Pedersen (eds), *Tradition and Agency: Tracing Cultural Continuity and Invention* (Aarhus: Aarhus University Press, 2005), pp. 11–50.

Otto, T. and P. Pedersen (eds), *Tradition and Agency: Tracing Cultural Continuity and Invention* (Aarhus: Aarhus University Press, 2005).

Ozaslan, N. and A. Akalin, 'Architecture and Image: The Example of Turkey', *Middle Eastern Studies*, 47:6 (2011), pp. 911–22.

Özkan, S., 'Introduction: Regionalism within Modernism', in R. Powell (ed.), *Regionalism in Architecture* (Singapore: Concept Media/The Aga Khan Award for Architecture, 1985), pp. 8–16.

Paidar, P., 'Gender of Democracy: The Encounter between Feminism and Reformism in Contemporary Iran', UNRISD Democracy, Governance and Human Rights Programme Paper 6 (2001).

Pagden, A., 'The "Defence of Civilization" in Eighteenth-Century Social Theory', *History of the Human Sciences*, 1:1 (1988), pp. 33–45.

Pahlavi, M. R., *The White Revolution* (Tehran: Imperial Pahlavi Library, 1967).

Pahlavi, M. R., Selection from the Shahanshah Aryamehr's Speeches and Writings on Culture, Tehran 1975.

Papchinski, M. and M. Simon (eds), *Ideological Equals: Women Architects in Socialist Europe 1945–1989* (London and New York: Routledge, 2017).

Parsa, M., *Social Origins of the Iranian Revolution* (New Brunswick, NJ, and London: Rutgers University Press, 1989).

Parvin, M. and A. N. Zamani, 'Political Economy of Growth and Destruction: A Statistical Interpretation of the Iranian Case', *Iranian Studies*, 12:1/2 (Winter/Spring, 1979), pp. 43–78.

Pedret, A., 'Within the Text of Kahn', master's thesis, Massachusetts Institute of Technology, 1993.

Pedret, A., *Team 10: An Archival History* (Abingdon: Routledge, 2013).

Peet, R. and E. Hartwick, *Theories of Development: Contentions, Arguments, Alternatives* (New York: The Guildford Press, 2009).

Phillips, M. S., 'Introduction: What Is Tradition When It Is Not Invented? A Historiographical Introduction', in M. S. Phillips and G. Schochet (eds), *Questions of Tradition* (Toronto: University of Toronto Press, 2004), pp. 3–30.

Phillips, M. S. and G. Schochet (eds), *Questions of Tradition* (Toronto: University of Toronto Press, 2004).

Pickering, M., 'Experience as Horizon: Koselleck, Expectation and Historical Time', *Cultural Studies*, 18:2–3 (2004), pp. 271–89.

Pickering, M. and E. Keightley, 'The Modalities of Nostalgia', *Current Sociology*, 54:6 (2006), pp. 919–41.

Pilat, S. Z., *Reconstructing Italy: The Ina-Casa Neighborhoods of the Postwar Era* (Oxford and New York: Routledge, 2014).

Pope, A. U., *Introducing Iranian Architecture* (Oxford: Oxford University Press, 1969).

Popp, R., 'An Application of Modernization Theory during the Cold War? The Case of Pahlavi Iran', *The International History Review*, 30:1 (2008), pp. 76–98.

Powell, R. (ed.), *Regionalism in Architecture* (Singapore: Concept Media/The Aga Khan Award for Architecture, 1985).

Powell, R. (ed.), *The Architecture of Housing* (Singapore: Aga Khan Awards, 1990).

Rabbat, N., 'What is Islamic Architecture Anyway?', *Journal of Art Historiography*, 6 (2012), pp. 1–15.

Rad, H. A., 'A Study of the Architecture of Nader Ardalan in Terms of Tradition and Modernity in the Islamic Context', PhD diss., University of New South Wales, 2015.

Radcliffe, S. A. (ed.), *Culture and Development in a Globalizing World: Geographies, Actors and Paradigms* (Abingdon: Routledge, 2006).

Radwan, N., 'Hassan Fathy and the Arts', Hassan Fathy seminar on the occasion of the fifth anniversary of the Bibliotheca Alexandrina, Alexandria, 25 October 2007, https://doc.rero.ch/record/8381/files/Bibalex.pdf (accessed 4 June 2018).

Ramazani, R. K., 'Iran's "White Revolution": A Study in Political Development', *International Journal of Middle Eastern Studies*, 5 (1974), pp. 124–39.

Ranger, T., 'The Invention of Tradition Revisited: The Case of Colonial Africa', in T. Ranger and O. Vaughan (eds), *Legitimacy and the State in Twentieth-Century Africa* (New York: Springer, 1993, pp. 62–111).

Ranger, T. and O. Vaughan (eds), *Legitimacy and the State in Twentieth-Century Africa* (New York: Springer, 1993).

Rapoport, A., *House Form and Culture* (Eaglewood Cliffs, NJ: Prentice-Hall, 1969).

Rapoport, A., *Human Aspects of Urban Form: Towards a Man–Environment Approach to Urban Form and Design* (Oxford: Pergamon Press, 1977).

Razavi, R., 'The Cultural Revolution in Iran, with Close Regard to the Universities, and Its Impact on the Student Movement', *Middle Eastern Studies*, 45:1 (2009), pp. 1–17.

Reid, D. G., *Tourism, Globalization and Development: Responsible Tourism Planning* (London and Sterling, VA: Pluto Press, 2003).

Reilly, W. (ed.), *Sustainable Landscape Design in Arid Climates* (Geneva: Aga Khan Trust for Culture, 1989).

Relph, E., *Place and Placelessness* (London: Pion, 1976).

Rico T., 'After Words: A Dedichotimization in Heritage Discourse', in K. L. Samuels and T. Rico (eds), *Heritage Keywords: Rhetoric and Redescription in Cultural Heritage* (Boulder, CO: University Press of Colorado, 2015), pp. 285–92.

Rico, T. (ed.), *The Making of Islamic Heritage: Muslim Pasts and Heritage Presents* (Singapore: Palgrave MacMillan, 2017).

Rizvi, K., 'Religious Icon and National Symbol: The Tomb of Ayatollah Komeini in Iran', *Muqarnas*, 20 (2003), pp. 209–24.

Rizvi, K., *The Transnational Mosque: Architecture and Historical Memory in the Contemporary Middle East* (Chapel Hill, NC: The University of North Carolina Press, 2015).

Robertson, J. T., *Shahestan Pahlavi: A New City Centre for Tehran, Book 1: The Master Plan* (London: Llewelyn-Davies International, Planning Consultants, 1976).

Rossi, A., *The Architecture of the City* (Cambridge, MA: MIT Press, 1982).

Roudbari, S., 'The Transnational Transformation of Architecture Practice: Iranian Architects in the New Geography of Professional Authority, 1945–2012', PhD diss., University of California, Berkeley, 2013, http://search.proquest.com.dbgw.lis.curtin.edu.au/docview/1526494875/abstract/AE714019B149437DPQ/1?accountid=10382 (accessed 1 April 2018).

Roudbari, S., 'Instituting Architecture: A History of Transnationalism in Iran's Architecture Profession, 1945–95', in M. Gharipour (ed.), *The Historiography of Persian Architecture* (London and New York: Routledge, 2016), pp. 287–332.

Roudbari, S., 'Renegade Cosmopolitans: Iranian Architects, Professional Power, and the State', *Iranian Studies*, 51:6 (2018), pp. 1–26.

Rudofsky, B., *Architecture without Architects: A Short Introduction to Non-pedigreed Architecture* (Albuquerque, NM: University of New Mexico Press, 1964).

Rudolph, P., 'Regionalism in Architecture', *Perspecta*, 4 (1957), pp. 12–19.

Rykwert, J., 'The Idea of a Town', *Forum*, 3 (1963), pp. 99–148.

Rykwert, J., *The Idea of a Town: The Anthropology of Urban Form in Rome, Italy and the Ancient World* (London: Faber and Faber, 1976).

Sabatino, M., 'The Primitive in Modern Architecture and Urbanism', *The Journal of Architecture*, 13:4 (2008), pp. 355–64.

Sadoughianzadeh, M., 'Gender Structure and Spatial Organization: Iranian Traditional Spaces', *SAGE Open*, 3:4 (2013), pp. 1–12.

Sadr, E. I., 'To Whisper in the King's Ear: Economists in Pahlavi and Islamic Iran', PhD diss., Graduate School of the University of Maryland, 2013, https://drum.lib.umd.edu/handle/1903/13977?show=full (accessed 8 December 2018).

Said, E. W., 'Invention, Memory and Place', *Critical Inquiry*, 26:2 (Winter, 2000), pp. 175–92.

Salazar, N. B. and Y. Zhu, 'Heritage and Tourism', in L. Meskell (ed.), *Global Heritage: A Reader* (Oxford: Wiley-Blackwell, 2015), pp. 240–58.

Samuels, K. L. and T. Rico (eds), *Heritage Keywords: Rhetoric and Redescription in Cultural Heritage* (Boulder, CO: University Press of Colorado, 2015).

Saremi, A.-A., 'Recherche d'un Nouveau Vocabulaire', *l'Architecture d'Aujourd'hui*, 195 (1978), p. 28.

Schayegh, C., 'Iran's Global Long 1970s: An Empire Project, Civilizational Developmentalism, and the Crisis of the Global North', in R. Alvandi (ed.), *The Age of Aryamehr: Late Pahlavi Iran and Its Global Entanglements* (London: Gingko Library, 2018), pp. 492–548.

Schech, S., 'Culture and Development', in V. Desai and R. B. Potter (eds), *The Companion to Development Studies*, 3rd edn (London and New York: Routledge, 2014), pp. 50–4.

Schech, S. and J. Haggis, *Culture and Development: A Critical Introduction* (Oxford: Wiley-Blackwell, 2000).

Schenkluhn, W., 'Bermerkungen zum Begriff des Architektur-Zitats: Zur Erinnerung an Hans-Joachim Kunst (1929–2007)' [Remarks on the Concept of the Architectural Citation: In Memory of Hans-Joachim Kunst (1929–2007)], *Ars*, 41:1 (2008), pp. 3–13.

Schneider, T. and J. Till, 'Beyond Discourse: Notes on Spatial Agency', *Footprint*, 4 (2009), pp. 97–111.
Schochet, G., 'Tradition as Politics and the Politics of Tradition', in M. S. Phillips and G. Schochet (eds), *Questions of Tradition* (Toronto: University of Toronto Press, 2004), pp. 296–322.
Schutz, A. And T. Luckmann, *The Structures of the Life World*, trans. R. M. Zaner and H. T. Engelhardt (London: Heinemann, 1973).
Scott, F., 'Bernard Rudofsky: Allegories of Nomadism and Dwelling', in S. W. Goldhagen and R. Legault (eds), *Anxious Modernisms: Experimentation in Postwar Architectural Culture* (Cambridge, MA: MIT Press, 2000), pp. 215–38.
Seamon, D., *A Geography of the Lifeworld: Movement, Rest and Encounter* (London: Croom Helm, 1979).
Secondi, G. (ed.), *The Development Economics Reader* (London: Routledge, 2008).
Sedgwick, M., *Against the Modern World: Traditionalism and the Secret Intellectual History of the Twentieth Century* (Oxford: Oxford University Press, 2004).
Sen, A., *Development as Freedom* (Oxford: Oxford University Press, 2001).
Sen, A., 'How Does Culture Matter?', in M. Walton and V. Rao (eds), *Culture and Public Action: A Cross-disciplinary Dialogue on Development Policy* (Washington, DC: World Bank Publications, 2004), pp. 37–58.
Serageldin, I., 'Shushtar New Town', in I. Serageldin (ed.), *Space for Freedom: The Search for Architectural Excellence in Muslim Societies* (London: The Aga Khan Award for Architecture, Butterworth Architecture, 1989), pp. 156–66.
Serageldin, I. (ed.), *Space for Freedom: The Search for Architectural Excellence in Muslim Societies* (London: The Aga Khan Award for Architecture, Butterworth Architecture, 1989).
Shadar, H., 'Between East and West: Immigrants, Critical Regionalism and Public Housing', *The Journal of Architecture*, 9:1 (2004), pp. 23–48.
Shah, H., *The Production of Modernization: Daniel Lerner, Mass Media, and the Passing of Traditional Society* (Pennsylvania: Temple University Press, 2011).
Shamoradi, E. and E. Abdollahzadeh, 'Antinomies of Development: Heritage, Media and the Sivand Dam Controversy', in A. Mozaffari (ed.), *World Heritage in Iran: Perspectives on Pasargadae* (Surrey: Ashgate, 2014), pp. 225–54.
Sharify, N., *The Pahlavi National Library of the Future: Its Resources, Services, Programs, and Building Requirement: Final Report* (East Norwich, NY: Board of Consultants, Pahlavi National Library, 1976).
Shayegan, D., 'Corbin, Henri', *Encyclopaedia Iranica*, Volume VI, Fasc. 3, 2011 [1993], pp. 268–72, www.iranicaonline.org/articles/corbin-henry-b (accessed 9 November 2019).
Shils, E., 'Tradition', *Comparative Studies in Society and History*, 13:2, Special Issue on Tradition and Modernity (1971), pp. 122–59.
Shils, E., *Tradition* (Chicago, IL: The University of Chicago Press, 1981).
Shirazi, M. R., 'New Towns – Promises towards Sustainable Urban Form: From "Shushtar-No" to "Shahre Javan Community"', Young Cities Research Paper Series, Volume 7 (Berlin: Universitätsverlag der TU Berlin, 2013).
Shirazi, M. R., 'From Utopia to Dystopia: Shushtar-e-No, Endeavour Towards Paradigmatic Shift', in F. F. Arefian and S. H. I. Moeini (eds), *Urban Change in Iran: Stories of Rooted Histories and Ever-accelerating Developments* (Cham: Springer, 2016), pp. 121–36.

Shirazi, M. R., *Contemporary Architecture and Urbanism: Tradition, Modernity, and the 'Space-in-Between'* (Cham: Springer, 2018).

Simon, M., 'Hungarian Women Architects in the UIFA: The Ambiguities of Women's Professional Internationalism', in M. Papchinski and M. Simon (eds), *Ideological Equals: Women Architects in Socialist Europe 1945–1989* (London and New York: Routledge, 2017), pp. 157–71.

Skurvida, S., 'Iranian or Not: DisLocations of Contemporary Art and Its Histories', *Art Journal*, 74:3 (2015), pp. 73–7.

Smith, L., *Uses of Heritage* (London and New York: Routledge, 2006).

Smith, L. and G. Campbell, 'The Elephant in the Room: Heritage, Affect and Emotion', in W. Logan, M. N. Craith, and U. Kockel (eds), *A Companion to Heritage Studies* (Chicester, UK, and Malden, MA: Wiley-Blackwell, 2015), pp. 443–60.

Smith, N., *Uneven Development: Nature, Capital, and the Production of Space* (Athens, GA, and London: University of Georgia Press, 2008).

Smithson, A., *Team 10 Primer* (Cambridge, MA: MIT Press, 1968).

Sommer, R., 'Four Stops along an Architecture of Postwar America', *Perspecta*, Resurfacing Modernism (2001), pp. 76–89.

Spencer, J. and N. M. Seabra, 'Context, Identity and Architectural Design Thinking: Álvaro Siza's "Bairro da Malagueira"', in H. Casakin and F. Bernado (eds), *The Role of Place Identity in the Perception, Understanding, and Design of the Built Environment* (Sharjah, UAE: Bentham Science Publisher, 2012), pp. 194–208.

Staub, A. (ed.), *The Routledge Companion to Modernity, Space and Gender* (Abingdon: Routledge, 2018).

Steele, R., 'The Pahlavi National Library Project: Education and Modernization in Late Pahlavi Iran', *Iranian Studies*, 52:1–2 (2019), pp. 85–110, https://doi.org/10.1080/00210862.2018.1557512.

Stieber, N., 'Architecture between Disciplines', *Journal of the Society of Architectural Historians*, 62:2 (2003), pp. 176–7.

Stirling, J., *James Stirling: Buildings and Projects 1950–1974* (Oxford: Oxford University Press, 1974).

Sudjic, D., *The Edifice Complex: How the Rich and Powerful Shape the World* (New York: Penguin Press, 2005).

Tafuri, M., 'storicità di Louis Kahn', *Communità*, 117 (1964), p. 41.

Tarfuri, M., *L'architecture Dans Le Boudoir: The Language of Criticism and the Criticism of Language*, *Oppositions*, 3 (1974), pp. 37–62, reprinted in K. M. Hays, *Architecture's Desire: Reading the Late Avant-Garde* (Cambridge, MA: MIT Press, 2010), pp. 148–73.

Tafuri, M., *Architecture and Utopia: Design and Capitalist Development*, trans. B. L. La Penta (Cambridge, MA: MIT Press, 1976 [1973]).

Tafuri, M., *Theories and History of Architecture* (New York: Harper and Row, 1980 [Italian 1st edn 1968]).

Tafuri, M., *The Sphere and the Labyrinth: Avant-Gardes and Architecture from Piranesi to the 1970s*, trans. P. d'Acierno and R. Connolly (Cambridge, MA: MIT Press, 1987).

Tafuri, M., *History of Italian Architecture, 1944–1985*, trans. J. Levine (Cambridge, MA, and London: MIT Press, 1989).

Tafuri, M., 'Toward a Critique of Architectural Ideology', in K. M. Hays (ed.), *Architectural Theory Since 1968* (Cambridge, MA: MIT Press, 1998), pp. 2–35.

Tafuri, M. and F. D. Co, *Modern Architecture*, trans. R. E. Wolf (New York: Harry N. Abrams, 1979).

Tannock, S., 'Nostalgia Critique', *Cultural Studies*, 9:3 (1995), pp. 453–64.

Taragan, H., 'Architecture in Fact and Fiction: The Case of the New Gourna Village in Upper Egypt', *Muqarnas*, 16 (1999), pp. 169–78.

Taussig, M., 'Tactility and Distraction', *Cultural Anthropology*, 6:2 (1991), pp. 147–53.

Taussig, M., *Mimesis and Alterity: A Particular History of the Senses* (London and New York: Routledge, 2018).

Taylor, C., *Sources of the Self: The Making of the Modern Identity* (Cambridge: Cambridge University Press, 1989).

Telfer, D. J. and R. Sharpley, *Tourism and Development in the Developing World* (London: Routledge, 2007).

Teyssot, G., 'Aldo Van Eyck and the Rise of an Ethnographic Paradigm in the 1960s', *Joelho: Revista de Cultura Arquitectónica*, Intersecçóes: Antropologia e Arquitectura, 2 (April, 2011), pp. 50–67.

The Mandala Collaborative/Wallace, McHarg, Roberts, and Todd, 'Pardisan Plan for an Environmental Park in Tehran, prepared for the Department of Environment, Imperial Government of Iran' (Philadelphia, PA: Winchell Press, 1975).

Theocharopoulou, I., 'Nature and the People: The Vernacular and the Search for a *True* Greek Architecture', in J.-F. Lejeune and M. Sabatino (eds), *Modern Architecture and the Mediterranean: Vernacular Dialogues and Contested Identities* (London: Routledge, 2010), pp. 110–29.

Thomas, N., 'The Inversion of Tradition', *American Ethnologist*, 19:2 (1992), pp. 213–32.

Thompson, J. B., *Media and Modernity: A Social Theory of the Media* (Stanford, CA: Stanford University Press, 1995).

Thompson, J. B., 'Tradition and Self in a Mediated World', in P. Heelas, S. Lash, and P. Morris (eds), *Detraditionalization: Critical Reflections on Authority and Identity* (Cambridge, MA: Blackwell, 1996), pp. 89–108.

Tibaijuka, A. K., *Building Prosperity: Housing and Economic Development* (Abingdon: Routledge, 2013).

Tilaki, M. J. M., R. A. Justafa, M. H. Marzbali, A. Aldrin, and J. Ariffin, 'Challenges of the Informal Settlements in Developing Countries' Cities: A Case Study of Iran', *World Applied Sciences Journal*, 12 (2001), pp. 160–9.

Tipps, D. C., 'Modernization Theory and the Comparative Study of Societies: A Critical Perspective', *Comparative Studies in Society and History*, 15:2 (1973), pp. 199–226.

Tiven, B., 'Interview with Hossein Amanat', *Bidoun*, 28 (Spring, 2013), https://archive.bidoun.org/magazine/28-interviews/hossein-amanat-with-benjamin-tiven/.

Tolia-Kelly, D. P., E. Waterton, and S. Watson (eds), *Heritage, Affect and Emotion: Politics, Practices and Infrastructures* (London: Routledge, 2016).

Trigg, D., *The Memory of Place: A Phenomenology of the Uncanny* (Athens, OH: Ohio University Press, 2012).

Tsing, A. L., 'The Global Situation', *Cultural Anthropology*, 15:3 (2000), pp. 327–60.

Tsing, A. L., *Friction: An Ethnography of Global Connection* (Princeton, NJ: Princeton University Press, 2005).

Tuan, Y.-F., 'Topophilia: Personal Encounters with the Landscape', in P. W. English and R. C. Mayfield (eds), *Man, Space and Environment: Concepts in Contemporary Human Geography* (Oxford: Oxford University Press, 1972), pp. 534–38.

Tuan, Y.-F., 'Place: An Experiential Perspective', *Geographical Review*, 65 (1975), pp. 151–65.
Tulbure, N. S., 'Drinking and Nostalgia: Social Imagination in Postsocialist Romania', *Anthropology of East Europe Review*, 24:1 (Spring, 2006), pp. 85–93.
Tunbridge, J. E. and G. J. Ashworth, *Dissonant Heritage: The Management of the Past as a Resource in Conflict* (New York: John Wiley, 1996).
Turner, B. S., 'A Note on Nostalgia', *Theory, Culture & Society*, 4 (1987), pp. 147–56.
Turner, V., *The Ritual Process: Structure and Anti-structure* (New York: Aladine de Gruyter, 1969).
Turner, V., *The Forest of Symbols: Aspects of Ndembu ritual* (Ithaca, NY, and London: Cornell University Press, 1970).
Tzonis, A. and L. Lefaivre, with A. Alofsin, 'Die Frage des Regionalismus', in M. Andritsky, L. Burkhardt, and O. Hoffman (eds), *Für Eine Andere Architektur* (Frankfurt am Main: Fisher, 1981), pp. 121–34.
Tzonis, A. and L. Lefaivre, 'The Grid and the Pathway', *Architecture in Greece*, 15 (1981), pp. 164–78.
UNESCO, Convention concerning the protection of the world cultural and natural heritage, World heritage committee, third session Cairo and Luxor, 22–26 October 1979, Report of the rapporteur on the third session of the World Heritage Committee, Documents CC-79/CONF.003/13 and CC-79/CONF.003/3e, https://whc.unesco.org/archive/convention-en.pdf (accessed 11 December 2018).
UNESCO, *The 2005 Convention on the Protection and Promotion of the Diversity of Cultural Expressions* (Paris: UNESCO and Diversity of Cultural Expressions, 20 October 2005), http://en.unesco.org/creativity/sites/creativity/files/passeport-convention2005-web2.pdf (accessed 2 February 2019).
United Nations Conference on Human Settlements, 'UN Documents: Gathering a Body of Global Agreements', www.un-documents.net/a31r109.htm (accessed 2 May 2019).
Ungers, O., *Die Thematisierung der Architektur* (Dortmund: Technische Universität Dortmund and Walter A. Noebel, Niggli Verlag, 2009).
Urban, F., *Tower and Slab: Histories of Global Mass Housing* (Abingdon: Routledge, 2013).
Vakili, M., 'International Competition, International Archiecture', *Art and Architecture*, no. 45–46 (April–July, 1978), pp. 34–5.
van Eyck, A., 'Is Architecture Going to Reconcile Basic Values?', in O. Newman (ed.), *CIAM '59 in Otterloo* (Stuttgart: Kramer Verlag, 1961), pp. 26–35.
Venturi, R., D. Scott Brown, and S. Izenour, *Learning From Las Vegas: The Forgotten Symbolism of Architectural Form* (Cambridge, MA: MIT Press, 1977).
Vidler, A., 'The Scenes of the Street: Transformation in Ideal and Reality, 1750–1871', in S. Anderson (ed.), *On Streets: Streets as Elements of Urban Structure* (Cambridge, MA: MIT Press, 1978), pp. 29–112.
Vidler, A., *Histories of the Immediate Present* (Cambridge MA: MIT Press, 2008).
Vinegar, A. and M. J. Golec, *Relearning from Las Vegas* (Minneapolis, MN: University of Minnesota Press, 2009).
Vlaardingerbroek, B. and N. Taylor (eds), *Getting into Varsity: Comparability, Convergence and Congruence* (Amherst, NY: Cambria Press, 2010).
von Osten, M., 'In Colonial Modern Worlds', in T. Avermaete, S. Karakayali, and M. von Osten (eds), *Colonial Modern: Aesthetics of the Past, Rebellions for the Future* (London: Black Dog Publishing, 2010), pp. 5–10.

Walton, M. and V. Rao (eds), *Culture and Public Action: A Cross-disciplinary Dialogue on Development Policy* (Washington, DC: World Bank Publications, 2004).

Wang, N., 'Rethinking Authenticity in Tourism Experience', *Annals of Tourism Research*, 26:2 (1999), pp. 349–70.

Waterton, E. and S. Watson (eds), *The Palgrave Handbook of Contemporary Heritage Research* (New York: Palgrave, 2015).

Weigel, S., *Body- and Image-Space: Re-reading Walter Benjamin*, trans. G. Paul, R. McNicholl, and J. Gaines (London and New York: Routledge, 1996).

Wendelken, C., 'Putting Metabolism Back in Place: The Making of a Radically Decontextualised Architecture in Japan', in S. W. Goldhagen and R. Legault (eds), *Anxious Modernisms: Experimentation in Postwar Architectural Culture* (Cambridge, MA: MIT Press, 2000), pp. 279–99.

Weston, R., *Utzon: Inspiration, Vision, Architecture* (Copenhagen: Bløndal, 2002).

Willcocks, M. J., 'Agent or Client: Who Instigated the White Revolution of the Shah and the People of Iran, 1963?', PhD diss., University of Manchester, 2015.

Wilson, R. P., 'The Persian Garden: Bagh and Chahar Bagh', in E. B. MacDougall and R. Ettinghausen (eds), *The Islamic Garden* (Washington, DC: Dumbarton Oaks, 1976), pp. 69–86.

Winter, T., 'Heritage Diplomacy: Entangled Materialities of International Relations', *Future Anterior*, 13:1 (2016), pp. 16–34.

Woodbridge, S., '"Reflections of the Founding" Wurster Hall and the College of Environmental Design [Two Place Tales]', *Places*, 1:4 (1984), pp. 47–58.

Wright, G., 'Cultural History: Europeans, Americans, and the Meanings of Space', *Journal of the Society of Architectural Historians*, 64:4 (2005), pp. 436–40.

Wurman, R. S., *What Will Be Has Always Been: The Words of Louis I. Kahn* (New York: Rizzoli, 1986).

Zabihi, H., F. Habib, and K. Rahbarimanesh, 'Study of Relationship between Satisfaction Rate of the Residential Complexes and Their Impacts on Human Relations (Case Study of Some Residential Complexes in Tehran)', *American Journal of Scientific Research*, 67 (2012), pp. 36–49.

Zanjani, H., 'Housing in Iran', *Encyclopædia Iranica*, Volume XII, Fasc. 5, 2012 [2004], pp. 535–40, www.iranicaonline.org/articles/housing-in-iran (accessed 21 October 2018).

Zareh, H., *The Horizons of Wisdom in the Sphere of Tradition: A Conversation between Hamed Zare and Seyyed Hossein Nasr* (Tehran: Qoqnus Publishers, 2014).

Zhu, Y., 'Performing Heritage: Rethinking Authenticity in Tourism', *Annals of Tourism Research*, 39:3 (2012), pp. 1495–513.

Ziai, H., 'The Illuminationist Tradition', in S. H. Nasr and O. Leaman (eds), *History of Islamic Philosophy* (London: Routledge, 1995), pp. 465–96.

Ziya'i, H., 'Nasr, Seyyed Hossein', Oral History interview (Newton, MA: Foundation for Iranian Studies, 1982–83), https://fis-iran.org/en/content/nasr-seyyed-hossein (accessed 14 January 2018).

Works cited (Persian)

آشوری، د.، فلسفه و علم در شرق و غرب، *الفبا*، ۱:۶(۱۹۹۷).

آ.ا. [جلال آل احمد]، مسجد جدید قم: آبرویمعماری قرن تخیر، علم و زندگی، 1338 ش. 3، صص. 55–61.

اسدی، ع.، تهرانیان، م.، ع. عبدی و م. گودرزی (eds)، صداهایی که شنیده نشد: نگرش‌های اجتماعی-فرهنگی و توسعه‌ی نامتوازن در ایران گزارشی از یافته‌های طرح 'آینده نگری' (تهران: نشر نی، ۱۳۹۵).

احمدی، ح.، روابط ایران و عربستان در سده بیستم (دوره پهلوی)، مرکز اسناد و تاریخ دیپلماسی (تهران: مرکز چاپ و انتشارات وزارت امور خارجه، 1386).

بانی مسعود، ا.، معماری معاصر ایران (تهران: انتشارات هنر معماری قرن، ۱۳۹۴).

'پرونده ای برای داریوش شایگان اندیشمند و فیلسوف ایرانی'، هفته نامه صدا، ۱۴۸: ۱۴ بهمن ۱۳۹۶.

پور کرامتی، و.، 'اهداف برگزاری مسابقات'، در وزارت مسکن و شهرسازی-واحد امور مسکن، مسابقه طراحی مجموعه های مسکونی (تهران: وزارت مسکن و شهرسازی، ۱۳۶۸)، صص. ۱۹–۲۱.

پهلوی، م.، بسوی تمدن بزرگ (تهران: کتابخانه پهلوی، ۱۳۵۵).

شیخ زین الدین، ح.، 'مقدمه'، در وزارت مسکن و شهرسازی-واحد امور مسکن، مسابقه طراحی مجموعه های مسکونی، تهران: وزارت مسکن و شهرسازی، ۱۳۶۸، صص ۱۳–۱۶.

در باره مقاله مسجد جدید قم [بینا، ولی به قلم یوسف شریعتزاده]، علم و زندگی، 1338 ش. 4، صص. 60–62.

دانشور، ر.، باغی میان دو خیابان، چهار هزار و یک روز از زندگی کامران دیبا، نشر البرز، پاریس، ۱۳۸۸.

روشن نهاد، ن.، انقلاب فرهنگی در جمهوری اسلامی ایران (تهران: مرکز اسناد انقلاب اسلامی، ۱۳۸۳).

صارمی، س.ع.ا.، تار و پود و هنوز ... سرگذشت من و معماری ما (تهران: هنر معماری قرن، ۱۳۸۹).

مسابقه معماری فرهنگستانها: معرفی طرح های برنده، آبادی (۴:۱۳) تابستان ۱۳۷۳ ، صص. ۴–۱۷.

مسابقه معماری فرهنگستانها ، آبادی (۳:۱۲)، صص. ۴۹–۵۰.

مشهودی، س.، نگرشی بر کارکردها و نارسایی های کوی نهم آبان، مقاله شماره ۴۲، مرداد ۱۳۵۵، http://bit.ly/2WqCUFN (accessed 10 May 2018).

مدیر عامل شرکت توسعه فضاهای فرهنگی شهرداری تهران: مسجد 72 تن در نزدیکترین حریم مجاز میدان آزادی قرار دارد، ایسنا، دوشنبه / ۱۴ تیر ۱۳۹۵، قابل دسترس در :http://bit.ly/32tlw4U (accessed 16 January 2019).

ملایی، ع.، توانی، ل. ملکی، س. م. ح. محمدی (eds)، اسنادی از مرکز ایرانی مطالعه فرهنگ‌ها، 5 جلد، (تهران: پژوهشگاه علوم انسانی و مطالعات فرهنگی، ۱۳۹۶).

ملکی، ف.، پیرمردی که ۳۷سال است در میدان آزادی عکس یادگاری می‌گیرد، خبرگزاری مشرق، ۱۳۹۵/۵/۱۷ http://bit.ly/2WUd0tY، در، دریافت ۲۹ سپتامبر ۲۰۱۸.

هاشمی، م. م .، هویت اندیشان و میراث فکری احمد فردید، (تهران: کویر، ۱۳۸۳).

هوشیاریوسفی، ب.، معماری: فضای فرهنگی پانزده متر زیرزمین، مهر (فرهنگی، هنری، اجتماعی)، (21:1)، 3 آبان 1382، ص. 16.

آغاز ساخت مسجد هفتاد و تن در تهران، عصر ایران، 29 مرداد 1396.

وکیلی، م.، نقد، هنر و معماری، صص. 45–6.

'مروری کوتاه بر دیروز و امروزداریوش شایگان: فکر در ساحت نامتناهی ذکر '، هفته نامه صدا، سال ۱۸، ۱۴۸: ۱۴ بهمن ۱۳۹۶.

Index

Page numbers in **bold** refer to figures

72 Tan Mosque **159**, **160**, 166–8, **166**, **167**, 179n57, 214, 232

Abadi 198, 200, **201**, 206
Ābbās Ābād 5, 18–19, 180, 181, 187, **190**, 191, **191**, 194–5, 206–8, 214–16, 226, 232
Abolghasemi, Latif 208
Abu Dhabi 167
Adorno, T. 29, 40
Aga Khan, the 140n28, 234
Aga Khan Award for Islamic Architecture 57, 75, 85, 89–90, 120, 124, 200
Aga Khan Foundation 124
Aga Khan Institute 233, 235
Aga Khan Network for Development 233
Ahmadi, Behrouz 132–3, **133**, 143n82
AIAD 4
Al-e Ahmad, Jalal 119
Alexander, Christopher 119, 125
Alsayyad, N. 106
Amanat, Hossein 32, **33**, 71, 72, 149–50, 152–4, 168, 177n16, 216
American Agency for International Development 11–12
Amouzegar, Kourosh 62–3
ancient monuments, nationalist use 144n95
Ansari, Houshang 67
anti-modernism 119
anti-Westernism 31–5, 225–9
Antonokakis, Dimitri and Susana 92

Arabshabi House, Tehran 128–9, **128**
Arc de Triomphe, Paris 154
architectural congresses 2, 17, 46, 75n1, 102, 118, 225, 231
architectural discourse 2, 6, 10, 68, 97, 119–20, 136–8
architectural education 2, 118
architectural journals, purge 120
architectural profession 4–5
architectural scholarship 2, 3–6, 18
architectural trends 1
architecture
  and development 6
  and heritage 10, 227–8
  and the past 1, 7
  role of 10–11, 227–30
  and social change 5–6
  and tradition 228–9
Ardalan, Amir Houshang 120, 129–31, **130**
Ardalan, Nader 14, 32, 40–6, 59, 63–4, 65, 68, 69, 73, 76n10, 77n18, 77n27, 78n51, 80n79, 92, 108, 118–19, 136, 184, 185, 189, 195, 204, 206
  Iran Centre for Management Studies 41–5, **42**, 189, 229
  The Sense of Unity 40–1, 64, 119, 124, 125, 189, 195
art festivals 34–5, 56
Atek Architecture, Planning, and Engineering Consultants 189
Athens Charter 58, 65

Index

authenticity 15–18, 27–8, 30–2, 40, 41–2, 44, 45, 60–1, 73, 98, 106, 119, 120–1, 134, 135, 206
Aymonino, Carlo 94

Badi', Naser 61, 64, 65, 68
Bāgh-e Melli gate, Tehran 126–7, **127**
Bairro Malagueira 88
Bakema, Jaap 58, 68
Bakhtiar, Laleh 40, 41, 59, 72, 119, 124, 125, 189
Bavand Consulting Engineers 202, **204**
belonging, sense of 83
Benjamin, Walter 103, 147
Berliner, D. 29
Bidonville Mahieddine Grid 58
body-space 99
Bourdieu, Pierre 98
Boym, S. 45, 83, 167
Bryant, R. 29
Bu Ali Sina University 78n51, 80n79
built environment 1
　and heritage 10–11

Candilis, Georges 62, 68, 74, 80n79, 84, 206
Canetti, Elias 210
capitalism 121, 225
Casablanca 96
Centre for International Studies, MIT 12
Chamran, Mehdi 219n52, 221n91
Chandigarh project 72
Chogha-Zanbil 197, **197**
CIA 12
CIAM (*Congrés internationaux d'architecture moderne*) 57–8, 58, 59, 67
civil society 236n13
civilizational discourse 32–5, 233
Clifford, J. 45
Cold War 2, 12, 37, 56, 225, 233
collective architectural heritages 1
community 37, 43, 45, 57–8, 83, 97, 107, 214
Competitions 117–18, **118**, 120–3, **130**, 134, 134–5
constitution 116

consumerism 121
Corbin, Henri 31, 41
Cowen, M. P. 9
Critical Regionalism 5, 16, 19, 55, 59, 71, 74, 85–6, 90–1, 92, 206
critical theory 3
cultural conditioning 136
cultural continuity 19, 64, 68, 155
cultural difference 5
cultural homogenization, dangers of 2
cultural identity 16, 43, 56, 59, 65, 72, 122–4, 225
cultural planning 28
cultural policy 11, 28, 136
cultural production 8, 234
cultural re-awakening 73
Cultural Revolution 120
cultural transformation 13, 122
culturally appropriate housing 16–17, 17, 84, 114, 135
culture 5, 228
　authentic 28, 31–2
　debates around 31
　and development 1, 10, 63, 96
　formation of 8, 55–6
　and modernization 13, 63

DAZ Architects, Planners, and Engineers 85
dependency theory 8, 225
Derby Civic Centre 94
design
　and heritage 6–8, 228, 230, 232
　and nostalgia 83
Design Core 4S 190–1
design language 118
detraditionalization 7, 36, 46, 161
development 224–7
　and architecture 6
　critiques of 224, 225–6
　and culture 1, 10, 12, 63
　destabilizing effect of 55, 62, 66
　forms of 9–10
　and heritage 27, 227
　problems arising from 28, 114
　scalar dynamics 230–4
　and tradition 8–11, 223
　unevenness 164–5

development plans 10, 11, 12–13, 85, 87, 92, 225
development studies 227
developmental instabilities, mitigating 229–30
Dezful 85, 87–8, 99
Diba, Kamran 2, 5, 14, 17, 18, 59, 69, 71, 73, 75, 82, 85, 102, 136, 206
  exile 108
  Jondishapur University 92, **93**, 94
  see also Shushtar Now
domestic spaces, gendered 121
Doxiadis, Konstantinos 92, 96, 181
Drew, Jane 17, 59, 72
Dubai 164, 167, 192

earthen architecture, congresses of 16, 75n1
Écochard, Michel 59, 62
economic growth 12, 14–15, 28
education 11, 28
Eggener, Keith 91
Ekbatan development 17, 115, 150
Emami, F. 5, 19
engaged universals 8, 224–7, 235n4
environmental design 2, 3, 90–1, 134
environmentalism 2
Etemad, Giti 132, **132**
Eurocentrism 9
European Enlightenment 1, 9, 32, 33, 72, 206, 224
expertise, flow of 55

Faghih, Nasrin 59, 72, 127–9, **128**, 129
Fanon, Frantz 31
Farah, Queen 14, 34, 59, 61, 62, **62**, 75n1, 136, **147**
Fardid, Ahmad 32, 34, 40, 73
Farmanfarmaian 181
Fathy, Hassan 67, 73, 79n74, 80n82, 124
female privacy 121, 131
First World War 39
Ford Foundation 12
Foroughi, Mohsen 61, 63
Forum 119
Foucault, Michel 32

Frampton, Kenneth 59, 86
France 14, 81n111, 92
French North Africa 17
friction 8, 9, 18, 19, 30, 33, 38, 56, 175, 224, 226, 228
Fry, Drew, and Partners 17
Fry, Maxwell 72
Fuller, Buckminster 61, 79n66
functionalist rationality 206
futurology project, 1974 28

genius loci 68
Gerkan, Meinhard von **188**, 195–6, **196**, 197
Germany 14, 159
Ghaffari, Ali 120–1, 221n91
globalization 2, 7–8, 14, 16, 31, 59, 71, 75, 135, 231
Godard, André 152, 213
Green Movement 149, 177n13
Grigor, Talinn 4, 5–6, 10, 148–9, 154, 159–60, 174–5
Gruen, Victor 181, 189

Habibi, Rana 4
habitat 58, 59, 68–9, 82, 84, 87, 229
Habitat Bill of Rights 69–71, **70**, 74
Habitat du Plus Grand Nombre Grid 58
Hadid, Zaha 151, 235
Haji-Ghassemi, Kambiz 125, 202, 204
Hamedan 125, 131–3, **131**, **132**, **133**
Harrison, R. 11, 122, 228
Hartwick, E. 9
Harvey, D. 29, 230
Hashemi, R. S. 200
Heelas, P. 36
heritage 1, 3, 4, 6, 56, 59, 74–5, 119, 123, 224
  and architecture 10, 227–8
  and the built environment 10–11
  definition 223
  and design 6–8, 228, 230, 232
  design of 18, 119
  and development 27, 227
  employment of 137
  and housing competitions 134–6
  and Islamic identity discourses 134–6

official 122, 135
political component 11
production of 16–17
respect for 124–5
and Shahyad Arya-Mehr Tower 150, 155, 172, 176
heritage–design discourses 17–18
heritagization 6, 125
Hierarchy of Associations 68–9
historical consciousness 1, 6
historical sources 18
historicism 57, 65, 102, 187, 189, 202
historico-cultural processes 1
Hobsbawm, E. 37, 206
Hodjat, Mehdi 221n91
holistic design 16
Honar va Memari 61
housing 57, 67, 69, 75, 79n74, 225
  courtyard 121, 125
  culturally appropriate 16–17, 17, 67, 84, 114, 135
  industry 116
  Islamic 85, 116
  need for 74
  Pahlavi approach 115–16
  policy 116
  post-Revolution condition 115–20
  social 71
  totalitarian 97
  see also Shushtar Now
housing competitions 115, 118–20, 231
  and authenticity 120–1
  distribution 116, **117**, 134–5
  entries 125–34, **126, 130, 131, 132, 133**
  and heritage 134–6
  impact 137–8
  intentions 117–18, **118,** 120–3, 133–4, 135–6
  jury 117
  objectives 123–4
  social agenda 123–5
  timing 116
  Western influence 119
Housing Foundation of [the] Islamic Revolution 116, 140n15

Hoveida, Amir Abbas 181
Hutton, P. H. 46

identity 28, 29, 31, 35, 45, 123, 155, 215, 229
  cultural 16, 43, 56, 59–60, 65, 72, 123, 192, 225, 233
  Islamic 64, 125, 137
  Islamic discourses 134–6
  national 13, 18, 57, 75, 161, 192, 231
  regional 59
  and tradition 137
ideological programmes 134
ideological rhetoric 120, 123
image 98, 98–100, 102–3
Imam Khomeini Mosallā 180–1, 189–90, **190**, 192, 194, 206–7, 226
  architecture 210–11, **211, 212,** 213–14, 215, 216
  context 207, **207**
  location 208, 210
  and nostalgia 213
  project origins 208, **209**, 210, 221n88
Imam Sadegh University **42**, 43
immanent development 9
industrialization 87, 135
instrumentalism 44
intellectual environment 3
intentional development 9, 10
international collaboration 57, 213
International Congresses of Architecture 19, 46–7, 55–75
  context 56–7
  global exchanges 58–60
  impact 74–5
  Isfahan, 1970 59, 60–7, **61, 62,** 84
  Persepolis, 1974 59, 67–71, **70,** 82, 84, 85
  precedents 57–8
  Ramsar, 1976 71–3
  strands 60
International Council on Monuments and Sites 65
Iran Centre for Management Studies 41–5, **42**, 229
Iran Housing Corporation 87

Iranian Academies 19, 198, 200, **201**, 202, **202**, **203**, 204, **204**, **205**, 206, 215, 219n62
Iranian Centre for the Study of Cultures 34–5
Iranian Cultural Heritage Organization 208
Iranian exceptionalism 14
Iran–Iraq War 89, 92, 100, 102, 114, 166–8
Isfahan 16, 77n18, 77n27, 125, **126**, 129
  International Congress of Architecture, 1970 59, 60–7, **61**, **62**, 84
Islamic architectural heritage 18, 115
Islamic architecture 86, 118, 234–5
Islamic criteria 116
Islamism 229
Islamist agenda 18, 115
Islamization 136
Israel 57
Italy 14, 58, 81n111
Ivan Hasht-Behesht 202, **203**

Jafari, Mr 166–7
Jameson, F. 189
Jondishapur University 92, **93**, 94

Kahn, Louis 5, 43–4, 45, 62, 64–5, 68, 72, 78n51, 78n54, 94, 99–100, 102, 181, **182**, 184–5, **185**, 187, 189, 215, 216
Kalantari, Iradj 202
Karimi, Zahra Pamela 4, 6
Kashanijoo, Mr 102
Kazemi-Nejad, Nader 125, 131, **131**, 133
Kennedy, John F. 11–12
Khamenei, Ali 221n88
Khomeini, Ruhollah 116
Khosravi, Hamed 4
Khuzestan 85, 125, 129–31, **130**
Kuran, Aptullah 61, 62, 63, 202

Lähdesmäki, T. 230
Laleh Park 92
L'Architecture d'Aujourd'hui 127

Le Corbusier 57–8, 58, 72
Lefaivre, Liane 59, 92
Lerner, Daniel 38
Llewelyn-Davies International (LDI) 180, 184, **186**, 187–9, 190, **191**, 192, 207, 215, 216
Loos, Adolf 91
Lotfi, Bakhtyar 147, 174–5
Lynch, Kevin 192

McHarg, Ian 42
Mandala Collaborative, the 41, 181
Mandan Consulting Engineers 125, 129–31, **130**
Marefat, Mina 3–4, 21n12
Marxism 224
Mashhad 116, 125, 125–6, 129, 148
materialism 121
Mehrabad International Airport 150
Memar-Naqsh 202, 204, **205**
memory 82, 82–3, 97, 98, 148, 163, 176
Micara, Ludovico 200
migration 28, 44, 74, 85, 114, 116
Millward, W. 107
Mimar 233
Ministry for Housing and Urban Development 18, 115, 116, 198
Mirmiran, Hadi 190, 200, **201**, **202**, 216
Mirsepassi, Ali 27, 32
Moayyed-Ahd, Parviz 207, 208, **209**, 210
modernism 74
modernity 13, 37, 66, 121, 213, 230, 234
modernization 4, 6, 7, 31, 31–2, 32, 46, 66, 87, 102–3, 224, 234
  approaches to 8–9
  and culture 13, 63
  impact of 12–13
  rates of 56–7
  technological 3
  the White Revolution 11–15
modernization theory 12
Mohajeri, Shima 5, 19
Moholy Nagy, Sibyl 187, 189
monumental architecture 4
monuments 145, 148–9

moral community 31, 86, 97, 102, 124, 137, 231
Mosallā project 19
Motahhari, Morteza 39
Mozaffari, Ali 122, 169
Mumford, Lewis 62
museification 73

Nabavi, N. 31
Naqsh-e Jahan Pars Consulting Engineers 190, 200, **201**, **202**
Nasr, S. H. 38–40, 41, 44, 45, 46, 119
National Archaeological Museum 152
national identity 13, 18, 57, 75, 161, 192, 231
National Library 19, 180, 188, **188**, 190, 191, 194, 195–8, **196**, **197**, 215, 216
National Organization for Land and Housing 140n16
national scale 231–2
nationhood 137
nativism and nativist discourse 33, 61, 64, 73
Navaee, Kambiz 125
nostalgia 27–8, 42, 45, 67, 73–4, 102, 134, 135, 169, 215, 216, 229, 232, 235
  conceptualisation of 28–9
  deployment 30
  and design 83
  experience of 30
  facets of 29–30
  geopolitical 35
  and identity 29
  institutionalized 15
  populist expressions 213
  restorative 83, 125, 167
  role of 28, 29, 223, 231–2
  and Shahyad Arya-Mehr Tower 158, 159–60, 163, 164
  and Shushtar-Now 82, 83, 85, 86, 87–8, 96–8, 105–6
nostalgic space 129

oil boom 14, 87
oil crisis 1973 57

oil revenue 11, 14, 19, 181
Oliver, P. 2, 91
Omar Khayyám mausoleum, Nishapur 152, **153**
Opbouw group 58
Orientalism 32, 137
Ove Arup 150, 155
Özkan, Suha 59

Pahlbod, Mehrdad 198
pan-Islamic agenda 215
Pardisan Park, Tehran 42
Parham, Mehdi 31
Paris, Arc de Triomphe 154
participatory design 124
Pasargadae site museum 32, **33**
past, the
  architecture and 1, 7
  continuity with 6
  engagement with 7, 82, 134, 184, 215–16
  imagined continuity with 30
  production of 1
Peet, R. 9
performativity 98
Persepolis **34**, 60, **61**
  International Congress of Architecture, 1974 55, 59, 67–71, **70**, 82, 84, 85
Pirnia, Mohammad Karim 221n91
place, creation of 97
Plan Organization 181
Point Four plan 6, 12
political expression 31
population displacement 56
Portoghesi, Paolo 137
Pourfathi, Mohammad 168, **168**
Pour-Keramati, Valiollah 120–1, 122–3, 123–4
power relations 163, 227, 231
premodern architectural culture, valorization of 3
PREVI housing competition 84
Programme for the Grand Mosallā of Tehran, The 208
public buildings 94
public space 103–4
purge, Cultural Revolution 120

Quaroni, Ludovico 58, 59, 62, 63, 65, 74, 206
Queen's Special Office 181, 184

racial ideology 11
Radmard, Taghy 127–9, **128**, 200, **203**
Rafsanjani, Akbar Hashemi 221n88
Ramsar International Congress of Architecture, 1976 71–3, 225
Ranger, Terence 206
Rapoport, Amos 2, 91, 119
Rayward, John L. 181
reactive identification 38
regionalism 6, 59, 69, 71, 138
representational space 19
Revolution, 1979 4, 14, 17–18, 44, 46, 89, 92, 102, 114, 116, 137–8, **148**, 189, 196, 226
Reza Shah 4, 10, 136, 152, 178n31, 180, 198
Rizvi, K. 213
Robertson, Jaquelin 187, 207
Robertson–Llewellyn Davies International project 5, 19
romantic imperialism 233
Romantic movement 31
Rossi, Aldo 94, 175–6
Roudbari, Shawhin 4–5
Rowe, Colin 94
Rudofsky, Bernard 2, 72, 119
Rudolph, Paul 62, 68
Ryder, Sharon Lee 188–9
Rykwert, Joseph 119

Saarinen, Eero 154
Sacred Defence Museum 19, 190, 192, **193**, 194, 215, 216
Said, Edward 4, 32
Sardar-Afkhami, Ali 66
Saremi, Ali-Akbar 78n54, 125–9, **126**, **128**, 200, 202, **203**, 220n69
scalar dynamics 163–5, 230, 230–4
Schochet, G. 37
Second World War 12, 57, 63, 120,
Sert, José Luis 68–9, 69
sexual harassment 103–4

Seyhoun, Houshang 143n82, 150, 152, 153, 154, 157, 196
Shah, Mohammad Reza 5, 13, 136, 148, 150, 172, 178n31, 180, 181, 207
Shahestan Pahlavi project 176, 180–95, 214, 214–16, 218n26, 226
  afterlife 189–92, **190**, **191**, **192**, **193**, 194–5, **194**
  funding 181
  Kahn project 181, **182**
  Kahn-Tange joint plan 184, **185**, 189, 215, 216
  LDI master plan 184, **186**, 187–9, 190, **191**, 192, 207, 215, 216
  Mosallā *see* Imam Khomeini Mosallā site 181
  Tange project 181, 182, **183**
Shahyad 6 Bahman Museum **147**
Shahyad Arya-Mehr Tower 4, 18, 32, 72, 136, 145–77, 214, 216, 226, 232
  access 156–7
  aims 145–7
  architectural analysis 149–54, **152**, **153**
  colour scheme 157, 159–60
  conception 149–50
  contamination 166
  contesting 166–8, **166**, **167**
  context 156–9, **157**, **158**, **159**
  current state 155–60
  design 152–4, **153**, 175
  engagement with 149, 163–5, 175
  function 154–5, 155–6, 172, 174–5, 175–6
  and heritage 150, 155, 172, 176
  heritage registration document **151**
  imageability 161, 163
  Mosallā *see* Imam Khomeini Mosallā
  museum **147**, 150–1, 156, 168, **168**, **169**, 170–2, **170**, **171**, **172**, **173**, **174**
  and nostalgia 158, 159–60, 163, 164
  opening ceremony **146**, 150
  the platform 159–60, **160**
  during the Revolution **148**
  scalarity 163–5, 230

scholarship 148–9
symbolic function 160–1, **162**, 163–5
shared language 124–5
Sharestan Consulting Engineers 132–3, **133**
Shariati, Ali 42
Shariatzadeh, Yousef 196–8, **197**, **199**, 219n57
Sharify, Dr Nasser 195, 218n44
Shayegan, Dariush 27, 31, 34, 37
Sheikh Zeineddin, Hossein 120–1, 124–5, 138, 141n35, 142n67, 202
Shenton, R. W. 9
Shiraz Arts Festival 34, **34**
Shirazi, M. R. 5, 102
showpiece towns 73
Shushtar Now 17, 75, 82–108, **83**, **91**, 116, 120, 124, 126, 129–30, 136, 154, 225
  Aga Khan Award for Islamic Architecture 89–90
  central area **89**
  courtyard structure 84
  design 87–90, **88**, **89**, 99–100, **100**, **101**, 102, 105, 106–7
  destabilizing effect of 104–5
  as development project 87–96
  engagement of residents 82–3, 103–6
  failure 92, 94–5, 102, 107
  housing 85, 88, **90**, 96, 99, 105
  image 98–100, 102–3
  and nostalgia 82, 83, 85, 86, 87–8, 96–8, 105–6
  population 86
  project origins 83–6
  public buildings 94
  reception 89–92
  transformations 105
  transport system 89
Six-Day War 57
Siza, Alvaro 87–8, 91, 92
Skidmore Owings and Merrill 41
Smithson, Alison 59, 72
social change, and architecture 5–6
social criticism 30
social engagement 72
social habitat 84

social housing 71
social norms 116
social relations 103
social stability 116, 122–3
Society for National Heritage 5–6
Socna Engineers 131, **131**
Soviet Union 13, 225
space, gendered 121
spirituality 123
standard of living 56
Stieber, N. 3
Stirling, James 84, 94, 99, 127, 202
Sufism 39, 65
symbolism 11, 65, 73, 154, 161, 175

Tafuri, Manfredo 102, 185
Tajeer Architects 125, 125–9, **126**, 200, 202, **203**
Tange, Kenzo 5, 181, 184, **185**, 188, **188**, 189, 215, 216
Tāq-e Kasrā 213, 240, 177n2
Tarh-va-Memari Architects and Planners 132, **132**
Team Ten 57, 59, 65, 68, 72, 124
Tehran 4, 164
  Abbās Ābād 18–19, 180, 181, **190**, 191, **191**, 194–5, 206–7, 214–16, 226, 232
  Arabshabi House 128–9, **128**
  Bagh-e Melli gate 126–7, **127**
  housing estates 17
  Shahestan Pahlavi project 5, 18–19, 180–95, **182**, **183**, **185**, **186**, **188**, **190**, **191**, **192**, **193**, **194**
Tehran 80 Plan 189
Tehran Action Plan 181
Tehran Book Garden 190–1, **192**, 194, 215, 216
Tehran Centre for the Appreciation of Music 32
Tehran City Hall 188, **188**
Tehran Comprehensive Plan 181, 189
total environment 84
total environmental control 86
tradition 13, 35–40, 45–6, 56, 63–4, 65, 66, 68, 71, 106, 107
  and architecture 228–9

tradition (*cont.*)
  creative reinterpretation of 158
  definition 36
  and development 8–11, 223
  engagement with 37, 41–5, 46, 66, 136, 167
  historicization 123
  and identity 137
  invented 37–8, 206
  loss of 103
  mutability 36–7, 121
  revival of 125
  role of 35–6
  as static 38–40
  turn to 234
traditional civilization 40
Traditionalism 35, 38–40, 44, 119, 122, 123, 189, 230, 231, 234
transnational collaborations 19
transnational exchanges 8, 17, 41, 55–6, 58–60, 61, 73–5
  Isfahan congress, 1970 60–7, **61, 62**
  Persepolis congress, 1974 67–71, **70**
  Ramsar congress, 1976 71–3
Tsing, Anna 8, 19, 55–6, 224, 228, 232, 235n4
Tyng, Jane 72, 184
Tzonis, Alexander 59, 92

UNESCO 2, 16, 19, 55, 87, 233
Ungers, Oswald Matthias 62, 65
UN-Habitat 19
Union internationale des architectes 57
Union Internationale des Femmes Architectes 16, 71
United Kingdom 14
United Nations Conference on Human Settlements 59, 74
United States of America 14, 224
  American Agency for International Development 11–12
University of California, Berkeley 2
Urban Bill of Rights 85
Urban Land Act 116
Urban Land Organization 116
urbanism 10–11, 16, 55, 96, 119, 121, 226
urbanisme 58
urbanization 58, 74, 85
Utzon, Jørn 195

Vakili, Mansour 195
van Eyck, Aldo 58, 65, 68, 77n18, 84, 119
Vancouver Declaration on Human Settlements 59
Venice Biennale, 1980 137
Venice Charter 65
vernacular, the 2, 3, 9, 14–18, 28, 40, 46, 56, 59, 67, 69, 73–4, 81n111, 85–6, 90–2, 99–100, 108, 114, 119, 134, 137, 202, 206, 235
village, the 67, 68, 69, 74

Western ideas 3
Westernization 31–2
Westoxification 31–2, 32, 124
White Revolution, the 4, 11–16, 43, 55, 72, 87, 115, 116, 168, **170**, 195, 214, 225
women
  position of 4
  segregation 121, 131
women's rights 225
Wright, G. 3

Yom Kippur War 11

Zhu, Y. 98

EU authorised representative for GPSR:
Easy Access System Europe, Mustamäe tee 50,
10621 Tallinn, Estonia
gpsr.requests@easproject.com